MW00807052

The Lifeboat Strategy: Legally Protecting Wealth and Privacy in the 21st Century

Copyright © 2003 by Mark Nestmann. Third Edition, October 2007
ISBN 978-1-891266-31-7 (PDF)
ISBN 978-1-891266-30-0 (perfect bound)

All rights reserved. U.S. copyright law prohibits copying any portion of this publication or placing it on any electronic medium without publisher's written permission. Violators risk criminal penalties and US$50,000 damages.

This publication is sold with the understanding that it does not render legal or other professional services or advice. If legal advice or other expert assistance is required, the services of a competent professional should be sought.

Additional copies of this title are available.

Published by:

The Nestmann Group, Ltd.
2303 N. 44th St. #14-1025
Phoenix, AZ 85008 USA
Tel./Fax: +1 (602) 604-1524
E-mail: info@nestmann.com
Link: http://www.nestmann.com

About the author: Mark Nestmann, LL.M., is the president of The Nestmann Group, Ltd., a consultancy focusing on wealth preservation and international tax planning solutions. He holds a master of laws degree in international tax law from the Vienna (Austria) University School of Business and Economics.

Mark is an Associate Member of the American Bar Association (member of subcommittee on Foreign Activities of U.S. Taxpayers, Committee on Taxation) and member of the Society of Professional Journalists. His books and reports are sold at http://www.nestmann.com. To arrange for a consultation with The Nestmann Group, e-mail info@nestmann.com or call +1 (602) 604-1524.

Mark is also a member of The Sovereign Society's Council of Experts. **Link**: http://www.sovereignsociety.com.

TABLE OF CONTENTS

PREFACE

On every front, from boarding an airplane to opening a bank account, you and your wealth are under surveillance of an intensity that would have been unimaginable only a few short years ago. Identity theft…no fly lists…e-mail surveillance… data mining…many of today's most serious threats to privacy and wealth have exploded into prominence in the first decade of the 21st century.

At the same time, havens for wealth and privacy are under attack. Money laundering laws, more aggressive tax investigations, and the war on terrorism have led to intense domestic surveillance and pressure on offshore centers such as Switzerland to end bank secrecy.

The result of these converging trends is that many of the wealth and privacy preservation strategies you've read about in the past—including earlier editions of my own books—are obsolete.

I've designed this newest edition of *The Lifeboat Strategy* to provide practical strategies against today's threats to privacy and wealth. When you've finished reading it, you'll know simple techniques to stop identity thieves in their tracks, make your wealth legally disappear from the surveillance "radar screen," and understand how to protect wealth you simply can't afford to lose. Along the way, you'll learn dozens of hands-on methods you can use everyday to avoid unnecessarily scrutiny by sue-happy lawyers, the IRS, or someone holding a grudge against you.

No book of this length and level of detail can possibly be 100% error-free. Please contact me with your corrections, suggestions, criticism, or praise.

I am writing these words in October 2007. All the suggested strategies that are contained in this book are, to the best of my knowledge, legal as of October 1, 2007.

Updates to publications from The Nestmann Group, Ltd. are posted at <u>http://www.nestmann.com</u>. Sign up to be notified of updates at <u>http://nestmann.com/mailman/listinfo/updates_nestmann.com</u>.

FOREWORD: HOW VULNERABLE ARE YOU?

1. Are you a U.S. citizen or permanent resident? ✓ Yes ___ No.
2. Is a U.S. passport the only international travel document you possess? ✓ Yes ___ No.
3. Have you been assigned a Social Security number? ✓ Yes ___ No.
4. Do you freely disclose details of your income and financial status to others? ___ Yes ✓ No.
5. Do you have accounts in your own name in U.S. bank or brokerage accounts exceeding US$100,000 in value? ✓ Yes ✓ No.
6. Do you keep over US$10,000 in any bank or securities account to which you have Internet access? ___ Yes ✓ No.
7. Do you have any credit cards issued by U.S. financial institutions? ✓ Yes ___ No.
8. Do you own unmortgaged U.S. real estate in your own name? ✓ Yes ___ No.
9. Do you own rental real estate in your own name? ___ Yes ✓ No.
10. Do you have utility service in your name? ✓ Yes ___ No.
11. Do you receive mail at your residential address in your name? ✓ Yes ___ No.
12. Does your driver's license list your residential address? ✓ Yes ___ No.
13. Is your Social Security number printed on your driver's license or checks? ___ Yes ✓ No.
14. Have you ever applied for government assistance? ✓ Yes ___ No.
15. Do you receive income or benefits from any governmental entity? ✓ Yes ___ No.
16. Have you ever been convicted of a crime? ___ Yes ✓ No.
17. Have you ever declared bankruptcy? ___ Yes ✓ No.
18. Have you ever been involved in a divorce or a lawsuit? ✓ Yes ___ No.
19. Have you ever received money through a probate court? ___ Yes ✓ No.
20. Do you belong to a church or any organizations that are controversial or politically unpopular? ___ Yes ✓ No.
21. Are you licensed by any state (e.g., as an attorney, physician, etc.)? ___ Yes ✓ No.
22. Do you operate a motor vehicle? ✓ Yes ___ No.
23. Do you own an airplane, boat, or recreational vehicle? ___ Yes ✓ No.
24. Do you have teen-age children living in your household? ___ Yes ✓ No.
25. Do you use a personal computer with a high-speed Internet connection? ✓ Yes ___ No.
26. Do you have a net worth exceeding US$1 million? ✓ Yes ___ No.
27. Have you ever invested in a "tax shelter?" ✓ Yes ___ No.
28. Do you own a business as a sole proprietorship or part of a business organized as a general partnership? ___ Yes ✓ No.
29. Are you a director or officer of a closely held corporation? ___ Yes ✓ No.

Give yourself one point for every "yes" answer, zero points for every "no."
Your score: ____

0-7 points: Virtually unexposed. Congratulations! You have successfully shut off surveillance of your wealth and privacy.

8-13 points: Somewhat exposed. You have shut down more pathways to surveillance of your wealth and privacy than most Americans. But you can lower your profile even more.

14-19 points: Exposed. Your life is nearly an open book. You should take steps to lower your financial profile immediately.

20-29 points: Highly exposed. You need to take immediate steps to protect your wealth and privacy. You're an easy target for identity theft, lawsuits, and/or asset forfeitures.

CHAPTER ONE: THREATS TO PRIVACY AND WEALTH

All of us deal with privacy invaders on a daily basis. Unsolicited telephone sales calls, e-mail spam, and junk mail are simply part of modern life.

We learn to ignore these low-level privacy invasions. Only if they become impossible to ignore—e.g., spam releasing a virus on to your PC that renders it unusable—are we goaded into action.

One reason we ignore low-level privacy invasions is that we subconsciously think the battle is lost: that there's no point trying to protect privacy, because it's already compromised in so many ways.

It's true that the news on the privacy front isn't encouraging. Marketing specialists have perfected data mining techniques that categorize their target audience in minute detail. Newborn children must be identified with tax identification numbers. Laws to counter money laundering make it illegal to make certain transactions with your own lawfully earned, tax-paid assets. Civil forfeiture laws permit property seizures from owners who have committed no crime. Lawsuits against businesses and professionals are at an all-time high. Anti-terrorism laws have greatly expanded the government's ability to wiretap telephone conversations without a search warrant. Indeed, it's tempting to resign to the seemingly inevitable and pretend not to be concerned about privacy invasion.

Fortunately, there's no need to take a defeatist attitude. You're not helpless against privacy invaders. You can take steps to lower your profile to the marketing mavens and government bureaucrats who would track your every footstep. You can remove yourself from mailing lists and use "throwaway" e-mail addresses to reduce spam. You can use currency (cash) or conduct financial transactions outside your own country to maintain your privacy. Finally, you can use technology to fight technology; for nearly every technical advance that invades privacy, a corresponding advance has been developed to protect it.

After you finish reading this report, and begin to adopt the strategies it suggests, you'll find it becomes second nature not to reveal your Social Security number, to decline to participate in "marketing surveys" or "opinion polls," and to pay currency when making a purchase. You will have developed that most important defense against invasions of your wealth and privacy: a private attitude.

Your attitude, more than any other single factor, is the key to successfully maintaining your wealth and privacy in a public age.

The Threat to Privacy

All of us live a portion of our lives unseen by anyone else. We assign different values to this solitude. Each of us has a different sense of privacy, and the concept of privacy changes from one culture to the next—and from one generation to the next.

In our own era, as access to personal information has increased, expectations of privacy have waned and our tolerance for the privacy needs of others has declined. Information that a few decades ago was considered intensely personal is now routinely released for public consumption. Intimate details of a president's sexual behavior become front-page news, after being posted on the Internet. Ordinary citizens document every moment of their lives via Webcams or online blogs and share vicariously in others' lives by watching reality television shows.

Privacy is also a market phenomenon. People who value financial privacy willingly pay higher transaction fees to an offshore bank than they would to a domestic bank, so that their banking records are protected from disclosure. In contrast, people don't assign a high value to privacy may give it up if they perceive a benefit. For instance, grocery shoppers may pay lower prices for groceries if they use a shopper's card and consent to have their purchases surveyed by the supermarket owner.

However, the benefits we receive from innovations such as shopper's cards can easily become liabilities. Databases set up to track consumer purchases by shoppers, tolls paid electronically on a highway, and any purchase made with a credit card, are now used to gather evidence in criminal and tax investigations, along with lawsuits. These databases are also targets of identity thieves.

One reason that privacy is disappearing in the United States is that there is no legal framework to protect it. U.S. federal privacy protection is a piecemeal affair combining constitutional law, congressional statutes, administrative regulations, and court decisions. There is even more variation between the states.

In other countries, the legislative framework to protect privacy is stronger. In the European Union, a data protection directive came into effect in 1995 imposing minimum standards for privacy laws in 15 (now 27) EU countries.[1]

I believe that privacy invasions by government are much more serious than those motivated by the profit motive. The man on the phone trying to sell you penny stocks doesn't have a gun to your head, but the Treasury Department analyst looking at your assets and your financial transactions on a computer screen can set in motion a chain of events that could lead to your indefinite imprisonment and a freeze of all your financial assets.

We are at the cusp of an era where wholesale government surveillance is possible. The National Security Agency can eavesdrop on every phone call, looking for patterns of communication or keywords that might indicate a conversation between terrorists. Networks of closed circuit television cameras can track every person in an area, and with face identification software, identify them, and record their movements for later analysis. Numerous cities now have license plate scanners installed that keep records of every vehicle that passes, and save that data for later analysis.

That this power can be abused is without question. Wayne Madsen observes:

In 1940, the German Army invaded Denmark, Norway, the Netherlands, Belgium, Luxembourg, and France. While the military exploits of the Wehrmacht received widespread attention, the surreptitious achievements of a specialized branch of the [Nazi] SS, the SD (Sicherheitsdienst des Reichsfuhrers or Security Service of the Chief of the SS in the Reich) received much less notice. All the invaded countries maintained advanced systems of paper records on their citizens. Some of these were held by local governments such as town clerks' offices, while others were held by churches, private clubs, organizations, and national government ministries. These records were seized by the SD shortly after occupation.

SD information analysts proceeded to examine closely birth records, voting records, and business records ... The results of these personal data analyses are now well known. Jews and those of Jewish descent, Jehovah's Witnesses, seminary students, Gypsies, the mentally retarded, Socialists, Communists, pacifists, Liberal Republicans, Catholic Action and Catholic Youth members, Protestant theologians, and homosexuals were rounded up by the SD's sister service, the Gestapo, for shipment to concentration camps and in most cases to their deaths.[2]

The Nazis identified their victims from paper records. How much more efficient would their extermination efforts have been had they been equipped with today's data mining software and the rapidly advancing network of law and technology designed to monitor our personal and financial transactions?

Fewer Refuges for Private Wealth

Only a few decades ago, the bulk of individual or family wealth was in a home, its furnishings, the value of any land, crops and animals, plus perhaps a few gold and silver coins.

Today, wealth is represented in many more forms, among them paper currency, holdings in bank and brokerage accounts, etc. Most of these forms of wealth are intangible. They can be bought and sold, or transferred, at the blink of an eye. This makes intangible wealth much more convenient for financial transactions than tangible wealth.

Intangible wealth represents a claim to an underlying asset—debt issued by a corporation or government, for instance, or ownership in a company. This claim takes the form of a stock or bond, issued originally in paper form, but now, more often than not, in the form of a book entry on the electronic ledger of a bank or broker.

The characteristics that make intangible forms of wealth attractive for financial transactions also make them vulnerable. Tangible assets are much harder to deal with: real estate is immobile and relatively illiquid; animals and crops must be maintained. Intangible wealth is both more mobile and often much more liquid than tangible wealth. In the event of a legal dispute, these characteristics make it much more attractive to potential creditors.

Because intangible wealth is often represented by nothing more than blips on a computer screen, its custodians have developed elaborate systems to track it. In the United States, information about these holdings can become a matter of public record in many ways: lawsuit, divorce, data sharing between companies, etc. In addition, investigators, the IRS and many other government agencies can also learn what intangible wealth you have, and where you keep it, without going to court.

Privacy for Sale

Wealthy people can afford to place legal and financial obstacles in the path of any would-be privacy invader. By placing their money in offshore entities, living as expatriates outside their own countries, doing business through corporate vehicles that shield their identity, and leaving bookkeeping details to trusted attorneys, the wealthy can live practically anonymous lives.

The very poor also lead relatively private lives, especially if they refuse government assistance. The illegal alien or the homeless street person is likely not to file income tax returns, be assigned a Social Security number, or apply for a driver's license. Their lives may be a desperate battle against hunger and despair. But it's a more private existence than most middle-class residents of the United States have.

Most likely, you fall somewhere in the middle of these two extremes. Your public image is likely to reside in hundreds of government and corporate databases. Credit bureaus, banks, tax authorities, administrators of social benefit programs, educational institutions, and perhaps the military and criminal justice system all contain snapshots of your life, from the day you were born to the day you die.

What Records Do "They" Keep on You?

So-called "public" records were, until a few years ago, possible to retrieve only with a visit to the local courthouse. Today, they're compiled in ever-increasing detail by marketing and data mining companies, and made available over the Internet.

The information exodus from the filing cabinet to the data bank has blurred the boundary between public and private information. Computers excel at analyzing information that individuals willingly share in order to obtain credit, go to work, receive welfare benefits, or purchase insurance coverage. Most of this information was once considered private, as were the conclusions banks, insurance companies, etc. reached after analyzing it.

This information is no longer private; a result not only of technological innovation, but also of laws that were never designed for the information age, or that quickly became outdated. Data mining software can cross-reference information residing in computers to create an amazingly detailed portrait of your wealth, your religious beliefs, and your lifestyle.

The array of records now considered public and available to an investigator is mind-boggling:

- Voter registration records
- Marriage license records
- Building and occupancy permits
- Business licenses
- Workers compensation information
- Property tax records
- Medical records
- Sheriff and county prosecutor records
- County fire marshal records
- Utility company records
- Real estate property records
- Litigation history
- Divorce records
- Personal injury suits
- State tax cases
- Professional licensing boards
- Bankruptcy records
- Corporate registration records
- Probate records
- Telephone bills

The information in these records can be used for deadly purposes. In 1999, a man obsessed by a high-school classmate tracked down and killed her after using the services of an information retrieval company. The killer paid US$204 to learn her birthday, Social Security number, and the name of her employer. Using this information, he murdered her as she left work.[3]

The information the killer obtained over the Internet about his victim only represents data available to the public. A great deal more information about individuals is available to law enforcement and intelligence agencies, as you'll learn in this book.

Public Images: Are You Being Watched?

Surveillance of personal, business, or political rivals has existed since the dawn of mankind. But it was not until the mid-19th century that technology made remote surveillance possible. The development of the telegraph during this period was accompanied by the invention of devices that could monitor telegraph signals. Wiretaps were used by both sides in the Civil War, and, when the telephone was invented in the 1870s, spread to this technology as well.

Remote listening devices that could be planted anywhere were also perfected, and by the early 1950s, the development of the transistor accelerated miniaturization. "Bugs" were invented that could be planted in cufflinks, tie clasps and, as every James Bond fan realizes, even martini olives.

Today, electronic surveillance has matured to the point where a camera the size of a pinhead can provide both a visual and audio record of your activities. Digital cable boxes monitor the viewing habits of television audiences. Conventions display an incredible array of technological wizardry devoted to the latest developments in electronic surveillance.

Although privacy isn't extinct, technology has made it an endangered species.

Government Invasions of Privacy and Wealth

Only a century ago, most people were known only by their name and occupation. Official records of your great-grandparents' existence, for instance, were likely limited to birth records, baptismal records, death records, census records, the purchase of a home, and perhaps the payment of property tax. Even this information was generally filed and forgotten, because of the considerable expense involved in paying clerks to organize it.

As technology progressed, the economic incentives for governments and corporations to use the information gathered on private citizens rapidly increased. The invention of the typewriter and devices capable of reading punched cards in the 19th century reduced the costs of compiling and organizing information. But it was the development of the digital computer in the 20th century that made it practical to collect, store, collate and distribute data on a truly massive scale.

Until the end of World War II, most personal information on Americans physically resided in their homes. Outside the home, the records maintained by banks, schools, insurance companies, etc. were in paper form and retrieved only to process a transaction or claim. In general, police could retrieve these records only if they could persuade a judge to issue a search warrant, based on probable cause, that the requested records provided evidence of a crime.

By the 1950s, as computers became an integral part of American society, entrepreneurs discovered a profitable business: compiling information on individual Americans in electronic form and making it available for a fee. Some of the first large-scale users of computer technology were credit bureaus. By contracting with financial institutions, department stores, local governments, etc., credit bureaus created vast libraries of information on individual Americans—information that had never before been conveniently accessible.

As technology progressed, governments began using computers to increase efficiency and productivity. It only seemed rational to place computers where they could be used to relieve clerks of dull, repetitive jobs. By the 1950s, officials at the IRS and Social Security Administration pointed to computerization of these agencies as models for other government agencies to follow.

These computer systems were frequently upgraded, and adapted to keep pace with the increasing obligations the government assumed. From a privacy standpoint, some of the most important new responsibilities were laws relating to financial surveillance. Beginning with the Bank Secrecy Act (1970),[4] Congress passed an increasingly complex series of laws intended to fight crime and later, to prevent the "laundering" of money.

To keep up with the increasing flow of data from the nation's banks, brokerage houses, money transfer services and casinos to the government, the IRS, FBI, and other law enforcement agencies required almost continuous computer upgrades. These occurred in rapid succession, and are still taking place. In addition, a unique "personal identifier" was needed to track individual financial transactions. The most logical choice was the Social Security number, once assigned to Americans upon entering the workplace, and now assigned at birth.

The SSN thus evolved into a universal identifying code for U.S. citizens. Knowing your SSN, anyone using one of thousands of Internet-based information services can learn where you live; where you work; what property you own; where you bank and the balance of your account; what stockbroker you use; the value of your investments; if you have ever been sued; and much more. Recent innovations make even the knowledge of a Social Security number unnecessary; information can be retrieved merely knowing your name, your address, or your driver's license number.

How Privacy and Wealth are Lost

The "global surveillance infrastructure" this book documents threatens your privacy and wealth in a variety of ways. This section contains a brief survey.

50,000 Lawsuits, Each Day

Battles waged in U.S. courtrooms over divorces, wills and other money matters are proliferating. More than 80% of the world's lawyers practice in the United States. Over 50,000 lawsuits are filed **every day** in the United States.[5] Each year, the "tort system" costs the U.S. economy nearly US$1 trillion.[6]

Why are lawsuits so prevalent in the United States? There are many reasons. One important factor is that unlike most other countries, U.S. lawyers can take cases on **contingency**, which means that the attorney receives no fees unless money is recovered from the defendant. As a result, persons with a chip on their shoulder can sue you. To encourage even more lawsuits, companies have now been formed to invest in selected U.S. lawsuits by buying a share of the settlement based on the merits of the case.

Once source of litigation is the concept of "strict liability," which holds that even if you were in no way negligent, you may still be liable for damages in a lawsuit.[7] Another is the concept of "joint and several liability," whereby someone suing you may recover all damages awarded from you, regardless of your individual share of the liability. In this manner, if you are 1% responsible for a US$10 million loss, you may be required to compensate the successful litigant the full US$10 million.[8]

Other sources of liability are federal and state laws that give plaintiffs a cause of action to recover damages against employers, landlords, and other businesses. Some of the most important of these laws are the Americans with Disabilities Act,[9] the Fair Credit Reporting Act,[10] and the Racketeer Influenced and Corrupt Organizations Act,[11] but there are many others.

High-income people who display their wealth openly are often subject to unwanted litigation. Disputes among ex-spouses, business partners, and relatives following the death of a wealthy family member are also frequent sources of litigation. Professionals—doctors, lawyers, engineers, etc.—are targets as well.

Lawsuits are privacy destroyers. One reason is that information disclosed in a lawsuit is usually a matter of public record. And through the judicial process, a plaintiff (the person suing) is entitled to use a compulsory legal document called a **subpoena** to obtain books, records, and other documents (e.g., records held by accountants, banks, brokers, etc.).

This process is called **discovery**. If you refuse to cooperate, the court can compel discovery with fines and even arrest. If you lie, and are later found out, you may be charged with perjury, a criminal offense. You may not refuse to answer the questions, unless there is a possibility of criminal prosecution.

Think you can count on the judge in a lawsuit to be "fair?" Then consider this quote from former West Virginia Supreme Court Justice Richard Neely:

As long as I am allowed to redistribute wealth from out-of-state companies to injured in-state plaintiffs, I shall continue to do so. Not only is my sleep enhanced when I give someone else's money away, but so is my job security, because in-state plaintiffs, their families, and their friends will re-elect me. It should be obvious that the in-state local plaintiff, his witnesses, and his friends, can all vote for the judge, while the out-of-state defendant can't even be relied upon to send a campaign donation.[12]

Your Lending Records for Sale

Almost everyone needs to borrow money sometime. But doing so can result in a significant loss of control over crucial personal and financial information. Your credit records can also be used to determine your eligibility for a job,[13] or even to decide whether you'll be allowed to board an airplane.[14]

A typical loan application will require that you disclose:

- Your name and residential address;
- The name and address of your employer and how much you're paid;
- Information about your spouse and children; and
- A detailed listing of all debts you owe.

If you're borrowing a substantial sum of money, you may be required to submit a financial statement. This is a formal listing of all your assets and liabilities.

This information may be disclosed under a variety of circumstances. To begin with, the lender to share this data with affiliated companies. Your repayment record is carefully tracked not only by the lender, but also by organizations the lender belongs to, including credit bureaus. The lender may also make an official public record of the loan through a county recorder's office.

If you default on the loan and are sued, the loan application can be introduced as evidence, making it a matter of public record that anyone can review. Further, in a lawsuit, the opposing attorney can subpoena loan applications to verify any statements of your net worth you've made in discovery.

Your Medical Records For Sale

Whatever, in connection with my professional practice or not in connection with it, I see or hear, in the life of men, which ought not to be spoken of abroad, I will not divulge, as reckoning that all such should be kept secret.

—A portion of the oath of Hippocrates

In Hippocrates' day, in ancient Greece, medical technology was non-existent. An extract of willow bark might be given to relieve pain and swelling. The foxglove plant might be administered to relieve chest pains of a person suffering from heart disease. A patient would pay the physician a modest fee out of his own pocket, or perform some services on his behalf.

Similar fee arrangements were routine in the United States until very recently. I have childhood memories of my father, who practiced medicine for over 40 years, bartering his professional services in exchange for goods or services provided by his patients. One time a patient brought him a bushel of tomatoes. Another patient gave him several large sacks of candy, which I eager consumed.

In today's modern medical system, few individuals can afford to pay for treatment out of their own savings. And the informal barter arrangements physicians used for thousands of years are today considered tax evasion.

Insurance billing for medical services is a fact of life. Insurers demand detailed information from physicians, including mental health counselors and doctors, to justify continued treatment. According to Paul Appelbaum, vice president of the American Psychiatric Association:

Managed care companies are requesting much more information than they need to make coverage decisions, including "comments about suicide attempts, extramarital affairs, job-related problems and drug or alcohol abuse."[15]

It was once possible to restrict disclosure of sensitive medical information by not making an insurance claim for a condition that you'd rather keep private. However, under current U.S. law, medical records are released to the federal government, data-processing companies, insurers, hospitals, doctors, and credit bureaus, in many cases without your consent.[16]

Employer Spying—On and Off the Job

Employers have long kept a watchful eye on employees during company hours. The "punch clock," which required employees to clock in at the beginning and end of the workday, came into use more than a century ago. But in recent years, monitoring has evolved from simple confirmation of physical presence into much more detailed surveillance of employee activities on—or off—the clock.

There are few privacy rights in the U.S. workplace. In most states, employers can:

- Prohibit you from speaking your opinion;
- Read your e-mail and monitor your keystrokes and Web-surfing habits at work;

- Search you or your office;
- Require you to submit to lie detector (polygraph) tests, if you work for the government or the tests are administered in connection with an ongoing investigation involving an economic loss to your employer;
- Monitor your credit record;
- Conduct random drug tests;
- Listen in on your telephone conversations at work;
- Require you to undergo medical or psychological examinations to determine your fitness for continued employment;
- Prohibit you from smoking tobacco or drinking alcohol; and
- Conduct surveillance if you make a worker's compensation claim to determine the claim's validity.

In most states, if you refuse to consent to such restrictions, you may be dismissed. [17]

You have a right to inspect files government agencies and credit bureaus keep on you. But you have no such right to inspect your own employment records (except in a few states).

Employers take many of these precautions to avoid lawsuits. For instance, if an employee downloads or otherwise brings sexually explicit materials into the office, an employer may be sued for sexual harassment. A racist opinion voiced by an employee at work may lead to a lawsuit. So might an accident involving an employee who uses illicit drugs.

Police Records: There for the Taking

Police agencies maintain detailed information on individuals suspected, accused, or convicted of crimes. You have no assurance that these records are accurate. And, in many cases, they're not maintained securely.

In the United States, the largest law enforcement database is the FBI's National Crime Information Center (NCIC) database. The NCIC stores information regarding open arrest warrants, arrests, and dispositions regarding felonies and serious misdemeanors. As of 2003, it contained information on 52 million individuals. More than 80,000 law enforcement agencies nationwide have access to the NCIC database. Prospective employers and licensing boards throughout the United States have access as well. [18] The NCIC delivers information on suspected criminals more than five million times daily.

In 2006, the FBI proposed expanding the NCIC by adding records of juvenile crimes and minor misdemeanor offenses. This will expose persons with minor offenses in their pasts to a nationwide search by employers and licensing boards. [19] Another initiative involving the NCIC comes from the Department of Justice, which is building a massive database to permit police throughout the United States to search millions of case files from the FBI, Drug Enforcement Administration and other federal law enforcement agencies. The "OneDOJ" program merges investigative reports, criminal-history information, details of offenses, and the names, addresses and other information of criminal suspects or targets into one giant database. [20]

These efforts raise significant civil liberties concerns, because the NCIC database is notoriously inaccurate. A study in 2000 showed that nearly half the records contained errors, including omissions as basic as whether a criminal suspect was convicted or exonerated. [21] Perhaps that's why in 2003, the FBI announced that it would no longer enforce a requirement that information added to NCIC database be accurate or timely. [22]

There's also long history of unauthorized access to the NCIC. While federal law generally prohibits public access to law enforcement and intelligence databases, it's often available "at the right price" or to persons "with the right connections." Among other examples, nearly 100 Michigan police officers, dispatchers, federal agents, and security guards have illegally accessed police databases to stalk women, threaten motorists, and settle scores.[23] In 2001, a former FBI employee pleaded guilty to illegally disclosing "hundreds of different FBI records and documents pertaining to criminal cases and grand jury investigations."[24]

The NCIC, of course, is only one law enforcement database. There are many others, and there is no evidence that most of them are any more accurate or better protected than NCIC.

Identity Theft: The World's Fastest Growing Crime

Imagine having creditors hounding you to pay debts you never incurred—foreclosing on your legitimate property, hauling you into court, or even asking police to take you into custody. You can't buy a house, rent a car, or open a bank account, all because "the computer" shows that you're a deadbeat. You know it's not true, but convincing anyone else that the computer is wrong can almost be impossible.

This nightmare is called identity theft. And it's the fastest growing crime in America. Approximately 15 million Americans were victimized by some sort of identity-theft related fraud in the 12 months ending in mid-2006, according to a survey by Gartner, Inc.[25] That's up 50% from the 12-month period ending in mid-2005. A few examples:

- Linda Tapia, a schoolteacher's aide who lives in California, discovered that someone had run up US$60,000 in unpaid bills under her name, including a US$22,000 car.[26]
- Jessica Grant had excellent credit, until a woman in Texas applied for credit 19 times using Grant's name and Social Security number (SSN).[27]
- Los Angeles resident Linda Weaver was billed US$60,000 for an amputation of her foot that never occurred. When she contested the bill, hospital officials refused to give her access to her own medical records to learn who had stolen her identity.[28]

A "typical" victim's financial losses can run US$36,000. And this doesn't include what victims have to pay to creditors defrauded by imposters. It only includes legal expenses, lost wages, and lost time.

The damage to identity theft victims is compounded when bogus information is transferred between credit bureaus or other companies. Even if the original mistake is corrected, it can be difficult or impossible to persuade companies or law enforcement to remove the incorrect information or drop a criminal investigation.

Erroneous data can lead to decisions to deny a person the most basic privileges. Private data banks indexed by SSN track worker's compensation claims or "problem" tenants. A "hit" based on an erroneous report can make it difficult or impossible to obtain employment or housing.

One factor leading to the explosion in identity theft is the proliferation of information in the hands of banks, retailers, and private data warehouses. Computer hackers and fraudsters target the databases on which this data resides, often with devastating results. For instance, in 2007, retailer TJX, which owns T.J. Maxx and Marshall's, revealed that data from 45.7 million credit and debit cards had been stolen in a computer security breach.[29]

Another identity theft scam tries to get you to launder money for the same criminals who steal your identity. Victims risk not only identity theft, but also criminal prosecution for wire fraud and money laundering. Scammers offer positions on online job sites such as "finance manager" or "accountant." In most cases, the job boils down to wiring stolen money from one account to another. [30]

Fortunately, it's easy to protect yourself from most common means of identity theft. The most important measures include sending and receiving your mail in a locked mailbox and avoiding disclosure of your SSN. These simple steps go a long way toward protecting your privacy. Chapter 3 contains additional suggestions.

High-Tech Surveillance

The technology available to monitor even the smallest details of everyday life has advanced to the point that the descriptions in Orwell's *1984* no longer seem remote. The following examples are hardly exhaustive, but give a feel for what's in store.

- At U.S. border crossings, customs officials use "gamma ray scanners" to check tanker trucks for contraband, scanning right through the vehicle's metal sides;[31]
- At some airport security checkpoints, officials are now equipped with body scan x-ray devices that see through clothing;[32]
- Sophisticated closed circuit televisions employing face scanning technology now scan public areas to identify suspected terrorists or criminals;[33]
- Police are using thermal imaging devices to scan houses for unusual heat sources that could indicate indoor marijuana growing operations. Houses can be scanned while police sit in their cruisers on the street. (The U.S. Supreme Court, however, has ruled that police can't conduct such scans without first obtaining search warrants);[34]
- The U.S. government plans to dramatically expand the domestic use of spy satellites that can see through clouds, buildings and underground bunkers, purportedly as an anti-terrorist measure.[35]

National ID Cards Through the "Back Door"

Imagine walking down the street to the corner store for a newspaper and being stopped by police. The police demand to see your identification. You aren't carrying it with you. You're immediately arrested and placed into custody.

Is this a totalitarian nightmare of East Germany or the Soviet Union? No, this is everyday life in dozens of countries that have already issued their citizens national ID cards that must be carried at all times. Failing to present the card upon demand is specifically an offense in many of these countries.[36]

Once a system of universal identification is established, it's a short step to requiring people to have and carry ID cards.

The tragic events of Sept. 11, 2001 led to renewed calls for national ID cards. Smart cards with massive quantities of embedded data about the holder have emerged as a proposed cure-all to prevent future terrorist incidents. This is despite the fact that most of the Sept. 11 hijackers were traveling with stolen travel documents that would have allowed them to obtain their national ID card in a fake name.

In the United States, the 2005 Real ID Act[37] establishes "national uniform standards" for driver's licenses. This will result in national identification cards coming in through the "back door," as you'll learn in Chapter 2.[38]

Proponents of national ID cards claim that they can be used for uses other than security: as a convenient way of receiving government benefits, for instance. This multiple use aspect of national ID cards illustrates a common process in privacy invasion: "surveillance creep." A technology or law intended for one purpose, winds up being used for many others.

A classic example is the Social Security card. Once stamped "not for identification," the number on your Social Security card is now required to file a tax return, open a bank account and to obtain a driver's license. Will "smart" national ID cards be any different?

One way to sell a national ID initiative is on the basis of user convenience. A *de facto* national ID system is already available to U.S. persons who travel internationally. You provide the Immigration and Naturalization Service (INS) with biographical data—home address, date of birth, etc.—and the INS photographs an image of your hand and electronically records it onto a plastic card.

This voluntary system, called INSPASS, is designed to demonstrate the feasibility of including machine-readable biographical and biometric data on U.S. passports. And all newly issued U.S. passports come with a microchip embedded in the cover. Data on the chip includes your name, date of birth and a digitized version of your photo. Unfortunately, the data isn't encrypted and can be read remotely. This raises the possibility of rings of identity thieves using sophisticated "skimmers" to retrieve this data.[39]

Another rationale governments use to justify national IDs is to crack down on black markets and the underground, tax-free economy. And with a microchip ID card that can also be used as a debit or credit card, governments could even eliminate a paper currency. It's a short step from "debit/credit cards accepted here" to "Sorry, we only take debit/credit cards."

Closed Circuit Television and "Surveillance Creep"

One of the fastest growing surveillance technologies is closed circuit television (CCTV). In city centers and other locations thought to be security risks or attract crime, CCTV is increasingly popular.

The United Kingdom has perhaps more CCTV cameras than any other country. At the end of 2006, there were an estimated 4.2 million CCTV cameras in Britain, one for every 14 people. More than 300 separate cameras might capture an individual in a major city like London on an average day.[40]

In the U.K. city of Middlesbrough, hidden CCTV cameras actually appear to scold you if you litter, are drunk, urinate in public, or engage in other "anti-social behaviors." The unexpected broadcast comes via a loudspeaker controlled by a CCTV control center staff—and delivered in the voice of a child.[41]

More surveillance creep: Software is being developed to spot when someone's on-camera behavior hints they may be about to commit a crime. Microphones are being built in to CCTV units to record conversations. Software automatically scans CCTV footage for suspicious behavior and matches it with mug shots. Police have proposed equipping CCTV units with "x-ray vision" that see through clothing in a bid to thwart terrorism. And thousands of security Webcams are now accessible via a simple query on search engines.[42]

Your Car is Spying on You

When you start your car, you might not think of the privacy implications. But many vehicles now contain global positioning system (GPS) technology that can pinpoint your location, wherever you travel.

GPS, originally conceived for the U.S. military, has evolved into a multi-billion-dollar industry. General Motors' **OnStar** system is now installed in millions of vehicles. Police and government agencies can track any of these vehicles—and in the United States, the courts have ruled that investigators don't need a warrant.[43] The FBI and other police agencies can also use these factory-installed tracking systems to eavesdrop on passengers.[44]

Car rental companies use GPS devices to pinpoint a driver's location and speed. The companies can set boundaries for their vehicles, so they know when cars are taken across state or provincial borders. The system can even deactivate a vehicle's ignition if it's been stolen, driven too fast, or operated in a location prohibited by the rental contract.

In another use for GPS, car insurance companies are rewarding drivers that don't use their cars often with lower rates. Naturally, the insurance companies want proof that the cars aren't being driven. Rather than inspect the odometers, the high-tech solution is to track the car by GPS satellite.[45]

GPS isn't the only threat to privacy in your car. "Black box" surveillance systems are now installed in most newly manufactured automobiles. Among other information, the box records a vehicle's speed, acceleration, etc. in much the same manner as the boxes placed in commercial airliners. In an accident, the readers just before the accident can determine if the vehicle was operated unsafely.

Another threat to vehicle privacy are automatic toll collection systems. Millions of U.S. drivers use a system called **E-Z Pass**. Subscribers open prepaid accounts, then receive special tags for their cars' windshields. When a car with one of these tags cruises through a suitably equipped toll plaza, the toll is automatically debited. The E-Z Pass system transponders record the time and location each time a toll is collected. The data is not private: police already use information recorded by E-Z Pass and similar systems in investigations.[46] Increasingly, the records are also available in civil litigation.[47]

Your Cell Phone is Spying on You

Pursuant to federal **E911 requirements**, all cell phones must contain technology permitting their location to be tracked within 100 meters of their actual position. Even more precise location information—within a few feet—is possible if the cell phone is equipped with a GPS chip. This information is continuously transmitted to the cellular provider whenever the cell phone is switched on.[48]

Do-it-yourself surveillance is possible, too. Web sites like **ULocate** (http://www.ulocate.com) show a cell phone's location and the speed at which it's moving, superimposed on a detailed digital street map.

GPS critics say the technology could lead to "geo-slavery." University of Kansas research professor Jerome Dobson worries that once GPS devices are miniaturized to the point that they can be implanted under someone's skin,

[W]e are only one technological step from placing a transponder in there that burns or stings a person if they step off a prescribed path by a meter. Or if they stay too long in one place. Or cross the path of another person they are prohibited from seeing, or if they congregate with other people.[49]

Biometric Surveillance and Its Risks

After Sept. 11, 2001, proposals were advanced for automatic face recognition systems at airports, a national ID card containing a electronic fingerprint imprint, and retinal scans when checking in at the gate. However, biometrics, in combination with the other technologies that are explored in this book, presents unique dangers to privacy.

Fingerprinting is one of the oldest biometric technologies, and one of the most accurate. Once reserved for suspected criminals, demands for ordinary Americans not implicated in any crime to submit fingerprints are now commonplace. If you've walked into a bank to cash a check recently, you may have seen signs that say, "No thumb-print, no cash." Many banks now require a fingerprint to cash a non-account holder's check and a few banks even require customers opening new accounts to provide fingerprints.

The proliferation of fingerprinting in both the private and public sector is yet another example of surveillance creep, not accompanied by any debate over the implications of the everyday use of such technology.

However, fingerprinting is not foolproof. In 2004, FBI examiners concluded that a fingerprint linked to a bombing in Spain that left 191 dead came from Portland lawyer Brandon Mayfield. Indeed, the FBI was so sure of their finding that they called it "100% identification." But Spanish police later discovered that the fingerprint tied to Mayfield actually came from an Algerian man.[50]

DNA profiling. Every human being shares about 99% of the same genetic make-up. The remaining 1% is what makes each of us unique. The ability to identify patterns within DNA that are unique to each individual (except identical twins) has revolutionized forensic investigation. It has been used to convict murderers, clear those wrongly accused of murder, to identify the victims of war, and settle paternity disputes, among many other applications.

Governments worldwide are now seeking to establish national DNA databanks in which DNA samples from various segments of the population will be stored.

Initially, the proposals were limited to persons convicted of violent sexual crimes. Then, in another example of surveillance creep, the conditions were eased so that the databases would contain DNA samples from all violent criminals. For instance, in 2004, a U.S. federal appeals court upheld the compulsory DNA profiling of certain convicted federal offenders. Although the court's ruling was limited to convicted felons, civil liberties experts now believe that the decision will be a precedent for authorizing the government to collect DNA samples from everyone, guilty and innocent alike.[51] Indeed, Canada, France, and Germany have already experienced DNA dragnets where thousands of people were asked to provide samples of their DNA in murder investigations.[52]

But the real question is: for what other purposes will these databases be used? Will erosion of the legal concept of "innocent until proven guilty" be reversed on the questionable assertion that the presence of DNA at a crime makes all defenses irrelevant? Will insurance carriers eventually gain access to our DNA "fingerprints?" And most chilling of all, will future totalitarian governments use them to impose their twisted vision of genetic perfection, forcing "non-perfect" humans to undergo genetic "repair" or even euthanasia?

Face recognition. CCTV camera networks can be modified to recognize faces. While this technology is still in its embryonic stages, it promises to eventually permit a person's face to be compared against a database of known criminal suspects. If there is a match, police can arrest the suspect. Another use of the technology is to identify people who attempt to use forged documents to obtain official identification.

It's easy to fool today's face recognition software with changes in hairstyle or facial hair, aging, weight gain or loss, or simple disguises. Experts say the technology's error rate is up to 50% if photographs are taken without proper lighting or even if the subject is smiling.[53] Still, face recognition technology is improving. Research published in 2006, sponsored by the National Institute of Standards and Technology, demonstrates that machine recognition of human faces improved tenfold between 2002 and 2006.[54]

Implantable microchips. What's next, you might ask—a microchip implanted in your forehead or the back of your hand? Indeed, such a device has now been perfected and is approved by the U.S. Food and Drug Administration. Proponents see a huge market for implantable chips as the ultimate defense against identity theft or kidnapping and a valuable convenience as well. The **VeriChip**, manufactured by Applied Digital Solutions Inc., is implanted in your hand and can store personal data for identification or safety purposes, particularly for those with medical conditions such as Alzheimer's disease.[55] Hundreds of individuals have already been "chipped." More recently, the company proposed using implantable microchips to identify immigrants and guest workers.[56]

More surveillance creep: the chips don't have to just carry medical information—they can contain information about anything. For instance, with an e-commerce application called "VeriPay," rather than swipe a card or pay cash, you can buy anything with a mere wave of your hand. At the Baja Beach Club in Spain, patrons with a VeriPay microchip implant pay for cocktails with a swipe of the arm. If a swipe of the wrist requires too much effort, prototypes exist that can scan your purchases of products containing a compatible RFID (radio frequency identity) chip, and deduct the balance from your bank account, as you walk through the door.[57]

A world with most humans living with implantable microchips could evolve into the ultimate police state. Microchips would replace all current forms of ID such as passports, driver's licenses, social security, and credit/debit cards. You might not be able to withdraw money from the bank without it, receive benefits from the government without it, or buy or sell anything without it. The chip would also include data on your family history, address, occupation, criminal record, income tax information etc. At the touch of a button, your assets could be frozen, medical treatment denied, etc. The ultimate punishment would be to have your chip deactivated. In that case, you could no longer exist, since all personal and financial interactions would require verification of identity and confirmation of sufficient assets to complete a transaction.

Is this the future of surveillance? If it is, "privacy" will be a quaint—and meaningless—concept.

Big Brother is Watching You on the Internet

If someone could secretly stand behind you and monitor everything you've done on your PC, what would they discover about you that you would prefer to keep private? Thanks to new surveillance techniques, that's an appropriate comparison of the threat you face unless you take advance precautions:

- **The swap or page file Windows creates writes data in memory to disk.** Data you entered months or years ago can in many cases be retrieved long after you think it's gone.

- **When you hit "delete," file(s) aren't actually removed.** The index to that data is merely changed to indicate that the space it occupies on your hard disk is available for future use.
- **Formatting a disk doesn't remove the data that was stored on it.** Using the right software, a disk can be "unformatted" to recover the data in its entirety.

All versions of the Windows operating system are insecure, including the newest one, Vista. Other operating systems using a graphical interface (e.g., Mac OS) are also vulnerable, but the popularity of Windows makes PCs using this operating system most vulnerable.

In addition, all multitasking operating systems create huge temporary files in their normal operation. These temporary files are often anything but "temporary" and represent a significant threat to privacy and security.

When you connect to the Internet, the problem multiplies, because each log in can be traced via your **IP Address**, which your Internet Service Provider assigns you. If you use an "always on" Internet connection, your IP address usually stays the same. That makes you an even more attractive target. Anyone who can retrieve your IP Address can probably figure out who you are, unless you've taken advance precautions.

Many PCs—especially laptops—now come equipped with wireless networking capability. This makes it possible to log into the Internet at "hot spots" in airports and other locations. However, hot spots are magnets for identity thieves and hackers, because the connections often aren't encrypted, giving other users the ability to monitor the wireless signals coming and going from your laptop. Similar threats face home or office users of wireless networks.

Even bigger threats lurk in your e-mail and on the World Wide Web. Many types of "malicious mobile code" are spread via e-mail or booby-trapped Web pages. Vulnerabilities in Windows, for instance, allow viruses and other "malware" to spread to computers over the Internet. Each year, viruses cause billions of dollars of damage to infected PCs and networks.

Two other rapidly growing threats are **botnet** and **phishing** attacks. Hackers can secretly make your PC part of a botnet through an infected Web page or e-mail attachment. The botnet silently takes control of your PC. Once your PC is compromised in this manner, it's used by organized crime syndicates to distribute child pornography or for other illicit purposes, while insulating those responsible from being detected.[58] In a phishing attack, you receive an e-mail purported to come from a financial institution or other trusted source. The message tries to trick you into logging onto a phony Web site impersonating a legitimate Web site and disclosing personal data such as your name, address, and SSN. The Web site operators then use this information to steal your identity.[59]

One of the biggest threats to privacy and security on the Internet is the explosion in technology facilitating interaction. Chat rooms, Web cams, blogs, "social networking" Web sites and the like expose information that is permanently archived at Web sites such as http://www.archive.org for future retrieval. Disclosure of this information has already led to loss of employment opportunities, lawsuits, and even criminal investigations.[60]

The most recent threat to computer privacy in the United States is a requirement that came into effect in 2007 stipulating that domestic Internet Service Providers make their networks "wiretap friendly." Essentially, this requires that networks be designed so that law enforcement authorities can monitor your online activity without intervention by the network. The requirements apply to universities, public libraries, Internet cafés, and other institutions that operate networks connected to the Internet.[61]

Conclusion

What are the most significant threats to privacy and wealth in the 21st century?

As annoying as the proliferation of surveillance technologies are in private hands, a far larger danger exists when governments use these technologies. There is a long history of private-public surveillance partnerships, as you'll learn in Chapter 2. These partnerships, many of them occurring out of the public eye, have already resulted in significant losses of privacy and autonomy.

An even larger danger, however, is when a population is conditioned to demand less privacy and greater surveillance over their wealth as the price for "security." This is precisely the threat today, as the United States and other countries systematically dismantle longstanding privacy and civil liberties protections to fight a poorly defined war on terrorism.

CHAPTER TWO: THE U.S. AND GLOBAL SURVEILLANCE INFRASTRUCTURE

The United States with its worldwide network of spy satellites and listening stations has the world's most extensive electronic surveillance infrastructure. U.S. law mandates extensive disclosure for many types of financial transactions and imposes severe penalties for non-compliance, giving the United States the world's most pervasive financial surveillance system.

U.S. communications and financial surveillance networks now operate globally. The impact of these surveillance networks on persons seeking to preserve privacy is profound.

Wealth and Privacy at Home
U.S. Constitution: No "Right to Privacy"

Stop throwing the Constitution in my face. It's just a goddamned piece of paper!

—President George W. Bush (2005)[62]

While the U.S. Constitution contains several implied privacy rights, U.S. law supports no right to financial privacy and only a limited right to personal privacy.

In U.S. law, courts have the power to create binding legal precedent with their decisions. This power is inherited from the common law of England. U.S. courts have frequently been called upon to make law in the realm of privacy, because the laws enacted to protect it are so inadequate.

Privacy legislation usually passes only when questionable information handling practices are related to highly visible or newsworthy events. For instance, the Video Privacy Protection Act of 1988 came into being only after records of videos rented by U.S. Supreme Court nominee Robert Bork were leaked to newspapers. As a result, under U.S. law, your video rental records have far greater legal protection than your medical or financial records.

Although the word "privacy" doesn't appear in the U.S. Constitution, there are several rights defined in the Bill of Rights that relate to privacy:

- The right to free association (First Amendment);
- A prohibition against illegal searches and seizures (Fourth Amendment);
- A prohibition against compelled testimony against oneself (Fifth Amendment);
- A guarantee that property not be taken without "just compensation" (Fifth Amendment);
- The ban on unreasonable punishment and excessive fines (Eighth Amendment);
- The reservation of unenumerated rights to the people (Ninth Amendment);
- The prohibition against states enacting laws abridging or otherwise interfering with their citizens' rights without due process (Fourteenth Amendment)

In addition to these constitutional provisions, U.S. courts have recognized four causes of actions that constitute an invasion of privacy:

- Intrusion (e.g., eavesdropping or repeated aggravating phone calls);
- Public disclosure of private facts, especially facts that can embarrass or threaten the safety of the victim, even if the information is true;
- Appropriating a person's name or likeness for commercial gain without that person's permission; and
- Casting a person in a false light.[63]

These causes of action are much stronger in relation to invasions of privacy by individuals or businesses than by government. With few exceptions, governments at all levels in the United States have assigned themselves an almost unlimited right to invade privacy, as justified by the need to regulate interstate commerce, fight crime, combat terrorism, etc.

Filburn's Sorrow: No Limits to Interstate Commerce

The **Commerce Clause** of the U.S. Constitution reads:

The Congress shall have Power ...To regulate Commerce with foreign Nations, and among the several States, and with the Indian Tribes.

The U.S. Supreme Court has held that the Commerce Clause gives the government the authority to regulate any activity with the potential to have an effect on commerce between states, even if the activity takes place at home and the goods or services produced never leave your property. In its 1942 *Filburn* ruling, the court ruled that the government could prohibit farmers from growing crops on their own land for their own consumption, if the cultivation exceeded official production quotas.[64]

In 2005, using *Filburn* as precedent, the Supreme Court ruled that the federal government can regulate through prohibition the theoretical economic transactions of individuals who grow and consume medical marijuana on their own property.[65] Given this reasoning, what can stop the government from saying that you don't have the right to make a free choice in any activity it chooses to regulate? Nothing, unless in the future, the Commerce Clause is interpreted more narrowly.

Fourth Amendment: More and More Warrantless Searches

The Fourth Amendment to the U.S. Constitution provides:

The right of the people to be secure in their persons, houses, papers, and effects, against unreasonable searches and seizures, shall not be violated, and no warrants shall issue, but upon probable cause, supported by oath or affirmation, and particularly describing the place to be searched, and the persons and things to be seized.

"Probable cause," according to *Black's Law Dictionary*, is

...reasonable cause; having more evidence for than against ... more than mere suspicion but less than the quantum of evidence required for conviction.

Over the years, the definition of what constitutes a "search" requiring probable cause has become progressively narrower. According to the U.S. Supreme Court, an involuntary blood test ordinarily requires probable cause to conduct[66] (e.g., to determine if an individual is legally intoxicated), but taking a voice sample doesn't require it[67] Similarly, obtaining handwriting samples[68] and fingerprints don't constitute a Fourth Amendment search.[69]

The Supreme Court has ruled that finger scrapings—material that can be scraped out from underneath your fingernails and may contain microscopic evidence that can be used against you—constitute a search.[70] However, police may shave large amounts of hair from your head, neck, and shoulders, without a warrant, probable cause, or any other basis for suspecting that the hair would provide evidence of crime.[71]

You have the most protection against "unreasonable" searches and seizures in your own home. There is an enhanced zone of privacy at home, originating in the decision in 1604 of an English court, which established the principle,

...that the house of every one is to him as his castle and fortress, as well for his defense against injury and violence, as for his repose.[72]

U.S courts have held that the Fourth Amendment protects a "zone of privacy" around your home from which you can reasonably exclude others. Police must have probable cause of a crime to enter that space without your consent, along with the dwelling itself. This area is known as the **curtilage**. The Supreme Court defines curtilage as "the area [that] harbors the intimate activity associated with the sanctity of a man's home and the privacy of life."[73]

You may therefore refuse consent for a warrantless search of your home, unless police have probable cause that evidence of a crime is being destroyed.[74] Police must also obtain warrants before using high-tech devices that search through walls.[75] However, the curtilage doesn't include outbuildings or fields within in a property line, even when "No Trespassing" signs are posted.[76]

Paradoxically, asserting your right to refuse a warrantless search may constitute probable cause for one. In one case, a homeowner was asked by police for permission to search his home. He refused and declined to talk to police until an attorney was present. Police presented this "evidence" to a county magistrate and obtained a search warrant for the home. Based on the results of the search, the homeowner was tried and convicted on criminal charges. A U.S. federal appeals court ruled that while the warrant was improperly issued, police reliance upon it to search the home was permissible.[77]

No expectation of privacy extends to documents or other items once they leave your home. For instance, there is no expectation of privacy for trash placed out for collection, since we "knowingly expose it to the public" and "voluntarily turn it over to third parties."[78]

Nor does the concept of curtilage apply to communications made from your home via postal mail, telephone, e-mail, or the Internet. These communications can be monitored, recorded or examined under whatever legal rationale Congress imposes, with or without a warrant, as you'll learn later in this chapter.

For more information on what constitutes a "search" under U.S. law, and how to avoid giving up your right to be free of an unreasonable search, see Chapter 3.

Fifth Amendment: The "Right to Silence" is Disappearing

The Fifth Amendment provides, in part:

No person shall ... be compelled in any criminal case to be a witness against himself.

An 1886 Supreme Court decision, *Boyd vs. United States*,[79] held that the Fourth and Fifth Amendments create a "zone of privacy" which protects an individual and his personal records from compelled production. But in 1984, after a series of decisions that minimized the impact of *Boyd,* the Supreme Court virtually overturned it. The court concluded that, "The Fifth Amendment provides absolutely no protection for the contents of private papers of any kind."[80]

This means that if the government subpoenas records you compile voluntarily or under compulsion of law (e.g., tax records), you must release them, or face a contempt citation. Those records may then be used against you in a civil or criminal proceeding. However, the government must know that the records actually exist.[81] Nor does Fifth Amendment extend to personal records that may tend to incriminate you, if a third party, such as a financial institution, holds them.[82]

The "right to silence" also doesn't apply to persons that are under investigation, but haven't been arrested. Oliverio Martinez thought he was dying after a police officer shot him five times, leaving him blind and paralyzed. Martinez begged police not to question him as he awaited medical treatment, but the Supreme Court ruled that the right to remain silent doesn't apply when authorities aggressively, or even coercively, interrogate someone they're not prosecuting.[83]

Grand Juries: What You Say Can Be Used Against You

A skilled prosecutor could indict a ham sandwich.

--Judge Thomas W. Brothers, Davidson County, Tennessee

The Fifth Amendment states in part:

No person shall be held to answer for a capital, or otherwise infamous crime, unless on a presentment or indictment of a grand jury.

The grand jury system is heavily tilted against a witness or defendant. If you're subpoenaed to testify at a grand jury proceeding, you aren't permitted to have your attorney accompany you (except in a few states). No judge is present; no referee between you and the prosecutor exists. Unless provided immunity, anything you say can be used against you.

The grand jury hears only one side of the story—the prosecutor's. A prosecutor may present the same case to a grand jury repeatedly, until the statute of limitations expires. In cases with no statute of limitations, grand jury probes can last a lifetime. The prosecutor isn't only the advocate, but also the legal adviser to the grand jury, which must determine, without hearing evidence from the defense, whether you should be charged with a crime. Moreover, the Supreme Court has ruled that a judge may not dismiss an indictment merely because prosecutors fail to disclose evidence to a Grand Jury suggesting that you're innocent.[84]

Historically, disclosure of grand jury testimony was permitted only to those directly involved in the enforcement of criminal law, or by court order. Secrecy is critical to the grand jury's investigative effectiveness, but secrecy also serves to minimize the harm that may be caused by grand jury investigations.

This status has changed, thanks to the USA PATRIOT Act.[85] This law permits disclosures of grand jury material without a court order for purposes unrelated to the enforcement of federal criminal law. This exemption is justified by the war on terrorism.

Presumption of Innocence Lost

Although the U.S. Constitution does not state it explicitly, U.S. courts have recognized for more than a century that the presumption of innocence is constitutionally protected. In a normal criminal proceeding, your presumption of innocence can be overcome only by evidence proving guilt "beyond a reasonable doubt." In a civil proceeding, the prevailing side must demonstrate by the "preponderance of the evidence" that its claims are more likely than not to be true.

In 1895, the Supreme Court traced the presumption of innocence as a legal concept dating to biblical times. The court declared:

The principle that there is a presumption of innocence in favor of the accused is the undoubted law, axiomatic and elementary, and its enforcement lies at the foundation of the administration of our criminal law.[86]

In 2005, however, the Supreme Court ruled that in relation to a U.S. citizen held as an alleged "enemy combatant," the standard of due process guaranteed under the Constitution:

...would not be offended by a presumption in favor of the Government's evidence, so long as that presumption remained a rebuttable one and fair opportunity for rebuttal were provided.[87]

Those defending this decision say that the reversal only applies to suspected terrorists. This is nonsense. The government defines who is not a terrorist, and can change its definition any time. When combined with laws such as the Military Commissions Act (2005),[88] which allows the president to throw anyone in prison, including U.S. citizens, with no judicial process whatsoever, the Supreme Court has reversed not only 200 years of U.S. legal precedent, but centuries of Western legal tradition.

How *Roe vs. Wade* Devastated Privacy

The Ninth Amendment is perhaps the most important amendment in the Bill of Rights. It's certainly the most ignored amendment, especially by the Supreme Court, when it comes to our "expectation of privacy" under the U.S. Constitution.

The Ninth Amendment reads:

The enumeration in the Constitution, of certain rights, shall not be construed to deny or disparage others retained by the people.

Many privacy advocates hail the 1973 Supreme Court decision in *Roe vs. Wade*[89] as a victory for privacy rights, specifically, a woman's right to choose to have an abortion. But the decision was a disaster for financial privacy. That's because in coming to its conclusion, the Supreme Court avoided taking the approach it had in previous privacy-related cases of citing the Ninth Amendment as the basis for its decision.[90] Instead, the *Roe* court found a qualified right to abortion in the Fourteenth Amendment's due process clause, which reads:

No State shall make or enforce any law which shall abridge the privileges or immunities of citizens of the United States; nor shall any State deprive any person of life, liberty, or property, without due process.

It avoided relying on Ninth Amendment, which not only has much broader language reserving unenumerated or "natural" rights to the people, but specifically applies to the federal government.

A few years later, when litigants challenged the constitutionality of the Bank Secrecy Act, a law which requires banks to act as unpaid spies on their customers to enforce federal money laundering laws, the *Roe* court held that bank customers had no "expectation of privacy" for information shared with a third party. No such expectation exists even if the common law, state constitutions, and private contracts require it. Nor do customers have the right to challenge the law.[91] Then in 1984, the *Roe* court overturned its own century-old decision protecting "private papers" kept at home.[92]

As it stands today, any U.S. business must turn over your private information at government demand. In some cases, neither probable cause of wrongdoing nor a search warrant is necessary. Police, military, and intelligence agencies can then "data mine" this personal information and examine it for anomalies that might reveal the need for further investigation.

Wealth, Privacy and the Nanny State

Until 1913, most law-abiding Americans could go through life and hardly notice the existence of the federal government. They could live wherever they wanted and imbibe any substance without fear of prosecution. Americans weren't required to have an official number or identity card. International travel was possible without a passport or any official permission. The use of currency or gold and silver coins in commerce wasn't suspect; indeed, there was no real alternative.

In 1913, though, there were two developments with profoundly negative impacts on privacy and wealth: the beginning of the federal income tax and the inauguration of the Federal Reserve System. A year later, Congress enacted the first statute regulating the sale of narcotic drugs. These early efforts began a long-term trend of assigning to government the responsibility of protecting people from themselves, and to provide a reliable source of funding for this responsibility.

Typically, Congress establishes an agency to deal with a perceived problem. Once it is established, it tends to grow. As it grows, the agency justifies its existence by calling for greater powers to regulate, innovate, etc.—always, of course, for the public good.

When the government can't prohibit something that it believes is "bad," it often imposes high taxes on the targeted product or behavior. This often results in the government becoming addicted to the new tax revenue from the behavior it wishes to discourage. The pattern of condemnation, prohibition, and taxation often creates alliances of parties with wildly differing agendas who jointly support policies that don't work as advertised.

This section provides several examples of how efforts to establish the "Nanny State" in the United States have resulted in a significant loss of privacy.

Social Security Act (1935)

In 1934, President Franklin Roosevelt announced an initiative to provide for the retirement needs of older Americans. The result was the Social Security program; an entitlement which seven decades later is the single largest item in the federal budget.

No Contractual Right to Social Security Benefits

Do you have a legal right to receive Social Security benefits because you paid money into the program? In 1960, the Supreme Court said "no" (*Flemming vs. Nestor, 363 U.S. 603* (1960). In a case involving an individual who was denied Social Security benefits because of his past membership in the Communist Party, the Supreme Court defined the benefits not as a contractual obligation, but as **welfare**. According to the ruling:

The Social Security system could accurately be described as a form of social insurance, enacted pursuant to Congress' power to "spend money in aid of the general welfare."

While the law denying Social Security benefits to ex-Communists was long ago repealed, the principle that there is no contractual obligation to beneficiaries hasn't changed. Congress can end benefits to any class of people it chooses, any time. For instance, in 2005, the Supreme Court upheld a law stipulating that the government can seize a person's Social Security benefits to pay off student loans (*Lockhart vs. United States*, 546 U.S. 142 (2005)).

Americans have been hoodwinked into "volunteering" into a "social security" scheme to which they have no contractual right to the funds we've paid in, and which they can be deprived of any time. As such, the Social Security system is a monumental scam: not only because it's essentially a Ponzi Scheme, but because any insurance company that claimed it could deprive contractholders of their entitlement would be shut down by the courts as a fraud.

While the concept of "old age security" is an attractive one, Social Security suffers from a fundamental problem: it's a "pay as you go" system. Benefits aren't "banked" for payment to the persons who earned them. Rather, much like a Ponzi scheme, earlier "investors" have first access to the funds taken in.

Ponzi schemes work as long as the numbers of persons paying into the system and those receiving payouts from them stay in the same approximate proportion. However, with Social Security, the proportion of people paying in to the system to beneficiaries is now at a historic low, and in the next 25-50 years will go lower still. The enormous gap between the benefits promised future retirees, and the resources available to meet those promises, requires a long-term infusion of trillions of dollars.[93]

The consequences to privacy and wealth of this continuing need for cash are immense. "Defections" from Social Security must be prevented. Preventing defections means, among other initiatives, that as many persons be brought into the system as possible, and not permitted to leave. At Social Security's inception, only workers in commercial and industrial occupations were covered. The military, the self-employed, and agricultural and domestic workers were exempt. Over time, Congress brought all these worker categories into the system.

In 1988, Congress enacted the Family Support Act, which mandated that states require parents to submit Social Security numbers (SSNs) to obtain birth certificates for their children. Even if the parents don't apply for a SSN for their baby, the government knows the parents' SSNs, and is alerted to the new arrival. No defections are allowed. Parents must also place the SSNs of their children on their tax returns in order to obtain deductions for them, assuring a cradle-to-grave identification card for every U.S. citizen.

The Social Security system diminishes privacy in other ways, due to the process of surveillance creep described in Chapter 1. Any public agency that administers taxes, general public assistance, driver's licenses, or motor vehicle registrations may require SSN disclosure. A federal appeals court has ruled that a state may deny a driver's license to a person who declines to provide a SSN.[94] Federal legislation also requires states to collect SSNs to administer various federal mandates; e.g., before issuing professional, occupational or marriage licenses.

Private companies find SSNs useful to identify their

customers. There are few restrictions on the private use of SSNs, or on government retrieval of data held by private companies that use the number as an identifier. Since banks and other non-governmental entities can legally turn away customers who refuse to supply SSNs, their use in the private sector is taken for granted in everything from medical insurance to credit applications.

The use of SSNs as a universal identifier presents many opportunities for impersonation and fraud. Confidential data may often be retrieved over the phone from banks, credit card companies, and insurance companies by anyone who provides a name and matching SSN, since knowledge of a person's SSN is often equated with proof of his identity.

This danger would be less serious if it were difficult to obtain other people's SSNs; it isn't. Given a name and address, private investigators or credit-reporting agencies can usually obtain a person's SSN. Corrupt employees of the Social Security Administration (SSA) sell personal data to investigators.[95] Many people list SSNs on checks. Employees in a large (but decreasing) number of companies must show their SSN on their ID badges. Doctors and other professionals often list their SSNs on their stationary or on prescription forms. Most government agencies use the SSN as an identification number, although in 2006, the Bush administration instructed federal agencies not to rely on SSNs for identification purposes.[96]

The (No) Privacy Act

Periodically, Congress becomes concerned about how the information that the bureaucracies it has created is used, and turns that concern into new legislation.

The Privacy Act (1974)[97] was such a law. Enacted shortly after Richard Nixon resigned the presidency, the act was designed to regulate the use of secret databases by executive agencies controlled by the president, many of them keyed to SSNs. It was supposed to give individuals access to information about them in government records and to protect that information from unauthorized disclosure.

The law stipulates that no federal agency may disclose information contained in a "system of records" to any other person or agency except by written request and with the prior written consent of the individual to whom the records pertain. Moreover, disclosure is permissible only "for a purpose that is compatible with the purposes for which it was collected." Federal agencies must maintain a list of disclosures, and citizens have the right to examine their files and challenge information they believe to be inaccurate.

However, there are gaping loopholes in these requirements. No notification or consent is required:

- If a transfer of information is a "routine use";
- If information is to be provided to another agency for civil or criminal law enforcement;
- If "national security" is at stake; or
- For data exchange with state and local authorities.

Almost from its inception, government bureaucrats plotted to overcome the restrictions of the Privacy Act. In 1977, the Carter administration initiated **Project Match**, a program to compare names of federal employees with those of welfare recipients. The matches were keyed to employee and welfare recipient SSNs.

Project Match violated the Privacy Act in at least three ways:

1. Records couldn't be disclosed to another agency without the permission of the individual on whom the record was being kept;
2. Records couldn't be used for purposes inconsistent with the purpose for which they were originally collected; and
3. Information couldn't be disclosed without an indication that a specific violation had occurred or might occur.

However, the matches proceeded in spite of these violations.

In 1984, Congress came full-circle in passing the Deficit Reduction Act.[98] This legislation avoided violating the Privacy Act by requiring states—which were not subject to the act's authority—to conduct computer matches to eliminate fraud and duplication in federal entitlement programs.

The Computer Matching and Privacy Protection Act (1988)[99] authorized even greater computer matching. States and federal agencies now could access a wide range of private and public databases to fight entitlement fraud: court records, credit bureau records, Drug Enforcement Administration, Educational Testing Service, Immigration and Naturalization Service, IRS, Medicare, Medicaid, Medical Information Bureau, motor vehicle records, National Driver Registry, National Parent Locator, National Crime Information Center, Passport Office, Social Security Administration, etc.

Joint federal-state enforcement efforts made possible by the act include initiatives:

*   By the Department of Transportation to create a nationwide database of driver's license holders designed to prevent persons who have had their license suspended in one state from obtaining a license in another state;
*   By the IRS to create an Individual Master File on every taxpayer and withhold tax refunds to persons who owe the federal government money; and
*   By the Customs Service to supply data on customs declarations to state tax authorities, so that states can impose sales taxes on imported goods.

New exemptions to the Privacy Act are constantly applied for, and approved. For instance, when the Treasury Department's financial intelligence unit, the Financial Crimes Enforcement Network (FinCEN), was created by executive order in 1990, the agency exempted itself from the Privacy Act's requirements that it:

*   Disclose the contents of its databases;
*   Permit public access to its databases;
*   Allow individuals to determine whether the agency maintained records containing information about them;
*   Permit individuals the right to amend incorrect information in a FinCEN database;
*   Not collect information beyond that "relevant and necessary to accomplish a FinCEN purpose"; and
*   Maintain records to a discernible standard of accuracy.

In 1996, the Personal Responsibility and Work Opportunity Act[100] further weakened the Privacy Act by creating the Federal Child Support Registry. The database logs the names of every parent ordered by a state court to pay child support. By cross-checking those names with a national database of newly hired workers, states can track down and withhold wages from the paychecks of more than five million parents who don't pay child support. All matches are keyed to SSNs.

The act requires banks to search their databases every three months for matches against state-provided lists of parents that have fallen behind in child support payments. As you'd expect, the results are often inaccurate. State authorities have seized the bank accounts of hundreds of men who were later determined not to be the fathers of the children in question. Since the law makes it illegal for banks to notify depositors of this practice, the first warning you may get that your account is affected is when it's mistakenly frozen.

Even the President of the United States, the official whom the drafters of the Privacy Act most wanted to be subject to this law, claims to be exempt from it. In 2000, a federal judge accused President Bill Clinton of violating the Privacy Act. His defense was that the White House is exempt from the law.[101]

Many agencies routinely co-mingle ordinary records with those having law enforcement or national security applications, thus exempting all such records from Privacy Act reporting requirements. The USA PATRIOT Act (2001) mandated such sharing of law enforcement and intelligence data, making the Privacy Act even less relevant.

The Privacy Act's gaping loopholes, and the cavalier attitude government officials toward it, have resulted in the law having little practical effect on government efforts to gather and cross-reference information on citizens, all tied to your SSN. When was the last time you received a notification that records about you were being released pursuant to the Privacy Act? I've never received such a notification—have you?

Your National ID, Disguised as a Driver's License

In 2005, Congress enacted the Real ID Act. Starting in 2013, no state driver's license that fails to conform to federally mandated "minimum standards" can be used for any federal "official purpose," such as boarding an airplane, buying a firearm, obtaining federal benefits, or even entering a federal courthouse. With this requirement, the United States is paving the way for a national ID card and internal passport; two of the ways totalitarian nations track their citizens.

The law's minimum standards require that state driver's licenses be machine-readable. The licenses must also contain your residential address. This data need not be protected in any way; states may publish your home address in plain text on the face of the license. Together, the machine-readable and residential address requirements will make identity theft much easier.

A major selling point of Real ID is that it will be difficult to forge the high-security driver's licenses to be created under its guidelines. However, a hard-to-forge ID card is an extremely valuable document, if its security can be compromised. The record of governments in producing "impossible to forge" ID documents is very poor, as described in Chapter 1.

But perhaps the most threatening aspect of this law is its creation of the equivalent of a national database to include details on nearly 250 million licensed drivers. The database will be created from a series of interlinking systems operated and administered by the states. Each state must provide electronic access to all other states to information contained in its motor vehicle database. An interlinked system is a far greater security risk than a decentralized one with each state issuing ID cards according to its own rules.

Since there's no requirement that the data on your Real ID be protected in any way, private companies are likely to use the information in it at will. Every retailer that requires identification will swipe your Real ID and then sell the data to information aggregators to be data mined at will.

Several states have refused to enforce the Real ID Act due to the high cost of implementing its requirements, estimated at more than US$23 billion.[102] While opposition to the law may succeed in minor delays in its implementation, the trend toward a national ID card may be unstoppable.

Securities Acts: Protecting Americans from Foreign Investments

For centuries, individuals have participated passively in financial ventures. And for just as long, their promoters have occasionally provided erroneous or fraudulent information to induce prospects to buy. Objects of speculation that have led to spectacular public losses include the Dutch East India Company tulip mania (1636-1640); British government debt (1763); and foreign bonds traded in London (1825).[103]

In the United States, state laws requiring registration of both securities and those persons selling them date from 1911. Securities promoters challenged the state laws on constitutional grounds, but in 1917, the U.S. Supreme Court upheld the securities laws of Ohio, South Dakota, and Michigan in three related cases.[104]

The first federal securities law, the Securities Act (1933),[105] was enacted after newspapers reported widespread fraud and corruption within the securities industry that helped feed speculation in the run-up to the Great Depression. A new federal agency, the Securities and Exchange Commission (SEC), was created to regulate the securities markets. However, federal securities legislation did not preempt state legislation. Nothing was done to deal with the massive expense and duplication of effort inherent in a system requiring companies to register both with the federal government and in each state in which they wished to raise money. This problem persists to the present day.

The 1934 Securities and Exchange Act[106] imposed the first laws against "insider trading." This is, essentially, any use of information for profit by persons with knowledge about a publicly traded company not available to the public. The problem is that the SEC never defined "insider trading." It feared that whatever definition it devised would be too narrow to sufficiently limit the types of "insider" activity the agency was trying to prohibit.

Here's a classic example of the "cure" being arguably worse than the disease. An individual intimately familiar with the operations of a company is in a better position to profit from that company than a person who lacks such familiarity. But by refusing to define insider trading, the SEC makes any investor who obtains inside knowledge about a company and invests based on that knowledge into a criminal.

Indeed, neither Congress nor the SEC bothered to define the term "security." It was left to the courts to do so, and in 1946, the Supreme Court ruled that a security is

...a contract, transaction or scheme whereby a person invests money in a common enterprise and is led to expect profits solely from the efforts of the promoter or a third party, it being immaterial whether the shares in the enterprise are evidenced by formal certificates or by nominal interests in the physical assets employed in the enterprise.[107]

Decades later, the collapse of Enron, WorldCom, Tyco, and other companies exposed conflicts of interest and compensation practices based on fraudulent incentives in publicly traded companies. Hundreds of billions of shareholder value disappeared, almost overnight. These revelations led to the enactment of the Sarbanes-Oxley Act (SOX)[108] in 2002. Rather than restore confidence in public companies, though, the act has forced domestic companies to raise capital from venture capitalists and prompted foreign firms to withdraw from U.S. securities markets altogether. In 2000, nine of every ten dollars raised by foreign companies were raised in the United States. In 2005, of the largest 25 public offerings globally, only one took place in the United States.[109]

Another effect of SEC regulation of the securities market is that U.S. investors are effectively prohibited from purchasing many non-U.S. investments. Most issuers of foreign securities won't allow U.S. residents to purchase them directly, for fear of coming under SEC jurisdiction. Fortunately, there are still ways U.S. residents can purchase foreign securities; you'll learn about them in Chapter 5.

Credit Abuse: You Don't Own Your Data

Do you have the quaint idea that information about you belongs to you? While the concept that your data is your property is an attractive one for those who care about privacy, the reality is very different.

Take credit reports, for instance. They're gold mines of information. Your credit report, keyed to your SSN, contains your birth date, current and previous addresses, telephone number, credit payment status, and employment. It also lists judgments, state and federal tax liens, repossessions, bankruptcies, lawsuits and criminal convictions, all keyed to your name and Social Security number, and available at the touch of a button.

Your credit report is compiled from many different sources. Companies that have granted you credit make regular reports about your accounts and payment history to the three main credit bureaus: **Equifax, Experian,** and **Trans Union**. Banks, credit card companies, department stores, hospitals, auto financing companies, etc., all provide information to credit bureaus about your payment history.

When you apply for credit, a lender will usually ask permission to obtain a credit history, ordinarily from one or more of the three major credit bureaus. The decision to grant you credit is based on a number of factors that comprise a "points" total. The scoring system was once kept secret by credit grantors, but in recent years, some of the formulas have been made public. (See, e.g., http://www.myfico.com.)

Credit bureaus perform an essential function in our mobile society. When individuals did not travel widely beyond their birthplace, the decision to grant credit was a matter of judging a person's reputation, often based on personal knowledge. However, credit grantors today most often deal with strangers. This makes a mechanism that allows them to check a person's creditworthiness essential.

Credit bureaus originated in the early the 20th century. A group of retailers would form a credit bureau so that each store wouldn't have to separately evaluate applicants for credit. But when a person relocated to another community, the application process had to be repeated. To facilitate these information exchanges, credit bureaus began to form affiliations. After World War II, national credit bureaus developed. By the 1960s, credit records were placed on computers. And thanks to computers, credit bureaus could provide a near-instant risk evaluation on most applicants for credit.

However, as with any other transition involving the manipulation of vast quantities of personal information, problems cropped up. Many individuals were denied credit based on outdated or inaccurate information. In response to these problems, in 1970, Congress enacted the Fair Credit Reporting Act.[110]

The law was designed to ensure that credit bureaus would provide accurate, up-to-date information, and that the data would be used only for its intended purpose. It stipulated that information constituting a "consumer credit report" could only be sold or transferred to those with a "legitimate business need for the information in connection with a business transaction involving the consumer." However, the act failed to define what is meant by "legitimate business need" or what constitutes a "business transaction." Not even the term "credit report" was precisely defined. It was left to the information industry and the Federal Trade Commission (FTC), the agency assigned to enforce the law, to define these terms.

Under the law and regulations issued to interpret it now in effect, you have the right to inspect your credit records and to contest inaccurate data. Credit bureaus must promptly investigate the claim and delete unverified data. If you're refused employment or credit due to negative information disclosed in a credit report, you have the right to inspect the report at no charge, within 60 days of disclosure. The Fair and Accurate Credit Transactions Act (2003)[111] requires that you be provided with one free copy of your credit report each year from all three major credit bureaus.

Even though these privacy protections appear substantial, there are many exceptions. "Consumer reporting agencies" (e.g., credit bureaus) may furnish credit reports, without your consent:

- In response to a court order or administrative subpoena (an assertion that credit records are relevant to an ongoing investigation);
- In connection with a credit transaction involving the consumer, or a review or collection action regarding such transactions;
- In an application for employment or insurance coverage; and
- To determine eligibility for a license or other benefit granted by a government agency required by law to consider an applicant's financial status.

The scope of these exceptions might surprise you. But even without them, you probably give written instructions permitting distribution of credit data more often than you might think. Credit card agreements authorize issuers to "make credit, employment, and investigative inquiries as deemed appropriate for the extension of credit or collection of amounts owing on the account." Signing the agreement gives the issuer authorization to obtain credit records and to review bank account balances to determine if you have sufficient funds to pay their bills.

Credit bureaus also generate and sell lists for use in "pre-approved" credit and insurance offers. If you receive an offer in the mail that you have been pre-approved for credit, this is the most likely source. However, the term "pre-approved" is misleading. If you respond to the offer, the credit-grantor will review your credit report to make certain you meet its lending criteria. You will be turned down if you don't qualify, and that fact may be noted on your credit report.

Credit bureaus also market "credit risk evaluation services." These mathematical models calculate the probability of a credit applicant falling behind on payments or declaring bankruptcy. Employers, banks, landlords, and government agencies use such services to evaluate prospective employees, customers, tenants, and investigative targets.

Since 2000, credit bureaus have been forbidden to sell information from credit reports to direct marketing companies without your permission. But credit bureaus work around the restriction by selling information not deemed "credit records." For instance, a credit bureau might sell mailing lists based on information gathered from consumer surveys, census data and public records.

Chapter 3 contains numerous suggestions to reduce the privacy invasion associated with the use of credit records.

Opt-Out of Data Sharing...if You Can

The Gramm-Leach-Bliley Act (1999)[112] overturned a 65-year-old prohibition against banks, securities firms, and insurance companies affiliating with one another. The end of this prohibition is a welcome one, as it ends the longstanding sanction against banks being able to buy or sell securities on behalf of their clients—a prohibition found almost nowhere else in the world.

However, a less publicized outcome of the act is that it loosens controls over the use of your personal data. The act gives you the right to opt out of exchanges of your personal financial data held by a company with unaffiliated third parties. But no such right exists if the company shares the data with **affiliate** companies. If your bank owns an insurance company, for instance, it might learn when you make an insurance claim for a heart attack and then cancel your line of credit. Some major banks have hundreds of affiliates. Companies can also avoid the opt-out provisions by entering into joint marketing agreements with non-affiliates.

In any event, few consumers bother to opt out. This may be because the "privacy notices" sent by companies to consumers advising them of their right to opt out don't make this right particularly clear. One privacy notice I received had the notification printed in six-point type; the size of the phrase "opt out" at the end of this sentence. Opt out.

Credit Repair Scams

In an age where good credit is essential to purchasing a home, buying a car or getting a job, it isn't surprising that companies have sprung up to assist consumers in "repairing" their credit. In return for large front-end fees, these companies guarantee they can remove negative information from your credit report, even if the information is accurate.

Unfortunately, many credit repair services are scams. One common scam provides instructions on how to secure a federal ID number (usually used by businesses) and use that in place of a Social Security number to apply for credit. Because credit bureaus rely on a SSN to match an application with a record in their databases, promoters claim that there will be no match between the person applying for credit and the consumer with the existing negative credit record. In a variation of the scam, promoters sell instructions on how to obtain a false SSN and use it to "start fresh" with a new credit identity—often at the expense of a co-worker, friend, or relative.

Police have shut down dozens of credit repair operations, but because of the demand for good credit, new ones continue to pop up. If you do business with a credit repair company that uses fraudulent means to "fix" your credit, you may be subject to both civil and criminal sanctions. It's a federal crime to lie on a loan or credit application, to misrepresent your SSN, and to obtain an Employer Identification Number from the IRS under false pretenses. Individuals taking these steps at the advice of credit repair services have prosecuted for mail fraud and wire fraud, among other crimes.

Data Mining: Big Business Marries Big Brother

Almost every piece of personal information that you might want to keep private—your bank statements, your telephone records, and your e-mail messages—is for sale.

As I described in Chapter 1, federal, state and local governments maintain many types of public records. An increasing number of these records are now available over the Internet. The Fair Credit Reporting Act doesn't regulate trade in public records, as data assembled from them are not "credit reports."

Companies such as **ChoicePoint, Acxiom, LexisNexis, Westlaw,** and **Seisint** exemplify the evolution of this trade in public records. ChoicePoint, for instance, has compiled more than 20 billion records on virtually every American into a series of searchable databases. These include property records; driver records; motor vehicle records; boating, records of pilot and professional licenses; and court records showing bankruptcies, liens, judgments and divorce. While you're permitted to access some of ChoicePoint's databases under the Fair Credit Reporting Act to insure that the records are accurate, other databases are off-limits. You're not legally entitled to review or make corrections to data that other companies and government agencies—including the FBI—can purchase and use to make decisions about you.

ChoicePoint's **AutoTrackXP** product, part of the company's Government and Law Enforcement Suite, is billed as providing:

Internet access to more than 17 billion current and historical records on individuals and businesses, and allows users to browse through those records instantly. With as little information as a name or Social Security number, users can cross-reference public and proprietary records including identity verification information, relatives and associates, corporate information, real property records, deed transfers and much more.[113]

ChoicePoint has numerous government clients, including the FBI and other intelligence agencies. Government use of data aggregators such as ChoicePoint, in effect, outsources government data-collection, effectively bypassing legislation such as the Privacy Act. When government officials buy that data or subscribe to data not incorporated into a government database, Privacy Act rules don't apply.

Yet, the reports ChoicePoint produces are riddled with errors—and in many cases, you have no right to contest them. A 2005 study revealed that **100%** of individuals who obtained a copy of a background check report prepared by ChoicePoint discovered serious errors in it. Most participants found errors in even the most basic biographical information: name, social security number, address and phone number.[114]

Another problem is poor security over the data maintained by data aggregators. In 2005, ChoicePoint sold more than 145,000 of its reports to identity thieves posing as legitimate businesses.[115]

In response to these problems, data aggregators have promised to improve accuracy and security of the reports they provide. ChoicePoint, for instance, is offering free credit reports and a free report-monitoring service to the 145,000 persons whose data was compromised in 2005.

Yet, there is a long way to go. There is little evidence that records maintained by data aggregators are much more accurate than they were in 2005, and state and federal law enforcement agencies still rely on them heavily, with little or no oversight.

Why Data Mining for Terrorists Will Never Work

One of the most innovative ways that information compiled by credit bureaus and data aggregators is used is through **data mining.** This is a data analysis technique that defines how an individual fits into a group, and predicts behavior based on characteristics of that group.

Direct marketers use data mining to pinpoint consumer tastes. Building upon experience derived from cross-matching government records to ferret out welfare fraud or tax evasion, government agencies today data mining to analyze thousands of databases containing billions of records of both U.S. citizens and non-citizens alike.

Most people first learned about data mining in 2002, when news of a secret government data-mining program called **Total Information Awareness** (TIA) hit the headlines. The idea was simple: compile as much data as possible on as many people as possible from as many data sources as possible, organize it so that it's searchable, then sift through it with super-computers to investigate patterns that might indicate terrorist plots. All transactions of everyday life—travel and telephone records, bank account transactions, e-mail messages, etc. would become part of what former Admiral (and convicted felon) John Poindexter, who headed up the TIA initiative, called a "virtual, centralized, grand database."[116]

Public outrage led to the shutdown of the TIA program, yet data mining hardly died. Indeed, as of 2004, according to the General Accountability Office (GAO), 122 federal data mining programs operate using personal information compiled by government agencies.[117] And this is only the tip of the iceberg, because the tally didn't include classified programs like the TIA.

According to the GAO, the most important uses of data mining by the federal government are designed to:

- Improve service or performance;
- Detect fraud, waste, and abuse;
- Analyze scientific and research information;
- Manage human resources;
- Detect criminal activities or patterns; and
- Analyze intelligence and detect terrorist activities.

In 2006, reports emerged that the TIA program had been resurrected by the National Security Agency (NSA), the super-secret intelligence arm of the Department of Defense. Evidence now suggests this technology has been further developed to enhance the effectiveness of the NSA's terrorist surveillance program, described later in this chapter.[118]

The promise of data mining is compelling, and for some purposes, it's very effective. It works best when there's a well-defined profile of whatever you're searching for, a substantial number of "events" (e.g., terrorist attacks, efforts to defraud a government agency, etc.) and minimal consequences for "false positives" (e.g., when the data mining software misidentifies someone as a terrorist, a tax cheat, etc.)

An example of an effective application for data mining is credit card fraud. All credit card companies now data mine their transaction databases, looking for patterns of spending that might indicate a stolen card. Since a credit card thief generally purchases a large number of expensive items in a short period after the theft, identifying fraudulent use with data mining software is relatively easy. The consequence of a false positive—mistakenly identifying a credit card as stolen—is that the legitimate owner temporarily can't use it. But this can be corrected when the owner contacts the credit card issuer to inform them of the mistake.

The same can't be said, unfortunately, when it comes to identifying terrorists through data mining. Terrorists don't fit an easily identifiable profile. While most terrorists are male and under 40, nearly two billion people fit this profile. There are also an exceedingly small number of actual terrorists, and they deliberately obscure their trail to avoid detection. All these factors make data mining to identify terrorism an expensive waste of time. According to security expert Bruce Schneier:

Data mining [for terrorists] is like searching for a needle in a haystack. Let's look at some numbers. We'll be optimistic. We'll assume the system has a 1 in 100 false positive rate (99% accurate), and a 1 in 1,000 false negative rate (99.9% accurate). Assume one trillion possible indicators to sift through: that's about ten events—e-mails, phone calls, purchases, Web surfings, whatever—per person in the U.S. per day. Also, assume that 10 of them are actually terrorists plotting. This unrealistically accurate system will generate one billion false alarms for every real terrorist plot it uncovers. Every day of every year, the police will have to investigate 27 million potential plots in order to find the one real terrorist plot per month. Raise that false-positive accuracy to an absurd 99.9999% and you're still chasing 2,750 false alarms per day -- but that will inevitably raise your false negatives, and you're going to miss some of those ten real plots.[119]

The federal government surely knows these facts. Yet, it persists in claiming that data mining will somehow help identify terrorists. Why?

It turns out that looking for other types of people who are not as rare as terrorists is much more plausible using data mining technologies. For instance, lots of people don't approve of the way the government is fighting the so-called War on Terrorism. Some of these people may subscribe to publications that criticize the War on Terrorism; make phone calls to other people who don't like it, etc. Since all of these records are "mined" by various federal agencies, it would be easy for the government to use this information to identify opponents of this war.

In other words, while data mining is almost useless for identifying terrorists, it's an effective way for the government to engage in political intelligence gathering. And that's how I think it's being used.

Medicare and the End of Medical Privacy

Medicare was a centerpiece of President Lyndon B. Johnson's "Great Society" programs. I remember the day in 1966 that President Johnson signed the Medicare statute[120] into law. My father, then a practicing physician, told me that the law would lead to "socialized medicine." While I was too young to appreciate what he meant, he was correct in his prediction.

The idea of individual physicians accepting less than their usual fees to treat the indigent or those who simply can't afford medical services is a longstanding tradition in the medical profession. But health care, like any other service, is subject to the laws of supply and demand. When the cost of health care falls, the demand for it increases. When governments decide that health care is an "entitlement," available at little or no cost, it should come as no surprise that demand service soars, and the quality of care falls. And, in the case of Medicare, that's exactly what has happened, with the following consequences:

- **Medicare is a "pay as you go" Ponzi-scheme system.** It's subject to the same demographic time bomb as the Social Security system. Recent studies show that Medicare's long-term funding is more precarious even than Social Security's.[121]

- **Medicare is a privacy destroyer.** The confidential relationship between doctor and patient doesn't exist when Medicare pays the bills. Physicians who fail to disclose patient information demanded by Medicare are subject to fines, forfeitures, even imprisonment.
- **Medicare has spawned an explosion in health care fraud.** When patients are no longer responsible for paying their own health care costs, they have little incentive to economize. As a result, fraud has soared under the Medicare program.
- **Medicare results in doctors being treated like criminals.** To fight Medicare fraud, federal prosecutors have turned the same legal weapons used in racketeering and narcotics prosecutions against doctors, hospitals, and other health care providers. As the U.S. Attorney prosecuting a physician in Ohio remarked: "The seizure of assets is a common tactic in the war on drugs. It will now become one of our major weapons in the war on health care fraud."[122]

The Lucrative Business of Selling Your Medical Records

The **Health Insurance Portability and Accountability Act**, enacted in 1996 (HIPPA), purports to protect the privacy of medical records. But it gives government agencies, insurance companies, direct mail marketers, and law enforcement agencies access to confidential medical information. And doctors' hands are tied—they must turn over your records on request, or face sanctions.

It wasn't supposed to be this way. The original 2001 regulations issued under HIPPA required a patient's consent for most uses of "protected health information," including its use for such common activities as treatment, billing and "other healthcare operations." In 2002, however, the Department of Health and Human Services substituted the words "regulatory permission" for "patient consent," thereby opening the floodgates for the disclosure of previously confidential health information.

Because of this seemingly small change, according to the Privacy Rights Foundation, some 800,000 companies, government agencies, and other organizations can tap into your personal medical information almost at will. And they're not required to tell you what they do with it.[123] Your medical information can be exchanged not only among doctors and other health care providers, but also to "covered entities," including business affiliates of health care organizations such as data clearinghouses, accounting firms, law firms, credit bureaus, and banks.

For instance, a federal rule that went into effect in 2006 allows creditors to obtain or use medical information for determining creditworthiness. The rule stipulates that credit-grantors can't use medical data in determining eligibility for a loan or in setting loan terms. However, credit-grantors who have such information can share it with their "affiliates." This converts the data into credit information, not medical data, which can then be used to determine eligibility for credit.[124]

Another result of this proliferation of medical data is an epidemic in medical identity theft. Research conducted by the World Privacy Forum suggests that through mid-2006, as many as 500,000 Americans had been victims of medical identity theft. The results can also be deadly: One woman found that her blood type had been changed in the hospital record.[125] What's more, once your medical identity is stolen, it's hard to set the record straight, since medical information is now so widely distributed. With computerized medical or claims records, erroneous data remains on archived backup files indefinitely.

Chapter 3 contains suggestions on how to protect your medical privacy under HIPPA and other federal legislation purporting to protect privacy.

Privacy and Your Communications

A record of your communications (be they written, oral or electronic) provides a highly revealing portrait. Many biographies have been written based on the subject's correspondence. What you write, and whom you correspond with, can be equally revealing.

Your telephone and electronic communications are no less revealing. Records of your telephone conversations, e-mail logs and data you leave behind on the Internet provide anyone who cares to investigate with a remarkably detailed picture of your work, your interests, your passions, your economic status, your lifestyle, and much more.

The Quiet Erosion of Postal Privacy

Throughout history, governments have viewed control over written communications as essential to both national security and unity.

In colonial America, correspondents depended on friends, merchants, and Native Americans to carry messages. However, most correspondence was between the colonists and England. It was largely to handle this mail that, in 1639, the first postal service in the colonies appeared.

In 1707, the British government assumed the rights to the North American postal service. But by the American Revolution, the colonists distrusted the Royal Mail. British authorities routinely opened correspondence and confiscated any materials deemed subversive. Benjamin Franklin and other colonial leaders responded by setting up their own mail service, the predecessor of the U.S. Postal Service. In 1775, Franklin was appointed the first U.S. Postmaster General.

The first U.S. President, George Washington, appreciated the political benefits of a postal monopoly. A monopoly was also justified in his mind by the belief that private postal services would never deliver to sparsely populated areas. Without a monopoly, proponents argued, the government would be left with unprofitable rural routes and massive losses.

But establishing that monopoly took decades. In many cities, private postal delivery companies provided better delivery services than the Postal Service—daily and sometimes even more frequent mail pickup and delivery, for instance. Many private postal carriers companies even issued their own stamps.

The **Private Express Statutes** (1792)[126] sought to establish a government monopoly over the delivery of first-class mail. However, exemptions in the law allowed private carriers to deliver packages and later, overnight mail. **Mail receiving services** also carved out an exemption.

Despite the postal monopoly, you have greater privacy protection for correspondence sent by first-class mail than by a courier service. The U.S. Supreme Court has ruled that first-class mail such as letters and sealed packages subject to letter postage—as distinguished from newspapers, magazines, pamphlets, and other printed matter—may not be opened, unless a warrant backed by probable cause is issued.[127]

However, since 2002, the Customs Service has been empowered to conduct warrantless searches of international first-class mail. And in 2006, President Bush quietly asserted a new government prerogative to open domestic mail without a warrant, probable cause, or even suspicion that it contains dangerous materials or contraband. The only requirement is that the mail opening be related to "foreign intelligence collection."[128]

Still, for the moment, the best way to protect the <u>privacy of your correspondence is to use first class mail, not a courier service.</u> This is because the confidentiality of a private courier service is governed by the terms of the contract between the service and the customer. All private courier services reserve the right to inspect the contents of packages and routinely cooperate with law enforcement in this regard. For instance, FedEx grants U.S. Customs inspectors access to the company's database of international shipments, including names and address of shippers, package origin and destination, credit card information and payment details (names of banks).[129] In addition, the courts have consistently said that private messengers may open packages prior to delivery.[130]

Another way that police can track your correspondence is if you use a color printer. At the request of the U.S. Secret Service, printer manufacturers encode the serial number and the manufacturer's name as nearly invisible markings on color documents. These codes ostensibly exist to track counterfeiters, but may also be used to track ordinary correspondence.[131]

Police Can Track Your Correspondence without a Warrant

A **postal mail cover** provides police and investigative agencies substantial information about your correspondence, under surprisingly lenient circumstances.

A mail cover provides a written record of all data appearing on the outside of any class of mail. This includes the addressee, sender, return address, place and date of postmark, and class of mail for all mail being delivered to a given address. Mail covers expire after 30 days, but can be extended indefinitely.[132]

No mail is opened in a mail cover. Therefore, the Postal Service doesn't consider Fourth Amendment limitations on search and seizure to apply. No warrant is required, and as a result, there is no judicial supervision of the practice.

Mail covers are administered by the Postal Inspection Service and may be initiated to protect national security, locate a fugitive, investigate a postal offense, or obtain evidence of the commission or attempted commission of a crime. Mail covers may only be used in criminal investigations, except in cases involving civil forfeitures.

Mail covers frequently target international correspondence. In the 1960s, the IRS photocopied all correspondence between Switzerland and the United States. It matched the postal codes on the envelopes with the names and addresses of Swiss banks and audited people who had received correspondence from these banks. Many account-holders were prosecuted for income tax evasion.

Statistical data on how often mail covers are used is considered secret. In 2006, *Salon* magazine filed a Freedom of Information Act to obtain information on mail-cover trends and statistics. The Postal Service rejected this request, citing "the interest of national defense or foreign policy."[133]

When Can the Government Open Your Mail?

Postal authorities can open domestic mail without a warrant in several situations. The broadest authority comes under the "foreign intelligence collection" exception to privacy asserted by President George W. Bush, noted earlier in this section.

Domestic mail can also be inspected if it fits into broad "suspicious package profiles" created by the Postal Inspection Service. Drug-sniffing dogs may inspect all packages sent to or from "source areas for the distribution of narcotics and/or controlled substances." Court testimony indicates that every major city in the United States is considered such a "source area."[134] The positive reaction of the dogs provides probable cause for the packages to be opened. Many packages opened contain no drugs, only currency, which may be seized if it contains narcotics residues. Once currency is discovered, its confiscation is virtually guaranteed, as numerous scientific studies have shown that the overwhelming majority of currency circulating in the United States is tainted with such residues.[135]

The Postal Service may also detain mail while a law enforcement agency decides if it has probable cause to examine the contents.

A long history exists of illegal opening of first class mail by intelligence agencies. Between 1940 and 1973, the FBI and CIA engaged in at least 12 separate mail-opening programs, in violation of federal law. In a single program alone, more than 215,000 communications were intercepted, opened, and photographed.[136] While the CIA conducted its mail-opening campaign, it told the Postal Service that it was merely conducting mail covers of targeted addresses. CIA agents deceived postal officials by opening mail and resealing it.

Based on its discoveries, the CIA built a database of 1.5 million people whose names were listed in the illegally opened correspondence. This operation was curtailed in 1973 in the wake of the Watergate scandal, although unofficial reports of illegal mail opening by U.S. intelligence agencies continue.

Chapter 3 contains numerous suggestions for protecting the privacy of your postal correspondence.

Electronic Monitoring: Expanding the Surveillance State

The evil incident to invasion of the privacy of the telephone is far greater than that involved in tampering with the mails. Whenever a telephone line is tapped, the privacy of the persons at both ends of the line is invaded, and all conversations between them upon any subject, and although proper, confidential, and privileged, may be overheard. Moreover, the tapping of one man's telephone line involves the tapping of the telephone of every other person whom he may call, or who may call him. As a means of espionage, writs of assistance and general warrants are but puny instruments of tyranny and oppression when compared with wiretapping.

—Dissent of Justice Louis Brandeis, *Olmstead vs. United States*, 277 U.S. 438 (1928).

The invention of the telegraph in the 1840s made possible a level of surveillance never anticipated by the authors of the U.S. Constitution. Police could not intrude into the privacy of a person's home without a warrant based on probable cause. But with the wiretap, a window into that home opened as soon as the surveillance subject sent a telegram, or a few decades later, made a telephone call. Wiretaps also made remote and (eventually) automatic surveillance possible.

Some states passed anti-telegraph wiretapping laws as early as the 1850s. Businesses sent telegrams in code so to avoid tipping off their competitors. In the 1880s, anti-telephone wiretapping laws followed as millions of businesses and consumers began installing telephones in their offices and homes. Still, wiretaps, then, as now, often went undetected.

In 1928, the Supreme Court ruled that police wiretapping without court authorization didn't violate the Fourth Amendment's ban or unreasonable search and seizure.[137] For the next 40 years, there were few if any practical limits on the government's authority to conduct wiretaps:

- For at least three decades, beginning in the 1930s, the FBI recorded the telephone conversations of Eleanor Roosevelt, without a warrant.
- The FBI began its surveillance campaign against civil rights leader Martin Luther King in 1963, immediately after his civil rights march on Washington, D.C. It bugged his bedroom, tapped his phone, and fed the results of the surveillance to the press.
- The FBI also eavesdropped on members of the Supreme Court in the 1950s and 1960s, according to documents filed in a 1988 lawsuit. Agents listened in on the conversations of Chief Justice Earl Warren and associate justices William O. Douglas, Abe Fortas, and Potter Stewart.[138]

But in 1967, the Supreme Court reversed course and ruled in its *Katz* decision that police could not eavesdrop on even one side of a telephone conversation without a warrant. The language employed by the court was unusually sweeping. This was possibly a reaction to the personal knowledge of the justices that the FBI was monitoring their telephone calls and possibly their deliberations.[139]

A year later, to set up a procedure under which wiretaps could lawfully occur, Congress as part of anti-crime legislation, enacted the **Safe Streets Act**.[140] Title III of the act prohibits electronic surveillance without a warrant supported by probable cause and bans the sale of fully assembled electronic surveillance devices.

The act covers two groups of surveillance devices: wiretaps and "bugs." A **wiretap** is the act, process, or equipment used to monitor and/or record the content of messages transmitted over wires or through the air without degrading the quality of transmission or interfering with it in any way, without detection. The product of a wiretap is the content of messages so transmitted. A **bug** is a device or system used to monitor all target area audio. The product of a bug is target area audio.

Except under the large number of exceptions to the general rule (primarily related to foreign intelligence or terrorism investigations), before issuing a wiretap warrant, a judge must find that:

- "Normal investigative procedures have been tried and have failed or reasonably appear to be unlikely to succeed if tried or to be too dangerous;"
- There is probable cause for believing "that an individual is committing, has committed, or is about to commit" one of a list of specific crimes;
- The wiretap will intercept particular communications about the enumerated offense; and
- The communications facilities to be tapped are either being used in the commission of the crime or are commonly used by the suspect.[141]

Exemptions to the act apply to telephone companies and other "electronic communication services," which have unlimited authority to listen in on conversations or data transmissions to prevent fraud:

...[A]n officer, employee, or agent of wire or electronic communication service [may] ... intercept, disclose, or use that communication in the normal course of his employment while engaged in any

activity which is a necessary incident to the rendition of his service or to the protection of the rights or property of the provider of that service.[142]

This latter exemption leaves room for substantial mischief. "REMOBS" or "remote observation" equipment used by telephone companies to monitor telephone connection quality is programmed to switch over to the next conversation every minute or so, after insuring that the sound quality is acceptable. However, the switching circuit can easily be disabled, resulting in a telephone tap. This is virtually impossible to detect remotely.[143]

Other exceptions to the requirement for a wiretap warrant include:

- The Federal Communications Commission may monitor transmissions if at least one party to a conversation (including law enforcement) is aware of the monitoring;
- Evidence taken from illegally tapped phones may be used in the trial of a U.S. citizen charged in crimes against U.S. government property or employees overseas; and
- In an "emergency situation" that involves immediate danger of death or serious physical injury to any person, conspiratorial activities threatening the national security interest, or conspiratorial activities characteristic of organized crime. Under these conditions, police may listen in for up to 48 hours before submitting an application for a wiretap warrant.

It's Easy to Wiretap: Just Point and Click

Only a small number of legally authorized wiretaps occur each year. In 2006, federal and state courts authorized only 1,839 wiretaps,[144] plus another 2,176 "national security" wiretaps.[145] State and federal courts approved every single application for wiretaps in 2006, although the federal government withdrew five applications for "national security" wiretaps.

According to the *2006 Wiretap Report:*

- The most common location specified in wiretap applications was a "portable device, carried by/on individual;"
- Telephone intercepts (including land line, cellular, cordless and mobile) accounted for 96% of intercepts installed in 2006 (most of the remainder were for telephone calls made over the Internet); and
- 80% of all applications for intercepts cited a drug offense as the most serious crime under investigation.

Legally authorized wiretaps take place through a sophisticated, point-and-click surveillance system constructed by the FBI that performs instant wiretaps on almost any communications device, including wire-line phones, cell phones, text message systems and push-to-talk systems.[146]

Wiretaps themselves are much more comprehensive than they once were. Instead of recording only what a particular suspect is saying, the FBI now assembles transcripts of telephone conversations, e-mail messages, etc. into massive databases. Those databases can subsequently be queried for names, e-mail addresses, or keywords.[147]

Law enforcement officials may also "clone" your cell phone to monitor your communications. After obtaining a wiretap warrant, they obtain an exact duplicate of your cell phone, including the number. Every time you use your cell phone, police receive the calls or messages and records them.[148]

Top 10 Electronic Eavesdropping Threats

Engineer and counter-surveillance expert James Ross of Ross Engineering ranks the following, in order of their importance, as eavesdropping threats:

1. Telephone modified to transmit room audio;
2. Listening devices that transmit signals through the power grid;
3. Listening devices that transmit radio signals to a waiting receiver;
4. Listening devices that transmit signals over telephone lines;
5. Telephone tap using radio transmitter;
6. Listening device activated remotely with a radio signal
7. Listening devices that transmit "exotically modulated" radio signals to a waiting receiver
8. Wired microphone
9. Reprogrammed PBX
10. Telephone tap not using a radio transmitter.

According to Ross, the first eight threats can be detected and neutralized by a trained, experienced, and well-equipped counter-surveillance professional. A reprogrammed PBX will have to be checked by someone knowledgeable with the specific PBX's software.

Wiretaps installed on a telephone switch (i.e., law enforcement wiretaps) are virtually undetectable. Wiretaps that don't use a radio transmitter can generally be detected only if specialized counter-surveillance equipment is in place on the line before the tap is installed. Usually, a physical search is impossible because the wiring isn't accessible.

However, illegal wiretaps, according to electronic surveillance expert James Ross, are much more common:

If you count ECHELON [Chapter 3] and REMOBs wiretaps, the ratio is thousands or ten of thousands of illegal wiretaps to each legitimate one.[149]

Not only divorce lawyers and corporate spooks conduct illegal wiretaps. The U.S. government has used them for decades. Illegal wiretapping of journalists, war protestors, civil rights activists, etc. is well documented, over a series of presidential administrations.[150] Four decades later, the Bush administration engaged in arguably illegal wiretapping of terrorist suspects, until Congress approved the Terrorist Surveillance Program in 2007.[151]

Illegal wiretaps installed by private parties are typically established in the same building as the target telephone, frequently in a telephone closet. This type of surveillance is common in divorce cases and corporate espionage. A wire pair is added to monitor conversations on the target line. Typically, the wiretap takes power from the line itself. Contrary to popular opinion, a properly installed wiretap doesn't cause "pops" or "clicks" on the line or otherwise degrade sound quality. And despite the hundreds of "wiretap detection" devices on the market, wiretaps are almost impossible to detect electronically.

Other telephone monitoring techniques don't require wiretaps. One ingenious method is an ordinary extension telephone. An eavesdropper asks the telephone company to install an extension phone to an existing line. When the target picks up the phone, the surveillance tape begins rolling. Executives who install private lines that bypass a central PBX are particularly susceptible to this attack.

One of the most commonly encountered surveillance devices is a modified telephone that functions as a combined wiretap and room bug. It operates normally but conducts room audio over spare wires in the telephone cable. Many telephones are room bugs as built. They may be remotely activated by telephone to transmit all room audio.

How to Turn Your Cell Phone Into a "Bug"

Cell phones may also be converted into room bugs. Many cellular telephones have an auto answer feature and allow you to turn off the ringer. Let's say you're in settlement negotiations in a lawsuit. To learn your opponent's strategy, all you need to do is to say something like, "Give me your very best proposal when I return," and leave the room. Leave your auto-answer cell phone in the

44

room, with the ringer turned "off." When you've left the room, dial your cell phone, and listen while the other side reveals its strategy.

It's also possible to turn a cell phone into a room bug by installing the appropriate software in it. Your cellular service provider or others with the requisite knowledge can do this remotely, without your knowledge. This is possible even if the phone is switched off. This attack is increasingly common in corporate espionage situations and has been court-approved for use in criminal investigations.[152]

Commercial software such as **Flexi Spy Pro** is also available for this purpose. The only way this form of surveillance can be defeated is by removing the battery from your cell phone.

Build Your Own Bug for $15 or Less

Battery-powered bugs are the most portable, because they don't need to be hard-wired into an electrical grid. They may be installed on the underside of ashtrays, in wastebaskets, underneath desks, etc. Some, disguised as pens or some other common office item, can be installed in the presence of the target.

Hard-wired or **carrier current** bugs may be installed inside telephones, in light fixtures, electrical outlets, electric appliances, etc. They're generally sold as "baby monitors." Remove the plastic case and the device can be hidden anywhere in a building's electrical system. While not as flexible as battery-powered bugs, carrier current bugs are more difficult to detect electronically.

Bugs may be designed with microphones designed to fit into unusual locations. A flexible **tube mike** may be placed in electrical outlets, keyholes, air ducts, etc. A **spike mike** is more rigid and can penetrate relatively hard surfaces such as walls. A **contact mike** can be attached to any interior surface.

A person can be wired to record and/or transmit conversation. This is common in undercover investigations, and is increasingly common in corporate espionage. A microphone can be taped to your skin or installed in cufflinks or a tiepin. A pen or wristwatch can easily be transformed into a radio transmitter.[153]

Intercoms are easily bugged. All an eavesdropper must do to construct an intercom bug is attach an amplifier (about US$15 at Radio Shack) across the wires and connect the amplifier to speakers or a voice-activated tape recorder. Any office with an intercom speaker can be bugged in minutes.

Warrantless Wiretapping: Why, When, and How

We have a particular obligation to examine the NSA, in light of its tremendous potential for abuse . . .. The interception of international communications signals sent through the air is the job of NSA; and, thanks to modern technological developments, it does its job very well. The danger lies in the ability of the NSA to turn its awesome technology against domestic communications.

—Senator Frank Church, Oct. 29, 1975

In its 1967 *Katz* decision, the Supreme Court acknowledged that the president had the inherent authority to order warrantless surveillance in national security investigations. But by the early 1970s, evidence began to accumulate of widespread wiretapping of U.S. citizens by U.S. intelligence services. Hearings in 1975 and 1976 before the U.S. Senate focused on the National Security Agency, America's largest intelligence agency.

Witnesses described initiatives such as **Project Minaret**, in which the NSA monitored dissidents (especially individuals opposed to the Vietnam War) on "watch lists" provided by the FBI, CIA, Secret Service, and the Defense Intelligence Agency. Another major surveillance project was **Shamrock**, in which from 1945 to 1975 U.S. intelligence services inspected all overseas telegrams daily. According to the Committee's final report, Shamrock was the "largest governmental interception program affecting Americans, dwarfing the CIA's mail opening program by comparison."[154]

The NSA defended its actions, citing its "inherent presidential authority" to eavesdrop on anyone it viewed as a legitimate foreign intelligence target. In response to these sweeping claims, and to abuses uncovered in its hearings, Congress passed the Foreign Intelligence Surveillance Act (FISA).[155] The statute, until it was temporarily amended in 2007, applied when collecting information about foreign spies or terrorists was "a significant purpose" of surveillance, under one of two scenarios:

- **Without a court order.** Acting through the Attorney General, the President may authorize warrantless electronic surveillance for a period of one year. The surveillance must target only a foreign power or its agents. The purpose of the surveillance must be to gather foreign intelligence information, with no substantial likelihood that the contents of any communication to which a U.S. person is a party will be acquired. FISA also permits the "physical search" of the "premises, information, material, or property used exclusively by" a foreign power. The requirements and procedures for searches are nearly identical to those for electronic surveillance.

- **With a court order.** If a suspected foreign intelligence agent is within the United States, or is communicating with someone within the United States, the NSA (or other investigative agency) must obtain a warrant from a court established under the act: the **Foreign Intelligence Surveillance Court** (FISC). This court deliberates in secret and its decisions aren't published.[156]

The FISC rarely turns down a government wiretap request. Since 1979, it has approved more than 20,000 FISA wiretap requests. But in 2002, the FISC found that in more than 75 cases, the Justice Department had violated federal law in its use of FISA wiretaps. However, its decision was overruled by the U.S. Foreign Intelligence Surveillance Court of Review, which met for the first time ever to review the lower court decision.[157]

Numerous examples exist of FBI agents providing inaccurate information to the FISC to obtain FISA surveillance warrants. An internal FBI review in 2006 of the more than 2,000 surveillance warrants the bureau obtains each year confirmed dozens of inaccuracies in court submissions.[158]

Amendments to FISA enacted in the 2007 **Protect America Act**[159] temporarily expand the grounds under which the government can conduct intelligence-related surveillance without obtaining a FISA wiretap. This authority ends on Feb. 5, 2008, unless renewed by Congress. The amendments codify into law the "Terrorist Surveillance Program" (TSP) authorized by President George W. Bush in 2001.[160]

The TSP appears to take two forms:

- Warrantless wiretaps of conversations originating in, or terminating in, the United States, of individuals allegedly connected to terrorist groups or otherwise of interest to intelligence officials; and
- Mining the data streams of U.S. telecommunications companies to analyze transactional records of telephone and Internet traffic in search of patterns that might point to terrorist suspects.

Sneaky Caller ID Tricks

Caller ID is a service in which telephones report the number and name, if available, of the calling party. In areas equipped with caller ID service, all originating calls in which the service isn't blocked send a caller ID signal. In areas with "enhanced 911" emergency service, calls to emergency services are accompanied by transmission of certain medical records.

Area codes and phone numbers collected through caller ID may be linked with customer records and other databases. When a call comes in, the computer automatically consults a national white-pages database on CD-ROM, and displays the resulting name and address. Optional databases add a demographic profile of the caller's neighborhood. This data is displayed in seconds.

Some companies place enticing advertisements and wait for calls to come in on their WATS lines. They don't answer the phone, but record the caller's number, match it to an address with a reverse directory on CD-ROM, and sell the information to direct marketing companies. Government agencies also place such ads (often for illegal products or services such as child pornography) to gather names of people who may later be targeted for investigations.

Caller ID is now global. You should assume that any call you place from your home or office telephone can be traced to that location, unless you follow the precautions in Chapter 3.

Various caller ID "blocking" services are available. However, caller ID blocking is disabled whenever you call police or other emergency services and possibly in other circumstances as well. Don't count on caller ID blocking to protect your privacy.

Caller ID "spoofing" services now exist and are discussed in Chapter 3. They effectively block transmission of originating telephone numbers, but are under attack by state and federal prosecutors and regulatory agencies.

A technology distinct from caller ID, but with similar capabilities, is automatic number identification. It permits an originating number to be displayed on calls to 800 (WATS) and 900 exchanges. Caller ID blocking doesn't block ANI.

While billed as essential to fight the "war on terror," the Protect America Act doesn't limit the NSA's domestic spying efforts to terrorist investigations. Instead, all that's required is that "foreign intelligence retrieval" be a "significant purpose" of the surveillance. The law places the authority for such surveillance in the hands of the attorney general—not the FISC. The court's only role is to review surveillance that's already been conducted, and intervene if the procedures set out in the act haven't been followed.

"Foreign intelligence retrieval" encompasses far more than listening in on suspected terrorists. Employees of the White House or the State Department, apparently, were frequent targets of the original TSP, before it was "legalized" in the Protect America Act.[161] In addition, the NSA conducts surveillance on the activities of foreign companies engaged in high-tech research. The results of this surveillance are passed on to politically connected U.S. companies.[162]

Secrets of Your Dialing Records

Your telephone dialing records and other transactional data about your telephonic communications provide a comprehensive record of calls made and the length of conversations. Analysis of this information, even without listening to the content of your conversations, reveals a great deal about you. The information retrieved is analogous to that obtained in a mail cover of your correspondence.

No expectation of privacy extends to these records, or to records of calls received. In the 1979 *Smith vs. Maryland* case, the Supreme Court declared:

[I]t is doubtful that telephone users in general have any expectation of privacy regarding the numbers they dial, since they typically know that they must convey phone numbers to the telephone company and that the company has facilities for recording this information and does in fact record it for various legitimate business purposes...When petitioner voluntarily conveyed numerical information to the phone company and "exposed" that information to its equipment in the normal course of business, he assumed the risk that the company would reveal the information to the police.[163]

E-mail transaction and Web browsing records—although not the contents of the messages—may also be retrieved under the same legal standard, as you'll learn later in this chapter.

A **dialed number recorder** provides police with a record of calls made to other numbers. This device records every digit you dial at your phone. In earlier times, a device that had a similar but more limited function was called a **pen register**. Anything you enter from your telephone keypad—credit card numbers, passwords, etc.—can be monitored. A **trap and trace** device records the originating number of incoming calls. To obtain a court order to install either of these surveillance devices, police must merely certify that the order is relevant to a criminal investigation. While the subject of such an investigation must be notified, the government may request a 30-day notification delay, which in practice may be extended indefinitely.

Your telephone company may also sell your dialing records for marketing purposes. In 2000, the Supreme Court declined to review a lower court ruling that overturned a federal regulation requiring telephone companies to obtain customer approval before doing so.[164]

Hundreds of companies buy and sell private telephone records. One of the most frequently used strategies to obtain someone's phone records is to impersonate that person. Such "pretexting" is now illegal, but persists.[165] Moreover, pretexting is illegal only if carried out by a private company. Government agencies may freely impersonate you to obtain your telephone records.

E-Mail and Cellular Phones Have Little Privacy Protection

In 1986, Congress enacted the Electronic Communications Privacy Act (EPCA).[166] The act extends privacy protection to radio paging devices, electronic mail, cellular telephones, cordless telephones, private communication carriers, and computer transmissions. The law also makes it unlawful to intentionally access stored electronic or wire communication to obtain, alter, or prevent authorized access to such communication.

However, in reality, the EPCA provides very little privacy protection. One of its most glaring deficiencies is that the EPCA codifies the *Smith vs. Maryland* decision into a statute. Thus, the government can obtain basic subscriber information for telephone, e-mail, Web browsing, or other electronic services, including name, address, and toll records, simply by issuing a subpoena.

The USA PATRIOT Act significantly expands this authority. Police can now obtain "records of session times and durations," as well as records of "any temporarily assigned network address." This data makes it faster and easier to identify computer users and trace their Internet communications. Investigators may obtain through a subpoena the "means and source of payment" that a customer uses to pay for an account with a communications provider, "including any credit card or bank account number." The PATRIOT Act amendments also stipulate that the pen register/trap and trace language of the EPCA applies to cell phones, an Internet user account or e-mail address, etc.[167]

Another glaring exception applies to e-mail or voice messages stored on an Internet service provider's or telephone company's computers. To read your stored e-mails on Yahoo, G-Mail, etc., or listen to your stored voice messages, police need only demonstrate that the information sought is relevant to an investigation. They don't have to establish that there's probable cause of any crime.

This exception may also apply in civil cases. In 2007, a U.S. district court ruled that in a copyright dispute, the party alleging infringement may conduct ongoing surveillance of another party's stored e-mail messages, without violating federal wiretap laws.[168] Legal authorization isn't required. But other types of private monitoring remain illegal—an individual eavesdropping on their spouse, for instance.[169]

Subscriber information and transactional data may also be disclosed under the following circumstances:

- If one party to the communication consents to such disclosure;
- If information is inadvertently disclosed to police and contains evidence of a crime, it may be used to investigate or prosecute that crime;
- By an employer monitoring use by an employee of the employer's computer system;
- If a service provider requires your permission to disclose this data as a condition of service. AT&T, for instance, reserves the right to use any information in its billing records without restriction. Its policy appears to allow the collection of Web browsing and video-viewing records, and disclosing that information to any third party.[170]

Another innovation of the EPCA is the so-called "roving" wiretap, which allows police to monitor calls made to or from multiple phones. The original legislation permitted roving wiretaps only in terror investigations, but they're now permissible in all criminal inquiries. To obtain a roving wiretap order, the government need only demonstrate that a surveillance target's use of multiple phones has the "effect" of preventing interception under an ordinary wiretap order.

The USA PATRIOT Act further loosened restrictions on roving wiretaps, by eliminating the requirement that authorities must confirm the surveillance target is actually using the device being monitored. This allows entire banks of pay telephones at airports, railway stations, etc. to be wiretapped continuously in the expectation that a roving wiretap target might use one of the phones. Similarly, every PC in an Internet café or other public connection point may be monitored in the expectation that the target of a roving wiretap order may use one such PC.

Finally, the protection the EPCA provides cellular and cordless telephone calls is more illusory than real. Monitoring cellular and cordless conversations is in some cases so easy as to make the wiretap laws unenforceable. This is particularly true with older analog cellular and cordless phones. While digitally encrypted cordless and cellular phones are difficult for amateurs to monitor, the government and organized crime can overcome most commercial phone encryption schemes.

What's more, only a US$500 fine is imposed for monitoring such calls. According to a fact sheet published by the Federal Communications Commission in 1999:

To the extent that [cellular and cordless] conversations are radio transmissions, there would be no violation of [the law] if there were no divulgence or beneficial use of the conversation.[171]

The newest cell phones feature not only a mobile phone, but also provide Internet access, a digital camera, an appointment book, and an address book. They also allow you to send and receive "text messages." If you're arrested, police may be able to copy this information, and indeed the entire contents of your cell phone, without a warrant.[172]

The expanded functions of cell phones have also proven to be irresistible to hackers. In 2005, hackers retrieved heiress Paris Hilton's address book and posted the celebrity-rich listing on the Internet, along with the photos she had taken with her cell phone's digital camera.[173]

Building Surveillance From the Ground Up

If it's up to the FBI and the NSA, the only medium of communications they won't be able to tap will be two tin cans and a string.

—Barry Steinhardt, American Civil Liberties Union

Suppose you want to send a message to someone that only that person can read. A mathematical process called **encryption** makes this possible. Encryption scrambles the message using mathematical formulas that make the message unreadable to anyone except for someone possessing the **key** to "decrypt" it. Encryption programs are now available that even the super-computers used by national intelligence agencies cannot decipher messages created with them, at least not without an exhaustive effort.

By the early 1990s, U.S. intelligence officials were deeply concerned about the increasing use of encryption technology. In 1993, the Clinton administration announced the development of an encryption device called the **Clipper Chip**. Its purported advantage was that it provided a standard for securing private voice communication. With Clipper, however, the government would hold a copy of the keys used to unlock the communication.

After a researcher discovered a secret "back door" in the Clipper design that allowed messages to be read without first obtaining the keys, Congress refused to go along with the scheme.[174] But U.S. intelligence services were determined to develop more "tappable" electronic networks. Rather than requiring surveillance to be built into individual telephones or PCs, they instead proposed that surveillance be built into all telephone and computer networks.

The outcome of this proposal was the **Communications Assistance for Law Enforcement Act** (CALEA).[175] The law establishes a legal duty for telecommunications carriers to assist in monitoring communications for law enforcement or intelligence purposes by building wiretapping capabilities into their networks and equipment. Neither the surveillance subjects, nor the companies themselves, are supposed to be aware that surveillance is occurring.

CALEA also requires U.S. cell phone manufacturers to equip all cell phones and cell phone networks with technology to precisely identify the location of cell phones. The FBI and other law enforcement agencies want to use this technology to track the location of any suspected criminal using a cell phone, without a warrant. To date, law enforcement has a mixed record on this score, although the rules were loosened in 2001 after enactment of the USA PATRIOT Act.

In 2007, CALEA's requirements were extended to universities, public libraries, Internet cafés, and other institutions that operate networks connected to the Internet. As with other communication networks covered by CALEA, wiretaps of Internet networks must occur at the flip of a switch (or perhaps the click of a mouse), without intervention by the network. These provisions also cover companies that provide phone service over the Internet via "Voice over Internet Protocol" or VoIP.

The inevitable consequence of requiring surveillance to be built into telephone networks, and now the Internet, is to erode security for everyone using these networks. While CALEA made wiretapping easier, U.S. telecom networks are now much more vulnerable to illegal wiretaps. This vulnerability has already been exploited by foreign intelligence agencies, international organized crime and possibly international terrorist networks. According to Fox News:

What troubles investigators most, particularly in the investigation of the World Trade Center attack, is that on a number of cases, suspects that they had sought to wiretap and survey immediately changed their telecommunications processes. They started acting much differently as soon as those supposedly secret wiretaps went into place.[176]

This was not the first time that back doors in U.S. communications networks have stymied criminal investigations. In a 1997 drug trafficking case in Los Angeles, a narcotics cartel targeted by the Drug Enforcement Administration was able to "completely compromise the communications of the FBI, the Secret Service, the DEA and the LAPD," according to a secret government report leaked to the media.

A few years later, revelations emerged that the White House telephone system was completely compromised by an unnamed foreign intelligence service, widely believed to the Israeli Mossad.[177] Israeli companies allegedly tied to Mossad manufacture most of the wiretapping equipment used in the U.S. and many other countries.

In a 2005 Greek wiretapping scandal, hackers bypassed the authorization mechanisms of the national eavesdropping system and activated the "lawful interception" mode in the mobile network. They then redirected about 100 phone numbers maintained by high-level government officials to a switch they controlled. It is unknown who was behind the break-in—what is known is that when you build surveillance into communication systems, you invite intruders to use that surveillance for their own purposes.[178]

ECHELON: Electronic Monitoring Goes Global

There was of course no way of knowing whether you were being watched at any given moment. How often, or on what system, the Thought Police plugged in on any individual wire was guesswork. It was even conceivable that they watched everybody all the time ... You had to live—did live, from habit that became instinct—in the assumption that every sound you made was overheard...every movement scrutinized.

—George Orwell, *1984*

After World War II, the U.S. and U.K. governments, acting through the North Atlantic Treaty Organization (NATO), constructed a sophisticated eavesdropping network to gather electronic intelligence from the former Soviet Union, and later, the People's Republic of China. When the Soviet Union collapsed in 1989, this surveillance network wasn't disbanded. Indeed, in the years since the end of the Cold War, it has become even more sophisticated.

Proponents of this surveillance infrastructure claim that it's required to fight terrorism, drug trafficking, and other global ills. However, it's also used to monitor political dissidents, civil liberties groups, and political enemies and to gather commercial intelligence for government-favored enterprises.

At the center of this global surveillance network is the National Security Agency (NSA), established by President Truman in 1952 by executive order, is the intelligence arm of the U.S. Department of Defense and the world's largest intelligence agency. Its mandate is the global monitoring of voice and other communications through a global network of monitoring stations and satellites. While the agency's annual budget is a closely guarded secret, it's believed to exceed US$6 billion annually with more than 30,000 employees worldwide.[179]

Through a network of thousands of monitoring stations worldwide, dozens of spy satellites, and submarines capable of tapping undersea cables, the NSA can monitor almost any information transmitted over wire and (especially) through the air. Voice, data, Teletype, facsimile transmissions, and telephone pager signals are all monitored. So are mobile radio systems, local area network communications, radio PBXs and cordless and cellular telephones. To analyze this data, the NSA has built the world's largest computer complex at its headquarters at Fort Meade, Maryland.

Information from non-U.S. monitoring stations is shared with the NSA pursuant to the **U.K.-U.S.A. Agreement** (1947) between the United States, United Kingdom, Canada, Australia, and New Zealand. This agreement insures that all five nations share intelligence data captured throughout the world.[180]

All five of these nations have domestic laws in place prohibiting electronic surveillance of residents by their respective intelligence services. However, the U.K.-U.S.A. Agreement bypasses these laws by calling for all the signatories to jointly acquire and share all signals and communications intelligence. For instance, if the NSA wishes to monitor the telephone calls of someone in the United States, it can request that the Communications Security Establishment (CSE), Canada's spy agency, conduct the surveillance. The CSE acts in a similar manner: according to Mike Frost, a former Canadian intelligence agent, among the Canadian targets that Frost asked other countries to monitor was the wife of former Prime Minister Pierre Trudeau.[181]

Domestic laws mirror these provisions. For instance, the FISA statute, which regulates the collection of domestic intelligence by the NSA, stipulates that "electronic surveillance" means "the acquisition by an electronic, mechanical or other surveillance device" of the approved targets. But it doesn't define "acquisition." This task was left to the NSA, which it does in a top-secret document. "Acquisition," according to the document, is "the interception **by the NSA** through electronic means of a communication to which it isn't an intended party [emphasis added]."[182]

By inserting "by the NSA" in this definition, the NSA excluded from the act and the Foreign Intelligence Surveillance Court all interceptions received from any non-NSA source.

Of course, monitoring global communications accomplishes nothing without a means to analyze their content. More than two decades ago, an unpublished report from the House Government Operations Committee described how this is accomplished:

The NSA captures data as it is transmitted through the air and under the ground. Such messages are then processed through computers that are programmed to isolate encrypted messages, as well as messages containing "trigger" words, word combinations, entities, names, addresses and combinations of addresses. The intercepted messages that are in code or cipher are, whenever possible, solved. Those messages and messages selected by "target procedures" are then inspected by human analysts. Messages which the NSA electronically scans and judges to be of no interest to the NSA or its consumers [i.e., other federal agencies]—annually accounting for tens of millions of communications of U.S. citizens—are not considered by the NSA to have been intercepted or acquired.[183]

In the 1990s, after the collapse of the Soviet Union, reports surfaced claiming that the NSA's global surveillance network was being redirected to monitor human rights organizations and to gather economic intelligence. This effort, code-named ECHELON, is used mainly against non-military targets: organizations, businesses, and individuals in virtually every country.

In 1998, the European Union's Scientific and Technological Options Assessment Office (STOA) approved a comprehensive report on ECHELON. The report concluded that, "within Europe, all e-mail, telephone and fax communications are routinely intercepted by the U.S. National Security Agency."[184] It also revealed that the targets monitored included human rights organizations such as Amnesty International and Christian Aid. In 1999, STOA approved a follow-up report entitled *Interception Capabilities 2000*.[185] This report revealed that the NSA had developed systems:

> *... to collect, filter and analyze the forms of fast digital communications used by the Internet. Because most of the world's Internet capacity lies within the United States or connects to the United States, many communications in "cyberspace" will pass through intermediate sites within the United States. Communications from Europe to and from Asia, Oceania, Africa, or South America normally travel via the United States.*

Indeed, there appears to have been a deliberate strategy by the U.S. government to facilitate surveillance of this data stream, by encouraging U.S. telecommunications companies to increase the amount of international traffic routed through American-based switches.[186] For example, Internet traffic going between Latin America and Asia or Latin America and Europe is almost entirely routed through the United States.

Interception Capabilities 2000 also described how ECHELON gathers commercial intelligence on behalf of U.S. companies. CIA director James Woolsey confirmed this when he told a French newspaper that he was ordered by President Clinton in 1993 to transform the NSA's surveillance network into a tool for gathering economic intelligence.[187]

In 1999, Australia became the first country to officially acknowledge its participation in ECHELON. The director of the Australian Defense Signals Directorate, the Australian counterpart to the NSA, stated that the DSD "does cooperate with counterpart signals intelligence organizations overseas under the U.K.-U.S.A. relationship."[188] Shortly thereafter, Canada confirmed that it collects and analyzes foreign communications in a similar manner.[189]

These disclosures provoked worldwide outrage. The European Parliament in 2001 adopted 44 recommendations designed to offer Europeans greater protection against ECHELON.[190] One of the most practical suggestions was for individuals who send sensitive information by e-mail to encrypt those messages to prevent others from reading them. You'll read more about encryption in Chapter 3.

While the NSA didn't change any of its information-gathering practices, it did go on a campaign to repair its public image, spending millions of taxpayer dollars in the process. Then-NSA Director Michael Hayden categorically denied the agency was monitoring Americans without first seeking a special warrant in the process called for by FISA.[191] These denials, of course, were false.

The Global Blueprint for Surveillance

The U.K.-U.S.A. Treaty is only one of many agreements that provide a legal framework for the international coordination of global surveillance.

In 1994, the United States enacted the Communications Assistance for Law Enforcement Act (CALEA), described earlier in this chapter. CALEA requires that companies which electronic communications companies construct equipment and networks to facilitate government surveillance.

In quick succession, several other nations introduced legislation remarkably similar to the U.S. law. In 1999, the U.K. civil liberties organization Statewatch revealed the reason for the sudden flurry of surveillance legislation: a behind-the-scenes effort by a FBI-funded consortium of national law enforcement and intelligence agencies called the International Law Enforcement Telecommunications Seminar

(ILETS). Since 1993, the ILETS have brought together police from 20 countries to formulate a legal agenda for global surveillance.[192]

The ILETS requirements published for national surveillance systems stipulate that:

"Law enforcement agencies" [must have] access not just to the content of a communication, but also "associated data," "post-connection" signals (e.g.: conference calling or call transfer), all numbers called, all numbers called by-in both cases even if a connection is not made-plus "real time [i.e., as it occurs], full time monitoring capability," the location of mobile subscribers, simultaneous and multiple interceptions "by more than one law enforcement agency" and "roaming" by mobile phone users...

Network operators and service providers [must] provide ... permanent "interfaces from which the intercepted communications can be transmitted to the law enforcement monitoring facility." And, if they provide "encoding, compression or encryption," ... they must provide it [decoded] to law enforcement ... Finally, they [must] ensure that: "neither the interception target nor any other unauthorized person is aware of any changes made to fulfill the interception order ... [and] ... not to disclose information on how interceptions are carried out ... The European Union will be able to trawl the airwaves for "subversive" thoughts and "dissident" views, and, with its partners, across the globe."[193]

In 2006, the European Union incorporated most of the ILETS requirements when the European Parliament ratified the Directive on Data Retention[194] which requires telephone companies, Internet Service Providers and other electronic communication services to maintain records of customer e-mails, telephone calls, Web surfing habits, etc.[195] Information such as the date, destination and duration of mobile calls, for example, must be stored for at least six months and made available to police on demand.

Another ILETS initiative was to require all nations to set out legal procedures for Internet surveillance. Following its recommendations, in 1997, the Council of Europe, a group of more than 40 countries, including all 15 members of the EU, asked a committee of experts to "draft a binding legal instrument" dealing with international computer crime. Four years later, the final draft was approved.[196]

Under the Convention, police in one signatory country can force authorities in another signatory to investigate any alleged crime that involves, in even the most remote way, computers or the Internet. Signatories must criminalize acts such as hacking and the production, sale or distribution of hacking tools. The Convention also expands criminal liability for theft of intellectual property and grants new powers of search and seizure to law enforcement, including the power to force Internet service providers to preserve customer usage records and to monitor online activities in real time. It also requires signatories to enact laws that would force PC users to disclose their private encryption keys (used to make "plaintext" documents unreadable to unauthorized users) upon demand.

The equivalent of these requirements in the physical world would be to require valid return addresses on all postal mail, installing cameras in all phone booths, making all currency traceable and giving the government the right to demand the keys to any dwelling upon request.

The Convention also lacks a **dual-criminality** provision, under which an activity must be considered a crime in both countries before one state can demand cooperation from another. Thus, the Convention requires law enforcement authorities in a signatory country to cooperate with a foreign inquiry, even when such activity in question is perfectly legal in the requested country.

What happens when information is turned over to one of the many countries in which organized crime syndicates have infiltrated law enforcement agencies? Once fraudsters gain access to your billing and browsing records, they can steal your identity. Plus they'll be able to crack down on any of their own citizens with the temerity to speak up in opposition.

In 2006, the U.S. Senate ratified the Convention, but reserved the right to deny cooperation requests when they violate U.S. free speech or other rights.[197]

"Policy Laundering"

The use of behind-the-scenes meetings such as ILETS and treaties such as the Cybercrime Treaty to create "minimum standards" for surveillance is a fundamental challenge to civil liberties worldwide. Policies that would never be approved through the domestic political process are instead put into place through international agreements. Countries that refused to meet whatever minimums standards are put into place due to concerns about civil liberties are subject to "naming and shaming," blacklists, etc. Critics of this process have dubbed it **policy laundering**.[198]

While organizations such as ILETS are funded by national governments, they undermine national laws and international human rights treaties by taking on what is equivalent to a treaty-making role without the legal capacity to make treaties. The minimum standards they espouse often conflict with such laws and treaties. However, these standards are postulated as essential to create a "level playing field."

You'll read more about policy laundering with respect to the international enforcement of tax and money laundering laws in Chapter 6.

Privacy and Your Property

The right to private property is a bedrock principle of western civilization. Yet, this principle is under attack on many fronts, as you'll learn in this section.

Central Banking Erodes Privacy

The core principle of all central banks is that governments can issue currency and other debt instruments without having the instruments backed by gold or some other tangible asset. This inevitably results in depreciation of the currency. If a central bank doesn't float a great deal of unbacked debt, the national currency may depreciate very slowly. If it floats too much debt, the result is currency destruction, a process that awaits every "fiat" or paper backed currency ever issued. Indeed, the U.S. dollar has depreciated more than 95% in value since the formation of the Federal Reserve in 1913.

While some would argue that the stimulus a central bank provides is essential to "jump-start" economies, and to prevent recessions or depressions, the resulting inflation has profound consequences. One consequence, largely overlooked, is to privacy.

When the United States first became a nation, many forms of money were accepted as "legal tender." Over time, the government gradually restricted the ability of businesses and individuals to require payment in any form other than government-issued currency. These restrictions culminated in 1933, when President Franklin D. Roosevelt invalidated "gold clauses" in contracts calling for obligations to be settled in gold.[199]

The inflation fiat money engenders also results in "bracket creep" in legislation designed to restrict privacy. The "currency reporting requirements" established by the Bank Secrecy Act are an example. For nearly 40 years, U.S. law has required banks and other credit institutions to submit reports to the U.S. Treasury Department of people depositing or withdrawing large sums of currency to or from their accounts. The reporting threshold was originally set at US$5,000; in 1984, the threshold was increased to US$10,000.

The value of US$10,000, however, has fallen by more than half since 1984, resulting in a huge increase in the number of forms filed and set off investigations of people innocent of any wrongdoing, but suspected of criminal behavior merely on the basis of depositing or withdrawing their own money.

The IRS: The Greatest Privacy Invader of All

A hand from Washington will be stretched out and placed upon every man's business; the eye of the federal inspector will be in every man's counting house. The [income tax] law will of necessity have inquisitorial features, and it will provide penalties. It will create a complicated machinery. Under it, businessmen will be hauled into courts distant from their homes. Heavy fines imposed by distant and unfamiliar tribunals will constantly menace the taxpayer. An army of federal inspectors, spies and detectives will compel men of business to show their books and disclose the secrets of their affairs. They will dictate forms of bookkeeping. They will require statements and affidavits. On the one hand, the inspector can blackmail the taxpayer and on the other, he can profit by selling his secret to his competitor.

—Richard E. Byrd, Speaker of the Virginia House of Delegates, speaking in opposition to the federal income tax (1910)

The United States had few taxes in its early history. From 1791 to 1802, the government supported itself with taxes on distilled spirits, tobacco, and slaves, among other items. These taxes were expanded during the War of 1812, but in 1817, Congress ended all internal taxes, instead deciding to rely on import tariffs to provide federal funding.

The Civil War brought the first U.S. income tax. Like today's income tax, it was a graduated or progressive tax, with the rates imposed increasing with declared income. In addition, income was withheld at source as an "emergency measure," an initiative renewed during World War II and subsequently made permanent. The Civil War also brought about additional sales and excise taxes. An inheritance tax also made its debut.[200]

After the Civil War, Congress abolished the income tax, only to impose it again in 1894. Then, in 1895, the Supreme Court declared the income tax to be unconstitutional for several reasons, including that taxing higher incomes at a higher rate was an unconstitutional attack on property.[201]

In response, Congress enacted a Constitutional amendment overturning the Supreme Court decision, and in 1913, the 16th Amendment came into effect. Some "tax protestors" argue that the 16th Amendment was not properly ratified. U.S. courts have uniformly rejected these arguments.[202]

Today, U.S. citizens and residents must report and pay a progressive income tax on their worldwide income, wherever they reside. Gift and estate taxes also apply to a U.S. person's worldwide assets. Other factors that may produce U.S. tax liability include residence, domicile, marital status, source of income, location of assets, timing, and status of beneficiaries.[203]

Eliminating U.S. taxation requires eliminating each of these criteria. For U.S. citizens, this requires giving up citizenship and abandoning U.S. residence, among other requirements. Chapter 5 contains a detailed examination of this admittedly radical option.

Submission of a tax return provides data that with the aid of computers allows the creation of financial dossiers on every taxpayer. The IRS analyzes individual returns compared to other returns of people with similar income and occupations. This **Discriminant Inventory Function (DIF)** system identifies returns that have a potential for adjustment. A computer makes this examination, and if the software detects differences that exceed predetermined variances, the return becomes subject to review by a human agent. Every tax return filed with the IRS undergoes such analysis. The effective audit rate for U.S. tax returns is therefore 100%.

The Awesome Collection Powers of the IRS

The IRS estimates that the difference between what Americans owe in federal taxes and what they actually pay is about $345 billion annually. This sum represents taxes assessed or otherwise calculated, but not paid.[204] According to the IRS, the enormous size of the tax gap is justification for much stricter enforcement of tax laws.

Congress has responded by providing the IRS with collection powers greater than any other federal agency. The IRS need not demonstrate its assessments are accurate before imposing taxes. To collect assessments, the IRS may, without a trial or judgment:

- Sell your principle residence at auction and use the proceeds to pay off taxes that it claims you owe;
- Seize your bank accounts, securities accounts and property in your safety deposit box;
- Seize your wages and salaries, forcing you to support your family on no more than the applicable standard deduction (no more than a few hundred dollars monthly); and
- Confiscate your Social Security or pension checks, even if they are your sole source of income.

An uncollected tax assessment automatically imposes a lien against all your property and property rights, including all property acquired after imposition of the lien. Property you own, or are deemed to own, is subject to seizure by "any means." Property exempt from seizure under state laws, such as homestead statutes, isn't exempt from an IRS lien.

The lien follows your property wherever you transfer it. If you sell or otherwise convey your property to a third party, the transfer is void unless the person who acquired it can prove that he did not know of the lien and paid fair market value for the property. If a third party such as a bank holds the property for you in trust, the third party subject to the lien and relieved of liability only if it surrenders the property. Failure to surrender renders the third party personally liable to pay the lien up to the full value of the property.

These powers have often been misused and continue to be misused. Between 1969 and 1973, the Nixon administration's secret IRS Special Services Staff audited more than 11,000 suspected "enemies" of Richard Nixon.[205] And, while enactment of the Taxpayer Bills of Rights, discussed later in this section, have decreased the number of abusive tax investigations, these initiatives haven't eliminated them. IRS audits of political enemies continued during the administration of Bill Clinton (1992-2000).[206]

The Outrageous Code

The text of the Internal Revenue Code (IRC), Title 26 of the U.S. Code, fills nearly than 3,000 pages. Much of the Code and regulations issued pursuant to it consists of reporting requirements, data from which helps create IRS taxpayer dossiers. These regulations occupy several thousand more pages, and the *Internal Revenue Manual*, which sets out IRS procedures, fills an entire bookshelf.

According to the *Tax Complexity Factbook*, compiled by a congressional committee in 2000:

A comprehensive volume of federal tax rules and regulations spans over 46,000 pages, more than twice the length of tax rules and regulations in the 1970s. The Tax Code itself fills 2,840 pages, and contains about 2.8 million words. In comparison, the Bible has 1,340 pages, and about 800,000 words.

The IRS estimates that Americans will spend 6.1 billion hours—over 3 million person-years— complying with the federal tax system in 2000. Over half of individual taxpayers now use a paid preparer for their income tax return, up from less than 20% in 1960. The costs of federal tax compliance are in the order of US$200 billion, or at least 10% of total tax revenue collected by the government. Small businesses have particularly high tax compliance costs. One study found that small businesses face compliance costs that are more than three times larger than taxes paid.

The IRS receives over 110 million phone calls each year for help by taxpayers. In 1999, the IRS was only able to answer 73% of the inquiries correctly. Individuals and businesses had to deal with 481 separate IRS tax forms in 1999, a rise of 20% from 403 forms in 1990. Between 1986 and 1998, Congress made about 6,500 changes to the tax code in 61 separate pieces of legislation.[207]

But the biggest problem of the Tax Code isn't its length or complexity, but its inconsistency, unpredictability and retroactive application. A good example is the Tax Reform Act of 1986.[208] This law had the beneficial effect of reducing the top tax rate to 28% (later increased to 35%), broadening the tax base, and simplifying the Tax Code. However, it also retroactively closed a number of "tax shelters." While few Americans may have objected to wealthy speculators paying additional taxes, the act retroactively disqualified deductions and extended depreciation schedules used by hundreds of thousands of taxpayers.

The end of these tax shelters meant that hundreds of billions of dollars invested into real estate and other ventures no longer enjoyed a tax-favored status. Real estate values collapsed, as the favorable tax policy afforded this investment was a large part of its economic value. This led in turn to the collapse of hundreds of banks and savings & loan institutions and a federal bailout that eventually cost taxpayers nearly US$1 trillion.

In 1994, the Supreme Court ruled that retroactive amendments to the Tax Code are permissible, despite the U.S. Constitution's prohibition of *ex post facto* laws.[209] *Ex post facto* laws are unconstitutional only when criminal activities are involved. The Constitution doesn't apply if "only" money or property is at risk.

It's Easy to Commit a Tax Crime

Every year, several thousand taxpayers are indicted for criminal tax offenses: tax evasion, tax fraud, failure to file, or money laundering. More than 90% of IRS criminal prosecutions end in convictions or plea agreements.

Over the years, the IRS has gained more and more weapons in its arsenal of criminal sanctions. If you're indicted for tax evasion and/or failure to file a tax return, the indictment may also include perjury and fraud charges.

Perjury can be as simple as making a statement or delivering a document to the IRS that it believes is false. Your knowledge need not be proven directly, but may be inferred by the surrounding circumstances. Violations are punishable by a fine up to US$10,000 (US$50,000 for corporations) and up to one year in prison for misdemeanor perjury.[210] The tax fraud and false statements statutes apply to more serious violations.[211] The penalty is a fine up to US$10,000 (US$50,000 for corporations) or up to three years imprisonment, plus the costs of prosecuting the case.

The felony perjury statute[212] makes it a crime to willfully make any false statement on any matter within the jurisdiction of any department or agency of the federal government and carries a fine up to US$10,000, up to five years imprisonment, or both. This law covers any false statement or document given to any representative of the federal government, in any inquiry.

Submitting a fraudulent asset listing in an IRS collection proceeding may trigger a felony perjury prosecution. Another common cause of action involves submitting a false withholding Form W-9 to an employer. For instance, a taxpayer may claim 10 deductions when he may only legitimately claim two or three. Even submitting a false return where there is no tax liability can result in prosecution.

Increasingly, the IRS alleges "tax fraud" in taxpayer prosecutions. This is particularly relevant in efforts by the IRS to enforce U.S. tax laws globally. The government has ratified numerous international treaties in which signatories must set aside confidentiality laws to provide mutual legal assistance if tax fraud is alleged. However, many of the treaties exempt tax offenses from coverage, except those that are fraud-related. Therefore, the IRS tries to allege fraud in international tax investigations. Under the IRS definition, simple tax evasion exists only in the rare case when the agency doesn't allege the taxpayer submitted false documents or declarations. You'll learn more about such treaties in Chapters 6 and 7.

Gathering evidence against taxpayers for criminal prosecutions is easier for the IRS than for most other federal agencies. In 1982, Congress eliminated the constitutional requirement that evidence gathering in a criminal tax investigation be supported by a warrant backed by probable cause. Instead, the IRS was given the authority to use administrative subpoenas to gather evidence. To obtain such a subpoena, the IRS need only demonstrate that:

- The investigation will be conducted pursuant to a legitimate purpose;
- The inquiry will be relevant to that purpose;
- The information sought isn't in the possession of the IRS; and
- The administrative steps required by the Tax Code have been followed.

The courts dismissed all constitutional challenges to the this law, culminating in a ruling where a federal appeals court held that absent an explicit congressional grant of professional privilege, the IRS authority to gather information from third parties couldn't be obstructed.[213]

Taxpayer Rights—and Wrongs

Beginning in 1988 and continuing until 1997, Congress held a series of hearings that exposed wrongdoing by the IRS. Dozens of witnesses testified as to how ordinary law-abiding taxpayers are hounded by unjust tax collection efforts. These hearings resulted in three so-called **Taxpayer Bills of Rights** (TBORs).

The first Taxpayer Bill of Rights (TBOR-I)[214] came into effect in 1988. Its most important provisions:

- Require the IRS to waive any penalty imposed because of underpayment of tax if the underpayment was caused by erroneous written IRS advice;
- Increase from 10 days to 30 days the advance written notice the IRS must give a taxpayer before seizing property, except for emergency jeopardy assessments;
- Prohibit the IRS from evaluating employees on the basis of how much tax they collect;
- Require the IRS to explain in detail how any interest or penalties attached to a notice of tax deficiency were calculated;
- Bar the IRS from backing out of an agreement to settle a tax obligation on an installment plan; and
- Increase the value of income and property that are exempt from IRS seizure.

In 1996, President Bill Clinton signed TBOR-II.[215] Its most important provisions:

- Make it easier for taxpayers to collect attorneys' fees from the IRS for malicious collection efforts;
- Require the IRS to take all necessary steps" to remove adverse information from credit reporting agencies upon withdrawal of taxpayer liens; and
- Authorize taxpayers to sue for up to US$500,000 in damages if any federal employee offers a tax preparer a more favorable settlement of his own tax liabilities if he informs on his clients, in any situation not involving criminal conduct or tax fraud.

Finally, in 1998, Congress enacted TBOR-III.[216] The most important provision of this law was to shift the burden of proof in certain civil tax cases from taxpayers to the IRS. However, this provision applies only in the small minority of cases that actually go to trial. In addition, taxpayers must first exhaust all available administrative remedies within the IRS.

This can be a significant expense. In many cases, it's less expensive and faster to file a petition for relief with the Tax Court where the taxpayer bears the burden of proof. And to prevail, taxpayers must demonstrate that they have:

- Complied with all the applicable laws and regulations;
- Maintained all relevant records; and
- Fully cooperated with all "reasonable" requests by the IRS for meetings, interviews, witnesses, information, and documentation.

Another change creates a confidentiality privilege for accountants. However, this privilege exists only for Certified Public Accountants (CPAs) and "Enrolled Agents" certified to represent taxpayers before the IRS. In addition, the privilege doesn't apply:

- To any proceedings other than tax proceedings before the IRS;
- In criminal matters before the IRS; and
- With regard to promoters of a "tax shelters."[217]

Unfortunately, none of these laws deal with some of the most pervasive problems associated with the U.S. tax collection system:

- The IRS need not prove that tax assessments are correct before seizing taxpayer property;
- Retroactive application of tax laws persists, despite language in TBOR-II purporting to deal with this problem. That law doesn't apply with respect to regulations designed to "prevent abuse" or if "internal regulations of the Treasury Department" call for such retroactive application;

- Tax records are increasingly disclosed for non-tax purposes. The IRS made an astounding **4.6 billion** disclosures of taxpayer returns or return information in 2004, in accordance with the Tax Code;[218]
- Lax security of IRS databases can easily lead to identity theft. For instance, a police officer checking up on money laundering reports can also review personal tax returns, in violation of federal law;[219] and
- Despite a 1997 law designed to prevent "browsing" of taxpayer returns by IRS employees, the practice persists.[220]

Tax Shelters: The New Reality

Tax shelters were pervasive in the 1970s and 1980s, but in the 1990s, Big 4 accounting firms started to aggressively market tax avoidance plans to high-net-worth clients and corporations. The firms would in many cases also provide "opinion letters" stating that in their view the strategy would likely withstand a challenge from the IRS. These arrangements allegedly resulted in the loss of billions of dollars in tax revenues.

According to the IRS, the following elements may characterize an "abusive" tax shelter:

- The claimed tax benefits far outweigh the economic benefits;
- The transaction has no real profit potential other than the tax benefits;
- Shelter assets don't actually exist or are insured for less than their purchase price;
- There is no non-tax justification for the way profits and losses; The investment plan involves hiding the economic reality of the transaction;
- The promoter offers to backdate documents or instructs participants to backdate checks covering their investment;
- The promoter promises that any debt taken on in the arrangement will never have to be repaid; and/or
- The transaction involves moving U.S. source income through foreign corporations incorporated in a tax haven that are owned by U.S. shareholders.[221]

The marketing of tax shelters spurred the Treasury Department to institute an approach that it hoped would end the "tax shelter" industry once and for all. Legislation in 2004 imposed significant new disclosure rules for a number of transactions frequently used in conjunction with tax shelters.[222] There are substantial penalties for failing to report these transactions.

In 2005, the IRS published Circular 230,[223] which contains regulations imposing much higher standards on tax advisors, particularly with respect to strategies that might reduce taxes. The regulations restrict the ability of tax practitioners to issue "covered opinions" (opinions that taxpayers can use to avoid penalties) and to market tax shelters. Practitioners must also inform the IRS when they create certain types of tax shelters for clients.[224]

Circular 230 has substantially increased the cost of obtaining tax advice, and substantially reduced the willingness of tax practitioners to engage in aggressive planning, because they may be subject to substantial civil penalties for doing so.[225]

Chapter 3 contains suggestions to avoid being penalized by the IRS for participation in a tax shelter.

Tax Avoidance vs. Tax Evasion

A growing number of U.S. persons refuse to pay income tax, claiming that the IRS has no authority to collect it from them. Some estimates place the number of non-filers as high as 30 million, although the vast majority of these individuals already have taxes deducted from their wages, and simply don't bother to file a return.

There are many strands to the so-called "untax" movement, but the common thread is a belief that the IRS has no legal authority to impose taxes. The arguments are essentially the same ones applied unsuccessfully by people who claim that the 16th Amendment was not legitimately made part of U.S. law.

Unfortunately for untax adherents, with a handful of exceptions, the courts have not supported their claims. In addition, the IRS has in almost every case prevailed in cases against persons who refuse to file a tax return on the basis that they are not liable to taxes.

However, every taxpayer has a right to try to avoid taxes. But when does completely legal tax avoidance turn into illegal tax evasion? The answer seems intuitive: evasion is driving around a tollbooth to enter a toll road without paying. Avoidance is taking an alternate free route. This fundamental difference couldn't be clearer. And the courts have repeatedly stated: Tax avoidance is legal. Tax evasion isn't. Justice Felix Frankfurter of the U.S. Supreme Court wrote:

As to the astuteness of taxpayers in ordering their affairs as to minimize taxes, we have said that, 'The very meaning of a line in the law is that you intentionally may go as close to it as you can if you do not pass it.' This is so because nobody owes any public duty to pay more than the law demands. Taxes are enforced extractions, not voluntary contributions.[226]

This principle is also recognized in other legal systems. In the House of Lords, the highest court for the United Kingdom and for many other Commonwealth countries, Lord Clyde stated:

No man in this country is under the smallest obligation, moral or other, so as to arrange his legal relations to his business or to his property as to enable the Inland Revenue to put the largest possible shovel in his stores...And the taxpayer is...entitled to be astute to prevent, so far as he honestly can, the depletion of his means by the Revenue.[227]

Yet, despite this ringing legal affirmation of tax avoidance, in practice, it's not always easy to tell the difference between evasion and avoidance. The line changes with amendments to tax laws, so that yesterday's legal avoidance can easily become today's tax evasion. And not knowing the difference can cost you dearly.

A simple benchmark to determine the difference between legal tax avoidance and illegal tax evasion is: "If I were to read about this technique or instrument in the newspaper, or hear about it from a friend, would I be skeptical, or not?" Two schemes that I've repeatedly encountered over the years don't meet the common sense test:

- **The sovereignty scheme.** Here you give up all ties to federal and state governments by renouncing your Social Security number, your driver's license, etc. Subsequently, you take additional steps to establish yourself as a "sovereign individual." At this point, supposedly, you're no longer required to pay U.S. taxes, even if you continue to reside in the United States.

- **The Pure Trust scheme.** Here, you transfer all your assets to a trust that is supposedly based on "common law" rather than statutory law. All income from this trust, because it purportedly isn't governed by statute, is supposedly tax-free.

I use these examples up because, despite numerous and successful prosecutions by the IRS, these schemes continue to proliferate. For details of other, similar, schemes, see http://www.quatloos.com.

Fortunately, the Tax Code remains riddled with loopholes; it's still possible to shelter income from taxes with many types of investments. Some of the most persistent loopholes relate to domestic energy production, life insurance, and the construction of low-income housing. There are many, many more; for guidance, consult your tax advisor. Just stay away from tax schemes that fail the common sense test or that otherwise promise benefits that appear unreal.

The End of Bank Secrecy in the United States

Although most people don't know it, U.S. financial institutions are required by the federal government to spy on their customers. This is a consequence of the **Financial Recordkeeping, Currency and Foreign Transactions Reporting Act**, more often referred to as the Bank Secrecy Act (BSA).[228]

First enacted in 1970, and extensively amended since then, the BSA represents a comprehensive federal effort to track currency and foreign financial transactions. It strips away secrecy from the vast majority of financial transactions by Americans, and increasingly, by anyone in the world doing business in U.S. dollars. The result is that bankers and other financial professionals no longer work solely in the interests of their customers. Instead, their highest duty, reinforced by civil and criminal sanctions, is to act as unpaid undercover police agents. The duty of discretion and care for customers has been supplanted by an overriding duty to conduct surveillance and notify the government in the event of any suspicious behavior. Amendments to the BSA have extended this obligation to many other U.S. trades and businesses.

The BSA requires U.S. depository institutions (i.e., banks or savings & loans), businesses, and/or persons to report:

- Any transaction or series of "related" transactions in currency exceeding US$10,000 with a U.S. depository institution (FinCEN Form 104);
- Any transaction or series of "related" transactions exceeding US$10,000 in currency and/or other "monetary instruments" (cashier's checks, money orders, and travelers' checks) in "designated reporting transactions" with any U.S. trade or business (IRS Form 8300 for trades and businesses and Form 8362 for casinos). Nearly 16 million Forms 104, 8300 and 8362 were filed in the 12-month period ending in June 2006;
- Any transportation of more than US$10,000 in currency, negotiable securities or certain monetary instruments across a U.S. border (FinCEN Form 105);
- The existence of foreign bank, securities, or "other financial accounts" with a cumulative balance exceeding US$10,000. Such accounts must be disclosed each year on Schedule B of IRS Form 1040 and on Treasury Form TD F 90-22.1.
- Any "suspicious activity" by a customer of a depository institution; securities or futures broker; casino or card club; insurance company; or money services business in transactions above thresholds ranging from US$2,000-US$10,000.

Penalties for violations of these requirements are draconian. Persons "willfully" violating the act may be fined up to US$500,000, imprisoned up to 10 years, and forfeit all property "involved in" or "facilitating" such violations.[229] The forfeiture sanctions in criminal violations of the BSA can involve all property with even the most tenuous connection to the offense. Officers, directors, and employees of financial institutions are personally liable for violations in which they knowingly participate. Informants providing information leading to a criminal fine, civil penalty or forfeiture that exceeds US$50,000 may receive commissions up to 25% of that sum, with a maximum reward of US$150,000.[230]

Congress enacted the BSA because it concluded that records of currency transactions have a "high degree of usefulness in criminal, tax, and regulatory investigations." However, there is no requirement that illegal or untaxed earnings be involved.[231] Unreported transactions or accounts involving lawfully earned, after-tax earnings can result in forfeiture, civil fines, and/or imprisonment.[232] Any effort to avoid these requirements by "structuring" a single transaction into smaller transactions under the reporting thresholds is also a crime.[233]

Two agencies oversee enforcement of the BSA: the IRS and the Treasury Department's intelligence bureau, the Financial Crimes Enforcement Network (FinCEN). FinCEN compiles data collected by both agencies in its "Bank Secrecy Act database," analyzes the millions of forms filed pursuant to the act, and combines that data with information drawn from government, private, and foreign databases. In doing so, the agency creates a dossier of individuals who engage in large transactions in currency or currency equivalents, or any other pattern of activity deemed suspicious, then matches these profiles against the typical behavioral profiles of tax evaders, money launderers, etc.

Because BSA filings aren't considered "tax return" information, they're not subject to the statutory privacy protection that tax returns enjoy. Indeed, the data may be disclosed to any other government agency, to state and local law enforcement officials and even to foreign governments. However, BSA filings generally aren't subject to disclosure in civil lawsuits.[234]

No "Expectation of Privacy" in Financial Records

The courts dismissed most legal challenges to the BSA, culminating in a 1974 case before the Supreme Court. The California Banker's Association claimed that the BSA's mandatory reporting provisions forced bank customers to submit evidence that could be used against them, thus violating constitutional privileges against compulsory self-incrimination (Fifth Amendment) and unreasonable search (Fourth Amendment). However, the court held that the association had no standing to challenge the act's constitutionality, as it could not invoke a depositor's Fourth or Fifth Amendment rights.[235] The courts also dismissed challenges to the act brought by individuals on First Amendment[236] and (again) on Fifth Amendment grounds.[237]

These rulings set the stage for a 1976 Supreme Court decision in a case involving a man named Mitch Miller, who was convicted of illegally manufacturing whisky. Miller's bank was served with secret subpoenas requiring it to turn over his account records to the government. The bank complied without notifying Miller or contesting the subpoenas. Armed with this information, the government indicted Miller for various offenses connected to failure to pay whisky tax, and obtained a conviction.

Miller's attorney argued that the subpoenas violated the Fourth Amendment. But the Supreme Court ruled that:

The depositor takes the risk, in revealing his affairs to another, that the information will be conveyed by the person to the government.[238]

In the *California Banker's Association* case, the Supreme Court had ruled that a bank could not invoke the rights of a depositor to challenge disclosure of account information to the government. In *Miller*, the court concluded that the depositor had no such right. In effect, under U.S. law, any information conveyed to a third party loses all constitutional protection, barring a statute restricting such disclosure.

In 1980, the Supreme Court extended this principle to illegal seizures. During a 1970s IRS investigation of offshore banks, a banker from the Bahamas briefly visited the United States. During his visit, the IRS lured him out of his hotel room. While he was gone, IRS agents conducted a warrantless search of his room and photocopied banking records in his briefcase. The records included evidence that a U.S. person had an account at the bank. Based on this illegally obtained evidence, that depositor was convicted of failing to report a foreign bank account. The Supreme Court upheld his conviction.[239]

U.S. courts may invalidate indictments or convictions obtained through governmental misconduct when the misconduct is "shocking to the conscience of the court."[240] Here, the Court concluded that the misconduct couldn't be used to suppress evidence obtained in violation of the constitutional rights of a third party; i.e., the banker whose briefcase was stolen.

Your Right to Financial Privacy is Virtually Non-Existent

In the Right to Financial Privacy Act (RFPA),[241] enacted in 1978, Congress sought to reinstate some of the constitutional protections lost in Supreme Court decisions relating to the BSA.

Generally, the RFPA requires federal agencies to provide individuals with a notice and an opportunity to object before a bank or other specified institution can disclose personal financial information. However, the RFPA is so riddled with exceptions that it provides almost no meaningful protection for financial privacy:

- The RFPA exempts most corporations, trusts, or limited partnerships from any protection by defining a "customer" as an individual or partnership of not more than five partners;
- A state agency can obtain financial records and share them with its federal counterparts without violating the RFPA;
- The RFPA doesn't restrict state or local government investigations, or investigations by FinCEN;
- Many government agencies, including FinCEN, the Homeland Security Administration and others, have obtained formal exemptions from the RFPA; and
- The RFPA imposes only a US$100 fine on the culpable party, "without regard to the volume of records involved." Contrast this penalty to fines of up to US$500,000 and prison sentences up to ten years that may be imposed on people who fail to comply with the BSA's reporting provisions.

Other exemptions make the notification and challenge requirements essentially nonexistent. They include:

- All disclosures to the IRS, including unwritten (i.e., verbal) summonses to banks;[242]
- All disclosures in accordance with federal statutes or regulations;
- All disclosures in litigation involving the government; and
- All disclosures to any intelligence or counterintelligence agency in any investigation related to international terrorism.

Indeed, it's almost laughably easy for government agencies to obtain financial records. All that's necessary is that they create an administrative, judicial, or grand jury subpoena certifying that the records are relevant to an ongoing investigation. While the RFPA stipulates that the customer must be informed of the investigation, in practice, such notification may be deferred indefinitely.

The Crime of "Structuring"

Amendments to the BSA in 1986 created a new crime: **structuring**. This is any act taken to evade (or avoid) completing a currency transaction report (CTR).[243]

Structuring convictions may be punished by up to a five-year prison sentence, a US$250,000 fine, and the forfeiture of all property involved in or facilitating the transaction. Merely violating the law is sufficient to be imprisoned; you need not be aware that seeking financial privacy is illegal. Nor is it necessary that "dirty" or untaxed funds be involved. Penalties are doubled for violations that occur in connection with another crime.

The act of structuring is undefined in law. The statute makes illegal any attempt to protect financial privacy by engaging in transactions in currency or other reportable monetary instruments that individually are lower than BSA reporting thresholds, but ultimately exceed those thresholds. Regulations stipulate that a person who deposits US$9,000 in currency into an account on two consecutive days commits a structuring offense. But 12 consecutive US$900 deposits may be structuring as well. The regulations don't address this possibility, or any of an infinite number of other possibilities.[244]

It's also a structuring crime to cross a U.S. border in a "related" series of crossings in which more than US$10,000 in currency is transported without completing FinCEN Form 105.

A good example of the draconian effect of the structuring statute on people who realize that a reporting requirement exists, but don't realize avoiding it's illegal, is illustrated in the following hypothetical situation, as postulated by an agent with the IRS Criminal Investigation Division.

An elderly widow with substantial assets in a bank account wishes to give cash gifts to her three grandchildren of US$8,000 each. When she approaches the bank teller and asks to withdraw US$24,000 in cash, she is told this requires the completion of a Currency Transaction Report.

Since the widow doesn't want to file a form that may "red-flag" her account, she breaks up the US$24,000 cash withdrawal into three transactions of US$8,000 each. She goes to the bank three days in a row, each day to a different branch, and withdraws US$8,000 each day. She then goes to each of her grandchildren's banks and deposits the cash in an account in each of their names.

Based on the widow's conduct, the bank informs the IRS of the suspected structured transaction on a Criminal Referral Form. The monies deposited into her grandchildren's account are subject to civil forfeiture and she faces potential criminal indictment for violation of Section 5324.[245]

Nor has the government made any effort to alert people to the structuring statute, although the Treasury Department proposed a publicity campaign after its enactment. The March 11, 1988 *Federal Register* included the following suggestions:

1. Require that a short notice of the provisions of Section 5324 [i.e., the anti-structuring statute] be posted at every location where customers may conduct cash transactions; e.g., bank teller's windows, casino gaming tables and cages.

2. Require that a short Treasury form notice of the provisions of Section 5324 be handed to any person conducting currency transactions over a certain amount; e.g., US$1,000 or US$3,000. Currency transactions would include deposits to accounts and purchases of monetary instruments such as cashier's checks, official bank checks, money orders, or travelers' checks.

3. Require that all deposit tickets be imprinted with a short Treasury form notice of the provisions of Section 5324 that a person making a currency deposit over a certain amount; i.e., US$1,000 or US$3,000, sign the back of the deposit slip as an acknowledgement of reading such notice.

4. Require that a short Treasury form notice of the provisions of Section 5324 be sent to all customers by a certain date and to all new customers upon the opening of an account.

5. Require that a short Treasury form notice of the provisions of Section 5324 be included periodically, e.g., quarterly, in all customers' monthly statements of accounts, and upon opening a new account. In the event that financial institutions receive inquiries from customers as the result of any of the above proposals, Treasury could make available a form to give to customers giving a more detailed explanation of the provisions of Section 5324 and a toll-free number for the customer to call for further information.

None of these suggestions were implemented. The government has made no effort whatsoever to inform customers that any attempt to avoid reporting deposits or withdrawals of currency or other monetary instruments is illegal.

One of the first individuals prosecuted for structuring was Charles Scanio, who in 1988 attempted to pay off a US$13,000 loan in currency without filing a CTR. The government made no claim that Scanio had any criminal intent, or that the funds he used were in any way tied to criminal activity, but still obtained a conviction. Scanio's attorneys argued that the structuring statute was unconstitutionally vague and that there was no statute of limitations or specific currency limit stated in it, but the court rejected these claims.[246]

In the 1991 *Aversa* case, in imposing sentence upon a defendant convicted of structuring, a federal judge delivered a scathing critique of the government's use of the statute. Aversa's alleged crime was conspiring with a friend to hide income from Aversa's wife. The scheme triggered reports of suspicious transactions in Aversa and his friend's bank accounts. Judge Martin Loughlin was particularly critical of the circus atmosphere surrounding the U.S. District Attorney's office when the indictment against Aversa was announced at a press conference. The implication was that prosecutors had broken up a major money-laundering ring. Judge Loughlin wrote:

Defendants should never have been prosecuted for structuring currency transactions...where evidence showed that defendants were not attempting to avoid paying tax on money or disguise where it came from...The evidence shows that [Aversa] did not believe that [he] was breaking any law... This is a case that was never contemplated by the drafters of the statute and that never should have been brought by the U.S. Attorney. There is only one explanation for the bringing of these charges—it was easy.[247]

Judge Loughlin felt he had no choice but to sentence Aversa to a mandatory prison term, but in 1993, a federal appeals court vacated Aversa's conviction because he had not "willfully" violated the statute. The court ruled that a willful act is "one committed in violation of a known legal standard or in consequence of a defendant's reckless disregard of such a duty." Since Aversa had no knowledge of the structuring statute, he could not be held criminally responsible for violating it.

A year later, in 1994, the Supreme Court overturned the structuring conviction of a gambler named Ratzlaf because he had not acted willfully.[248] However, an amendment to the BSA later that year overturned the *Ratzlaf* decision and eliminated the willfulness requirement.

Financial Institutions Must Spy

Under the BSA, U.S. financial institutions are required to complete a currency transaction report (CTR) by completing FinCEN Form 104 for currency transactions larger than US$10,000.[249] "Financial institutions" are defined not only as banks or other depository institutions, but also as brokers or dealers in securities, money transmitters, currency exchangers, check cashers, and issuers and sellers of money orders and traveler's checks.

Instructions for Form 104 state:

Who Must File. Each financial institution ... must file FinCEN Form 104 ... for each deposit, withdrawal, exchange of currency, or other payment or transfer, by, through or to the financial institution which involves a transaction in currency of more than US$10,000. Multiple transactions must be treated as a single transaction if the financial institution has knowledge that (1) they are by or on behalf of the same person, and (2) they result in either currency received (Cash In) or currency disbursed (Cash Out) by the financial institution totaling more than US$10,000 during any one business day ... Generally, financial institutions are defined as banks, other types of depository institutions, brokers or dealers in securities, money transmitters, currency exchangers, check cashers, and issuers and sellers of money orders and traveler's checks.

Form 104 defines "currency" as "the coin and paper money of the United States or any other country, which is circulated and customarily used and accepted as money." A "transaction in currency" is:

The physical transfer of currency from one person to another. This does not include a transfer of funds by means of bank check, bank draft, wire transfer, or other written order that does not involve the physical transfer of currency.

U.S. persons for whom banks complete Form 104 must provide their address, SSN and a government-issued photo ID. Non-resident aliens must identify themselves with a passport, alien ID card or other official document showing nationality and residence.

In the early years following the BSA's enactment, banks didn't enforce it vigorously. However, well-publicized crackdowns followed. Numerous banks have paid multi-million fines for permitting depositors to withdraw their own lawfully earned, tax-paid money without filing CTRs.[250]

In certain cases, U.S. financial institutions must monitor transactions smaller than US$10,000 in currency. Banks and S&Ls, along with the U.S. Postal Service, must verify your identity and retain a record of the transaction for five years when issuing or selling "monetary instruments" (bank checks and drafts, cashier's checks, money orders and traveler's checks) if purchased with currency in amounts between US$3,000 and US$10,000.[251]

Businesses Must Spy

The obligation of ordinary U.S. businesses to help enforce the BSA's currency reporting provisions expanded dramatically the USA PATRIOT Act. Businesses that receive or disburse more than

US$10,000 in currency in a single transaction, or a series of "related" transactions, must file another type of CTR, Form 8300. Casinos must complete Form 8362,[252] a modified version of this form. The return is due the 15th day after the cash is received, or sooner. A business must notify affected customers that it's submitting this form to the IRS.

In cities that are subject to **Geographical Targeting Orders**, businesses may be subject to significantly lower reporting thresholds. In past GTOs, reporting requirements have been lowered to US$750 for "money transmitting businesses."

Instructions for Form 8300 state:

Each person engaged in a trade or business who, in the course of that trade or business, receives more than US$10,000 in cash in one transaction or in two or more related transactions, must file Form 8300. Any transactions conducted between a payer (or its agent) and the recipient in a 24-hour period are related transactions. Transactions are considered related even if they occur over a period of more than 24 hours if the recipient knows, or has reason to know, that each transaction is one of a series of connected transactions.

Note that the reporting obligations apply to transactions only "in the course of that trade or business." If you're a physician, and someone pays you US$11,000 in currency for the provision of medical services, you're obligated to complete Form 8300. But if you sell someone a used car for US$11,000, you're not required to file Form 8300, since the sale occurs outside the course of your trade or business.

Businesses that buy or sell "consumer durables," collectibles, or are engaged in the travel or entertainment industry have expanded reporting obligations. They must not only report transactions in currency, but also in other monetary instruments that constitute what the Treasury Department calls **designated reporting transactions**. For designated reporting transactions, "cash" not only includes "U.S. and foreign coin and currency received in any transaction," but also, according to Treasury Publication 1544, the following **monetary instruments**:

A cashier's check, money order, bank draft, or traveler's check having a face amount of US$10,000 or less that is received in a designated reporting transaction (defined below), or that is received in any transaction in which the recipient knows that the instrument is being used in an attempt to avoid the reporting of the transaction.

A **designated reporting transaction** is:

A retail sale (or the receipt of funds by a broker or other intermediary in connection with a retail sale) of a consumer durable, a collectible, or a travel or entertainment activity.

- *Retail sale. Any sale (whether or not the sale is for resale or for any other purpose) made in the course of a trade or business if that trade or business principally consists of making sales to ultimate consumers.*
- *Consumer durable. An item of tangible personal property of a type that, under ordinary usage, can reasonably be expected to remain useful for at least 1 year, and that has a sales price of more than $10,000.*
- *Collectible. Any work of art, rug, antique, metal, gem, stamp, coin, etc.*
- *Travel or entertainment activity. An item of travel or entertainment that pertains to a single trip or event if the combined sales price of the item and all other items relating to the same trip or event that are sold in the same transaction (or related transactions) exceeds $10,000.*

69

Exceptions. A cashier's check, money order, bank draft or traveler's check is not considered received in a designated reporting transaction if it constitutes the proceeds of a bank loan or if it is received as a payment on certain promissory notes, installment sales contracts, or down payment plans.

A cashier's check, bank draft, traveler's check, or money order with a face amount of more than US$10,000 isn't treated as cash and a business doesn't have to file Form 8300 when it receives them. These items are not defined as cash because, if purchased with currency, the bank or other financial institution that issued them must file Form 104.

Businesses affected by the BSA must also track installment currency sales. According to federal regulations, "multiple currency deposits" or "currency installment" payments that are "related" are counted as a single transaction. If an initial payment is less than US$10,000, the business that receives it must track subsequent payments made within one year of the initial payment. If the total aggregate payments exceed US$10,000 within one year, the transaction must be reported on Form 8300.

Civil penalties for failing to file Form 8300 range from US$50 (for simple negligence) to US$25,000 or more if the failure is due to an intentional or willful disregard of the reporting requirements. Violations may also be subject to criminal prosecution, which may result in imprisonment of up to five years or fines of up to US$250,000 for individuals and US$500,000 for corporations, or both. "Willful ignorance" of multiple currency transactions over US$10,000 being related is also a crime.

Sting operations involving undercover agents from the IRS Criminal Investigation target businesses that frequently deal in currency; car dealerships, precious metals dealers, jewelry dealers, etc. Typically, agents approach a merchant and try to convince him to accept more than US$10,000 in currency or other monetary instruments without completing Form 8300.[253]

Most targeted industries now realize that they're required to file Form 8300 for receipt of currency or monetary instruments above US$10,000. As a result, the IRS now instigates technical reporting violations. For instance, an undercover agent may pay currency for a car, and then casually mention that the purchase is for another person. This information must be noted on Form 8300 and the identity of the real purchaser disclosed. If the information isn't included, both the individual who completes the form inaccurately, and the business itself, may be subject to civil and/or criminal penalties.

Attorneys have also been targeted for enforcement of these requirements. The courts have repeatedly upheld the authority of the IRS to demand client-identification information from attorneys on Form 8300 when they receive payments of US$10,000 or more in currency.[254] The IRS may impose a civil penalty of US$25,000 or more against the attorney for failure to comply.

International Investments and Money Movements Under Scrutiny

The BSA requires U.S. persons holding a cumulative total of US$10,000 or more in certain "foreign financial accounts" to report the existence of these accounts annually on Schedule B of their federal income tax return and make an annual filing of Treasury Form TD F 90-22.1. Schedule B must be completed even if interest and dividend income is less than the reporting threshold for this schedule.

Form TD F 90-22.1, the foreign bank account reporting, or **FBAR** Form, is submitted to a Treasury Department intelligence center in Detroit and its data then conveyed to the Financial Crimes Enforcement Network.[255]

The BSA also requires any person transporting, causing to transport, or mailing more than US$10,000 in currency or monetary instruments across a U.S. border to declare that fact on FinCEN Form 105.[256] Structuring a single transaction over US$10,000 into smaller related transactions, each under US$10,000, is illegal.

These requirements, and exceptions to them, are discussed further in Chapter 5.

Software Holds Your Money Hostage

When the FBI tried to design a profile of how a bank might be used by terrorists, it only came up with one main characteristic: large deposits with withdrawals of cash in a series of small amounts. ... Such a profile matches a quarter of the customers of most [American] banks.

—Derek Sambrook, *Offshore Pilot Quarterly*, March 2005

The BSA requires certain trades and businesses classified as "financial institutions" to notify FinCEN of any suspicious transactions in which their customers engage. Reporting is mandatory for suspicious transactions larger than US$5,000 and optional for smaller transactions. The threshold is US$2,000 for money transmitters.[257] Other types of businesses may **voluntarily** file Form 8300 and designate a particular transaction as "suspicious."

You have no right to sue any business that files a **Suspicious Activities Report** (SAR) pursuant to these requirements, even if the suspicions are false or fabricated[258] or in bad faith.[259]

SAR requirements were once restricted to banks and credit unions, but have now been extended to many other businesses. Currently, the following types of businesses must file SARs if you engage in behavior or transactions deemed suspect:

- Banks and other depository institutions (Form TD F 90-22.47, to be replaced by FinCEN Form 111);
- Brokers or dealers in securities (FinCEN Form 101);
- Insurance companies (IRS Form 8300 marked "suspicious transaction," to be replaced by FinCEN Form 108);
- Futures commission merchants and introducing brokers in commodities (FinCEN Form 101);
- Money services businesses (FinCEN Form 109); and
- Casinos (FinCEN Form 102)

Links to all of these forms are posted at http://www.fincen.gov/reg_bsaforms.html.

Under the USA PATRIOT Act, the obligation to report suspicious transactions can at any time be extended to other businesses deemed "financial institutions" via regulation. Currently, the Treasury Department is considering a requirement that travel agencies, car dealers, and real estate professionals report suspicious transactions.[260]

The businesses covered by these requirements must file SARs secretly, without your knowledge or consent. The reports are made available electronically to every U.S. Attorney's Office and to dozens of law enforcement agencies. No court order, warrant, subpoena, or even written request is needed to access a report. Law enforcement agencies can, and allegedly do, "troll" through suspicious activities reports (SARs) whenever they want.

Businesses subject to SAR requirements must watch for dozens of behavioral patterns by their customers—none of which are illegal, but when taken as a pattern, may indicate criminal activity. If the government determines after-the-fact that a business failed to heed these indicia of wrongdoing, it may take these indicia as **proven facts** to support its action. Since businesses don't know in advance which customers, if any, are engaged in illegal activity, all customers are subjected to pervasive, systematic, and continuous surveillance.

Prosecutors aren't required to prove any direct knowledge of wrongdoing to obtain a criminal conviction against persons subject to SAR requirements. They merely must show that a defendant institution or employee avoided knowledge of certain facts.[261] In one case, bankers were convicted of money laundering and bank fraud without the government even demonstrating they "ought to have known" about their customers' illegal activities. Instead, the government demonstrated that the defendant bankers had violated bank policies requiring employees to understand a customer's business and be alert to unusual transactions.[262]

The *Code of Federal Regulations* outlines the procedures banks must follow:

(1) Every bank shall file with the Treasury Department, to the extent and in the manner required by this section, a report of any suspicious transaction relevant to a possible violation of law or regulation. A bank may also file with the Treasury Department by using the Suspicious Activity Report specified in paragraph (b)(1) of this section or otherwise, a report of any suspicious transaction that it believes is relevant to the possible violation of any law or regulation but whose reporting is not required by this section.

(2) A transaction requires reporting under the terms of this section if it is conducted or attempted by, at, or through the bank, it involves or aggregates at least $5,000 in funds or other assets, and the bank knows, suspects, or has reason to suspect that: (i) The transaction involves funds derived from illegal activities or is intended or conducted in order to hide or disguise funds or assets derived from illegal activities (including, without limitation, the ownership, nature, source, location, or control of such funds or assets) as part of a plan to violate or evade any federal law or regulation or to avoid any transaction reporting requirement under federal law or regulation; (ii) The transaction is designed to evade any requirements of this part or of any other regulations promulgated under the Bank Secrecy Act ... or (iii) The transaction has no business or apparent lawful purpose or is not the sort in which the particular customer would normally be expected to engage, and the bank knows of no reasonable explanation for the transaction after examining the available facts, including the background and possible purpose of the transaction.[263]

From a financial institution's perspective, a policy to detect and report suspicious transactions isn't enough. The policy must work every time. A single mistake can result in a criminal prosecution against the person making the mistake and/or sanctions against the bank.[264]

One way to avert problems is to avoid the suspicious transactions to which financial institutions have been alerted. According to Michael Zeldin, former director of the U.S. Department of Justice's Asset Forfeiture Office, financial institutions should be aware of the following "non-industry-specific red flags" that may indicate criminal activity:

- Loans to offshore companies that have no apparent connection to the customer's business;
- Large currency transactions from businesses that are not typically cash-intensive;
- Large wire transfers with offshore banks or businesses, especially if no connection to the customer's business is obvious;

- Loans secured by obligations to offshore banks;
- Established financial relationships with bank secrecy or tax haven countries;
- Frequent or large wire transfers for people with no account relationship with the financial institution;
- Brokered deposit transactions where the broker's fees are paid for from the proceeds of related loans;
- Loan production/sales used as a basis for officer bonuses;
- Solicitation by people who reportedly have access to millions of dollars from a confidential source, readily available for loans and/or deposits in U.S. financial institutions. (Rates and terms quoted are usually more favorable than funds available through normal sources);
- Financial statements showing concentrations of closely held companies or businesses that lack audited financial statements to support their stated value;
- Loan proceeds used for purposes other than those stated;
- Attempts to use currency to complete a transaction when such transactions are typically handled by checks or other monetary instruments;
- Attempts to use monetary instruments endorsed to a third party to make purchases or investments;
- Customers who are more concerned with cancellation privileges than with return on investment;
- Reluctance to provide adequate identification information when opening an account or making a purchase;
- Purchases (especially by currency/bank check/money order) that appear to be beyond the purchaser's means;
- Customers whose business or residence isn't near the financial institution or business at which they make a transaction, especially when branches are located closer to customer;
- Businesses whose financial statements are inconsistent with similar businesses and (especially for large businesses) whose financial statements are not prepared by an accountant; and
- Customers with backgrounds inconsistent with proposed business activities or purchases.[265]

Additional suggestions for evaluating suspicious transactions come from a booklet distributed by the Treasury Department to all U.S. banks entitled *Money Laundering: A Banker's Guide to Avoiding Problems:*

- Opening accounts in several different names, none larger than US$10,000;
- Paying down a delinquent loan all at once;
- Objecting to completing Currency Transaction Reports;
- Changing currency from small to large denominations;
- Buying cashier's checks, money orders or travelers' checks for less than the reporting limit;
- Coming to the bank with another customer, and each making a currency transaction under the US$10,000 ceiling;
- Making deposits in currency, then having the money wired somewhere else;
- Ordering internal transfers between accounts, followed by large outlays;
- Appearing to use an account as a temporary repository for funds transferred overseas;
- Making a transaction that involves a large number of US$50 and US$100 bills; and
- Making a transaction without counting the currency first.[266]

According to the American Bankers Association, the following situation is also suspicious and should be reported:

You are the personal banker for a successful local businessman in your small town. Three months ago, he opened a checking account for his 12-year-old son. You have noticed that about one *month ago, the businessman began depositing a significant amount of business receipts into his son's account. The account balance has grown from US$150 to US$36,000. You have just received a call from the businessman. He has asked you to wire transfer US$35,000 from the account to a major New York bank to the account of Spring Trust. You have never heard of Spring Trust.*

Is this a suspicious transaction? Yes, definitely, according to Charles Morley, head of the consulting firm The Morley Group and a former IRS agent and Senate investigator. "We're not just talking drugs and drug cash," said Morley. "The businessman may be trying to evade taxes. Or he may wish to hide money from his spouse."[267]

The United States Postal Service operates one of the most vigorous suspicious activity reporting programs. In its **Eagle Eye** program, the Postal Service trains clerks to closely monitor individuals who purchase money orders. A guiding principle of the program is: "It's better to report 10 legal transactions than to let one illegal transaction get by... if it seems suspicious to you, then it is suspicious."[268]

These incredibly broad provisions threaten every law-abiding citizen. Consider Walter Soehnge, of Providence, R.I., who found himself under suspicion of terrorist activity because he paid off a US$6,500 credit card bill. Because this was much larger than his normal monthly payment, it was reported to Department of Homeland Security as a potentially "terrorist-related transaction."[269] After considerable inconvenience, Mr. Soehnge was able to regain access to his account. However, what happened to him could happen to almost anyone.

For instance, say that you have an average balance in your bank account of US$2,500. One day, you sell your vehicle for US$7,500 in currency and deposit the proceeds in your bank account. Is the transaction suspicious? It could be, according to the regulations: the transaction exceeds US$5,000 and it's "not the sort in which the particular customer would be expected to engage."

Given the draconian penalties that apply to businesses for not filing SARs, it's hardly surprising that the numbers filed are increasing exponentially: from 62.388 in 1996 to 919,230 in 2005, according to FinCEN.[270] Some banks even set quotas for increased numbers of SARs to be filed each reporting period. However, the overwhelming majority SAR reports were for innocent activity, as demonstrated by the fact that of the nearly 700,000 SARs filed in 2004, fewer than 900 were actually passed on by the collecting federal agency to a law enforcement agency for follow-up.[271] **In other words, nearly 99.9% of SARs don't lead to a criminal investigation.**

But the collateral damage is huge. In one case, a mistaken report caused the accounts of 1,100 innocent depositors to be frozen. Allegations have also surfaced that SARs are being made available (illegally) to private investigators and others. According to a letter sent to FinCEN by Merrill-Lynch:

FinCEN's SAR database is widely accessible to federal and state agencies, and consequently, further dissemination of the information is difficult to control. As FinCEN is aware, there have been instances where SAR information has been disclosed by government agencies to third parties (including the suspect) during...an investigation, where SAR information has been leaked to the press and where SAR information has been disclosed in connection with the obtaining of a seizure warrant or other court proceedings.[272]

The more reports filed, the greater the chance for such foul-ups. Especially since FinCEN itself has trouble entering the data it gets accurately. A 1999 audit found that in one case, US$5,000 was entered as US$5 million.[273]

Given the magnitude of the efforts required to unearth suspicious activities, much of the compliance effort in this regard involves the development of sophisticated software tools. These tools aren't particularly effective at distinguishing truly criminal activity from activity that simply doesn't match with a customer's previous account activity. In both cases, the account will be flagged and potentially frozen.

According to Suheim Sheikh, the CEO of an Indian software firm:

Anti-money laundering software will change international banking forever. Governments across the world will have their eyes on bank customers. Since the software can monitor so many accounts, so many transactions, all kinds of people will be scrutinized, even those who in theory are just regular people. By default, not just money laundering but anything that violates the law, like tax evasion, will be hard to hide.[274]

Civil Forfeiture: Policing for Profit

If an ox gores a man that he [shall] die, the ox shall be stoned, and his flesh shall not be eaten...When this ancient concept is recalled, our understanding of the law of forfeiture of chattels is more easily understood.

--United States vs. One 1963 Cadillac, 250 F. Supp. 183, 185 (W.D. Mo. 1966).

Drawing upon the biblical tradition of the "goring ox," as expounded in Exodus 21:28, for more than two centuries U.S. federal courts have justified the confiscation of property from owners who are not guilty of any crime, and indeed, are never accused of one. This concept of "guilty property" is known as **civil forfeiture**.

The "goring ox" concept described in Exodus 21:28 was derived from both Jewish tradition and Athenian law, by which any instrument causing death was considered accursed, and was destroyed.[275] By A.D. 1000, this tradition had evolved in England into a concept known as ***deodand***, which held that any object causing the death of a person was forfeited to the Crown. The forfeiture occurred even if the object's owner was not responsible for the death. But, unlike the ox in Exodus, which was stoned to death, the medieval *deodand* wasn't destroyed.

Eventually, the principle was established that any personal property causing the death of a person would be forfeited to the Crown. In this manner, *deodand* evolved from a religious injunction into a revenue raising measure, thereby corrupting the biblical command that the flesh of the ox "shall not be eaten."[276]

Over time, *deodand* was criticized both for its unfairness and because it did not compensate the families of accidental death victims. In 1846, the English Parliament repealed the practice. However, the repeal only affected the legal form of *deodand*, and not the underlying principle that property could be held accountable for a crime without reference to its owner's culpability. That principle, which was inherited in U.S. law, is fundamental to the law of civil forfeiture.

Civil forfeiture statutes were seldom employed for the first 200 years of U.S. history. This was in large part due to the unpopularity in colonial America of the English Navigation Acts.[277] These laws required that all goods imported into or exported out of English colonies be shipped in English-owned vessels. The captain and at least three-fourths of the crew were required to be English or residents of English colonies.

Having even one crewmember less than the three-quarters majority required could make the entire vessel and its cargo forfeitable. Proceedings were *in rem*, thus perpetuating the guilty property fiction of deodand. From the profits of these sales, trial costs were deducted, and commissions, typically 5%, were awarded to the officers of the court. The informer or prosecutor, the colonial governor, and the crown typically each received one-third of the balance.

Proceedings under the Navigation Acts took place in the crown's vice-Admiralty courts, which employed no juries. With only one judge to convince, and with the court receiving a commission when the prosecution prevailed, the odds were against the property owner. John Adams and other American leaders of the revolutionary period bitterly criticized the denial of jury trials in these proceedings.[278]

Despite this history, civil forfeiture became part of U.S. law almost from the inception of the republic. Beginning in 1789, Congress enacted a series of statutes authorizing the confiscation of ships and/or their cargoes for non-payment of customs duties and piracy, and later, for involvement in the slave trade. As with forfeitures under the Navigation Acts, the defendant in prosecutions under these statutes was the property, not its owner

Because civil forfeitures were relatively rare for the first 200 years of U.S. history, the statutes authorizing them remained obscure. But, when challenged, the courts usually upheld them. The *deodand* principle underlay these laws, as confirmed by the Supreme Court, which in an 1827 case declared that in forfeiture *in rem*, "The thing is primarily considered the offender." That decision also confirmed that no criminal conviction was necessary for confiscation to occur and that property of people entirely innocent of any wrongdoing whatsoever could be forfeited. [279]

In 1878, the Supreme Court upheld the confiscation of real and personal property used in connection with a distillery, due to violations of revenue laws by the company renting the property from the owner.[280] In 1921, during the Prohibition Era, the court upheld the confiscation of an innocent lienholder's interest in an automobile used illegally to transport distilled spirits.[281] And in 1996, the court upheld a Michigan statute providing for the civil forfeiture of any property involved in a crime, even if its owner is innocent of any wrongdoing.[282]

Civil Forfeiture Becomes a Cash Cow

Until 1978, civil forfeiture was used primarily to seize property involved in customs offense, but that year, Congress expanded its scope to permit confiscation of the proceeds of drug transactions.[283] This was a revolutionary change, for it marked the evolution of civil forfeiture into a punishment occurring without any of the safeguards due a defendant in a criminal proceeding.

Even larger changes came in the 1984 anti-crime bill, which provided for:

- The civil forfeiture of property derived from, connected to or facilitating drug-related offenses, including real estate;
- The payment of informant commissions to individuals who provided information leading to forfeitures under this statute; and
- The creation of an "Asset Forfeiture Fund" at the Department of Justice to share forfeited revenues with other agencies.[284]

But perhaps the most important innovation of the 1984 law was the concept of **adoption**. Under this process, when local or state police authorities seize property, they may turn it over to the federal government for processing under federal law. Then, at the discretion of the Department of Justice, up to 80%

of the proceeds are returned to the federal, state, local, or county agency initiating the seizure.[285] Forfeited assets may also be shared with foreign governments, a policy that has been effective in obtaining cooperation in asset forfeiture from foreign law-enforcement agencies.

This procedure bypasses state and foreign laws and constitutional provisions that would otherwise provide a legal barrier against the confiscation of property without a criminal conviction or that provide that forfeited assets be used for specific purposes not related to law enforcement; e.g., education.[286] The direct disbursement of forfeited revenues to law enforcement agencies and the reliance on forfeited proceeds as a revenue-raising device has been widely criticized as equivalent to "bounty hunting,"[287] but the practice continues. In 1989, the Supreme Court declared that the government has a legitimate financial interest in maximizing forfeiture to raise revenue.[288]

An even larger expansion of civil forfeiture authority came with the 1986 anti-money laundering statute.[289] The act provided authorized civil forfeiture of all property representing the proceeds of, involved in or facilitating a "specified unlawful activity." Violations of nearly 300 federal crimes are now considered "specified unlawful activity."[290] The 1986 act, in effect, expands the scope of civil forfeiture from customs and narcotics violations to any criminal offense that involves money.

Civil forfeiture laws provide the government with several unique advantages. A seizure or asset freeze is authorized in an *ex parte* hearing (without the defendant or defendant's lawyer being present) before a judge, magistrate, or administrator. Except when real property is involved, the property owner need not be informed of this hearing, and thus may not attend it, much less contest the seizure.[291]

The combination of lax procedural requirements and the potential to raise significant revenues has led an enormous increase in the property seized in civil forfeiture cases since 1984. Yet only a handful of procedural limits exist on this draconian legal procedure:

- In 1992, the Supreme Court ruled that lienholders on property allegedly obtained from or used to facilitate illegal activity have the right to appeal seizures by federal authorities.[292]

Do You Fit the Profile?

According to Richard Miller, *Drug Warriors and Their Prey* (Greenwood Publishing, 1996), the following profiles are all court-approved reasons to search individuals and seize their property:

- *Having a pale complexion*
- *Having a dark complexion*
- *Having a Hispanic appearance*
- *Being between the ages of 25 and 35*
- *Acting nervous*
- *Acting calm*
- *Carrying US$100 bills*
- *Carrying US$50 bills*
- *Carrying US$20 bills*
- *Carrying US$10 bills*
- *Carrying US$5 bills*
- *Wearing a pager*
- *Wearing casual clothing*
- *Wearing clothing with a bulge in it*
- *Wearing "a lot of gold jewelry"*
- *Wearing perfume*
- *Being a female who wears platform shoes*
- *Being a female who carries a condom in her purse*
- *Running up large electric bills*
- *Having a heat source in a house*
- *Having window covering that hinders someone from peering inside a residence*
- *Having a telephone answering machine message recorded by someone other than the person who is the phone subscriber*
- *Owning a dog*
- *Having a home security system*
- *Having a recreational vehicle motor home*
- *Driving a rental car*
- *Driving with an unfolded road map*
- *Driving a car with out-of-state license plates*
- *Having McDonald's fast food bags on a car floor*
- *"Scrupulous obedience to traffic laws"*
- *Failing to twist around in car to watch as a marked patrol car passes routinely in the opposite direction*
- *"Sitting very erect" in a car*
- *Being a foreigner without friends or relatives in the United States*
- *Being a foreigner who does not speak English*
- *Returning from a visit to Mexico without having bought souvenirs.*
- *Flying to or from any city*
- *Arriving at an airport and buying a ticket shortly before one's flight departs*
- *Paying currency for an airline ticket*
- *Buying a one-way ticket*
- *Buying a round trip ticket*
- *Buying a first class ticket*

- *Making a trip on more than one airline*
- *Flying nonstop*
- *Changing planes*
- *Having new luggage*
- *Having no luggage*
- *Traveling with a companion*
- *Traveling without a companion and meeting no one at the destination airport*
- *Acting as if you are looking for a person you expected to meet at the destination airport*
- *Being among the first passengers off an airplane*
- *Being among the last passengers off an airplane*
- *Being among the middle group of passengers off an airplane*
- *Looking at one's wristwatch*
- *Lacking a confirmed hotel reservation*
- *Using a telephone soon after leaving an airplane*
- *Walking quickly*
- *Walking slowly*
- *Leaving an airport without loitering*
- *Renting a motel room under a name that seems Hispanic or African-American*
- *Renting a motel room adjoining one of a traveling companion*
- *Using currency to pay for a motel room*
- *Looking at a police officer*
- *Not looking at a police officer*
- *"Looking around at other people"*

...[B]eing a citizen is sufficient cause to suspect a person of criminal conduct, thereby constricting civil liberties protections for that person. That situation is hard to distinguish from the legal status of citizens of Nazi Germany.

Former federal appellate Judge George Pratt compared the DEA drug courier profile to Humpty Dumpty's worldview in Lewis Carroll's *Through the Looking Glass*:

In our "Looking-Glass" world of drug enforcement, the DEA apparently seeks "to be master" by having "drug courier profile" mean, like a word means to Humpty Dumpty, "just what I choose it to mean—neither more nor less." (United States vs. Hooper, 935 F. 2d 484, 499 (2d Cir. 1991).

Laws that require no evidence of illegal activity for their enforcement, but the mere triggering of an arbitrary profile are an unprecedented threat to civil liberties. The threat is made more acute when combined with the rapid expansion in the government's legal authority and technological ability to monitor personal and financial activities, as documented throughout this book.

- In 1993, the Supreme Court ruled that, absent extraordinary circumstances, the due process requirements of the U.S. Constitution require notice and a hearing before seizure of real property.[293]
- In 1993, the Supreme Court held that civil forfeiture could be "punishment," thus subjecting civil forfeitures to the Eighth Amendment's limitation on "excessive fines."[294] However, the court refused to overturn the property seizure at issue, leaving it to lower courts to determine when a civil forfeiture may constitute an excessive fine. Moreover, in a subsequent decision, the Supreme Court ruled that civil forfeitures did not constitute "punishment" for purposes of the double jeopardy clause of the U.S. Constitution.[295]

These legal limitations to civil forfeiture are wholly inadequate, and in numerous cases, civil forfeitures have gone spectacularly wrong. In one 2004 incident, sheriff's deputies in Campbell County, Tennessee tortured a criminal suspect until he agreed to sign a statement agreeing to turn over his assets to the county.[296] While torture may not be an everyday occurrence in civil forfeiture cases, there are thousands of documented abuses of the procedure. Here's a small sample:

- In 1999, narcotics investigators in El Monte, California, shot and killed a 65-year grandfather in the back as he knelt on the floor at his bedside. Officers then confiscated the man's life savings and dragged his surviving family members to the police station for interrogation. Later, the city admitted that neither the victim nor his family had anything to do with drug trafficking.[297]
- In Bradenton, Florida, police have an ongoing policy of confiscating currency and property from people arrested for drug possession and other crimes. Arrested persons are coerced into signing a "forfeiture contract" waiving their right to contest the seizure in court. Those who hesitate to sign the contract are threatened with imprisonment.[298]
- In Illinois, a married couple was arrested in 2006 for carrying out a scheme in

78

which they would shake down people coming to the state's attorney's office trying to reclaim property seized during criminal investigations.[299]

- In New York City and many other cities, vehicles may be forfeited if an intoxicated driver operates them. The innocence of the owner or lienholder of the vehicle isn't a defense to forfeiture.[300]

When the government seizes your property under a civil forfeiture law, it doesn't need to prove you did anything wrong. All it needs to do is to demonstrate, by a preponderance of the evidence, is that your property is subject to forfeiture.

Currency (cash) is particularly vulnerable to this argument. U.S. courts have repeatedly ruled that possession of a large sum of currency is "strong evidence" of a connection to trafficking in illegal drugs. Merely possessing currency provides the government with sufficient evidence to seize it, unless you can provide clear and credible evidence that it's NOT connected to illegal drugs.

And even then, you might still lose it, as illustrated by the confiscation of US$124,700 from three motorists in Nebraska. During a traffic stop in 2003, Nebraska state troopers asked permission from Emiliano Gomez Gonzolez, the driver of a rented vehicle, to search the car. Gonzolez gave them permission, and during the search, the troopers found bundles of currency totaling $124,700. Later, a drug-sniffing dog "alerted" to the presence of narcotics residue on the money. Based on this "evidence" of narcotics related activity, police seized the currency, despite the fact that numerous scientific studies have demonstrated that as much as 96% of circulating U.S. currency is contaminated with narcotics residues.[301]

Gonzolez contested the forfeiture, and at trial, testified that after pooling his own legitimately earned currency with that of two partners in the produce business, he flew to Chicago to purchase a refrigerated truck. Both partners' testimony backed Gonzolez' account of the legitimate source and intended use of the defendant currency, which the government never contested.

The trial court believed Gonzolez' story and ordered the currency returned to him. But on appeal, the Eighth U.S. Circuit Court of Appeals overturned the trial court's decision and awarded the money to the government.[302] The government neither convicted nor accused any of the owners of the seized currency of any crime. Nor did police find any drugs, drug paraphernalia, or drug records connected to the seized currency.

Protecting Innocent Owners—or Not?

One of the most controversial aspects of civil forfeiture is the potential for innocent owners to be deprived of their property. One study revealed that in 80% or more of civil forfeiture cases, the owners were never charged with any crime.

Some civil forfeiture statutes provide exemptions for innocent owners and lienholders, but demonstrating innocent ownership was difficult. Owners may be required to prove much more than they aren't criminals. They may also be required to demonstrate that they took all reasonable steps to prevent illegal activity on their property.

In addition, they may need to prove that they are the "actual" owner of the property and that they exercise "dominion" over that property. This provision makes it difficult for absentee owners or anyone owning property through a corporation or other legal entity to make an innocent owner claim. And if a civil forfeiture statute lacks an innocent owner provision, the owner has no claim.

Another problem is that some civil forfeiture statutes permit the government to use hearsay evidence to establish probable cause to seize property. Tips from confidential informants, whose testimony can't be directly challenged, may be used as evidence in civil forfeiture cases. Once the government establishes probable cause, the burden shifts to the owner to demonstrate that the property isn't linked to criminal activity.

At the federal level, these procedural shortcomings were partially corrected in the Civil Asset Forfeiture Reform Act (CAFRA), a 2000 law[303] that significantly reforms federal civil forfeiture law, including:

- Shifting the burden of proof to the government by requiring it to show that property is forfeitable by a preponderance of the evidence;
- Abolishing the requirement that claimants post a bond before they can contest a civil forfeiture;
- Requiring (in most cases) warrants backed by probable cause to seize property for forfeiture;
- Making it easier to qualify as an innocent owner;
- Allowing for release of seized property in hardship cases;
- Allowing the appointment of counsel for indigent claimants (although no money has been appropriated to fund this mandate);
- Requiring payment of reasonable attorneys fees in cases where claimants prevail; and
- Allowing an action for damages against the government for harm to seized property while under the government's control.

However, CAFRA doesn't end the practice of seizing agencies being allowed to keep the assets they confiscate. Nor does it affect state and local forfeiture statutes or ordinances, or end the practice of adoption. CAFRA also doesn't apply to "national-emergency" type civil forfeitures under the International Emergency Economic Powers Act (IEEPA). Such forfeitures are exempted from virtually all of the evidentiary and due process requirements of federal forfeiture law.[304] You'll read more about the IEEPA later in this chapter. CAFRA even contains a provision for "automatic forfeiture," which requires that U.S. persons contesting civil forfeitures make available any records of investments maintained in a "bank secrecy jurisdiction" or face dismissal of the claim.

If you've been the victim of a civil forfeiture, or want to learn more about this procedure, the organization Forfeiture Endangers American Rights (FEAR) and its Web site http://www.fear.org are excellent resources. FEAR is also the publisher of *FEAR's Asset Forfeiture Defense Manual*, the only legal analysis that focuses on defense strategies to defeat a civil forfeiture.

Who's a "Racketeer?" Look in the Mirror

In medieval England, a convicted felon's property could be seized by anyone with the strength to hunt down and kill him. This legal concept was known as **outlawry.** Over time, outlawry evolved into a sanction by which all real property was forfeited to the crown upon conviction of high treason. For all other felonies, it **escheated** (reverted to) the lord of the convicted felon. The forfeiture was said to be *in personam* ("against the person").

Because outlawry under English law evolved into a political sanction against the enemies of the crown, the U.S. founding fathers opposed it. Article III, Section 3, of the U.S. Constitution states:

The Congress shall have Power to declare the Punishment of Treason, but no Attainder of Treason shall work Corruption of Blood, or Forfeiture except during the Life of the Person attainted.

This seemingly cryptic clause states that the loss of all civil rights by a person convicted of treason (**attainder**) doesn't prevent that person's family from inheriting his property after his death (**corruption of blood**).

In 1790, Congress adopted a statute eliminating the possibility of corruption of blood, or any **forfeiture of estate**, after a criminal conviction. [305] (Criminal forfeiture combined with corruption of blood was referred to as forfeiture of estate because of its complete divestiture of property and all property rights.) In 1970, the **Racketeer Influenced and Corrupt Organizations Act** (RICO)[306] ended the 180-year U.S. prohibition of criminal forfeiture. RICO makes it unlawful for any person (an individual, corporation, etc.) to use a pattern of criminal activity (defined as two or more **predicate offenses**) or the proceeds of such offenses to invest in, acquire control over, or conduct the affairs of, any formal or informal interstate enterprise.

Criminal forfeiture is an *in personam* action brought against an individual found guilty of a criminal offense. Only after a guilty verdict is rendered is a criminal forfeiture possible. Unlike a civil forfeiture, a defendant in a criminal forfeiture prosecution is entitled to all the procedural protections associated with the criminal process. Criminal forfeitures are considered constitutional on the basis that they don't represent forfeiture of estate. Instead, the statute authorizes only the return of illegally obtained monies and any properties or interests purchased with or connected to the tainted funds.[307]

Also in 1970, Congress enacted the Comprehensive Drug Abuse Prevention and Control Act. [308] It included a **Continuing Criminal Enterprise** statute, which was aimed at dismantling narcotics trafficking syndicates. [309] The criminal forfeiture provisions of this law are similar to those of RICO.[310]

The next major revision in criminal forfeiture law came in 1986, with the **Money Laundering Control Act**.[311] Criminal forfeitures under this law extend to virtually any crime in which there is an economic motive, along with violations of the Bank Secrecy Act. RICO's requirement for a "pattern of criminal activity" is no longer necessary. A single conviction for any of nearly 300 laws can lead to forfeiture of all funds linked in even the most remote way to the crime.

Since the laundering statute also provides for civil forfeiture, if the government doesn't win a criminal conviction, it may institute a civil forfeiture action. Alternatively, the government may carry on simultaneous civil and criminal forfeiture proceedings against the same property. This is a common tactic when the government is seeking to gather evidence to use against criminal defendants. Information that individuals disclose to prove that they are innocent owners, for instance, can then be used against used against them in a related criminal proceeding.

Criminal forfeiture law was again expanded in 2000 with the enactment of the Civil Asset Forfeiture Reform Act discussed earlier in this chapter. Prior to CAFRA, criminal proceeds could only be forfeited if there was a specific statute authorizing such forfeiture for a given crime, or if the government sought forfeiture as part of a money laundering case. With CAFRA, the government can include a criminal forfeiture allegation in virtually every indictment that charges at least one of the offenses listed in the money laundering statute. By making the proceeds of all crimes denoted as "specified unlawful activity" subject to forfeiture, CAFRA effectively gives the government the authority to seek the forfeiture of the proceeds of virtually all serious federal crimes, and a number of state and foreign crimes as well.

RICO Forfeiture: Few Limits

The RICO Act was the culmination of longstanding efforts to enact legislation to dismantle organized crime syndicates. Until RICO, no federal statute made it illegal to operate a "corrupt organization." Prosecutors might obtain convictions for crimes committed by individual members of organized crime syndicates, but could not attack the organization directly.

RICO's criminal forfeiture provisions provide prosecutors with the power to seize essentially all your assets prior to trial, and its civil provisions provide for the recovery of triple a victim's actual damages.

The RICO statute doesn't define the term "racketeering." However, the Interstate and Foreign Travel or Transportation in Aid of Racketeering Enterprises, or "Travel Act," defines racketeering as:

...the intent to distribute the proceeds of any unlawful activity; or commit any crime of violence to further any unlawful activity; or otherwise promote, manage, establish, carry on, or facilitate the promotion, management, establishment, or carrying on, of any unlawful activity.[312]

The following federal and state offenses, among many others, constitute RICO predicate offenses:

- Bribery (18 U.S.C. § 201)
- Counterfeiting (18 U.S.C. §§ 471-473)
- Embezzlement from pension and welfare funds (18 U.S.C. § 664)
- Extortionate credit transactions (18 U.S.C. §§ 891-894)
- Mail fraud (18 U.S.C. § 1341)
- Wire fraud (18 U.S.C. § 1343)
- Reproduction or sale of naturalization or citizenship papers (18 §§ U.S.C. 1426-1427)
- Obstruction of justice (18 U.S.C. § 1503)
- Fraud and misuse of visas, permits, and other documents (18 U.S.C. § 1546),
- Racketeering (18 U.S.C. § 1952)
- Interstate transportation of stolen property (18 U.S.C. §§ 2314-2315)
- Criminal infringement of a copyright (18 U.S.C. § 2319)
- Any offense involving fraud connected with a case under Title 11 (bankruptcy), securities fraud, or the felonious manufacture, importation, receipt, fraudulent concealment, buying, selling, or otherwise dealing in narcotic or other dangerous drugs, punishable under any U.S. law
- Any act indictable under the Currency and Foreign Transactions Reporting Act (18 U.S.C. § 1829(b) and 31 U.S.C. § 5311-5326)
- Any act or threat of murder, kidnapping, gambling, arson, robbery, bribery, extortion, dealing in obscene matter, or dealing in narcotic or other dangerous drugs chargeable under state law and punishable by imprisonment for more than one year.[313]

Criminal forfeiture after a RICO conviction is mandatory. The determination in the forfeiture is whether your interest in property is sufficiently linked to the offense. If the assets deemed linked to the crime aren't available for forfeiture, the court may order the forfeiture of **substitute assets** the defendant owns.

A criminal forfeiture order has far greater power than an ordinary civil judgment. It reaches property that would otherwise be protected under state laws protecting your home from seizure (e.g., homestead laws) and also may extend to annuity contracts and pension assets (see Chapter 4).

The Eighth Amendment, which prohibits "excessive fines" from being imposed in criminal cases, requires that RICO forfeitures be roughly proportional to the crime. However, "rough proportionality" leaves enormous discretion to the court. In 1993, the Supreme Court reviewed a RICO case in which the defendant was sentenced to a six-year prison term and forfeited his US$9 million business after he was convicted of selling four magazines and three videos found to be obscene.[314] The court questioned whether the forfeiture was proportionate to the crime committed, and sent the case back to a lower court for reconsideration.

Amendments to RICO in 1984 codify the **relation-back doctrine** with respect to criminal forfeiture. Under this legal fiction of English law, as inherited in U.S. law, all title to forfeitable assets transfers to the government the moment an offense is committed, before conviction. The major consequence of the relation-back doctrine is that property can be seized prior to a RICO conviction. Unless the defendant can prove it won't ultimately be forfeitable, the property isn't available for the defendant's use. A federal court, upon application of the government, may approve restraining orders or take any other action to preserve the availability of property for forfeiture. No notice or hearing need be provided, if the government can demonstrate that such notice would jeopardize the availability of the property for forfeiture.

The consequence of the relation-back doctrine, combined with the seizure of property before conviction, can be to deny you the use of your assets to pay living expenses or hire defense counsel. In 1989, the Supreme Court ruled that pre-trial restraint of assets that could have been used to pay an attorney did not violate a defendant's Sixth Amendment right to an attorney.[315]

Under the relation-back doctrine, the government can invalidate past asset transfers, however legitimate, by linking the history of an asset to some unlawful act that occurred while the asset was in the custody of an earlier owner or user. Only people who can prove they had no knowledge of the source of the monies or property given or sold to them, or had title to the property prior to the date the predicate offense was allegedly committed, can prevail in a claim to recover their property. They must wait until a post-conviction hearing to assert their claims, which may be years after the funds are initially frozen.

If you attempt to pay attorney fees or living expenses out of property that isn't subject to a pre-trial asset freeze, recipients may be required to establish that they are a "bona fide purchaser for value of such property who at the time of purchase were reasonably without cause to believe that the property was subject to forfeiture." If the recipients of the payments can't meet this burden of proof, the money may be confiscated. Family members and business associates may therefore lose assets acquired before any indictment was issued, dating back to the time the assets were allegedly tainted.

The law relating to the pretrial restraint of **substitute-untainted assets** in criminal forfeiture cases under the relation-back doctrine is not settled. In some judicial districts, prosecutors may restrain substitute-untainted assets before conviction or even trial.[316] Other federal courts prohibit this tactic.[317] The Supreme Court will undoubtedly be called upon to settle this issue.

Are you a racketeer? You probably don't think you are. But don't be so sure. RICO defines a "pattern of racketeering activity" (i.e., a pattern of predicate offenses) as:

...[requiring] at least two acts of racketeering activity [predicate offenses] ... the last of which occurred within ten years (excluding any period of imprisonment) after the commission of a prior act of racketeering activity.

There's no requirement that you be convicted of the predicate offense. You don't even need to be indicted. It's sufficient that you "could have been indicted."

The many predicate offenses under which RICO actions can be brought pose a minefield for businesses. Mail and wire fraud are the most common RICO predicate offenses. At first glance, the elements of mail fraud or wire fraud appear substantial. The government must establish all three of the following factors:

- A scheme or artifice to defraud and obtain money or property by means of false pretenses, representations or promises;
- The use of the mails or interstate wires (i.e., the telephone or Internet) for the purpose of executing the scheme; and
- A specific intent to defraud, either by devising, participating, or abetting the scheme.

The courts have interpreted this language broadly. "Scheme to defraud" includes any trickery, deceit, half-truth, concealment of material facts, affirmative misrepresentation, or breach of fiduciary duties. "Intent to defraud" may be inferred by a pattern of conduct, including recklessness, or from the nature of the scheme itself.[318]

Recklessness is conscious disregard of a substantial and identifiable risk; a gross indifference to the consequences of one's acts. It isn't a defense to state, "I didn't know," or "I didn't intend to" when a pattern of conduct clearly indicates otherwise.

RICO's definition of "corrupt organization" therefore reaches many, if not most U.S. businesses. Your entire business might be considered corrupt, even if carried out for a legitimate purpose, if you or any other owner or other individual controlling or with a "source of influence" over the business have committed two or more predicate crimes in a 10-year period.

While the lower courts have often sought to restrict RICO's application, federal appellate courts and the Supreme Court have repeatedly noted the intent of Congress for RICO to be "broadly construed." So, broadly construed it has been. According to an in-depth study by Professor Gerard Lynch of the Columbia University School of Law, of RICO cases brought for prosecution:

[I]t is very difficult to distinguish these cases from the typical run of fraud cases that are prosecuted ... without the assistance of RICO ... The only apparent motivating factor for the use of RICO in these cases would appear to be prosecutorial interest in either the aggravated sentencing possible under RICO or the specific forfeiture remedy.[319]

The "RICO Divorce" and Other Abuses

RICO isn't purely a criminal statute. A prosecutor may bring simultaneous RICO criminal and civil actions against a defendant. While the federal government may only seek injunctive relief under civil RICO, private persons who file a RICO lawsuit, and prevail, are entitled to treble damages, in addition to actual costs and attorney fees.

Consider the facts leading to one such claim:

Two sisters owned a small tailoring business. When their sewing machines broke down, they called a repairman, who fixed the machines and mailed a bill. The bill was larger than the sisters had anticipated and listed repairs they believed were never performed. The sisters contacted a lawyer, who agreed that the invoice listed some questionable items, but didn't think there was enough money at stake to justify a lawsuit. Then the repairman sent another bill. The lawyer then could now demonstrate two incidents of mail fraud in a 10-year period. He filed a RICO case against the repairman.

A U.S. district court threw out the case, but the sisters successfully appealed.[320] An allegation of fraud under state law was transformed into a federal racketeering charge. Even though "intent to defraud" couldn't be proven, the lawsuit alleged that it could be inferred from the repairman's allegedly reckless conduct.

In the 1980s, some lower courts reacted to the proliferation of private RICO actions by imposing stringent requirements on people bringing such litigation. The Supreme Court removed such limitations in 1985, reasoning that it was not the court's responsibility to impose such requirements. Congress alone had this responsibility.[321] However, an alleged RICO violation must be the "proximate cause" of the damages claimed.[322]

Under civil RICO, all that's necessary to federalize a business or domestic dispute is to discover two suitable predicate acts that allegedly form a pattern, affect interstate commerce, and relate to one another.[323] Every financial transaction should therefore be reviewed in terms of its potential application as a RICO predicate offense. Every business should be evaluated as a potential corrupt organization.

Daniel J. Popeo, Chairman of the Washington Legal Foundation, describes how attorneys use RICO as a battering ram to force lucrative settlements in lawsuits:

RICO is the critical link in a progression of legal assaults that begin with the filing of multiple product liability and tort suits. After bringing the initial suits, the lawyers use the discovery process to find some way to allege a cover-up or fraud. When the company defends itself to the public and its shareholders, the trial lawyers mischaracterize these actions as predicate acts under RICO. They then level a RICO charge, which carries with it bad publicity and triple damages. If that doesn't force a company to open its checkbook, they launch the coup de grace, a shareholder derivative suit based on the RICO claims that exposes the company's senior management to personal liability. This whole scheme is unabashedly designed to force settlements.[324]

Litigants have thus sought to apply civil RICO in patent litigation; contract disputes; zoning disputes; religious conflicts; divorces; invasion of privacy claims; and landlord-tenant disputes. The Church of Scientology brought a RICO suit against a splinter church, alleging spiritual harm from alleged theft and distribution of religious manuscripts.[325] The National Organization for Women sued an anti-abortion group for damages under RICO in what was essentially an action for aggravated trespassing, although the Supreme Court eventually threw out the lawsuit.[326] In a "RICO divorce," an estranged wife claimed that her husband and officers of a corporation had conspired to misrepresent the value of stocks subject to community property laws.[327]

The Thought Crime of Money Laundering

The Bank Secrecy Act established perhaps the first thought crimes in U.S. law, stipulating that individuals who fail to report their suspicion of criminal activity are guilty of a crime.

The Money Laundering Control Act (MLCA) expands the concept of thought crime in U.S. law, in that it forbids doing business with anyone that you should have reasonably suspected of being a criminal. Indeed, to be found guilty of money laundering, you need not actually launder money—you only need to consider doing so.[328]

The term "money laundering" apparently derives from the ownership by organized crime syndicates of laundromats in the United States in the 1920s. Laundromats were ideal for appearing to give these groups an apparently legitimate source for their revenues. Legitimate proceeds could be intermingled with revenues from drugs, gambling or (during Prohibition) alcohol sales to make the illegal income appear clean. The first time the term money laundering appears to have used by a court, however, was in 1982.[329] Since then, the term has come into both legal and popular use worldwide.

Until 1986, no federal statute criminalized financial transactions tied to illegal activity. The Money Laundering Control Act (MLCA) explicitly did so, and in so doing dramatically expanded the ability of U.S. prosecutors to seize and forfeit property, anywhere in the world.[330] The statute subjects both would-be money launderers and the financial institutions they use for this purpose to criminal liability. There are three types of liability:

- **Transactional liability** for anyone who conducts or attempts to conduct transactions with laundered funds;
- **Transportation liability** for anyone who transmits, transports or transfers, or attempts to transport, transmit, or transfer laundered funds; and
- **Concealment liability** for anyone who conceals or disguises the nature, location, source, ownership, or control of property they believe to represent laundered funds.

Borrowing criminal sanctions from the RICO Act, the MLCA goes beyond RICO by requiring only one act (not a related pattern) to establish culpability. While a RICO defendant must commit two specific and connected RICO predicate offenses within a 10-year period to be convicted or subject to a judgment, a single financial transaction connected to what the act refers to as "specified unlawful activity" can result in a laundering conviction and/or forfeiture. A single fraudulent transaction may taint an entire business and all its proceeds from the time the transaction occurred or scheme to defraud began, and make the entire business subject to forfeiture.

Unlike the Bank Secrecy Act, currency or monetary instruments need not be involved in a money laundering offense. Any financial transaction tied to a specified unlawful activity qualifies, and there is no minimum threshold. The MLCA also makes it a crime to do business with a person with a criminal reputation, even if the specific illegal act committed by that person is unknown.

The common conception of money laundering is that of criminals moving money derived from crime into the financial system. However, the conduct criminalized by the laundering statute is much wider than this popular conception. It includes all monetary instruments and all financial transactions, in any form. Virtually any exchange of value between two parties is included.

Under the "concealment" element of the MLCA, actions such as concealing title to property,[331] depositing illegally earned funds in a geographically different location from where they were generated,[332] and disguising the source of funds by putting them in a legitimate business[333] all establish criminal liability. Even withdrawing money from your own bank account,[334] or placing money in a safety deposit box constitutes a "transaction" under the statute.

The act also provides for corporate criminal liability. A corporation may be criminally liable for the acts and omissions of its agents and employees who are acting within the scope of their authority so long as the acts are intended to benefit the corporation, at least in part.

The penalties for money laundering are almost unbelievably harsh: US$500,000 or twice the value of the property involved in the transaction, whichever is greater, or imprisonment for not more than 20 years, or both. In addition, any property "involved in" a money laundering offense is subject to civil or criminal forfeiture. However, the most severe money laundering sanctions are imposed only in cases of large scale drug money laundering or serious crime, not in cases of relatively small-scale fraud or theft.[335]

Amendments to the MLCA make attempts to launder money subject to the same sanctions. This makes undercover sting operations against suspected launderers possible.

The list of specified unlawful activities encompasses nearly 300 crimes. Most of them are punished much more lightly than money laundering itself. In most cases, the government can obtain punishment far exceeding the penalties associated to underlying criminal conduct by adding one or more money laundering counts to an indictment. The effect is not unlike prosecuting a person accused of assault and battery for murder.

Specified unlawful activities, among many others, include:

- Racketeering (18 U.S.C. § 1961) except an act which is indictable under subchapter II of chapter 53 of title 31;
- Fraud, or any scheme or attempt to defraud, by or against a foreign bank (as defined in paragraph 7 of section 1(b) of the International Banking Act of 1978));
- Bribery of a public official, or the misappropriation, theft, or embezzlement of public funds by or for the benefit of a public official;
- Smuggling or export control violations involving—(I) an item controlled on the United States Munitions List established under section 38 of the Arms Export Control Act (22 U.S.C. § 2778); or (II) an item controlled under regulations under the Export Administration Regulations (15 C.F.R. §§ 730-774);
- 18 U.S.C. § 115 (relating to influencing, impeding, or retaliating against a federal official by threatening or injuring a family member)
- 18 U.S.C. § 152 (concealment of assets; false oaths and claims; bribery)
- 18 U.S.C. § 215 (commissions or gifts for procuring loans)
- 18 U.S.C. §§ 500-503 (certain counterfeiting offenses)
- 18 U.S.C. § 545 (smuggling goods into the United States)
- 18 U.S.C. § 641 (offenses involving public money, property, or records)
- 18 U.S.C. § 656 (theft, embezzlement, or misapplication by bank officer or employee)
- 18 U.S.C. § 657 (offenses involving lending, credit, and insurance institutions)
- 18 U.S.C. § 666 (theft or bribery in programs receiving federal funds)
- 18 U.S.C. §§ 793, 794, or 798 (espionage)
- 18 U.S.C. § 875 (offenses involving interstate communications)
- 18 U.S.C. § 1014 (relating to fraudulent loan or credit applications)
- 18 U.S.C. § 1030 (relating to computer fraud and abuse),
- 18 U.S.C. § 1032 (relating to concealment of assets from conservator, receiver, or liquidating agent of financial institution)
- 18 U.S.C. § 1201 (kidnapping)
- 18 U.S.C. § 1203 (hostage taking)
- 18 U.S.C. § 1708 (theft from the mail)
- 18 U.S.C. §§ 2113-2114 (relating to bank and postal robbery and theft)
- 18 U.S.C. §§ 2113-2114 (bank and postal robbery and theft)
- 18 U.S.C. § 2319 (copyright infringement)
- 18 U.S.C. § 2320 (trafficking in counterfeit goods and services)
- 18 U.S.C. § 2332 (terrorist acts abroad against U.S. nationals)
- 18 U.S.C. § 2339A (relating to providing material support to terrorists)
- Section 206 (relating to penalties) of the International Emergency Economic Powers Act
- Section 16 (relating to offenses and punishment) of the Trading with the Enemy Act
- Any felony violation of the Foreign Corrupt Practices Act

- Any act or activity constituting an offense involving a federal health care offense.[336]

To be found guilty of money laundering, you need not know the precise crime that occurred. You only need to believe that the proceeds were generated through an offense that violated a state, federal or foreign law.[337] The knowledge requirement is satisfied by the **willful blindness** test; i.e., if you deliberately avoided knowledge of the alleged offense.

The risks of willful blindness are illustrated in the case of a realtor convicted of money laundering. Prosecutors argued that the realtor should have known that a homebuyer was a drug dealer because he paid for a house in cash, drove an expensive car, wore gold jewelry, carried a cellular phone, and had a tan. The trial judge threw out the defendant's conviction, but to avoid retrial, the realtor pleaded guilty to a lesser charge.[338]

Tax evasion isn't a specified unlawful activity. However, felony violations of the tax fraud and tax perjury sections of the tax code can be. For instance, failing to file a tax return that would have included illegally earned, unreported income doesn't constitute money laundering. But, filing a return that excludes such income or contains material misrepresentations relating to it may constitute tax fraud and/or perjury and thus violate the anti-laundering statute, with its much more severe penalties. For this reason, even routine tax inquiries can now lead to money laundering investigations. Indeed, a laundering violation could occur for conduct as simple as mailing the IRS information later proven false.[339]

The MLCA is also enforceable outside the United States, so long as the specified unlawful activity involves a U.S. citizen, or if the conduct is somehow connected to the United States. The law also criminalizes international funds transfers that involve tainted monies or in any way facilitate money laundering. A single international transfer of money derived in whole or in part illegally, or of legitimate funds intended to promote an illegal activity, may violate the law.[340]

Indeed, two criminal defense lawyers state that, "a single telephone call in the United States in furtherance of a scheme to defraud, coupled with the movement of the funds in the United States, would establish a domestic money-laundering violation."[341] The government is required only to establish that a defendant knew that a crime had been committed, anywhere in the world, and that the transmission of the funds was designed to disguise the nature, location, source, or ownership of the proceeds.[342] Indeed, the telephone call need not even be physically in the United States, if the government can prove the defendant "acted electronically" within U.S. borders.[343]

From "to Serve and Protect" to "Show Me the Money"

The civil forfeiture provisions of the MLCA stipulate that "any property, real or personal," is subject to civil forfeiture if it is purchased with proceeds of, facilitates, or is "involved in" specified unlawful activity.[344] The MLCA, in effect, expands the scope of civil forfeiture from customs and narcotics violations to any criminal offense that involves money.

The statute doesn't condition forfeiture on the involvement of the owner in the underlying crime. Rather, the focus is on the money itself—the defendant in a laundering civil forfeiture—and its connection to the underlying offense.

Historically, civil or *in rem* forfeiture was more restrictive than *in personam* criminal forfeiture because the legal theory of civil forfeiture gave it operation only against "guilty property."[345] U.S. *in rem* jurisdiction has now expanded to the point where law enforcement can seize funds passing through U.S. financial institutions, even if neither sender nor recipient are subject to U.S. jurisdiction and the seized funds represent the proceeds of activity outside the United States.[346] It's even possible for substitute property in other countries to be forfeited.[347]

Professor Steven Schwarcz asserts:

Congress has not only dramatically increased the number of crimes that support a forfeiture action, but also has required an ever-lessening relationship between the "culpable act" and the forfeitable property. As a result of the expansion of civil forfeiture, property subject to seizure in [civil] forfeiture actions is increasingly part of the mainstream economy rather than contraband.[348]

Former Department of Justice attorney David E. Smith, who drafted a 1984 law expanding the use of civil forfeiture, explains:

In a number of cases, the government is seeking forfeiture of entire legitimate business enterprises on the theory that the entire business "facilitated" structuring or money-laundering activity connected with that business. This broad view of the facilitation language allows prosecutors to seek civil forfeiture of legitimate businesses for the first time.[349]

Amendments to the MLCA authorize the civil forfeiture of "any identical property found in the same place or account" as the property involved in a laundering offense.[350] In other words, the government can use the civil forfeiture statutes to confiscate substitute assets—an innovation previously reserved in criminal forfeitures. This provision greatly expedites the international enforcement of U.S. civil forfeiture orders, because assets in the United States may be forfeited in place of those subject to forfeiture abroad.

The USA PATRIOT Act further expands the civil forfeiture provisions of the money laundering law, as summarized later in this chapter.

As in RICO, criminal forfeiture under the MLCA provides for the confiscation not only of assets generated through criminal activity, but all assets providing a "source of influence" over the enterprise. Prosecutors may forfeit substitute assets if the criminally tainted assets can't be seized. Also, as in RICO, pre-trial restraint or seizure of any property involved in or traceable to illegal transactions is permitted.

The MLCA's civil forfeiture provisions expand the universe of offenses for which civil forfeiture is a "remedy" to nearly 300 crimes. There is no requirement that every dollar of the proceeds be proven illegal or fraudulent for forfeiture to occur. If one is tainted, all may be tainted. Under this reasoning, depositing US$10 of "criminally derived proceeds" into a US$100,000 bank account may make the entire account forfeitable.[351] Clean inventory may be forfeited where it served to conceal or disguise the use of other inventory to launder criminal proceeds through the business.[352] An entire business and all its assets may be forfeited if the business is used to conceal or disguise the true nature or ownership of criminal proceeds.[353]

While such "ink drop" forfeitures are generally reversed on appeal, prosecutors continue to bring them before the courts. A notorious example was the prosecution of San Diego eye surgeon Jeffrey Rutgard, beginning in 1994. A gifted surgeon, Rutgard made millions of dollars by correcting the vision of patients previously believed to be untreatable. Many of his patients were over 65, and the large number of surgeries he billed to Medicare led to an investigation for Medicare fraud.

After an exhaustive investigation of 20,000 patient visits to Rutgard's office, prosecutors brought fraud charges involving fewer than 30 patients. One-third of these charges were dismissed. On the basis that 20 out of 20,000 patient visits, or 0.1%, were allegedly fraudulent, prosecutors argued that Dr. Rutgard's **entire practice** was a scheme to defraud insurance companies and the government. They claimed that the entire gross receipts from Rutgard's insurance and Medicare billings were fraudulent—virtually every dollar he had earned from his first day of practice.

A jury found Rutgard guilty of mail fraud and money laundering. But, it concluded that only US$46,000 of the US$16.2 million earned by Rutgard from billing insurance companies and Medicare was for medically "unnecessary" treatment. Even in these cases, patients' vision improved after surgery. Indeed, three medical experts testified that the surgery was medically necessary.

In addition, the government's own billing expert testified that Medicare's reimbursement procedures are ambiguous. Dr. Rutgard followed expert advice on how to comply with those procedures, but despite these mitigating circumstances, and the jury's conclusion that only US$46,000 of Rutgard's earnings were fraudulent, the judge ordered him to pay the entire US$16.2 million as "restitution," less US$7.5 million already seized. These funds were ordered forfeited to the United States. Rutgard was also sentenced to 11 years imprisonment.[354]

In 1997, the Ninth U.S. Circuit Court of Appeals confirmed in part Rutgard's conviction on mail fraud charges, but vacated his money laundering and criminal forfeiture conviction.[355] The court declared: "[W]e hold that the government failed to prove beyond a reasonable doubt or even by a preponderance of the evidence that Rutgard's entire practice was a fraud and that all its proceeds were the fruit of fraud.[356]"

Money Laundering and "Reputational Risk"

The corner grocer in a community is aware of the reputation of the local drug trafficker. That person comes to the store and buys five pounds of hamburger. The grocer has to know what he is coming in to buy groceries with is indeed the money derived from a particular designated crime. I don't have any problem whatsoever in holding the grocer accountable for money laundering.

—Florida Congressman Bill McCollum, Congressional Record, Oct. 18, 1986

Could you be imprisoned for selling hamburger to someone who has a reputation as a criminal? Congressman McCollum—one of the architects of the MLCA—thinks you should be. And section 1957 of the act reflects his wishes.

It's a money laundering violation to do business with people with **reputations** as criminals, even if you're ignorant of the specific illegal conduct. Unlike section 1956, section 1957 exempts transactions under US$10,000. However, any pattern of "related transactions" totaling US$10,000 or more in any 12-month period counts toward this amount. So, if over a period of several months, you do US$10,000 or more business, in any form, with a person with a reputation as a criminal, you could be held criminally accountable under the laundering statute.

Section 1957 provides, in part:

*(a) Whoever ... knowingly engages or attempts to engage in a monetary transaction in criminally derived property that is of a value greater than $10,000 and is derived from specified unlawful activity, shall be punished as proved in subsection (b); (b)(1) Except as provided in paragraph (2), the punishment for an offense under this section is a fine under title 18, United States Code, or imprisonment for not more than ten years or both. (2) The court may impose an alternate fine to that imposable under paragraph (1) of not more than twice the amount of the criminally derived property involved in the transaction. (c) **In a prosecution for an offense under this section, the Government is not required to prove the defendant***

knew that the offense from which the criminally derived property was derived was a specified unlawful activity [emphasis added].

> *... (f) As used in this section—(1) the term "monetary transaction" means the deposit, withdrawal, transfer, or exchange, in or affecting interstate or foreign commerce, of funds or a monetary instrument ... by, through, or to a financial institution ... (2) the term "criminally derived property" means any property constituting, or derived from, proceeds obtained from a criminal offense.*

While the sanctions under section 1957 are not as severe as under section 1956, the scope of liability is greater. This is because section 1957 affects not only financial transactions, but also virtually any transaction involving any form of monetary instrument. The intent to commit a crime or the design of concealing criminal proceeds is eliminated. Simply spending, depositing, or transferring allegedly tainted funds is sufficient, provided at least $10,000 is involved. Thus, section 1957 can be applied to any form of commercial transaction and financial act, no matter how innocent.

For instance, if a businessman commits a fraud, and his secretary knowingly deposits a check representing at least US$10,000 of the fraud proceeds in a bank account in the business' name, with no attempt to conceal anything, the secretary has committed a crime that is punished much more severely than the underlying fraud committed by her boss.[357]

Section 1957, as originally enacted, granted no exemptions based upon the kind of trade or business engaged in by a potential defendant or the purpose for which a particular "monetary transaction" was undertaken. Thus, the statute allowed the prosecution of defense attorneys who knowingly received more than US$10,000 in criminally derived funds as legal fees for representation of clients in criminal cases. Subsequent amendments exempt attorneys from the brunt of section 1957. They do so by exempting from the definition of "monetary transactions" all transactions "necessary to preserve a person's right to representation as guaranteed by the Sixth Amendment to the Constitution."[358] Still, attorneys hired by drug traffickers or other people involved in criminal activity are a frequent target of laundering prosecutions and fee forfeiture.[359] In addition, the exemption doesn't apply to legal fees received for representation of a client in any non-criminal matter.

The Explosive Growth of "Testilying"

The expansion in civil forfeiture under the MLCA, combined with the severe penalties, has led to serious prosecutorial abuse. The worst abuses started after 1988, when Congress amended the MLCA to provide for "sting" operations against suspected money launderers. Now, any financial transaction can be converted to money laundering provided that an undercover operative asserts that proceeds or property involved in the transaction have been derived from some form of unlawful activity.

The sting statute also makes it easy for unscrupulous prosecutors to forgo laundering prosecutions of hard-core criminals or drug traffickers, and to focus on easy targets such as lawyers and bankers.

A textbook example was the 2001 laundering conviction of criminal defense attorney M. Donald Cardwell. At trial, the Drug Enforcement Administration claimed that that Cardwell had laundered money for his clients for more than a decade. Prosecutors obtained a conviction that could have led to Cardwell's imprisonment and loss of his law license. However, U.S. District Judge Alvin W. Thompson concluded that "the government's entire prosecution was based on a mountain of skillfully crafted lies under oath" and reversed the conviction.[360]

Another example of prosecutorial misconduct came in the case of Esperanza de Saad, a South Florida banker who was the target of a sting in an international money laundering investigation. In setting aside de Saad's 1999 conviction for money laundering, the judge ruled that an undercover informant who testified against de Saad never represented that the funds he was seeking to "launder" were the proceeds of illegal activity.[361]

Since the penalties for laundering are so high in relation to the sentence for the underlying crime, prosecutors have learned to tack on a money laundering count in almost every conceivable case. This not only permits asset forfeiture when no forfeiture would be available for the underlying offense, but creates an incentive to "make a deal" with prosecutors. In many cases, criminal defendants facing laundering charges have falsely implicated others in return for leniency. Defense attorneys have dubbed this practice "testilying." In 1999, a federal appeals court affirmed that the government has the right to offer leniency to a prospective criminal defendant in exchange for testimony against a person charged with a similar crime. The Supreme Court refused to review the ruling. [362]

Despite the occasional acquittal, most laundering prosecutions result in a plea bargain by the defendant. The threatened penalties are so heavy that defendants usually feel they have no choice but to plead guilty. In many cases, defendants' assets are seized in advance of trial, leaving them indigent. Unless they plead guilty, they may be forced to accept the services of a public defender, who may never have previously been involved in a money laundering or forfeiture case.

FinCEN: Big Brother Gets Bigger

We're a lot like Big Brother.

—Brian Bruh, former Director of the Financial Crimes Enforcement Network

In 1988, the U.S. Congress authorized the creation of a Treasury Department intelligence unit with the legal and technological mandate to escalate the "war on drugs" to a new level. Its job would be to analyze data from the largest array of computerized databases ever assembled for law enforcement.

Two years later, the 1990 National Drug Control Strategy agenda included a proposal for massive interagency sharing[363] of data to "consolidate and coordinate all relevant intelligence gathered by law-enforcement agencies."[364] It also called for a state-of-the-art law enforcement and intelligence organization that would use these and other databases to employ the most modern techniques of computer profiling against international drug traffickers. Treasury Secretary Nicholas Brady put this strategy in motion in 1990 when he signed a Treasury Order creating the Financial Action Task Force (FinCEN).[365]

FinCEN's creation nearly went unnoticed and the few published articles appeared to be taken almost verbatim from Treasury press releases. Most media sources missed crucial provisions of the Treasury Order that set aside federal laws that would otherwise have provided oversight over the searches conducted and records maintained by FinCEN, such as the Privacy Act, the Right to Financial Privacy Act and the Freedom of Information Act. The media also ignored warnings from individuals such as Dr. Ron Paul (now a U.S. congressman), that FinCEN and its investigative techniques would effectively repeal the guarantees against unreasonable searches and seizures and self-incrimination in the U.S. Bill of Rights. Dr. Paul also warned, "FinCEN is a trial run for a world system."[366]

Dr. Paul's warnings were prophetic. FinCEN clones now operate in more than 100 countries, many of them inter-connected to FinCEN. Jurisdictions reluctant to form FIUs or take other measures to fight the "War on Money Laundering" (now the "war on terrorism") are now threatened by sanctions if they fail to dismantle legal or constitutional presumptions of innocence.

FIU development is funded in part by monies seized in asset forfeitures, which are facilitated by FinCEN and other FIUs. In 1996 testimony before Congress, former U.S. Treasury Secretary Lawrence Summers stated:

As part of our effort to obtain better intelligence ... we have recognized the need to improve the international tracking of the flow of laundered money ... Treasury has authorized FinCEN to use nearly US$700,000 in asset forfeiture funds to upgrade and expand significantly our communications with, technical assistance to and training of the other financial units—the counterparts of FinCEN—around the world.[367]

Initially, FinCEN's mission was to help detect narcotics traffickers as they laundered money. However, its efforts quickly expanded to initiatives involving not just drug money laundering, but all criminal activity; in particular, white-collar crimes and tax evasion, and later, terrorism. FinCEN has placed no limit on what data it might eventually collect or what activities, illicit or otherwise, might in the future be targeted.

Beginning in the 1990s, FinCEN expanded its role again as it began participating in the promulgation of government regulations to enforce the Bank Secrecy Act and Money Laundering Control Act, among other statutes. FinCEN also began a direct enforcement role, e.g., in assessing penalties against businesses deemed not to comply with federal anti-laundering laws.

FinCEN may be the world's most comprehensive source of financial intelligence. A pioneer in the use of data mining technology, FinCEN seeks out unexplained, atypical money flows. It creates a dossier of individuals who engage in large transactions in currency or currency equivalents, and then matches these profiles against the typical patterns of tax evaders, money launderers, etc. programmed into the system.[368]

FinCEN's analysis begins with the massive Currency and Banking Database, derived from filings of various forms pursuant to the BSA. It maintains more than 140 million computerized financial records compiled from 21,000 depository institutions and 200,000 non-bank financial institutions. Banks, casinos, brokerage firms, and money transmitters all must file reports with FinCEN on cash transactions over US$10,000. FinCEN is also the repository for "Suspicious Activity Reports" filed under the BSA.

FinCEN also has access to a variety of law enforcement databases, including those operated by the Drug Enforcement Agency and the Defense Department, in addition to commercial databases of public records. FinCEN may also use databases held by the Central Intelligence Agency, the National Security Agency, and the Defense Intelligence Agency.

FinCEN shares information with investigators from dozens of agencies, including the Bureau of Alcohol, Tobacco, and Firearms; the Drug Enforcement Administration; the Federal Bureau of Investigation; the U.S. Secret Service; the Internal Revenue Service; the Customs Service; and the U.S. Postal Inspection Service. Agents from all these agencies can investigate names, addresses, and Social Security numbers through FinCEN. State and local law enforcement agencies can access data from FinCEN remotely.

A FinCEN initiative called **Operation Gateway** (now renamed **BSA Direct**) gives state and local law enforcement direct access to some of Treasury's most sensitive financial databases, including those maintained by FinCEN. The system automatically creates a dossier of people suspected of crimes by any law-enforcement agency. The Gateway model is now being expanded globally with the worldwide development of financial intelligence units modeled on FinCEN.

In the hands of a totalitarian government, FinCEN could easily be converted into a startlingly efficient means of financial oppression. As one observer noted, "Long after the public appetite for social control recedes, the infrastructure of social control will be in place, up and running."[369]

The USA PATRIOT Act: Deconstructing the U.S. Constitution

History shows that democratic societies don't cope well with sudden crises. The greater the crisis, the swifter and more unthinking the solution politicians concoct. And the reaction of the United States in the wake of the attacks of Sept. 11, 2001 was no exception.

Only a few weeks after the attacks, a terrified U.S. Congress adopted the "Uniting and Strengthening America by Providing Appropriate Tools Required to Intercept and Obstruct Terrorism Act," or "USA PATRIOT Act."

One of the most disturbing aspects of this act is its broad definition of terrorism:

The term "terrorism" means an activity that—(i) involves a violent act or an act dangerous to human life, property, or infrastructure; and (ii) appears to be intended—(A) to intimidate or coerce a civilian population; (B) to influence the policy of a government by intimidation or coercion; or (C) to affect the conduct of a government by mass destruction, assassination, kidnapping, or hostage-taking.

This incredibly expansive definition allows the U.S. government to label practically all forms of domestic protest as "terrorism." The words "intimidate" and "coerce" could apply to any group or organization that actively disapproves of official U.S. policy. Indeed, it could be argued that any forms of organized protest is designed to "intimidate or coerce" a change in government policy.

Once someone is designated a terrorist under the act, one of the broadest forfeiture provisions in U.S. law comes into effect, in effect, providing all the sanctions available for criminal forfeiture, but in the legal context of civil forfeiture.[370] The act authorizes forfeiture of all assets belonging to anyone engaged in terrorism, any property affording any person a "source of influence" over a terrorist organization, and any property derived from or used to commit a terrorist act.

Prosecutors can seize and ultimately forfeit **all assets**, foreign or domestic, of the alleged terrorist or terrorist entity—whether or not those assets are connected to terrorism. Once the government makes its initial showing of probable cause, the property owner must prove by a preponderance of the evidence that the property is not subject to confiscation. Moreover, in the forfeiture trial, hearsay is admissible if the evidence is reliable, and compliance with the normal Rules of Evidence "may jeopardize the national security interests of the United States."[371]

An equally dangerous development tied to the USA PATRIOT Act is that the focus on money laundering efforts is no longer on finding criminal assets of suspected launderers, but rather, to trace legitimate assets. This is because individuals with legitimate sources of income often finance organizations deemed by the U.S. government to be supporting terrorism. "It's money-laundering in reverse," says Alan Abel, global practice leader of anti-money laundering compliance services at Price-Waterhouse-Coopers.

"It's money that starts out clean then gets dirty when it's put to its purpose. It's a very difficult thing to ferret out."[372]

Discovering such illicit purposes requires a very high level of surveillance. Banks and other financial institutions must now required to seek out and investigate all assets and transactions, legitimate or otherwise, to determine if funds might possibly be used for some terrorist purpose.

Other important provisions of the USA PATRIOT Act:

- Expand "know your customer" and suspicious activity reporting obligations to many more types of businesses;
- Require banks to cross-reference the identity of all customers against a government-provided "watch list" of known terrorists, suspected terrorists, and individuals being investigated for possible suspicious activity.
- Authorize the Treasury Department to demand identification of the foreign beneficial owners of correspondent accounts;
- Permit the Treasury Department to ban all U.S. business with any foreign bank or nation, without stipulating a specific threat they allegedly pose to the U.S. financial system;
- Permit U.S. courts to order a person whose property may be subject to civil forfeiture to return any property located outside the United States to the custody of the court, before trial;
- Ban offshore "shell banks" without staff or offices from all connections to the U.S. banking system;
- Expand the currency transaction reporting obligations of banks to any business designated by the U.S. Treasury;
- Permit U.S courts to take "any action necessary" to ensure that a bank account or other property of a defendant is available to satisfy a forfeiture order;
- Permit the sharing of grand jury information that involves foreign intelligence or counterintelligence with federal law enforcement, intelligence, protective, immigration, national defense or national security officials;
- Give U.S. intelligence officers the ability to share foreign intelligence information obtained as part of a criminal investigation with law enforcement;
- Expand the use of "sneak and peek warrants," which permit the government to search a home or business without informing the owner or resident, from investigations affecting national security, to investigations involving any federal crime or misdemeanor; and
- Expand the FBI's authority to issue "national security letters" (NSLs) that are comparable to subpoenas, but may be issued with no judicial review.

The Terrorist Excuse

While purporting to fight terrorism, at its root, the USA PATRIOT Act has much more to do with advancing the long-term agenda of those in Congress who seek to enforce U.S. anti-money laundering laws offshore.

A few months before the September 11 attacks, the minority staff of the Permanent Subcommittee on Investigations of the Senate's Governmental Affairs Committee, chaired by Senator Carl Levin (D-Mich.), issued a report alleging that billions of dollars are laundered each year through the U.S. correspondent accounts of foreign banks. (Correspondent accounts are used by foreign banks to conduct business in the United States or in U.S. dollars; e.g., to permit customers of the foreign bank to purchase or sell U.S. securities.) Among other provisions, the report recommended that:

...forfeiture protections in U.S. law should be amended to allow U.S. law enforcement officials to seize and extinguish claims to laundered funds in a foreign bank's U.S. correspondent account on the same basis as funds seized from other U.S. accounts. [373]

The September 11 attacks provided Levin and his congressional allies a perfect excuse to pursue this agenda, although no evidence exists that the attackers used correspondent accounts. Indeed, an exhaustive investigation concluded that bank accounts in Germany, the United States, Sudan, and Pakistan helped fund the September 11 attacks—not correspondent accounts.[374] Nonetheless, the recommendations in the Levin Report became the centerpiece of the anti-laundering provisions of the USA PATRIOT Act.

Any foreign bank with a U.S. correspondent account—virtually every bank in the world—is now at risk if an alleged criminal deposits funds there. The U.S. government may seize and forfeit an equivalent sum of money in the correspondent account, even if it can't trace the money to proceeds deposited in an account held by the foreign bank. The court hearing to authorize the seizure is secret, with no notice provided to the property owner.

The first time correspondence accounts were targeted, predictably, was in a non-terrorist context. A husband and wife allegedly involved in an insurance fraud in the United States opened a US$2 million bank account in Belize. The U.S. Department of Justice sought to freeze the account, but the Belize Supreme Court turned down the request. Once the USA PATRIOT Act was enacted, the Justice Department used its new authority to freeze US$1.7 million in the U.S. correspondent account of the Belize bank.[375]

A License to Snoop

Could you be the subject of a FBI inquiry because you checked out a biography of Osama bin Laden at your local library? Or if you requested a copy of Mao Tse Tung's *Little Red Book* (an infamous paean to the glories of Communism) through an inter-library loan? [376]

That's exactly the type of inquiries undertaken by the FBI under authority of the "national security letters" (NSL) provision of the USA PATRIOT Act. The NSL provision permits the FBI to demand virtually any record from a U.S. business or organization, without a warrant. Records that can be obtained include library records, telephone logs, e-mail logs, financial and bank records, and credit reports. To obtain a NSL, the FBI only needs to certify that the records are "sought for" or "relevant to" an investigation "to protect against international terrorism or clandestine intelligence activities." This has led to an explosive growth in NSLs, with the number issued increasing from 8,500 in 2000 to more than 47,000 in 2005.[377]

FBI officials may forever prohibit the recipient of a NSL from disclosing its existence "to any person" other than the recipient's lawyer, with five years imprisonment as the prescribed punishment. (Under the original legislation, the recipient of a NSL had no right to challenge it at all—although a 2005 amendment to the law now permits court challenges.[378]) Requested records have included library records, telephone logs, e-mail logs, financial and bank records and credit reports. The FBI may retain the records indefinitely, even when they prove irrelevant to an investigation. They may also be shared broadly, facilitating the creation of electronic dossiers on tens of thousands of Americans.

Most of the records requested with NSLs are from telephone and Internet companies. America Online, for instance, employs more than a dozen people, including several former prosecutors, handling almost 12,000 requests a year from federal, state, and local police agencies. Not all of these requests are under the authority of NSLs, but the number of records requested exploded after enactment of the USA PATRIOT Act.[379]

Even under the extraordinarily loose standards under which NSLs may be issued, an internal FBI audit completed in 2007 concluded that the bureau had illegally used them more than 1,000 times. The new audit covers just 10% of the bureau's national security investigations since 2002, and so the mistakes in the FBI's domestic surveillance efforts are undoubtedly much higher.[380]

NSLs also helped the Bush White House build what is essentially an "enemies list" on more than 10,000 people. The Bush administration reportedly uses this information to retaliate against those who disagree with its policies. Those on the list reportedly include filmmaker Michael Moore and Senator Barbara Boxer (D-Cal.).[381]

In 2007, a federal court ruled that the gag orders that can accompany NSLs violate the recipient's free speech rights. In addition, the law "offends the fundamental constitutional principles of checks and balances and separation of powers." However, the ruling will end the use of gag orders in NSLs only if upheld on appeal—a process that could take years.[382]

NSLs may also have extraterritorial effect. U.S. companies doing business in other countries receive NSLs requiring them to divulge information that is legally protected under foreign law. Some countries have enacted passed legislation designed to protect private information from disclosure in this situation, but U.S. companies continue to deal with dilemma of competing legal obligations in this context.[383]

Foreign Nationals with U.S. Accounts May Be Money Launderers

Hundreds of thousands of foreign nationals use U.S. bank accounts to avoid corruption, hyperinflation, currency controls, and even kidnapping in their own countries. For instance, shakedowns by corrupt police officials are common in some Latin American countries. In other countries, it's common for kidnappers to pay banks for the names and addresses of their largest depositors.

The USA PATRIOT Act makes criminals of many of these depositors, if they maintain bank accounts in the United States in violation of their domestic law. It does so with a provision making any "scheme or attempt to defraud, by or against a foreign bank," a specified unlawful activity under the MLCA. Since exchange controls and similar banking regulations are generally enforced, at least in part, by a nation's central bank, violation of such laws could arguably be considered a "scheme to defraud" a foreign bank.

Civil forfeiture is available for the government to use in this situation, as in all other money laundering offenses. If the government pursues a civil forfeiture, it must prove its case only by a preponderance of the evidence. Moreover, that "proof," as in the domestic context, can rest on the self-serving testimony of witnesses with interests adverse to those of the owner. In addition, as in all civil forfeitures under the USA PATRIOT Act, hearsay is admissible if the evidence is reliable, and compliance with the normal Rules of Evidence "may jeopardize the national security interests of the United States."

Just how would foreign investors mount a defense against such a charge? Would they dare enter the United States to do so, and risk arrest on criminal laundering charges? The government would appear to have an open and shut case where foreign investors maintain U.S. financial interests in violation of foreign law administered by a foreign central bank.

Privacy in National Emergencies and War

It is the genius of our Constitution that under its shelter of enduring institutions and rooted principles there is ample room for the rich fertility of American political invention.

—*Lyndon B. Johnson, former U.S. President*

In 1787, during the debates on the Constitution, Alexander Hamilton warned that a loss of liberty was a natural consequence of war. Americans would "resort for repose and security to institutions which have a tendency to destroy their civil and political rights," he wrote. "To be more safe they, at length, become willing to run the risk of being less free."

Just as Hamilton feared, the elastic constitution praised by President Johnson is most elastic in times of war and national emergency. As this section documents, using an instrument known as an **executive order**, the president may, at the stroke of a pen:

- **Freeze the property of any person, entity, or government in the United States.** This authority was used during the Civil War (1861-1865) to confiscate the property of sympathizers of the Confederacy, and was upheld by the Supreme Court. It was also used to freeze Swiss assets in 1941, six months before the United States entered World War II. In the last two decades, the U.S. assets of Iran, Libya, Kuwait, Serbia, Iraq, Nicaragua, South Africa, Panama and thousands of persons allegedly tied to terrorism have been frozen.
- **Eliminate the right of *habeas corpus* and bring accused political criminals before military tribunals for trial.** President Abraham Lincoln used this authority during the Civil War and imprisoned members of Congress who disagreed with him. President George W. Bush used this authority in the detentions of suspected terrorists at Guantanamo Bay, Cuba.
- **Imprison or detain individuals or an entire class of people without trial.** President John Adams jailed a congressman for criticizing his "continual grasp for power." During the Civil War, President Lincoln imprisoned up to 38,000 civilians suspected of undermining the Union cause. During World War II, President Franklin Roosevelt used this authority to send many Japanese-Americans living in the western United States to internment camps for the duration the war.
- **Impose national banking "holidays" closing all U.S. banks or restrict and ration currency withdrawals and the cashing of checks or drafts.** President Franklin Roosevelt used this authority in 1933 to close down the U.S. banking system after a run of bank failures.
- **Shut down all stock and commodity exchanges.** This authority was used in 1914 to shut down U.S. markets for four months at the eve of World War I.
- **Investigate, regulate, or prohibit the importing, exporting, or holding of currency, securities, or precious metals.** President Franklin Roosevelt invoked this authority in 1933 to mandate the sale of all privately held gold in the United States to the federal government.
- **Impose punitive taxes on inbound or outbound foreign investments.** This authority was used in the 1960s to shrink U.S. capital deficits and support the U.S. dollar.
- **Impose wage and price controls.** This authority was used in World Wars I and II, and more recently in 1971 by President Richard Nixon.

An executive order is the "law of the land" unless overridden by Congress within 30 days of its publication in the *Federal Register*. After that, it can only be overridden by the courts or by a two-thirds vote of Congress. Only two executive orders have been overturned by the courts: an order by President Harry S. Truman seizing strike-threatened steel mills during the Korean War [384] and an order by President

Clinton prohibiting federal contracts being awarded to companies that hire permanent replacements for striking employees.[385]

The Whiskey Rebellion (1794)

A little rebellion now and then is a good thing, and as necessary in the political world as storms in the physical. Unsuccessful rebellions, indeed, generally establish the encroachments on the rights of the people which have produced them. An observation of this truth should render honest republican governors so mild in their punishment of rebellions as not to discourage them too much. It is a medicine necessary for the sound health of the government.

—Thomas Jefferson, Letter to James Madison, Jan. 30, 1787

The first constitutional crisis of the American Republic resulted from protests by farmers in Pennsylvania, Maryland, and Virginia over a federal excise tax on distilled liquor. Farmers resented the tax because they had to pay it not only on whisky sold to the public, but that they consumed themselves.

In 1794, President Washington sent officers into the Allegheny Mountains, where farmers distilled much of their rye crop into whiskey, to collect the tax. Armed men met the tax collectors and turned them away. One officer was stripped of his clothing, smeared with hot tar, and covered in feathers. Local militias led the insurgents, with as many as 7,000 people under arms. They seized government buildings, robbed the mails, and burned buildings occupied by supporters of the federal government.

President Washington issued two proclamations ordering the insurgents to lay down their arms, with little effect. He then sent more than 12,000 troops to Pennsylvania that restored order after only a few minor skirmishes. Was Washington justified in calling out troops to crush the Whiskey Rebellion? Insisting the tax be collected at the still rather when sold was a provocation, but once Washington was faced with a large armed force in the heart of the United States, he had little choice to "preserve the union." Yet, this precedent took on a much more ominous tone when the same authority was employed 67 years later by President Abraham Lincoln.

Census Acts (1790-2000)

A nationwide population census on a regular basis is stipulated in Article I, Section 2, of the Constitution:

Representatives and direct taxes shall be apportioned among the several States which may be included within this Union, according to their respective numbers ... The actual Enumeration shall be made within three years after the first meeting of the Congress of the United States, and within every subsequent term of ten years, in such manner as they shall by law direct.

The first census in 1790 asked only for the name of the head of the family and the number of people in each household of the following descriptions: free white males of 16 years and upward, free white males under 16 years, free white females, all other free people (by sex and color), and slaves.

At each successive census, the number of questions increased. In 1840, Congress established a centralized census office and authorized the Bureau of the Census to collect statistics pertaining to "the pursuits, industry, education, and resources of the country." Concerns that confidential information might be divulged led to the Census Act of 1880, which placed upon census-takers an obligation of secrecy.[386]

Subsequent censuses were carried out according to statutes that make compliance mandatory, with penalties for refusal; and responses confidential, with penalties for disclosure.[387]

More recently, the 2000 census drew criticism, particularly the "long form" with 53 questions. The survey asked about such things as marital status, transportation choices, employment, and household plumbing. Critics claimed that the information the Census Bureau releases in statistical aggregate form is so detailed that, combined with other information, it could be used to identify individual respondents.[388]

Many people refused to answer the questions. No one, to my knowledge, was prosecuted for failing to do so, although enforcement tools were at the time limited to a US$100 fine for failure to answer census questions. (However, you can now be fined up to US$1,000 **per question** for any census question you don't answer or which you answer "incorrectly.")

While the Census Bureau loudly proclaims that the data it collects is secret, census data is routinely released in aggregate form. Direct marketing companies and anyone else with the inclination to do so can analyze a particular region, state, city or even nine-digit zip code to determine its average income, household makeup, age, etc.

More disturbing, though, is the practice of the Census Bureau of periodically releasing data to law enforcement or military authorities. For instance, in World War I, the Census Bureau helped law enforcement officials find the names and addresses of young men who refused to register for the draft.[389]

During World War II, the military commander in the Western United States ordered that all persons of Japanese descent report to "Assembly Centers" and "Relocation Centers." From there, nearly 112,000 Japanese-Americans were sent to internment camps, and their property confiscated. The military used information gathered by the Census Bureau to help round up these individuals. Indeed, the Census Bureau drew up detailed maps that showed where Japanese Americans lived.[390] In 1943, the Supreme Court approved the detention of these individuals and the confiscation of their property as being within the war powers of the president.[391]

Reports in 2004 revealed that the Census Bureau secretly shared data about persons of Arab ancestry with the Department of Homeland Security. Census officials claimed that only demographic data was released, such as the number of Arabs in a particular zip code, and not names, addresses, or other private details. However, the initiative was in some ways reminiscent of the Bureau's pinpointing of Japanese-American communities when internment camps were opened during World War II.[392]

In 2006, the Census Bureau began distributing "The American Community Survey." Up to one million households, receive this form annually. The 2008 version of this form is 28 pages long and asks you to reveal how much money you make, the value of your home, details of your health, etc. It also asks you to report on the activities of relatives, employers, and roommates. You can be fined up to US$1,000 for each question you fail to answer "incorrectly." While this information is supposed to be kept private, given the record of the Census Bureau, you have near-zero assurance that some justification won't be found to share the survey with the IRS, the Department of Justice, or immigration authorities. As past experience demonstrates, what you reveal on census forms can come back to haunt you.

Alien and Sedition Acts (1798)

Only a decade after French financial and military support helped colonial America throw off British rule, French agents were accused of seeking to undermine the Constitution and overthrow the government. This was due to the violence accompanying the French Revolution, which some Americans feared would be exported to the United States.

In response, Congress passed the Alien and Sedition Acts, which made it a crime to:

...write, print, utter or publish [any] false, scandalous and malicious writing or writings against the government of the United States, or either house of the Congress of the United States or the president of the United States.

Persons found guilty of violating the acts could be imprisoned and their property confiscated. The acts also gave the president the power to deport any alien viewed as "suspicious," without any due process whatsoever. Thomas Jefferson and James Madison denounced the acts as fundamental affronts to press freedom, as guaranteed by the First Amendment, and to due process. They declared the acts illegal, although they were forced to conceal their authorship of such criticism for fear of prosecution.

After Jefferson won the presidential election of 1800, he suspended all prosecutions brought under these measures and Congress compensated those persons whose property had been confiscated. In 1801, the acts expired and weren't renewed.

The fear of aliens that was so pervasive in late 18th century America is again present two centuries later. In criticizing the Alien and Sedition Acts, Madison warned citizens to be mindful of losses of liberty at home in the face of danger from abroad. It's a lesson America should again heed in the war on terrorism.

Civil War (1861-65)

The Civil War, the largest conflict ever waged in North America, brought about a bumper crop of emergency proclamations and legislation.

After southern forces attacked Fort Sumter, South Carolina on April 15, 1861, President Abraham Lincoln issued a proclamation establishing a blockade against secessionist states. Over the next few weeks, Lincoln issued proclamations ordering naval vessels to be constructed and to triple the size of the armed forces.

Lincoln also suspended the writ of *habeas corpus,* an action the Constitution permits in wartime. However, at the time, Congress had not declared war against the secessionist states. (The "Great Writ," which originated centuries ago in English law, permits a detained person to demand a court hearing to determine the legitimacy of his confinement.) The Lincoln administration eventually imprisoned as many as 38,000 citizens without accusing them of a crime, including members of Congress. It also shut down more than 300 opposition newspapers.[393]

Congress sanctioned none of Lincoln's actions in advance. However, most Americans supported Lincoln's actions, and when the president finally convened Congress, his actions were approved retroactively. Thus began a precedent that continues to the present day: in time of crisis, the president may utilize virtually any means necessary to deal with the crisis, with the expectation of congressional concurrence.

While Congress went along with most of Lincoln's emergency measures, the courts didn't. But in 1861, Lincoln ignored a Supreme Court order to produce a prisoner detained without charge under a writ of *habeas corpus.*[394] This was only the first of many court orders Lincoln ignored during the Civil War.

Presidential proclamations also declared that suspected war criminals could be tried before military tribunals, an initiative predating a similar proposal from President George W. Bush by 140 years. Military tribunals tried approximately 4,000 prisoners during the Civil War, and many of those found guilty were immediately executed.

In 1866, after the Civil War ended, the Supreme Court ruled that military tribunals couldn't try civilians so long as the civil courts were open. The case dealt with a civilian sentenced to death by a military court and hanged for "disloyal activities." The Court ruled that:

Martial rule can never exist where the courts are open, and in the proper and unobstructed exercise of their jurisdiction ... The Constitution...is a law for rulers and people, equally in war and in peace, and covers with its shield of protection all classes of men, at all times, and under all circumstances.[395]

The Lincoln administration also brought the nation several innovations that had an enormous effect on the development of a national surveillance infrastructure. These included the first military draft and the first income tax.

To finance the war, Lincoln also resorted to a method used by rulers throughout history: he debased the currency by printing enormous quantities of paper money. The result was runaway inflation. When many citizens refused to accept paper notes, Congress enacted a legal-tender law, which required people to accept the government's bills and notes at their face value, which at that time was defined in terms of gold. While the Supreme Court originally held the legal-tender law to be unconstitutional,[396] it subsequently overturned its own decision.[397]

Other significant proclamations and laws during the Civil War that profoundly affected civil liberties, property rights and privacy included:

- **Emancipation Proclamation (1863).** This, the most famous executive order issued by Lincoln, purported to free all slaves living in the Confederate states. Lincoln questioned the constitutionality of his own proclamation. To provide a veneer of legality over his proclamation, he sought the passage of the 13th Amendment, which outlawed slavery. This amendment was ratified in 1865.
- **Confiscation Acts (1861-1862).** These acts called for the civil forfeiture of property of anyone who gave aid or comfort to the Confederacy. During and after the war, the government confiscated millions of dollars of property. The Supreme Court held in 1871 that the laws were a legitimate exercise of the government's war powers.[398]
- **False Claims Act (1863).** This act, passed to deal with procurement fraud in purchases for the military, is dealt with in the next section.

False Claims Act (1863)

In 1863, Congressional hearings revealed widespread fraud by military contractors that included the supply of defective products, substitution of inferior material, and price gouging. In response, Congress adopted the False Claims Act,[399] a statute that encouraged informants to come forward to the government with accusations of fraud or waste and receive up to a 50% commission for any resulting fine or forfeiture.

The informant, termed the **relator** under the act, is said to act *qui tam*. *Black's Law Dictionary* defines this term as:

...an action brought by an informer, under a statute which establishes a penalty for the commission or omission of a certain act, and provides that the same shall be recoverable in a civil action, part of the penalty to go to any person who will bring such action and the remainder to the state or some other institution.

While the original False Claims Act was enacted to combat military contractor fraud, it applied to all government programs. As federal expenditures grew exponentially, so did the use of *qui tam* actions, brought by individual citizens acting as "private attorneys general." In 1986 amendments, Congress set the whistleblower's maximum share of the recovery to 30% and authorized treble damages to be awarded against defendants.[400] In 2005, Congress prodded states to enact their own False Claims Act by providing them with incentives to increase their share of recoveries in Medicaid fraud cases.[401] The inducements allow states to up their takes by 10% (40% total), provided their acts follow the federal model.

No one can debate the wisdom of insuring that government programs are run with as little fraud as possible. But, the constantly increasing size and scope of government makes fraud and abuse inevitable. And the prospect of private attorney generals bringing a case against a business—perhaps due to a dispute, personal conflict, or other non-fraud-related reason—is a real one.

Posse Comitatus Act (1878)

The concept of *posse comitatus* dates back more than 1,000 years to medieval England. The phrase translates as "posse of the county" or the power or force of the county. It is essentially the citizen's duty to aid local law enforcement in capturing criminals and maintaining order.

Over time, the responsibility of enforcing the law was turned over to government. But in times of crisis, governments have historically turned to the military to quell civil disturbances. In this United States, this has occurred on numerous occasions:

- 1787–Shay's Rebellion
- 1794–Whiskey Rebellion
- 1846–Anti-Catholic riots in Philadelphia
- 1850–Property destruction, looting and killings in Kansas
- 1854–Army used to enforce fugitive slave laws
- 1859–John Brown captured and turned over to federal authorities to be hanged
- 1863–Draft riots in New York
- 1865-77–Occupation of the defeated Confederacy

After the 1876 presidential election, decided by only one electoral vote, President Ulysses S. Grant sent federal troops to supervise elections in the South. The perceived misuse of the military in an election led Congress to enact the **Posse Comitatus Act** (PCA).[402] Among other provisions, this act bans the military from participating in arrests, searches, seizure of evidence and other police-type activity on U.S. soil.

There are several exceptions to the law:

- The Coast Guard and National Guard troops acting under the control of state governors;
- Federal troops acting pursuant to the federal authority to quell domestic violence, riots or insurrection; and

- Emergency military assistance in the event of the release of nuclear materials.

Since its enactment, the PCA has been viewed as essential to preserve the principle that the military must always be subject to civilian authority. Though it was ignored in wartime—in World War II, for instance, U.S. troops rounded up thousands of Japanese Americans into internment camps—it remained mostly intact until the 1980s:

- In 1981, as part of the war on drugs, Congress created an exception to the PCA to allow military interdiction of suspected narcotics shipments at U.S. borders.
- In 1989, Congress designated the Department of Defense as the "single lead agency" in drug interdiction efforts.
- Since 1994, the armed forces have provided state and local police with more than 12 million pieces of military equipment, including armored personnel carriers, grenade launchers, and machine guns. The military have also conducted classes for police special weapons and tactics (SWAT) teams in camouflage, survival skills, reconnaissance, and other martial arts.
- In 1998, the Pentagon established the Joint Task Force, Civil Support (JTF-CS). Its mission is mobilize all military resources, including more than one million troops and National Guard units, in response to the use or threatened use of weapons of mass destruction.

But the biggest challenge to the PCA came in 2006[403] in the form of amendments to an obscure law dating from 1807, the Insurrection Act.[404] The amendments authorize the president to deploy troops within the United States when, in the president's judgment, the authorities of the state are incapable of maintaining public order. This may occur **without** the consent of state authorities, essentially making the PCA irrelevant.

World War I (1914-1918)

During the presidency of Woodrow Wilson, the United States entered World War I. As with previous wars, Wilson enjoyed enormous popular support for the war and for his initiatives to punish those who opposed it. Indeed, with overwhelming public approval, Congress in 1917 passed a law that prohibited using the U.S. mail to send any material urging "treason, insurrection or forcible resistance to any law." An even more extreme statute, the **Espionage Act**[405] (also known as the Sedition Act), authorized fines and prison for anyone who sought to "utter, print, write or publish" any "disloyal, profane, scurrilous, or abusive language" about the government, the Constitution, or the military. Postal bans on newspapers escalated to arrests for even the mildest criticism of the government's war efforts.

More than 2,000 people were arrested and 1,055 convicted under the Espionage Act and related legislation. Socialist Eugene Debs received a 10-year prison sentence after making a speech opposing the war. Film producer Robert Goldstein faced the same penalty for making a film about the Revolutionary War that was deemed treasonous because it portrayed the British (a U.S. ally in World War I) in a negative light. Police in New Jersey arrested author Upton Sinclair for the "crime" of reading the U.S. Constitution to an audience.[406]

The law was also used to prosecute and convict an individual who printed leaflets that urged men to resist the draft. In unanimously upholding this conviction, the Supreme Court ruled:

When a nation is at war, many things that might be said in time of peace are such a hindrance to its effort that their utterance will not be endured so long as men fight and that no court could regard them as protected by any constitutional right.[407]

World War I also brought about unprecedented governmental control over the economy. The federal government nationalized the railroad, telephone and telegraph industries; it virtually took over the ocean shipping industry. It brought about the first significant confiscations of "enemy" property since the Civil War. The **Trading With the Enemy Act**[408] enacted in 1917, authorized most confiscations.

The end of World War I brought about the termination of most of the emergency legislation that accompanied it. But the government was much larger and Americans not so free compared to only a few years earlier. Wartime roundups of dissidents paved the way for the "Red Scares" a few years later. And massive government intervention in the communications and transportation industries as well as rent controls, military conscription, and the suppression of free speech all set dangerous precedents.

Moreover, major portions of the Espionage Act and Trading with the Enemy Act remain part of United States law. Indeed, the latter law has been extensively amended and used by subsequent presidents to shut down the U.S. banking system; force U.S. persons to sell precious metals to the government; and confiscate foreign-owned U.S. property.

The Roosevelt National Emergencies (1933-1945)

Until the administration of Franklin D. Roosevelt (1933-1945), presidents declared national emergencies only in wartime. But Roosevelt, facing the economic crisis of the Great Depression, used his "inherent" executive authority to make sweeping changes in U.S. laws in peacetime and in many cases, without the consent of Congress. And when war did come in 1941, Roosevelt expanded presidential executive authority to an unprecedented level.

Emergency Banking Act (1933)

Roosevelt's first emergency initiatives dealt with a banking crisis. At his inauguration in 1933, many U.S. banks were insolvent, a consequence of imprudent lending practices in the 1920s, combined with a ruinous decline in stock prices and property values beginning in 1929. "Bank runs" were common; Roosevelt feared a wholesale banking panic that would wreck the American financial system. And on the second day of his presidency, March 6, 1933, under the questionable authority of the Trading with the Enemy Act, Roosevelt issued an executive order declaring a "bank holiday" and closing all U.S. banks.[409]

Never before had a president imposed emergency powers during peacetime. And in declaring an **economic** emergency, Roosevelt established a pattern that was to be followed throughout the remainder of the 20th century, and beyond.

As did Lincoln and Wilson before him, Roosevelt enjoyed overwhelming public support for his actions. And just three days after Roosevelt issuing the executive order, Congress enacted legislation placing these emergency measures into a statute. The **Emergency Banking Relief Act**[410] made important changes to the president's authority under the Trading With the Enemy Act. Section 5(b) of the revised Act now read:

*During time of war **or during any other period of national emergency declared by the president**, the president may, through any agency that he may designate, or otherwise, investigate, regulate, or prohibit, under such rules and regulations as he may prescribe, by means of licenses or otherwise, any transactions in foreign exchange, transfers of credit between or payments by banking institutions as defined by the president, and export, hoarding, melting, or earmarking of gold and silver coin or bullion or currency, by any person within the United States or anyplace subject to the jurisdiction thereof [emphasis added].*

Roosevelt drew upon this authority to continue the bank closures he had initiated. He used it again on April 5, 1933, to issue an executive order requiring all U.S. persons to deliver all gold coin, bullion and gold certificates to the Federal Reserve. Anyone failing to comply could be fined up to US$10,000, jailed up to 10 years, or both.[411]

People turning in gold were reimbursed with currency at the official value of gold; US$20.67/ounce. Roosevelt then devalued the dollar to US$35/ounce. The government paid gold owners only about 65% of the market value of their holdings, in effect confiscating the remainder of the value. The prohibition on private gold ownership was later extended to silver, and did not end until 1975.

Roosevelt's order also voided any private or public contract containing a **gold clause**. Such clauses provide that monetary obligations are to be settled in gold, rather than paper money. Indeed, until Roosevelt's executive order, all federal obligations (e.g., government bonds) called for payment in gold coin of, or equal to, the "present standard of weight and fineness."

Congress rubber-stamped Roosevelt's executive order, but some bondholders demanded payment in gold rather than paper money. They sued the government, but in 1935, the U.S. Supreme Court upheld the constitutionality of the Gold Repeal Joint Resolution[412] that invalidated gold clauses. In four separate cases, the court upheld the resolution as a legitimate exercise of the power of Congress over the monetary system. The outcome: all parties to contracts containing gold clauses, including the many holders of U.S. government bonds stipulating payment in gold, were deprived of their property.[413]

World War II (1939-1945)

World War II began in Europe in 1939, but did not involve the United States until the Japanese navy launched aircraft that bombed Pearl Harbor, Hawaii, on Dec. 7, 1941.

In preparation for the yet-to-be-declared war, on May 27, 1941, President Roosevelt issued a proclamation of "unlimited" national emergency.[414] Roosevelt's executive order gave him essentially the powers of a dictator, and with the assistance of two **War Powers Acts**[415] enacted by Congress, he used them to that effect. The First War Powers Act granted the president broad powers to, among other things, "cause to be censored ... communications by mail, cable, radio, or other means of transmission passing between the United States and any foreign country." Dozens of newspapers shut down after this enactment, as the Postal Service refused to deliver them. The government banned some newspapers altogether.[416] The Second War Powers Act allowed the government to exercise broad economic powers, including seizing private property.

Roosevelt also used his emergency authority to ration gasoline and food, and to impose wage and price controls. The government also confiscated factories, indeed entire industries, on behalf of the war effort. Meanwhile, Congress raised income tax rates repeatedly, until the top rate reached 94%. Withholding of taxes from paychecks was introduced as a "temporary" emergency measure in 1943; it remains law 65 years later.

The Supreme Court refused to deny the government the powers it was exercising at the expense of private rights. For instance, in upholding emergency price controls, it declared:

National security might not be able to afford the luxuries of litigation and the long delays which preliminary hearings traditionally have entailed.[417]

The Supreme Court also ignored its own Civil War era ruling that proceedings before military tribunals couldn't occur while the civil courts were functioning. The case before the court concerned a group of German saboteurs, one of them a U.S. citizen, who were captured shortly after they surreptitiously entered the United States. When their lawyer demanded a jury trial in a civilian court, the Supreme Court concluded that a military trial was good enough.[418] The prisoners were tried and executed, except for one who became a FBI informant.

World War II carried government by emergency to new heights. In 1947, two years after the war ended, more than 100 wartime statutes remained in force. Official states of emergency also continued. Indeed, new emergency measures, including a rent-control act and a peacetime military-conscription law, came into force. It wasn't until 1952 that President Harry S. Truman terminated Roosevelt's original 1941 national emergency declarations.

Professor Edward S. Corwin noted that after World War II, the United States for the first time in its history did not return to a "peacetime Constitution." Now the Constitution included:

- Legislative power of indefinite scope;
- Executive power to stimulate constantly the use of this indefinite power for enlarged social ends;
- The right of Congress to delegate its powers to the president;
- A broad presidential prerogative to meet self-defined emergencies and to create executive agencies to assist in dealing with such emergencies; and
- Progressively expanding administrative instead of judicial enforcement of the law.[419]

Office of Foreign Assets Control (1962)

World War II brought with it a massive blockade of "enemy" assets, including property owned by German and Japanese nationals and corporations. Even the assets of neutral Switzerland were frozen, before the United States even entered the conflict.[420]

Wartime boards within the Treasury Department administered these emergency controls. But by the 1950s, in preparation for possible war with the Soviet Union and China, a more permanent solution to administer blocked assets seemed desirable. Spurred by the seizure of U.S. property in Cuba, and the desire to freeze Cuban assets in the United States in retaliation, Congress created the Office of Foreign Assets Control (OFAC).

Since its inception, OFAC's responsibilities have grown dramatically. OFAC now administers economic and trade sanctions against more than a dozen countries, under executive orders declared under presidential wartime and national emergency powers, as well as specific legislation. Comprehensive asset freezes and trade embargoes are in effect against Cuba, North Korea, Iran, the former Taliban regime in Afghanistan, and numerous other governments. OFAC also maintains a watchlist of more than 6,000 "specially designated nationals."[421]

With narrow exceptions, doing business with anyone on an OFAC watchlist can result in a 30-year prison sentence, a US$5 million criminal fine, or a civil penalty of up to US$1 million per incident. Even the smallest transactions are covered—there is no minimum threshold. If OFAC freezes your assets, you must apply for a "license" (exemption) to recover them. In some cases, it takes OFAC years to process a claim, with the entire process shrouded in secrecy.[422]

Businesses nationwide are racing to install "OFAC compliance software" to screen financial transactions against OFAC targets. As a result, an increasing number of people are being denied the opportunity to open a bank account, obtain health insurance, buy a home, rent an apartment, or find a new job. A Sacramento resident with the first and middle names of "Mohammed Ali" found this out the hard way. He contacted a local Western Union agent to collect a US$50 funds transfer. For three days, Western Union told him that it couldn't find the record. Then, an employee told him he couldn't get the money because he "had a Muslim name." While Mohammed Ali finally got his money, his first and middle names remain on the OFAC watch list, so there's no guarantee his ordeal won't be repeated again and again.[423]

Like other U.S. government watchlists, the one OFAC administers is basically useless. One screening of six million names in a health insurance company's database against the OFAC list resulted in 6,000 false positive matches—and not one real match. If OFAC's watchlist isn't effective at identifying suspect terrorists, what is it good for? One thing it's effective at is to keep people with names like "Mohammed" out of the United States, and to encourage them to leave if they're already here. And perhaps, that's what the watchlist is really designed to do.

The Nixon Emergencies (1969-1971)

President Richard Nixon used all the emergency powers of his predecessors to fight a war in Vietnam and deal with domestic crises. A few months after taking office in 1969, Nixon combined many of the powers granted under previous executive orders and the Trading with the Enemy Act into a single executive order.[424] This executive order stated that all power might be transferred to the president under "any national emergency type situation that might conceivably confront the nation." It authorized the president to "utilize non-industrial facilities in the event of an emergency in order to reduce requirements for new construction and to provide facilities in a minimum period of time." Going beyond any previous presidential peacetime emergency proclamations, these words authorized the confiscation of commercial and residential property without any declaration of war.

In 1969, Nixon issued executive orders escalating the Vietnam War by authorizing the secret bombing of Cambodia. In 1972, he ordered American warplanes to drop bomb major North Vietnamese cities. In both instances, he claimed to be acting under the authority of the Trading With the Enemy Act, as amended by the Emergency Banking Act.

Nixon used the Trading With the Enemy Act again in 1971 to control the balance of payments flow by imposing supplemental duties on some imported goods. He used this authority the same year to impose wage and price controls[425] and to terminate the right of foreign central banks to exchange dollars for gold.[426]

National Emergencies Act (1976)

In the mid-1970s, some members of Congress expressed concern over the ability of presidents to exercise emergency powers in peacetime, and failing to terminate declared national emergencies. These concerns were fueled by the perceived abuse of executive orders by President Nixon.

Senators Charles Mathias and Frank Church established a Senate subcommittee to study national emergency powers. Senate hearings identified 470 grants of emergency power and four proclamations of national emergency (1933, 1950, 1970 and 1971) still in effect. Each proclamation activated the whole collection of statutorily delegated emergency powers. The hearings also revealed that no process existed for terminating national emergency proclamations.[427]

In response to these findings, Mathias and Church proposed legislation to regulate future declarations of emergency. The resulting law, the National Emergencies Act,[428] was enacted in 1976. While the act effectively ended the states of emergency that were then in effect, it did not revoke any of the "inherent authority" that Presidents Lincoln, Wilson, Roosevelt and Nixon, among others, had claimed.

Indeed, the Supreme Court in 1983 overruled the most significant requirement of the act—requiring a concurrent congressional resolution before a presidential declaration of national emergency goes into effect.[429] The Supreme Court further eroded restraints on executive authority when it ruled in 1984 that the president could impose new restrictions on private travel to Cuba without declaring a national emergency.[430]

International Emergency Economic Powers Act (1977)

In 1977, Congress again tried to reign in the president's powers in national emergencies. However, the legislation resulting from their efforts merely placed a stamp of statutory approval on these powers.

The International Emergency Economic Powers Act (IEEPA) is probably the most important law used today authorizing the president to employ emergency powers. It allows the president to exercise controls over international economic transactions during any period of declared national emergency. In the event of an "unusual or extraordinary threat" to the U.S. economy if that threat exists "in whole or in substantial part outside the United States," this act authorizes the president to:

...require licenses for any activity; require anyone to keep and furnish any records; and investigate, regulate, prohibit, direct, compel, nullify, void, prevent, or prohibit any transaction, acquisition, holding, use, transfer, withdrawal, transportation, importation or exportation, dealing, or exercising any right, power, or privilege with respect to any property.[431]

Persons violating these rules are subject to civil fines of US$10,000 per violation. Criminal penalties for willful violations provide for up to a US$50,000 fine and 10-year prison sentence.

One of the first uses of the IEEPA came in 1979, after Islamic fundamentalists assumed power in Iran and held more than 50 employees of the U.S. embassy in hostage. President Jimmy Carter announced the seizure of more than US$12 billion of Iranian assets. Since then, presidents have used the IEEPA to impose trade restrictions or seize property in relation to Cuba, Nicaragua, South Africa, Libya, Panama, Iraq, the former Yugoslavia, Haiti, Angola and Serbia, among other countries.

In 1981, the Supreme Court gave broad approval to the IEEPA, concluding that the president can invoke emergency economic powers without a declaration of war or any other statutory authority.[432]

The civil forfeiture authority of the IEEPA is exempted from virtually all of the evidentiary and due process requirements of federal forfeiture law. Under the IEEPA, civil forfeitures occur administratively, without a court hearing. The owner of seized assets must prove that the property isn't subject to confiscation. **All** property owned by the subject of an IEEPA forfeiture may be seized, not just that associated with alleged illegal activity. The IEEPA also retains the worst aspects of civil forfeiture. No criminal charges need be filed against the owner of seized property, and there's no obligation for the government to distribute the seized assets to the victims of the alleged wrongdoing. Indeed, the Treasury can give the assets to any agency or person designated by the president "for the benefit of the United States."[433]

In 2004, the Supreme Court refused to review a lower court decision upholding this draconian procedure.[434]

In 2005, the Treasury Department issued a statement declaring that it has the authority under the IEEPA to seize or freeze any "financial instrument." All that is needed is a presidential proclamation of a national emergency.[435] In other words, the government can at any moment order the confiscation of any document or paper that has intrinsic value or embodies monetary value: stocks, bonds, bank accounts, mortgages, cash, precious metals, etc. It's highly unlikely these powers will ever be invoked on a large scale unless the United States experiences a truly nationwide disaster, such as a nuclear attack. However, they're already being invoked on a narrow basis, against specific targets, as you'll learn later in this section.

The Clinton Executive Orders (1992-2000)

Stroke of the pen, law of the land...kinda cool.

—Paul Begala, aide to President Clinton (1999)

While Presidents Ronald Reagan and George H. W. Bush made occasional use of executive orders, President Bill Clinton used them much more frequently, issuing more than 300 published executive orders.

Clinton also made extensive use of another kind of executive order that is generally not a matter of public record: a **Presidential Decision Directive** (PDD). PDDs are used to circulate decisions on national security issues and for this reason generally remain classified. About a dozen current PDDs relate to deployment of nuclear weapons. Several classified PDDs were devoted to Iraq, North Korea, China, Serbia, and the former Soviet Union.[436]

All modern presidents have used PDDs, but Clinton greatly expanded their use. While most of them remain classified, his administration released documents describing a few PDDs, most notably PDD 63 ("Protecting America's Critical Infrastructure.") This PDD is linked to a Clinton-era executive order, which proclaims that in a national emergency declared by the president, the Federal Emergency Management Agency (FEMA) has the authority to suspend the Constitution and take control of the U.S. government and its citizens.[437]

Among other provisions, PDD 63 provides for the government control of all national communications, including the Internet, and for the interception and monitoring of all electronic communications.

The Bush Executive Orders (2001-2008)

After the attacks of Sept. 11, 2001, the administration of George W. Bush immediately put into effect a series of executive orders based primarily on the Trading With the Enemy Act and the International Economic Emergency Powers Act:

- **Expansion of civil forfeiture authority.** In a series of executive orders, President Bush has significantly expanded the authority under which civil forfeitures may occur under the IEEPA. No judicial review is possible; any appeal must be made directly to the U.S. Treasury's OFAC, the decision of which is final.

110

- **Warrantless surveillance.** President Bush has acknowledged that under his authority, the NSA wiretapped the conversations of suspected terrorists, without a warrant, in violation of federal law. Congress enacted legislation to temporarily legalize this program in 2007, as described earlier in this chapter.
- **Monitoring of international money transfers.** Under the authority of the IEEPA, since 2001, the U.S. Treasury has monitored money transfers of more than US$6 trillion daily between nearly 8,000 financial institutions worldwide.
- **Mass detentions, military tribunals, and torture.** Acting under the authority of an executive order, later enacted as a statute, the Bush administration has detained several hundred people, including at least two U.S. citizens, without charging them with any crime. Most were forbidden from consulting with an attorney for years, and some were tortured.
- **Violations of attorney-client privilege.** A Justice Department surveillance directive gives the government the right to monitor confidential conversations between lawyers and any clients suspected of terrorism, without a court order.
- **Expanded spying on domestic political groups.** The Bush administration has relaxed restrictions on the FBI's spying on religious and political organizations in the United States. This initiative loosens one of the most fundamental restrictions on the conduct of the FBI.

Expansion of Civil Forfeiture Authority

On Sept. 23, 2001, President Bush issued a far-reaching executive order "Blocking Property and Prohibiting Transactions With Persons Who Commit, Threaten to commit or Support Terrorism."[438]

The order goes beyond U.S. borders in its impact. For the first time, the United States threatened retaliation against other governments that were in its opinion, "soft on terrorism." In addition, the order:

- Provides authority for the United States to deny access to U.S. financial markets and dollar clearing facilities to a country or financial institution that is alleged to harbor terrorist funds or facilitate transactions linked to terrorist acts;
- Lists dozens of organizations and individuals with which any person subject to U.S. jurisdiction is forbidden to have financial dealings;
- Calls for the global dismantling of financial privacy laws as an anti-terrorist measure;
- Voids all contracts with any person covered by this emergency order; and
- Excludes the U.S. government from any liability for harm caused by the application of the order

Acting under authority of Bush's order, the FBI and local police authorities began raiding U.S. businesses that allegedly played a role in funding domestic terrorist operations tied to Osama bin Laden's *al Qaeda* network. Code-named **Operation Greenquest**, the Treasury's financial intelligence unit, FinCEN, coordinated the initiative. Using undercover operations, electronic surveillance and other techniques, investigative teams examined so-called "underground financial systems," along with allegedly illicit charities and corrupt financial institutions. It also targeted other funding mechanisms for terrorists, including counterfeiting, credit card fraud, currency smuggling, and drug trafficking.

One of the most significant efforts of Operation Greenquest involved seizing the assets of the Holy Land Foundation, one of the largest Muslim charities in the United States, under authority of the IEEPA, effectively shutting it down. The charity challenged the government's action, but in 2004, the Supreme Court ruled that the charity had no right to challenge its designation as a "terrorist organization" before any court.[439]

Little doubt exists that the government will continue to label organizations it opposes as "terrorist," and seize their assets under the IEEPA. The government uses this mechanism because it short-circuits the legal process that would ordinarily be required in a civil or criminal proceeding before a court. Even absent an alleged connection to terrorism, the government can hold a secret hearing in federal court as authorized by the USA PATRIOT Act to conduct the seizure, without notifying the property owner.

In 2006, a U.S. district judge struck down part of Bush's Sept. 23, 2001 order. Judge Audrey Collins ruled that the order was too vague and infringed on the right of free association, guaranteed by the First Amendment to the U.S. Constitution.[440] Indeed, any person or group could be named a "terrorist" under the President's authority for any reason. Or, as Judge Collins observed, "for no reason." However, the government has appealed this decision, and while the appeal is pending, it continues to seize alleged "terrorist property."

Monitoring of International Money Transfers

Under a secret initiative launched shortly after Sept. 11, 2001, the Bush Administration has gained access to a database of international financial transfers.[441] Under authority of the IEEPA, the Treasury Department, under CIA supervision, issued a secret administrative subpoena to compel the Belgian-based Society for Worldwide Interbank Financial Telecommunication, or SWIFT, to open its records. This international banking consortium routes more than US$6 trillion daily between nearly 8,000 financial institutions worldwide. The use of the IEEPA permitted an end run around U.S. laws that generally require the government to show that specific records are relevant to an investigation of a specific person or group before demanding their release.

U.S. government officials claim that this "Terrorist Finance Tracking Program" (TFTP) investigates only transactions related to terrorist financing, but SWIFT itself says it can't extract the bits of data U.S. analysts seek. So, it has given the Treasury Department access to its entire database of detailed records on billions of bank-to-bank transfers.[442]

There are numerous possible uses of the SWIFT data unrelated to terrorism investigations. The data would be useful to help enforce U.S. economic sanctions administered by OFAC. The IRS could use it to investigate U.S. persons engaged in offshore transactions, and the CIA could use it to conduct economic espionage against foreign businesses.

While the European Union and the United States have reached a tentative deal that would require the data turned over from SWIFT to be used exclusively in anti-terror investigations, the agreement won't apply outside the 27 EU countries.[443] Consider the non-EU nation of Switzerland, where 99 banks and 254 other financial institutions are connected to SWIFT, with daily transactions of some US$160 billion. Although the Swiss Bankers Association claims the TFTP doesn't violate Swiss bank secrecy laws, there's little doubt that U.S. investigators now have extensive information about Swiss banking transactions.[444]

As with other data mining programs conducted to fight terrorism, the effectiveness of the TFTP is an open question. Underground networks that exist outside the banking system have long been used in Asian countries to transfer money internationally. Terrorists reportedly use these networks instead of dealing with banks, where their financial dealings are subject to far greater scrutiny.[445]

Mass Detentions, Military Tribunals and Torture

In November 2001, President Bush signed an executive order authorizing the president to designate any person who is not a U.S. citizen as an "enemy combatant" and imprison them indefinitely, without criminal charges or access to attorneys.[446] Several hundred persons have been detained pursuant to this order, mostly at Guantanamo Bay, Cuba. In 2002, the Bush administration claimed the authority to designate **U.S. citizens** as enemy combatants and hold them incommunicado without access to the civilian courts as well.[447]

The executive order also authorized the use of **military tribunals** against enemy combatants. Members of the tribunal serve as interrogator, prosecutor, defense counsel, judge, and when death sentences are imposed, as executioner. Military tribunals can conceal evidence by citing national security, make up their own rules, and find a defendant guilty even if a third of the officers disagree.[448]

While the Bush administration denied torturing terrorist suspects, the Department of Justice wrote a legal memo stating that in certain circumstances, "torture may be justified.[449] It also claimed that international conventions signed by the United States that prohibit torture don't apply to enemy combatants.[450] A revised policy, however, bans the use of torture.[451]

At the same time, though the Bush administration admitted using "stress and duress" techniques to interrogate detainees, including sleep deprivation, denial of medication for battle injuries, forcing them to stand or kneel for hours on end with hoods on, and subjecting them to loud noises and sudden flashes of light.[452] The Bush administration also admitted that it transfers prisoners to other countries where torture is permitted.[453]

Numerous court challenges resulted from these initiatives, and in 2006, the Supreme Court ruled that President Bush overstepped his authority to create military tribunals outside the auspices of the military justice system without congressional approval.[454] However, Congress shortly thereafter enacted the **Military Commissions Act**,[455] which overruled the court's decision. The law allows the president to throw anyone in prison, including U.S. citizens, without access to any court. If you're classified as an "enemy combatant," there's no requirement that a trial via military tribunal, or in civilian courts, ever take place. You can be held indefinitely, without ever being accused of a crime. In other words, the law repeals, or attempts to repeal, the constitutional principle of *habeas corpus*. The government argues that "rebellion," "invasion" and "public safety" justify its permanent suspension, at least with respect to "enemy combatants."

Attorney-Client Privilege Compromised

On Oct. 31, 2001, then-Attorney General John Ashcroft approved an emergency rule that permits the Justice Department to eavesdrop on the conversations of lawyers with clients in federal custody. This includes people detained but not charged with any crime, whenever deemed necessary to prevent any crime of violence.[456] Neither attorneys nor prisoners need be informed of the surveillance.

This rule not only eviscerates attorney client privilege, but also one of the most fundamental rights enjoyed by U.S. persons: the right of an accused person to legal counsel. According to Irwin Schwartz, president of the National Association of Criminal Defense Lawyers:

The [attorney's] Code of Professional Responsibility is quite clear: a lawyer must maintain confidentiality. If we can't speak with a client confidentially, we may not speak with him at all. And if we can't do that, the client is stripped of his Sixth Amendment right to have a lawyer.[457]

The government, however, refuses to notify attorneys if their conferences with clients are being monitored, citing national security concerns. When challenged, the Justice Department claims that to confirm or deny surveillance, "could itself tend to reveal classified information."[458]

In another threat to the Sixth Amendment, federal prosecutors are targeting attorneys representing clients accused of terrorist offenses. The most notorious case is that of civil rights attorney Lynne Stewart, who in 2005 was convicted of conspiracy, providing material support to terrorists, and defrauding the U.S. government. Essentially, the government alleged that public statements made by Stewart were in reality coded messages intended to be heard by her client's terrorist compatriots.

By convicting Stewart, the government sent a message that it can imprison lawyers who represent clients with unpopular beliefs. "The purpose of this prosecution," said Michael Ratner, president of the Center for Constitutional Rights, "was to send a message to lawyers who represent alleged terrorists that it's dangerous to do so."[459]

Can Freedom Be Exchanged for Security?

Shortly after the events of Sept. 11, 2001, Congressman Ron Paul observed:

The biggest problem with these new law enforcement powers is that they bear little relationship to fighting terrorism. Surveillance powers are greatly expanded, while checks and balances on government are greatly reduced. Most of the provisions have been sought after by domestic law enforcement agencies for years, not to fight terrorism, but rather to increase their police power over the American people. There is no evidence that our previously held civil liberties posed a barrier to the effective tracking or prosecution of terrorists. The federal government has made no showing that it failed to detect or prevent the recent terrorist strikes because of the civil liberties that will be compromised by this new legislation.[460]

Yet, most Americans remain willing to trade freedom for security. In doing so, they ignore the wise advise of Benjamin Franklin, who more than 200 years ago, observed, "The man who trades freedom for security does not deserve nor will he ever receive either."

CHAPTER THREE: PRESERVE PERSONAL AND FINANCIAL PRIVACY

Are there ways to achieve complete privacy and anonymity, and making your wealth invisible? Yes, but the effort may be extremely costly—and/or illegal. To obtain it, you must:

- Sell all domestic real estate and convert it to currency.
- Sell your motor vehicles and convert them to currency.
- Sell your business and convert it to currency.
- When your driver's license expires, don't renew it.
- Resign from all organizations that might have your name on a list.
- Cancel all subscriptions in your real name.
- Cancel all your credit card accounts.
- Close all your domestic bank accounts.
- Allow all your professional affiliations to lapse.
- Move to another state or province and find somewhere to live with all utilities, including the telephone, listed in another person's name. Pay rent in currency, of course.
- Don't register to vote.
- If you work, do odd jobs in the underground economy that can be performed without identifying yourself. Accept currency only—no checks. If you must accept a check, currency it at a check cashing service, not a bank. Go to a different check cashing service each time. It's more expensive this way, but tax authorities monitor regular customers of these services to determine if they file tax returns.
- Use a series of mail drops to receive your mail. Pay another person to complete the necessary paperwork, and then give you the key. Pick up your mail late at night when no one else might see you. Wear a cap that obscures your face so that if the mail drop is equipped with a closed circuit television system, you won't be recognized.
- Assume a new identity using techniques such as **ghosting** outlined in books such as *The Paper Trip* (vols. I, II and III).[461] Ghosting (assuming the identity of a person who is deceased) is illegal in the United States and increasingly easier to detect as identity theft countermeasures become more common.
- Stop filing income tax returns. This is illegal if you have income above the filing threshold.
- Use your new identity to obtain a driver's license in another state, using a hotel or mail drop in that state as your address. This is a federal felony if you obtain your new identity illegally.
- Apply for a passport using your new name. This too is a federal felony if you obtain your new identity illegally. Leave the section asking for a Social Security number blank. Have the passport mailed to an address that you use for this purpose only, and never use it again. When you receive your passport, keep it in a safe place, but not in a safety deposit box.

If you're discovered, take your passport and your currency and leave the country. At the border, don't declare your currency to Customs. This is a federal felony if you're carrying more than US$10,000 and is punishable by fines, forfeitures, and/or imprisonment (Chapter 2).

Why might you want to take such extremes to disappear? Perhaps someone is bent on revenge and has threatened to kill you. Perhaps you're caught in an impossible personal or financial situation and you feel that "going underground" is the only way out. Whatever the reason, these deep-cover techniques—some of the same ones that people enrolled in witness protection programs are advised to follow—make it difficult for an investigator or anyone else to find you.

Besides separating you from mainstream society, disappearing will make you appear to be a terrorist or criminal, especially if you break the law, as you must if you create a false identity.

I don't endorse any illegal act to achieve this level of anonymity. Fortunately, you can still lower your profile to theft, lawsuits, and the government by using common sense, remarkably simple, often inexpensive, and perfectly legal techniques you'll learn more about in this and the next chapters. I call these techniques "lifeboats" of privacy and wealth preservation.

It isn't easy to achieve privacy in an age of global surveillance. But with diligence and forethought, the lifeboat strategy makes it possible to live a lower-profile life, and reduce, if not eliminate, everyday threats to privacy and property.

How Much Privacy Do You Need?

Privacy isn't a life-and-death matter for me. I seek privacy to avoid notoriety, frivolous lawsuits, wasted time, unwanted visitors, etc. I don't hold the illusion that a person can disappear from government—the largest privacy invader of all—without breaking the law or moving to an out-of-the-way corner of the world where government doesn't exist.

Not being willing to do either, I compromise with government. I pay my taxes and advocate legal strategies to protect privacy. This makes me a "collaborator" in the view of some privacy militants, but in this age of global surveillance, I fear retribution more from government than I do from tax protestors and civil libertarians.

Some privacy seekers have ulterior motives. People who seek privacy to conceal criminal activity discredit similar efforts by everyone else. For instance, a manual discovered in a raid by British authorities on a group associated with the *al Qaeda* network, recommends that members obtain false identity cards and passports.[462]

We all pay for those who misuse privacy for criminal purposes or terrorism. Governments worldwide, with overwhelming public approval, are rapidly stamping out longstanding legal protections against warrantless searches, imprisonment without trial, etc. The USA-PATRIOT Act is only one example; there are many more.

Seeking ultimate privacy can also create a sense of paranoia that interferes with normal daily living. Paranoia can lead to paralysis, which is always destructive. You need to determine what you are or aren't willing to do, and then make rational decisions within these parameters.

Keep a Low Profile

The most obvious way to react to increasing violations of your wealth and privacy is to fight back in any manner possible. But such a strategy is usually counterproductive. By taking a militant pro-privacy stance, you call attention to yourself and invite even greater intrusions. Always keep this paradox in mind as you seek to reduce your exposure to the privacy invaders.

For more than two decades, I have deliberately taken such a stance in order to call attention to what I believe is an enormously serious problem. But for most people, it's better to live a life that on the surface is completely ordinary, selectively protecting privacy by avoiding compromising situations and events.

The lifeboat strategy is to live in such a way that a potential snooper won't see anything unusual on the surface—and will never bother to look any deeper. For instance, most people use credit cards; those persons living a low-profile existence will use them as well, but only for purchases that reveal little about their lifestyle, political or religious beliefs.

If you live in a mansion in the best part of town, send your children to the best private schools, make large contributions to charities in your own name, and drive an expensive car, your financial success is obvious. Your high profile makes it much more likely that a potential litigant will consider you as a target for a lawsuit, even with only the flimsiest of evidence—hoping you will offer a generous settlement.

How might you lower your profile? You can live in a middle-class neighborhood, renting a home that is modest on the outside, but impeccably furnished within. You can send your children to a local private school, rather than a nationally-recognized academy. You can drive a mid-priced automobile, but have it customized to your taste. If you must drive a luxury automobile, you can lease it so that ownership isn't in your name. You can give to your local church or charity anonymously and still claim a tax deduction for the contribution. Finally, you can use techniques and structures discussed throughout this and the next chapter to make it more difficult for a litigant to recover your assets. All these steps lower your profile to potential litigants, and lessen the probability you will be investigated or sued.

Keep Your Mouth Shut

Many people readily disclose confidential information in exchange for small rewards. In a 2006 survey, interviewers persuaded 81% of commuters outside a major London subway station to part with vital personal information in exchange for the opportunity to win a prize worth less than US$120. The interviewers extracted names, dates of birth, mothers' maiden names—information that an identity thief would have found immensely useful.[463]

But even without being offered the opportunity for compensation, it's amazing what people will tell you voluntarily. Who they're having an affair with. How much they get paid. What investments they purchase. And much more.

Not disclosing personal information is the first line of defense and an essential element of the lifeboat strategy. You have no way of knowing what a friend, lover, a casual acquaintance, or someone on the street who offers you a small reward will do with the information you disclose.

For that reason, steer discussions on confidential personal or financial matters to another subject. But this requires a degree of finesse to avoid raising suspicion that you're trying to hide something. For instance, if someone asks you about your investments, rather than saying, "none of your business," you could say something like, "you wouldn't want to take investment advice from me—my portfolio has done terribly, and talking about it just gets me upset." This accomplishes two objectives: it deflects the conversation away from your personal situation, and makes you appear a less attractive target.

If you're wealthy and known as such, you're already a target. But you need not discuss the details. Perhaps it's known in your community that "you" own 40 acres of prime land a few miles out of town. But it doesn't need to be common knowledge that you hold it through a family limited partnership tied to an offshore trust.

Especially keep your mouth shut with respect to anything you say to police or federal law enforcement agents. It is a felony under the federal perjury statute, punishable by fines and imprisonment, to lie to an authorized representative of the U.S. government.[464] Billionaire Martha Stewart is one of thousands of defendants convicted and imprisoned for perjury.[465]

The details of your privacy and asset protection plan should be known only to you and one or two trusted advisors. These advisors should be attorneys, or working under the direction of an attorney, because conversations with them and the work they produce will generally be protected by attorney-client privilege. However, this privilege isn't absolute, as you'll learn in later in this chapter.

You may choose to include your spouse or partner in your asset protection planning. Married couples have asset protection and tax avoidance opportunities that are not available to people who are not legally married. If you're married and are confident that your relationship won't end in a rancorous breakup, you should take advantage of these opportunities.

Discussions with your spouse are protected by a **spousal privilege** under the laws of all 50 states. If your spouse is called as a witness or summoned to a deposition, he or she can generally refuse to answer any questions relating to communications between the two of you. However, this protection is dissolved if you divorce and may not exist at all if you and your partner aren't legally married.

Keep a Small Circle of Friends

Maintaining a low profile means reducing the information that you might otherwise voluntarily give to casual acquaintances, salespeople, employers, etc.

Still, every person needs a trusted circle of friends in which to confide. In today's mobile society, many people are placed in the difficult position of establishing new relationships and making new friends. How do you go about this process without endangering your privacy?

In our forefathers' time, the answer would be simple: Join the local church. And today, you can still use this oldest and most familiar method to become acquainted with people who not only share your religious beliefs, but perhaps also your political and financial philosophy.

In the 21st century, religion plays a diminished role in the lives of many Americans. Not everyone is familiar or comfortable in a religious environment. Fortunately, there are alternatives to a church to which you can turn in order to build a trusted circle of friends.

One alternative is volunteer community groups. By becoming involved in efforts such as neighborhood watch groups, volunteer fire-fighting departments, community food cooperatives, etc., you're likely to encounter people who share your outlook and attitudes. If you have children, groups such as Parent-Teacher Associations, Boy Scouts and Girl Scouts, etc., are excellent places to meet other parents. Eventually, a few of these casual acquaintances may become friends.

As your friendships evolve, you will begin sharing more information about yourself and turning to these friends for guidance in meeting the challenges that you face in your life. Eventually, you will build that most valuable of assets: trust.

But one thing is certain: You should guard your privacy as if it were an irreplaceable resource. It is.

Prepare for Uncertainty

Nothing in life is certain. A traffic accident, lightning strike, or other event could end your life, or that of someone you depend upon, in an instant. Or the accident or sudden illness could leave you disabled. You could run over a child while driving, sparking a lawsuit. That's why you need to construct a basic succession and asset protection plan, no matter how old or how young you are.

This plan should include:

- **A testamentary document (will or trust).**
- **A medical power of attorney.** This document assigns a person you trust the authority to make medical decisions for you, if you're unable to make those decisions yourself.
- **A living will.** This document conveys your wishes to be kept alive (or not kept alive) by artificial means if you're terminally ill and can't make decisions for yourself.
- **A durable power of attorney.** This document designates a trusted family member or friend to make personal and financial decisions for you if you are incapacitated.
- **An asset protection plan.** Everyone has assets they simply "can't afford to lose." Protect them using the techniques you'll learn about in this and the next chapter—using retirement plans, domestic and offshore annuities, domestic and offshore trusts, etc.

Avoid Lawsuits

Nearly all lawsuits revolve around promises made, but supposedly not kept. The lifeboat strategy is to follow these two simple recommendations to avoid lawsuits:

1. Don't make promises you can't keep.
2. Keep the promises you make.

These rules are easy to repeat, but difficult to apply in real life. A practical example is when a friend or family member asks you to co-sign for a loan. The question you need to ask isn't, "Can I trust this person?" but, "Do I have the financial means to make good on this obligation?" It's unlikely you can force your friend or family member to pay off the loan, at least not without losing the friendship or straining family ties. You also have little or no control over what extraneous events might occur that would prevent the loan recipient from paying off the obligation.

Many lawsuits are frivolous, but most are not. If a person has unjustly suffered because of something you've done, it will be much less expensive to negotiate an amicable settlement, rather than go to court. It's also the right thing to do. Ethical behavior will prevent many, if not most lawsuits.

Another way to prevent lawsuits is to keep your mouth shut around someone you don't like. Don't be drawn into arguments. Just "grin and bear it," then try to avoid that individual's company in the future. Many lawsuits stem from petty disagreements that get out of hand.

To keep contractual disputes from ending up in court, have contracts drawn up outlining exactly what is to occur when the project or venture is complete. Invest in an attorney to draw up the contract based on your agreement. One of the most contentious issues in joint ventures is the division of assets. Make certain the contract identifies all assets (including those that are not obvious, such as the name of the joint venture), and describes precisely who gets what property. The contract should also stipulate that disagreements are to be handled through impartial, expert arbitration.

Your children's behavior may spark lawsuits. Did little Johnny hang toilet paper in the neighbor's tree on Halloween? When I pulled off such pranks as a child, I received a rebuke from the neighbor who caught me, and later, a spanking from my parents. Nowadays the neighbor might sue the parents for "emotional distress." Make certain your children know that their mischief could lead to financial catastrophe.

In today's world, much of this mischief may be conducted in cyberspace. For instance, you may be legally responsible if your child downloads copyrighted software, music, or videos without paying for them.[466]

An often-overlooked source of liability is your attitude. If you come across as aloof or arrogant, others may resent your success. In the eyes of a plaintiff's attorney or prosecutor, this makes you an easier target. On the other hand, if you have the "common touch" and are friendly to all, you're less likely to become a target.

I'm convinced this is one reason why my father, who practiced medicine for more than 40 years, was never sued for malpractice. Even though he certainly made mistakes during his career, his patients believed him to be a caring physician. He told me that he always took the time to explain to patients the possible consequences of their illness and what he believed to be the best way to treat it. He even maintained a listed telephone number so that patients could call him at our home. This hardly guaranteed his patients wouldn't sue him, but demonstrated a willingness to maintain an open line of communication.

The Private Divorce

The legal action that is both the most emotionally difficult, and the most invasive of privacy, is a divorce.

The best way to avoid divorce, of course, is to not get married. But marriage and family fulfill some of our most basic needs, so this recommendation isn't for everyone.

Like any lawsuit, in a divorce, the process of discovery, including depositions, submission of documents to the court, etc., can result in the disclosure of private information. The problem is that your spouse probably knows far more about you than the average litigant—and thus is more likely to disclose or force the disclosure of embarrassing or even incriminating facts.

Take a protective stance from the beginning. Lifeboat strategies include:

- **Obtaining a post office box or mail drop in your own name**. Bank statements, business documents, etc. that are in your name only should be directed to this address.
- **Obtaining your own safety deposit box**. Keep ownership documents relating to "your" property here, especially property acquired prior to marriage.
- **Filing taxes separately.** This may result in a higher tax bill, but doesn't require you to disclose information about your financial situation to your spouse. It can also be an effective strategy to limit the liability of an innocent spouse if the other spouse has significant unpaid tax obligations.
- **Using asset protection trusts (APTs).** A well-drafted APT that names your spouse as a beneficiary is an excellent way to keep your property separate from your spouse's property. This is especially important in community property states. In addition, an APT is a much more subtle way of protecting your property than a pre-nuptial agreement in that it doesn't shout to your spouse, "I

don't trust you." Your spouse probably won't realize that in a typical APT, he or she can be removed as a beneficiary.
- **Using custodial bank accounts.** Set up bank accounts in your children's name naming yourself as the custodian.

Pre-nuptial and **post-nuptial** agreements are worth considering, although they indicate a level of distrust at your spouse, and aren't always legally enforceable. If you opt for such an agreement, make certain that assets owned before the marriage are explicitly segregated. In addition, the agreement should specify how marital property will be divided if the marriage ends, including child support and alimony. Both spouses must make full disclosure of their assets, as failing to do so is the most common reason why courts invalidate such agreements.

If divorce is inevitable, the best strategy to avoid a lengthy, expensive, and privacy-invading court battle in a divorce is to convince your spouse that a "no-fault" divorce is in both of your best interests. You may be forced to give up more of your property than you want, but you will avoid court and the expense, embarrassment, and privacy invasion associated with it.

An excellent adjunct strategy is to hire a private judge or arbitrator to adjudicate the divorce, rather than go through the court system. This procedure is generally much less expensive than a full-fledged fight in court, although both spouses must explicitly consent to the process. When couples agree to arbitration or mediation before a private judge, only the final divorce decree is made public. Information released to the private judge or arbitrator never appears in any public record. It may be possible to edit or "redact" any personal information (such as Social Security numbers, bank account numbers, etc.) from the final decree.

However you settle a divorce, you should insist on a non-disclosure agreement from your former spouse to avoid the possibility of "kiss and tell" publicity in the future. Also, the final agreement should itself require mandatory arbitration or mediation in the event of a breach of contract by either party. This insures that any future disagreements are settled privately, not in open court.

Avoid Probate

Most people assume that the only way to insure that their property will be divided as they wish is with a will. While a will insures that property is distributed to your designated heirs, it doesn't avoid a system known as **probate**.

After your death, the executor named in your will presents it to the probate court with an inventory of your estate's assets and liabilities. After examining your will to insure that it's legally binding, the court places a legal advertisement in your town's newspaper. This advertisement invites creditors to submit claims against the estate. The notice also alerts anyone else who wishes to make a claim, such as an ex-spouse, a disinherited child, etc.

In some states, probate is inexpensive and heirs receive their property quickly. In others, it may involve large attorney fees and long delays in beneficiaries receiving their inheritance. Even moderately-sized estates can be ravaged by the need for detailed appraisals and seemingly endless hearings. In some states, fees are based on the size of the probated estate, not the amount of work done.

Probate is always a privacy invader. For prominent families, it can be a nightmare of competing claims, shouting reporters and expensive attorneys. For a spectacular example, read *Johnson vs. Johnson,* detailing the competing efforts to settle the estate of the heir to the Johnson Wax fortune.[467] Bypassing probate also saves your heirs time and the expense of paying a lawyer or executor to cut through legal red tape.

However, some portion of your property should always go through probate. This limits creditor access to your estate to a limited period, and bars creditors entirely after the statute of limitations has expired. But the lifeboat strategy is to pass the bulk of your estate to your heirs privately. One of the most effective tools for this purpose is the trust, which you'll learn more about later in this chapter.

23 Essential Strategies to Prevent Identity Theft

Most of us comply with requests from people we don't know when they ask for private information. We think nothing of handing our credit cards over to servers, clerks, and service station attendants. We provide our Social Security number when requested at doctor's offices, car dealerships, banks, and credit unions. Unfortunately, all of these disclosures raise our vulnerability to identity theft.

Consider the following lifeboat strategies to protect yourself:

1. **Don't disclose your SSN without good reason.** Your SSN is the "holy grail" of identity theft. Federal law requires that you disclose it when you accept employment or file a tax return. You must also disclose it when you obtain a driver's license. Disclosing your SSN is optional just about anywhere else, including when you open a bank or brokerage account, although a private company isn't legally obligated to provide you services should you refuse to disclose it. In many cases, it's possible to leave an entry on a form requesting your SSN blank. Alternatively, insert "N/A." Rarely is this omission challenged. If it is, ask if you can insert an alternative number (e.g., your driver's license number) on the form. Don't use a fictitious SSN; this is a federal crime.
2. **Don't disclose your date of birth and residential address, without understanding how this data will be used and how it will be secured.** As with your SSN, this information may be used to impersonate you. It's often possible to leave the section of a form requesting this information blank, or to insert alternative data (e.g., a post office box address instead of your residential address). When you order checks, don't publish your residential address on them. Instead, use the address of a post office box or mail receiving service, or leave your address off altogether.
3. **Don't complete customer surveys unless they offer a benefit you wish to obtain.** Data you disclose will be sold to direct marketing organizations. If you complete a customer survey, leave all questions related to your financial status blank.
4. **Send or receive mail from a locked mailbox.** Unlocked mailboxes are a prime target of identity thieves, who find it easy to obtain credit card numbers, bank account numbers, and SSNs. Consider getting your mail at a post office box or mail receiving service instead.
5. **Check your credit records at least annually.** Federal law requires credit bureaus to give consumers one free copy of their credit report annually. For more information, see http://www.annualcreditreport.com, call toll-free 1 (877) 322-8228 or download the written request form at https://www.annualcreditreport.com/cra/requestformfinal.pdf.
6. **Check records of other "credit reporting agencies" required by federal law to provide consumer access to the contents of their databases.** One of the most important of these companies is **ChoicePoint,** a major data aggregator (Chapter 2). You can obtain a free annual "public records" report from the company's ChoiceTrust consumer Web site at http://www.choicetrust.com. Also, check to see if **ChexSystems,** which has constructed a database of "negative data" on millions of bank customers, has you in its files. If you show up as a bad risk on ChexSystems' databases, banks may refuse to open an account for you, or place restrictions on your account. You're

entitled to a free copy of your ChexSystems report. For more information, call 1-800-428-9623, or go http://www.consumerdebit.com and click on the ChexSystems tab.

7. **When you receive your credit report, make sure that all credit cards and other extensions of credit in your name are really from you.** Challenge unfamiliar charges against your card and make the service or retail provider back up the authorization.

8. **Join a credit report monitoring service such as Trusted ID** (http://www.trustedid.com). You'll be asked to provide substantial additional information to "insure the accuracy" of their records. However, you're under no obligation to give a credit monitoring service any more information than they need to identify you. This means providing only your SSN, a non-residential contact address, plus whatever information you want them to correct (if any). Don't complete the rest of the multi-page questionnaire that will likely be included with your membership kit.

9. **Protect yourself from "pretexting."** One of the ways that identity thieves (along with lawyers, government investigators, and others) can gather personal information is to impersonate you when dealing with someone who has access to your data. To protect yourself from phone record pretexting, use a disposable phone (described later in this chapter) to prevent your calling records from falling into the wrong hands. Also, assign a hard-to-guess password (not your SSN) that anyone who contacts your telephone company, utility companies, banks, credit card companies, etc. must disclose in order to retrieve your personal data.

10. **Be cautious of what you discard in the trash.** As you learned in Chapter 2, there's no federal "right to privacy" for trash set out for collection (although some states do protect "trash privacy"). Purchase a crosscut shredder (about US$200) and shred any document before disposal that contains personally identifying information such as credit card numbers or your SSN. This includes documents as innocuous as an airline boarding pass, which can be used to retrieve your passport number, date of birth, residential address, etc.[468]

11. **Notify all companies that have granted you credit not to authorize new extensions of credit over the phone, but only in writing.** This is another way to protect yourself from having someone trying to steal your identity from impersonating you.

12. **When writing checks to pay your bills, don't write the complete account number on the check.** Instead, just insert the last few numbers. These digits are sufficient for authorized representatives to verify the account number. Anyone else handling your check won't have access to this information.

13. **Pay cash at large retail stores.** Huge data thefts such as that suffered by TJX (Chapter 1) demonstrate that hackers can penetrate retail stores' computer databases almost at will. And when they do, your credit card information, Social Security numbers and other personal data are at risk.

14. When creating passwords and personal identification numbers for bank accounts, never use the last four digits of your SSN or your date of birth. And don't write down passwords or PINs unless you do so in a code. For this purpose, it's probably safe to use a simple substitution code. For instance, each letter in the word "documents" could represent the digits 1-9. Any other letter could indicate a zero. Thus, if your PIN is 6908, you could record it as "ESAT."

15. **Copy every card or other document you carry in your wallet, your purse, or your car.** If they're stolen, you'll know exactly what's missing and whom you need to contact for a replacement.

16. **Remove information that could be used to steal your identity from court records.** Public access to court records is guaranteed in all states. In many cases, that includes unrestricted public access to financial statements, SSNs and other data that could be sued to steal your identity. If you're involved in a legal dispute, ask your attorney if it's possible to have the court record "sealed." If not, it may be possible to have SSNs and other sensitive data redacted from the court record. If the case is already closed, it may be necessary to reopen it in order to delete this data.

17. **Place a credit freeze on your credit bureau account.** This action "locks" your credit file, prohibiting new extensions of credit being issued in your name. When you sign up for a credit freeze, you're assigned a PIN with which you can lift the freeze when necessary. About 30 states

now authorize credit freezes. Two major credit bureaus (TransUnion and Equifax) now offer credit freezes in all 50 states.

18. **Keep bank statements, credit card bills and other records containing confidential information in a locked, secure location.** A locked filing cabinet is usually sufficient; a floor safe is even more secure.

19. **Guard against identity theft through online job or social networking Web sites.** Web sites such as Monster.com are now a preferred route for millions of job seekers to connect with prospective employers. And social networking Web sites such as MySpace.com are used by millions of people to communicate with one another. However, it's also easy for identity thieves to troll this data for illicit purposes. To protect yourself, don't reveal too much personal data. Never post your SSN, date of birth, or residential address online. If a prospective employer or recruiter contacts you, check them out carefully. Fake employers and recruiters are common, so insist on knowing more about the company or the recruiter before revealing personal information; e.g., by verifying a recruiter's membership in a national recruiting organization.

20. **Don't respond to unsolicited e-mails or telephone calls requesting personal information.** A government agency or financial institution will almost never communicate in this way. Chances are, the e-mailer or caller is trying to obtain information to steal your identity. If you're not certain, contact the agency or financial institution yourself, using contact details from previous communications or statements, or that you look up in a telephone directory or online. Don't contact the sender or caller using a number they provide; it could easily be set up explicitly for the purpose of identity theft.

21. **Don't disclose your credit card number on the phone unless you initiate the call.** An increasing number of unsolicited telephone calls come from identity thieves who are more interested in stealing your credit card details than in selling you a product or service.

22. **Watch for missing mail.** Make a list of bills you receive on a regular basis. If an expected bill doesn't arrive within a few days of when you expect it, a fraudster may have changed your billing address to delay having you notified of illicit purchases in your account. Check with the company you expected to receive a bill from to find out why it didn't arrive.

23. **Beware of copying sensitive information on a photocopier.** Most photocopiers manufactured after 2002 contain a hard disk that records what's been duplicated. If you photocopy tax returns or other confidential information at a commercial copy service, criminals can easily retrieve this data. To protect yourself, buy an inexpensive copier for use at home. You can also copy documents on a fax machine or scanner.

If you believe that you could be the victim of identity theft, take immediate action:

- **Close any accounts that have been tampered with or established fraudulently.** Call the security or fraud departments of each company where an account was opened or changed without your authorization. Follow up in writing, with copies of supporting documents. If you're not sure what to say in your letter, use the ID theft affidavit at http://www.ftc.gov/idtheft. Once you've done so, ask for verification that the disputed account has been closed and the fraudulent debts discharged.

- **Contact Experian (888-397-3742), Equifax (800-525-6285), and TransUnion (800-680-7289) and request that a "fraud alert" be placed on your credit record.** Under federal law, the alert must remain on your credit file for at least 90 days, unless you request that it be removed sooner. In serious cases of identity theft, you can request an "extended fraud alert" that can last for as long as seven years. Placing a fraud alert on your credit record entitles you to receive free copies of your credit reports. Look for inquiries from companies you haven't contacted, accounts you didn't open, and debts on your accounts that you can't explain.

- **If you live in a state that permits you to place a "credit freeze" on your credit file, do so at your earliest opportunity.** If you don't, contact TransUnion and Equifax (see previous bullet) and ask them to freeze your credit file.
- **File a police report.** Some credit grantors may want to see a copy of a police report as "proof" that you're a victim of identity theft.
- **Obtain a new SSN.** In extreme cases of identity theft—e.g., where your SSN is assigned to another person who has been arrested for a crime—it may be possible to obtain a replacement SSN. This will wipe out your credit history, so ask for a replacement SSN only if there is no realistic alternative. Contact the Social Security Administration at **800-772-1213** for more information.

For additional suggestions on preventing or dealing with identity theft, see the following Web sites: http://www.privacyrights.org/identity.htm; http://www.ftc.gov/bcp/edu/microsites/idtheft; and http://www.identitytheft.org.

Get Off Databases

The proliferation of data mining means that information about you is being used in many ways that you know nothing about. While in many cases you have little or no control over what happens to information after you release it, there are ways to limit the dissemination of your data.

The Gramm-Leach-Bliley Act requires "financial institutions" (banks, brokerage firms, insurance companies, credit card companies, etc.) to notify their customers about the personal information they collect and share with others and give them the opportunity to opt out of certain disclosures. This notification must occur at least once a year and generally comes in the form of a pamphlet entitled "Privacy Statement" or with similar wording. Follow the instructions in this statement to limit disclosure of your data.

Opting out doesn't prevent companies from sharing your "transaction and experience" data with other companies. You can, however, make a legally binding request that information about your "credit-worthiness" not be shared.

Also, remove yourself from databases used for data mining and for pre-screened credit offers. Note, however, that you can only remove "non-public" information; companies are under no obligation to stop selling "public" information (courthouse filings, real estate transaction records, etc.) tied to your identity. Nor are the companies under any obligation to stop sharing public or non-public information to their affiliates or with those companies with which they have "marketing agreements."

- **Pre-screened credit offers.** Trans Union, Experian, and Equifax, the three largest credit bureaus, sell lists to companies that may extend to you unsolicited offers of credit. If an identity thief intercepts these offers, someone may apply for credit in your name. To reduce the number of pre-screened credit and insurance offers you receive, visit http://www.optoutprescreen.com or call 888-567-8688 to opt-out of these offers.
- **Acxiom Corp. databases.** This firm develops and maintains databases containing information on most U.S. households. For the company's marketing and directory products, you may opt-out by e-mailing optoutus@acxiom.com or by calling 877-774-2094. For Axiom's directory, fraud detection and prevention, and background screening products, you may access your records and in some cases correct information found there. Access to these products costs US$5 and is available by contacting Acxiom at referencereport@acxiom.com or by calling 877-774-2094.
- **Mail Preference Service.** Contact this service to reduce the amount of unsolicited commercial mail ("junk mail") you receive from members of the Direct Marketing Association. There is a

US$1 fee for this service. Register online at https://www.dmaconsumers.org/cgi/offmailing or write to Direct Marketing Association, P.O. Box 282, Carmel, N.Y. 10512.

For additional suggestions on databases you might wish to have your name removed from, see http://www.junkbusters.com/optout.html. Also, review the suggestions in this chapter on protecting telephone records and keeping your correspondence private.

Avoid Shopper's Cards

Most major grocery chains now offer **shoppers' cards** to their customers. In exchange for giving the store a continuous record of your purchases, the store provides you with special offers, coupons tailored to your preferences, etc. According to David Sobel, general counsel for the Electronic Privacy Information Center, a Washington, D.C.-based public interest group, there is no way to stop stores from selling or sharing the information they collect:

For instance, a database could be purchased by a [health or life] insurance company and used to see what kind of food a person eats as an indication of lifestyle. Or an employer could use it to see if a prospective employee purchases alcohol or tobacco.[469]

The information can also be turned over to police and attorneys or used against you in a lawsuit. In California, a man shopping at a Southern California grocery store sued after falling in one of the aisles. It was reported (although the store denied it) that the store threatened to use his shopping history, which included purchases of alcoholic beverages, against him in court.[470] If you sign up for shoppers' cards, follow the example of former Assistant Secretary of Commerce Larry Irving: when he signed up for a Safeway Club card, he used a fake name. He was worried that the record of his purchases might somehow come back to haunt him.[471]

Avoid Searches and Seizures

Anyone can be targeted for search and seizure. If you have any doubt, reread "Do You Fit the Profile?" in Chapter 2. Even slowing down at the sight of a parked police car or driving a minivan can be factors that justify stopping a motorist, the Supreme Court has declared.[472]

One of the best ways to avoid being targeted is not to stand out. The lifeboat strategy is, to "blend with the crowd." If you're targeted for investigation, the lifeboat strategy is to place legal obstacles between you and the investigator(s) to prevent needless disclosure of information, while making it appear that you want to be cooperative. This requires considerable finesse, but is possible.

On the Street

When confronted by police, you're not obligated to answer any questions. The catch, of course, is that if you don't answer questions, you'll stand out. Still, the police won't generally ask permission to search you or your property unless you've done something to make them suspicious.

If you answer questions from police, don't lie or embellish the truth. Doing so can lead to perjury charges, as I've already described.

If police confront you in a public place, don't run away. Doing so gives police the right to chase you, and, given the tenor of the war on terror, you may be shot. Instead, make direct eye contact with the individual who's speaking to you. Interact only with the person addressing you. If you're wearing sunglasses, take them off.

Keep your hands visible. Don't make any sudden movements with any part of your body. This can be viewed as threatening and may itself establish probable cause for a search.

Be respectful. Answer non-threatening questions with short answers, but don't volunteer any information. Call the person addressing you "sir" or "ma'am." All these actions make you appear less of a threat.

Until recently, if police asked you your name, you were under no obligation to answer. However, the Supreme Court ruled in 2004 that you have no right to remain silent in this situation. If the law in your state requires it, you must disclose your name to police, or face whatever penalty applies.[473] In some states, giving a false name is a criminal offense.

On the other hand, you're under no legal obligation to show identification to police just because you're in a public place. But not producing ID will generate suspicion, so it's best if you do carry ID.

The best and lowest profile ID is a passport. A passport doesn't contain your address and thus avoids the question, "Do you live at this address?"

If you're asked why you're carrying a passport, you can say that you travel frequently and use it as an ID document. If you have dark skin or speak English with a foreign accent, you can say matter-of-factly that you have been advised that carrying your passport could avoid potential misunderstandings.

In Your Vehicle

If you're stopped in your vehicle, don't get out of it. Roll down the window and keep your hands in your lap.

When police approach your vehicle, they'll ask for your license and registration. Since the courts have ruled that driving is a "privilege" and not a right, you're obligated to carry these documents when you drive a motor vehicle. Ask permission to reach into the glove compartment (or wherever you keep the documents) to retrieve them. Keep any private items out of view; police don't need a search warrant to examine items in "plain view" that appear suspicious.[474]

Keep your license and registration in easy reach. In some states, police may conduct a warrantless search of your vehicle if you don't show them identification or registration papers. If the officer writes you a ticket, accept it quietly and don't argue. Listen to any instruction on paying the fine or contesting the ticket, and slowly drive away.

Later in this chapter, I recommend holding your vehicle in the name of a legal entity, such as a limited liability company. However, in some states (Arkansas is one), you give up the right to refuse a search of your vehicle if you don't own it.[475]

Police may ask you if you live at the address noted on your driver's license. I recommend never listing your residential address on your driver's license; use a mail receiving service instead. But answer honestly—"No sir, I don't live at that address." The next question is likely to be, "What is your residential address?" You have no legal obligation to answer this question, but if you do answer it, tell the truth.

Many U.S. persons don't reside full-time in one location. Others have recently moved to a new address. Still others live overseas and come back to the United States periodically to visit friends and family. Perhaps one of these situations applies to you. If asked where you live, you can then truthfully say something like, "I'm temporarily living overseas."

Assuming you're not intoxicated, that nothing suspicious-looking is in plain view, that you're not acting in a threatening manner, and that whatever ID you have supplied is accepted, this strategy will end most encounters with police. However, police may ask you to answer additional questions or to consent to a search of your vehicle or of your person. Such a request means the officer doesn't have sufficient evidence to search without your consent. In this case, you should assert your rights—but again, in a non-threatening manner.

Say something like, "Officer, I know you want to do your job, but I can't consent to a search." A likely response will be, "Why not? What do you have to hide?" You're under no obligation to answer this question. Instead, say something like, "Officer, am I under arrest? If not, I would respectfully ask that you permit me to leave." If there's no response, then announce, "Officer, if you're not detaining me, may I leave?" If the response is "yes," say "thank you" and leave immediately. If the response is ambiguous, or if your question is answered by another question, repeat your question: "Am I being detained, or may I leave now?"

If the response is "no," you're being detained. Police may detain you or your vehicle for brief periods without charging you with any crime. One U.S. federal appeals court ruled that a 17-minute traffic stop doesn't violate your rights.[476] There is, of course, now the "terrorist exception" to this rule, which permits police to detain suspected terrorists indefinitely (Chapter 2). So, avoid looking like a terrorist, particularly if you have dark skin. For men, this means being clean-shaven, with short hair; for women, it means not wearing your hair too short. Both sexes should wear Western clothing in public to avoid standing out.

If you're detained, you're under no obligation to answer any questions or consent to a search. You should point that out; but again, in a non-threatening way. One way to do it is to make a joke; e.g., "My lawyer would kill me if I consented to a search without him being present." An even better reason, which you shouldn't mention, is that police sometimes plant drugs on criminal suspects or their vehicles during a search, then arrest them.[477] Also, make sure to write down the names and badge numbers of all officers involved.

Specifically mention the word "lawyer." This will end many requests for a search or to answer questions. If not, tell the officer that you want to call your lawyer. Keep the number handy and carry a cell phone with you for such emergencies. If you don't have a lawyer, police have no obligation to appoint one for you if you're not under arrest. Just keep your mouth shut and don't consent to a search.

The officer then has another decision to make—whether to bring in a "drug dog." This can require waiting anywhere from 15 minutes to several hours. To induce you to consent to a search, the officer may say something like, "if you don't want to wait a long time for the dog to arrive, you should consent to a search." But even if the officer says a drug dog is on its way, you should continue asking if you're being detained. Again, while there is no "bright line" as to how long you can be detained, a wait of several hours is clearly unreasonable.

When the dog arrives, its handler will lead it to your vehicle. It will walk around the vehicle and then crawl on top of it. If the dog "alerts," this provides "probable cause" for a search to proceed. In 2005, the Supreme Court gave judicial approval to this practice nationwide.[478] Nearly 100% of the time, the dog will alert, because dog handlers are trained to induce alerts. The bottom line is that once a drug dog arrives, there is a virtual certainty that your vehicle will be searched. No lawyer needs to be present.

If police search you or your vehicle without your consent and find anything illegal, your attorney can argue that it was discovered through an illegal search and hence should be thrown out of court. Don't resist the search, but make it clear that you don't consent to the search. Simply say, "Officer, I will not resist this search, but I am not consenting to it."

If you're not carrying drugs or other contraband, the search of your car won't be fruitful and police will leave. However, if you're carrying more than a few hundred dollars in cash, it will be confiscated, although you won't be arrested. This is because nearly all cash contains narcotics residues, which the drug dog will detect. Police need not arrest you or present any evidence of narcotics involvement to keep the cash.[479]

If possible, count the cash yourself and ask for a receipt. This avoids situations in which part or all of seized cash "disappears" while in police custody. Call your lawyer as soon as possible.

If drugs or other contraband are found, you will be arrested. But you don't have to give a statement or answer any questions. Contact your lawyer or ask that one be appointed for you. You have a right to have your lawyer present when you're being questioned, and even then, you're under no obligation to answer questions.

If you're arrested, your car will be towed to a police impound facility and thoroughly searched. Be certain to check it for damage before you sign a statement that it was returned in good condition. Also, remember that it is now legal for police to plant a GPS tracking device in your vehicle when they return it to you, without obtaining a warrant.[480]

In Your Home or Office

The concept of curtilage (Chapter 1) insures that you have a higher expectation of privacy in your home or office than in a public place or in your vehicle. The lifeboat strategy is to not voluntarily allow police into your home or office, answer any questions, or consent to a search. Indeed, you're under no legal obligation to even answer the door.

If you do answer the door, and police wish to ask you questions, or conduct a search, you should refuse consent. But, again, be scrupulously polite. Ask for the officer's name, and use that name throughout your conversation. Say, "With all due respect, Officer Smith, I don't believe that I have any legal obligation to answer your questions." The response is likely to be, "Only people with something to hide refuse to answer questions." To which you should reply, "Officer Smith, am I under arrest?" If the reply is "no," simply say, "Officer Smith, I have nothing more to say. Good day." Then close the door.

In some cases, a police visit will have nothing to do with you personally. Police may be seeking information about a missing person or a crime committed nearby. In other instances, the purpose of their visit may be to ask you to turn down your stereo or stop your dog from barking. In these situations, you can end the encounter simply by acquiescing to the request. Only if police ask permission to enter your home, or ask personal questions, do you need to be prepared to exercise your constitutional rights.

You may be asked to accompany an investigating officer to be questioned at another location. In this situation, ask, "Officer Smith, am I under arrest?" If the response is negative, then say, "Officer Smith, if I'm not under arrest, I don't believe I have a legal obligation to go anywhere with you."

If police ask permission to "look around" your home or office, it means they don't have enough evidence to obtain a search warrant. Ask, "Officer Smith, do you have a search warrant?" If the answer is no, then say, "Officer Smith, if you don't have a search warrant, I don't believe I have a legal obligation to let you into my home (office)."

There are, however, a number of exceptions in which police may conduct a warrantless search of your home or office, without your consent:

- If police see evidence of any crime;[481]
- In emergencies (e.g., if someone has called for help).[482] However, police may not "manufacture" the emergency after attempting to enter a dwelling under false pretenses;[483]
- In some states (California is one), if you've applied for government assistance;[484]
- If police receive consent to search from a resident of the home. However, police cannot search when one resident invites them in but another tells them to go away;[485] and
- Under the USA PATRIOT Act, police may conduct warrantless "sneak and peek" searches of your home or office, even if terrorism or other national security issues aren't at stake.

If police have a warrant, they're under no obligation to announce themselves when they enter your home or office. Even if police fail to knock and simply knock down the door of a home to search it, as long as they have a warrant, evidence they seize is admissible in court.[486]

If you're arrested in your home or office, police can search the area "close by," which usually means the room in which you're arrested. They can't search the entire premises without a search warrant, your permission, or your employer's permission. However, police are known to invent permission for a search by someone who actually refused. Witnesses are essential for corroborating your refusal and to witness any illegal search.

If police insist on a search, again, you can't legally obstruct them, but any evidence discovered will be inadmissible in court if you make it clear you did not consent to it. Call your lawyer immediately.

If police have a search warrant, you must submit to the search. Again, call your lawyer immediately. Ask for a copy of the warrant; it will detail what is to be searched for. Don't consent to a search even at this point; this strategy will limit police to searching only as authorized by the warrant. Say "I don't consent to this search; however, I won't obstruct it."

Take notes, and if you have a video camera, videotape the search. Get the badge numbers of all uniformed officers and the names and contact information for any non-uniformed persons participating in the search.

At the Airport

After the events of Sept. 11, 2001, government officials moved quickly to secure U.S. airports and border crossings. This resulted in a handful of arrests for suspected terrorists, and a massive privacy invasion for everyone else.

When you check in at a U.S. airport, you must show a government-issued photo ID. There's no evidence this reduces terrorism, but a secret regulation requires this precaution—a regulation that a federal appeals court ruled you have no right to review.[487]

Next, your checked baggage is screened for bombs and other contraband. To avoid having your bag unnecessarily searched, avoid packing anything that resembles a "prohibited item" in your luggage (e.g., blasting caps, dynamite, fireworks, flares, plastic explosives, etc.). But there are some less obvious items to avoid as well. For instance, **peanut butter** has about the same density as some explosives.

Once you've checked your luggage, you must clear the security screening line. Even if you don't appear on a "terrorist watch list" and aren't carrying any of the constantly changing lists of items that are banned from carry-on luggage (see http://www.tsa.gov/travelers/airtravel/prohibited/permitted-prohibited-items.shtm for an updated list), you still might be detained for additional screening. Once you've begun the airport screening process, you have no legal right to revoke permission to search your carry-on luggage or your person.[488]

Avoid carrying anything that might result in you being detained or worse, being denied the right of boarding your flight. Enhanced searches and/or denial of boarding privileges have resulted from:

- **Carrying a suspicious book** (almanacs or anything with a picture of a bomb on it are particularly suspicious).
- **Wearing a provocative shirt.** Numerous travelers have reported being detained and in some cases being denied boarding for wearing shirts displaying images of bombs or explosives, or of controversial figures such as Chef Guevara or Karl Marx.
- **Making provocative statements.** Anything you say that indicates displeasure or impatience with the screening system may result in enhanced searches, denial of boarding privileges, or in extreme cases, arrest, and detention.

Be particularly cautious when carrying a laptop computer across an international border. Customs officials can seize and copy the contents of any laptop carried across a U.S. border.[489] There's no arrest, warrant or probable cause required. Copy your data to a USB drive and send it via a courier service to your destination. Encrypt the data using a program such as PGP Desktop (http://www.pgp.com). Then securely "wipe" any confidential information off your hard drive, along with the "free space," again using a program like PGP Desktop. (PGP and its capabilities are discussed later in this chapter).

The forensic programs used by Customs officials can retrieve files and images downloaded months or even years ago. If you've ever viewed anything controversial or illegal in your Web browser or newsreader, back up your data, use a utility like **Killdisk** (http://www.killdisk.com) to securely wipe everything on your hard drive. Reinstall the operating system according to the instructions in Killdisk or whatever utility you use for this purpose. If Customs conducts a warrantless inspection of your laptop, they won't find anything but the operating system and standard system files.

If You Want Privacy—Pay with Currency

Using currency (cash) is the single most effective strategy you can use to protect your financial privacy. The challenge is to use it without being suspected of being involved in money laundering, terrorism, or other illegal activity. Not to mention to avoid having it confiscated under civil forfeiture laws.

The best strategy is to pay currency for any purchase that reveals information about you you'd rather not be seen by the wrong set of eyes. For payments that you need to mail, use money orders.

Currency transactions larger than a few hundred dollars, however, may be viewed as suspicious. Always keep in mind the paradox of keeping a low profile: If you try too hard to maintain privacy, you will stand out and attract attention.

Also, don't forget that all trades and businesses must submit records of currency transactions larger than US$10,000 to the Treasury Department. Two or more "related" transactions must also be reported. (The most frequent type of related transaction is an installment purchase.) Businesses subject to "suspicious transaction" reporting requirements (Chapter 2) must complete a "Suspicious Activities Report" (SAR) for out-of-the-ordinary transactions of any kind (not just cash that exceed US$5,000. The threshold is US$2,000 for money transmitters.

Don't engage in multiple currency transactions with the same bank or company that exceed US$10,000. This avoids arrest and possible imprisonment for the crime of "structuring." If you must do so, ask to speak with a manager and tell that person something like, "If you need to file any kind of government form for this transaction, that's OK." In most cases, this statement eliminates the possibility of having a SAR filed on the transaction. Try to keep currency transactions well under the US$10,000 limit, to avoid any suspicion that you might be engaged in structuring.

Here are some additional tips for using currency:

- **When you pay currency, always have the bills ready.** Don't peel them off from a larger group of bills.
- **Use new bills.** The overwhelming majority of circulating currency contains drug residues on it, which gives police an excuse to confiscate it. Protect yourself by obtaining currency at the bank teller's window and asking for new bills, which should be free of drug residues. Don't mix old bills and new bills, since drug residues spread easily from one bill to another.
- **Avoid US$100s.** This is by far the most frequently counterfeited denomination. As a result, some banks and merchants examine transactions made with US$100s much more carefully than other denominations. Avoid the hassle by holding currency in denominations of US$20 or smaller.

There are risks associated with storage of currency. The most obvious risk is theft. Stolen currency is impossible to recover. Currency also deteriorates if it is not stored in a climate-controlled environment. If you keep significant quantities of currency at hand, carefully consider the storage alternatives you'll learn about later in this chapter.

14 Must-Do Strategies to Protect Postal Privacy

It's not easy to protect your privacy from a government monopoly, particularly in light of the anti-privacy initiatives taken in recent years against people renting post office boxes and using mail-receiving services. However, you can take some common-sense precautions:

1. **Don't use a return address.** This, plus delivering your letters to a public mailbox, guarantees anonymity. However, as I described in Chapter 2, mail sent to Canada won't be delivered without a return address.
2. **Type sensitive correspondence or use a laser printer.** Handwritten correspondence, even if unsigned, can easily be matched to a handwriting sample. Typing or printing correspondence, at least the outer envelope, prevents handwriting identification.
3. **If you own a laser printer, keep an old cartridge handy for sensitive correspondence, and then throw it away.** A photocopy of a typed or laser-printed original is harder to trace than the original. Avoid color laser printers and photocopiers, which embed an invisible code in the paper passing through them that can be traced back to the purchaser.

4. **Make your correspondence tamper-resistant**. An expert can surreptitiously open even the best-protected mail, but you can discourage casual examination by carefully taping the flaps and sides of your envelopes.

5. **Use foil lined envelopes to prevent someone from reading the contents of letters by applying oil to the envelope or holding it up to a light.** For a highly illuminating review of the techniques police and intelligence agencies use to surreptitiously read and/or open mail, read the *CIA Flaps and Seals Manual*.[490]

6. **Don't complete Postal Service change-of-address forms**. This information is forwarded to direct marketing companies, insuring a steady flow of junk mail. Instead, contact correspondents individually to let them know of your address change. If you do complete the form, list a post office box number or mail receiving service address on the form, not your home address. Or use the temporary, rather than permanent, change-of-address form. A temporary change of address can be valid for a year. And direct marketing companies don't have access to the temporary address change database.

7. **Be alert to a sudden decrease in the volume of mail you receive.** This might indicate that an identity thief has redirected your mail to a new address. There is no follow-up by the Postal Service to such requests to determine whether they're legitimate.

8. **Be alert to unusual patterns or delays in how you receive your correspondence.** An unusual delay in your correspondence, followed by a sudden influx of mail, may indicate a mail cover.

9. **Shred sensitive correspondence when disposing of it.** The Supreme Court has ruled that you have no reasonable expectation of privacy in trash placed out for collection.

10. **Use codes and ciphers, and change them frequently**. This is one of the oldest ways to protect correspondence. You can make up your own code, using indirect language, but natural sounding ones, so your correspondence doesn't sound contrived.

11. **Use an assumed name or company name in your correspondence.** This is legal in most situations as long as you have no intent to defraud anyone.

12. **Beware of sending currency through the mail.** The government seizes millions in currency each year from mailed envelopes and packages. Theft of currency is another problem. Dishonest postal employees target greeting cards, in particular, because they realize they often contain currency. Don't use the envelope supplied when you send a greeting card. Use a plain white one instead.

13. **Don't use a postage meter. Each postage meter is registered to a street address.** The Postal Service can quickly identify the address at which a suspicious metered letter or parcel originated.

14. **Check the routing of international correspondence not originating or being delivered to a U.S. address to insure it doesn't pass through the United States.** Many packages mailed to or from Canada, Mexico, or South America pass through the United States on their way to Asia or Europe. If it does, the package can be opened for warrantless inspection by U.S. Customs of Homeland Security authorities.[491]

Using Post Office Boxes and Mail Drops

Avoid receiving mail at your residential address, particularly if you have an unlocked mailbox. Particularly important correspondence to have delivered to a secured, locked mailbox includes:

- Anything containing your Social Security number;
- Financial statements from banks or brokers;
- Correspondence from controversial political organizations, affinity or religious groups;
- Publications frowned upon in mainstream society;
- Communications with lovers;
- Dealings with government officials; or
- Any other correspondence that might bring repercussions if discovered.

A post office box is an excellent alternative to receive your mail. For less than US$60/year, you can remain accessible by mail without giving out your home or office address. You can also use your post office box as a return address on parcels you send by private courier.

Post office boxes are not a privacy panacea. You must complete Postal Service Form 1093 before renting the box.[492] This requires a photo ID with your home or business address on it, plus one other form of ID. The Postal Service is also obliged to cooperate with other government agencies in any investigation of mail delivery.

One way to avoid having the box associated with your name is to open it in the name of a business entity. The Postal Service will want proof that the business exists at the street address you provide. You will also need to indicate on Form 1093 that the box is for "commercial use."

However, this recommendation violates Postal Service rules, which require that only persons listed on the application for service can receive mail at a post office box. As an alternative, request that correspondents send sensitive information to "Occupant" or "Current Resident," care of your post office box number. The Postal Service will usually deliver mail addressed in this manner. It may not deliver correspondence to a name or company not explicitly listed on your application.

You may find that you receive mail in the name of previous box-holders. This provides you with a convenient alias, but using that person's name is illegal if you use it to defraud anyone.

For some purposes, you cannot use a post office box, but need to supply a street address. This includes obtaining a driver's license, credit card, having your checks imprinted, package delivery and pick-up, etc. Companies such as The UPS Store provide these services and additional ones such as package delivery, fax messaging, etc. Such firms are collectively termed **mail receiving services** or **mail drops**. These businesses offer other services, such as packaging, fax service, etc. These are convenient, but if you value your privacy, you may not wish to show up too often.

It may be possible to use a mail drop to receive packages without a contract, although this service is harder to obtain than it once was. You'll pay a fee of US$3-$5 for each package you receive in this manner.

If you rent a private mailbox at a mail drop, you must complete U.S. Postal Service Form 1583, "Application for Delivery of Mail Through Agent." Form 1583 requests your name, address, and the address of the mail drop. You must provide a photo ID and list your home or business address.[493]

Mail drops charge higher fees than the Postal Service for receiving mail. But you obtain a higher level of service. For instance, you can arrange to be contacted when you receive a parcel. You may also be able to request that mail addressed to any name be delivered there. You can pick up the mail yourself, have someone else pick it up, or have it forwarded.

In addition, businesses can project a more positive image with a street address than with a post office box, while obtaining a secure location at which to receive correspondence. Police often recommend that battered women and other people "on the run" from abusive spouses or otherwise at risk for violent crime use a mail receiving service to protect their privacy.

The Postal Service has historically tried to restrict competition by mail drops, usually under the guise of "crime prevention" or "preventing fraud." However, it's legal to receive correspondence at a mail drop under a pseudonym. Nor is it necessary to have mail to a mail drop addressed in a format that makes it obvious the correspondence is being sent to a private mail box, rather than a residential address or business entity. Finally, other than the Postal Service, police, and other law enforcement officials, mail drop records are private.

If you receive mail from outside the United States, consider renting a box at a foreign mail drop. This service can remail correspondence to your domestic mail drop in its own envelope. This delays correspondence, but insures that sensitive overseas mail—e.g., account statements from foreign banks, etc.—isn't sent in original envelopes to a domestic address. It's a very effective way of frustrating a mail cover.

Foreign mail drops may offer other services, including precious metals brokering or storage, nominee checking accounts, etc. These services can be useful, but only if you have complete trust in the mail drop operator. Listings of U.S. and foreign mail drops are posted at http://www.escapeartist.com/global/maildrops.htm.

Setting up a post office box or a mail drop requires a permanent address. If you don't have one—e.g., you live in a motor home—you may need to pay a private individual to receive mail for you. You won't get all the services that some mail drops can offer, but the address will have a lower profile. If you travel extensively, the hotels at which you stay may be willing to receive and even store your mail for later pickup. Just ask.

General Delivery is another option. Your mail will be held for up to 30 days and can be picked up at any retail window. This period can be extended if you don't have a permanent address. Contact your local Postmaster for more information.

When Can the Postal Service Disclose Your Address?

The address you list on Forms 1093 and 1583—which will generally be your home address—may be disclosed "to an appropriate government agency, domestic or foreign, for law enforcement purposes."

Postal Service regulations for information contained on an application for a post office box (Form 1093) stipulate that information may also be released:

- To anyone authorized by law to serve judicial process;
- To a government agency, in performance of its duties;
- In response to a subpoena or court order; and
- When it pertains to a legal proceeding that involves the Postal Service.

The instructions for Form 1583 (necessary to complete when you apply for service at a mail drop) state:

We do not disclose your information without your consent to third parties, except for the following limited circumstances:

- *To a congressional office on your behalf;*
- *To financial entities regarding financial transaction issues;*
- *To a USPS auditor;*
- *To entities, including law enforcement, as required by law or in legal proceedings;*
- *To contractors and other entities aiding us to fulfill the service;*
- *For the purpose of identifying an address as an address of an agent who receives mail on behalf of other persons.*

Information concerning an individual who has filed an appropriate protective court order with the postmaster will not be disclosed except pursuant to court order.

A court order of protection is routinely issued to victims of domestic violence, stalking, etc. If you think you're entitled to such an order, talk to an attorney. It can be an invaluable aid in preserving your privacy, and perhaps your life.

Reclaim Telephone Privacy

In recent years, it has become increasingly difficult to communicate privately via the telephone. While police can't generally eavesdrop on your calls without a warrant, there is no legal expectation of privacy to **call detail records**—the telephone numbers you dial or where calls you receive originate.

Obtaining local telephone service from most carriers now requires proof of identification and a credit report. Local telephone service in your name at your home or business also raises your profile. Since service is tied to your physical address, it increases your vulnerability to burglary and other intrusions, particularly if you have a listed telephone number. Online reverse directories (e.g., http://www.reversephonedirectory.com) can instantly provide any curiosity-seeker—or burglar—your home address. Then a prospective burglar or stalker can use a service such as http://maps.yahoo.com to print a map showing exactly how to get there or even download a satellite image of your home,

Unlisted numbers provide a practical privacy advantage, but can often be obtained illegally through bribery or with the aid of a computer hacker.

Obtain Private Local, Cellular Service and Defeat Caller ID

Since you have little expectation of privacy with regular telephone service, the lifeboat strategy is to obtain private telephone service. For about a 50% premium over the local Bell provider, you can obtain local phone service without a credit check and in some cases without showing proof of identify.

While such companies target people with poor credit, the service is attractive to privacy-seekers. Most don't require you to submit a credit report or a Social Security number to obtain service. You simply provide the company your "name," the address at which you wish service to be connected, and pay the hook-up fee. To protect your privacy, pay with currency or a money order.

In the United States, one provider of this service is Ameritel, which does business under the name **1-800-RECONEX**: call (800) 732-6639. Another provider is **Q-Tel**: call (800) 527-3233.

For long distance calls, use pre-paid telephone cards, which can be purchased at any supermarket or office supply store. There are two types of prepaid cards: rechargeable and non-rechargeable. With a rechargeable card, you call into a central computer and add value to the card with a credit card or debit card number. Obviously, this compromises privacy.

A non-rechargeable card isn't as flexible, but is much more private. You can purchase it over-the-counter, anonymously, with currency. Throw it away when you're finished using it.

You can also purchase pre-paid private cellular service. The per-minute cost is significantly higher than if you have a service contract, but you can obtain your cell phone and purchase calling cards for it without a credit check and without showing proof of identify. **Cricket** (http://www.mycricket.com) and **Virgin** (http://www.virginmobileusa.com) are two U.S. providers of this service. However, if you rent pre-paid cellular service under an assumed name, you may have a lower legal expectation of privacy than if you use your real name.[494]

For phone accounts in your name, the call detail record accompanying your bill is very revealing. For landlines, the call detail lists every long-distance number you've dialed. For cellular phones, the call detail includes every incoming and outgoing call, local or long-distance. To protect your privacy, contact all carriers (both land lines and cell phones) and request that the call detail be removed from your bills.

To prevent telephone carriers from selling your calling records:

- **"Restrict" or "opt out" from all customer proprietary network information (CPNI) sharing.** This data includes the time, date, duration and destination number of each call, the type of network a consumer subscribes to, and any other information that appears on your telephone bill.
- **Place a password on your account to prevent access by someone impersonating you.**
- **Deactivate online access to your account.** Information brokers often obtain cell phone records by setting up online account access that customers have not themselves activated.

Caller ID has become ubiquitous in telephone communications. Caller ID blocking services aren't effective for the reasons discussed in Chapter 2. However, Internet-based systems ("spoofing services") that allow privacy seekers to assume the identity of another caller appear to be more effective. **Spoof card** (http://www.spoofcard.com) is a typical example. Spoofing services are now under attack. In 2006, the Federal Communications Commission began investigating Caller ID spoofing services for failing to provide caller information for interstate calls, as required by law. Prosecutors in some states have subpoenaed the records of several spoofing services to learn the identity of their customers.[495] Legislation to ban spoofing services is also pending in Congress.

Protect Cordless and Cellular Phone Conversations

Cordless phones send radio signals from the base unit to the handset and from the handset back to the base. Radio scanners, baby monitors, radios and other cordless phones can pick up the signals up to a half-mile or more from the point of transmission. Analog cordless phones are the least expensive, but have poor security—anyone within range of the phone can listen in on a radio scanner. Digital cordless phones that operate on higher frequencies (900 MHz, 2.4 GHz, or 5.8 GHz) are more secure, especially those using **digital spread spectrum** technology. This feature breaks apart the voice signal and spreads it over several channels during transmission, making it difficult to capture. However, the surveillance provisions of the CALEA statute (Chapter 2) mean that police can instantly compromise the encryption these phones provide.

Radio scanners can monitor calls from analog cellular phones, particularly older scanners or those illegally altered to pick up cell phone communications. Newer digital cell phones are more difficult to monitor without specialized equipment available to law enforcement, but generally not sold on the open market. Digital cellular service is available in most parts of the United States, but where it's not available, most cell phones will automatically switch over to analog mode, where conversations may be monitored on a radio scanner. Many prepaid cellular services still use analog phones, so you'll need to shop around to find a digital model. On the other hand, older analog models won't contain GPS chips inserted as tracking devices into modern digital cell phones.

To prevent your cell phone from secretly transmitting your conversations, even when switched off (Chapter 2), remove its battery when you're not making a call. Alternatively, keep the phone far enough away that a remotely activated microphone isn't likely to pick up your conversations.

"Unlock" Your Cell Phone for Cost Savings—and Privacy

To keep you as a customer, most cellular providers "lock" your phone so that you can't use it on another network. But if you purchase a cell phone with a SIM (Subscriber Identity Module) card, which holds the phone number and other information specific to your handset, you can probably "unlock" the phone. Doing so allows you switch out the SIM card and subscribe to another company's network. You may also be able to use your cell phone in another country without paying for expensive roaming service from your domestic carrier.

In the United States, many cell phones don't contain SIM chips. However, if you purchase a "tri-band" phone that can be used internationally, it will generally come with a SIM chip.

The easiest way to unlock your cell phone is to enter a series of number on the dial pad— typically an unlock code plus an identifying number unique to your phone. On some units, you need to connect the phone to a personal computer using special cables and software.

To find out how to unlock your cell phone, go to your calling network and ask for it. In many cases, though, phone companies won't provide this information and may even tell you it's illegal to unlock your cell phone. It isn't—in 2006, the U.S. Copyright Office confirmed that software-based unlocking services don't violate copyright laws.[496]

If your carrier refuses to help, fee-based services such as http://www.iunlock.com will unlock your cell phone. But it's better to have an independent telephone shop perform this task because you can bring your phone back if there's a problem.

To make a private call from your unlocked cell phone, simply use a SIM card that you purchased anonymously, over-the-counter, with cash. When you're finished, put the original card from your network provider back in the phone.

"Wipe" Your Cell Phone Before Disposing of it

Today's cell phones can be used to send and receive e-mail, browse the Internet, take photos, send text messages, etc. All these functions leave records that may be difficult to securely erase.

When you replace your cell phone—or if you simply want to protect your privacy on an ongoing basis—perform some basic maintenance to delete possibly sensitive information. Begin by removing your cell phone's SIM card, if it has one. The SIM card is uniquely tied to you, and if ends up in the wrong hands, you could be falsely tied to a crime committed by someone else.

Your call logs, text messages, photos, and other information likely reside in the phone's internal memory. If instructions to delete this data aren't in your cell phone's operating manual, see if they're posted at http://www.wirelessrecycling.com. This Web site lets you choose the brand and model number of your cell phone, and displays the exact commands needed to delete all data from it. Once you've followed instructions to delete this data, double-check to make sure your address book, call logs, and other data stores really are empty. Then you can sell your old phone on eBay, or donate it to a charity, with confidence that information on it can't come back to haunt you.

Communicate Anonymously with Your Phone

It's possible to communicate using your phone, without disclosing your phone number. Three services that facilitate such communication are:

J2 Communications (http://www.j2.com) provides a free and potentially anonymous way to receive faxes and voice messages via e-mail file attachments. With this service, you can view your faxes on your PC, print them, and forward them via e-mail. And you can listen to voice messages through your computer. When you sign up, you'll be asked for your name, e-mail address, etc. and postal code, but this data doesn't appear to be verified. You must use a valid e-mail address, but the address may be an anonymous one from a service provider such as **Hushmail** (http://www.hushmail.com).

Jangl (http://www.jangl.com) is a free service that allows you to communicate with anyone using your phone but without actually disclosing your phone number. You enter a valid e-mail address on the Jangl homepage, and you receive a Jangl phone number to leave a message for that person. Jangl delivers the message by e-mail, and provides a local number for the message recipient to call you back, without sharing your real number. As soon as the contact calls this number, Jangl forwards it to your real phone number. If you decide you don't want the person to contact you anymore, simply delete the number Jangl created.

PrivatePhone (http://www.privatephone.com) alerts you via e-mail or text message that you've received a message in an anonymous voice mailbox. You can listen to the message over the phone or online. PrivatePhone is free, but if you want to answer or forward calls, you must purchase a premium service.

Private Call Forwarding and Fax Service

For about US$20/month, you can obtain a private voice/fax mailbox that will forward incoming calls to another telephone number.

Callers dial one number and are transferred to another, without being aware of the transfer. The number you give callers is listed in the name of the voice mail provider, not your own name.

After you set up this service with your voice mail provider, you can distribute the assigned number to friends, business prospects, etc. When callers dial this number, they hear a message instructing them to either leave a message or dial zero to connect to "the office" or "the operator." If they dial zero, calls are re-routed to you, or to whomever you designate. Callers must identify themselves before anyone picks up the phone. If no one is available to take the call, the system requests callers to leave a message.

In addition to defeating reverse directory traces and eliminating unscreened calls, this system provides a key business benefit: you can reprogram the forwarding number any time. If you have calls routed to your home office, for instance, and later move to another location, your contact number can stay the same.

An increasing number of voice mail providers provide call-forwarding service. Look under "voice mail" in your telephone directory and find a company that doesn't require you to provide identification and permits you to prepay for service at least a year in advance.

This isn't a perfect strategy. If you use your real address for billing purposes, your identity may be traced. And whatever number you choose for the caller to connect to can also be traced. But if you have already obtained anonymous service for whatever number to which calls are forwarded, the risk of having this number tied to "you" is minimal.

Most voice mail services also offer private fax receiving services. Program the system to have the faxes sent to a local office services store. Or have them delivered to you via e-mail, if this service is available.

The Only Effective Way to Encrypt Your Phone Calls

Traditional phone encryption systems aren't effective to protect conversations from wiretaps, at least not from the government. Annual U.S. wiretap reports indicate that the government has never encountered a situation where they couldn't recover "plain text" from an encrypted telephone conversation.

That may change with the advent of encryption systems for voice communication over the Internet, via the "Voice over Internet Protocol" or VoIP. One of the best-known VoIP systems is **Skype** (http://www.skype.net), which automatically encrypts conversations. However, Skype won't release its "source code" so there's no way to know whether the company has programmed "back doors" into the software. Still, Skype is a good start to protect your conversations against casual eavesdropping.

A better solution may come from civil liberties hero Philip Zimmerman, who almost went to prison for developing Pretty Good Privacy (PGP), one of the first effective and trusted programs to encrypt e-mail messages. Zimmerman has developed a program called **Zfone** (http://zfoneproject.com) to encrypt VoIP calls. In an effort to demonstrate that there are no backdoors, Zimmermann has made Zfone's source code publicly available for review by experts. Zfone's early versions aren't easy to use, but they're improving fast.

Keep Hackers and Identity Thieves Out of Your PC

Your computer may be a sitting duck for online attack. Even if you're not connected to the Internet, any Windows-based personal computer creates potentially incriminating "temporary" files every time you use it.

Where do you start to protect yourself? That depends on how much security and privacy you need. If you have your computer and software registered in your own name and address, that information indisputably ties you to a particular computer and software. If you use your computer for highly confidential purposes, the lifeboat strategy is to purchase it anonymously and not register your software, or register it under a pseudonym.

Secrets of Your Hard Disk

The surface of your hard disk is divided into sequentially numbered sectors, each like a tiny concentric arc. The sector number, its physical position, and a description of the data stored in it are held in an index. Each sector may contain just one small piece of data, leaving some empty space, or data may extend over many sectors, filling all of them.

This filing structure can become fragmented with what were originally contiguous chunks of data scattered over the disk's surface. Apart from being a security hazard, this fragmentation can slow down your computer.

When you delete a file, the index is merely changed. The data doesn't actually disappear until new data is written to the sector. Even then, it may be only partially deleted. With the right software (e.g., **Norton SystemWorks** from http://www.symantec.com), this data can be recovered.

Further, every Windows-based computer uses more than its available memory (RAM) during processing. This temporary memory is held on the hard disk in a **swap** or **page file**. But data in the page file is stored on the hard disk the same way as other data. The page file still contains chunks of old data long after it's been used. Data in the page file also gets fragmented and scattered around your hard disk.

20 Steps to Configure Your PC for Privacy and Security

To insure that no stray or not-quite deleted data remains accessible, you must change some settings. The following suggestions are for Windows-based PCs. While these steps shouldn't damage your computer or its software, before you begin, make a full backup of your software and data.

1. **Maintain your swap file as a fixed-length file**. In Windows XP, open Control Panel, click "System," "Advanced," "Performance," "Advanced," and finally "Virtual Memory." Click on "Change." A box showing the amount of free space on your hard disk will appear, with two further boxes showing "Minimum" and "Maximum." Enter a figure three times the size of the amount of RAM in your system in these boxes. The figure should be the same in both boxes. Click "OK," then click "Yes." Ignore the warning message from Windows. Again, click "Yes," then close your control panel and reboot.

2. **Defragment your hard disk.** In Windows XP, click on "My Computer," then right click on your C: drive. Select "Sharing and Security," "Tools," and "Defragment Now."

3. **Remove all temporary files, folders, and files left by Windows system crashes**. Close down all programs. Click "Start," then "Find," then "Files or Folders." A window will open and a cursor will be flashing in the box marked "Named." Enter "*.tmp" (without the quotes) in the box, then click "Find Now." Press "Ctrl-A" to highlight the files displayed in the window, then press "Delete." Confirm by clicking yes.

4. **Use encryption software**. Sending e-mail is the equivalent of sending a postcard—just about anyone can read it during transit to its intended recipient. Protect yourself by using **Pretty Good Privacy** (PGP), which you can download at http://www.pgpi.com. PGP is a free program that converts your e-mail messages into unreadable gibberish that only the intended recipient of your message can decode. PGP also lets you encrypt files on your hard drive, so only you can access them. A commercial version, **PGP Desktop**, has additional features, most notably the ability to encrypt your entire hard drive. It's available at http://www.pgp.com.

5. **Install software designed to eliminate not-quite deleted data and run it regularly**. PGP contains a "free space wipe" function that performs this function.

6. **Obtain anonymous Internet service**. Most Internet Service Providers require a credit or debit card number to set up service. To protect your privacy, find one that allows you to pay for service in advance using a money order and, if you desire, using a pseudonym. One such company is **Anonymizer** with its **Anonymizer Dialup** service (http://www.anonymizer.com/consumer/products).

7. **Avoid surveillance by your Internet Service Provider (ISP)**. The USA PATRIOT Act authorizes the government to obtain extensive records of your Internet browsing and e-mail correspondence, without a warrant (although not the contents of the messages themselves). In addition, the nature of the

Internet makes it possible for surveillance to occur at multiple points on the electronic pathways from computer to computer. Protect yourself by using an **anonymous proxy server** from a non-U.S. service not subject to the USA PATRIOT Act, such as **Diclave** (http://www.diclave.net).

8. **Use anonymous e-mail addresses.** This prevents e-mail messages you'd prefer to keep private from being traced to you. Consider a free account with **Hushmail** (http://www.hushmail.com). Unlike competing services such as **Yahoo** (http://www.yahoo.com), **Hotmail** (http://www.hotmail.com), and **G-Mail** (http://www.gmail.com), Hushmail doesn't log the IP addresses of your messages in a way that can be associated with your e-mail address or identity.[497] In addition, since Hushmail isn't U.S-based, it's not subject to the USA PATRIOT Act.

9. **Use anti-virus software. Viruses** (and related programs such as **remote administrators, worms**, etc.) are usually spread by being attached to executable files; i.e., those ending with .bat, .com, or .exe. When you click on the file attachment, you launch the virus. To lessen the chance of your system becoming infected, install a virus detection program on it and update it regularly. A good choice is "AVG" (anti-virus) from http://www.grisoft.com.

10. **Use a firewall.** A firewall is software or hardware, or a combination of both, designed to prevent unauthorized access to or from a PC or network. All data entering or leaving the PC or network must pass through the firewall, which blocks data you haven't authorized to get through. Many firewalls, including the firewall that comes installed with Windows XP, filter only incoming data to your PC. They don't inspect outgoing data that a remote administration program hidden on your PC might be sending. One firewall that detects outgoing data is **Comodo** (http://www.comodo.com)

11. **Avoid "phishing" and "pfarming" scams.** In a phishing scam, you receive a bogus email, allegedly from a bank or online merchant. The message contains a link routing you to an authentic-looking, but phony, website where you're asked to enter sensitive information such as your password, your Social Security number, etc. If you enter this data, the fraudster has enough information available to steal your identity, or drain your account. In a pfarming scam, a hacker plants malicious software in the servers that direct traffic on the Internet. Even if you type in the correct address of a website, the software sends you to a bogus one, where thieves can steal your personal information.

Protect yourself from phishing scams by never entering personal information into an online form in response to an unsolicited e-mail message. If you're not sure, call the company sending you the e-mail. Don't call any number listed in the message, either. It's probably a fake listing. Instead, call the number on any statement the company has sent you, or look it up.

Pfarming scams are more difficult to detect, but it's difficult even for the best hackers to duplicate the "look and feel" of a commercial website. Also, be alert to misspellings. Another tip-off is if the website doesn't display the "lock" icon at the bottom of your screen. If you have any suspicion the website isn't real, again, call the company.

12. **Use browser-scrubbing software**. As you surf the Web, you pick up a trail of temporary files that your browser stores, sometimes indefinitely. One program that eliminates these files is **Window Washer** (http://www.webroot.com).

13. **Avoid spyware.** Many PC software applications carry a hidden payload: **spyware**. At its most benign, spyware may send your Web browsing records to unknown recipients for marketing, investigative or other purposes. At worst, spyware can allow a remote user to assume complete control of your PC. Any data on the PC—your e-mail, your Internet browsing records and any other confidential infor-

mation can be retrieved, modified, corrupted, or deleted with such programs, so-called **Trojan Horses** or **Trojans**.

Spyware usually comes bundled with free programs advertised as enhancing PC performance or speed. It is often distributed over instant messaging services. Even the popular "toolbars" from mainstream companies such as Google, Yahoo, or Microsoft, send back a record of your online activity to the company. Avoid any add-on program unless you are certain it doesn't contain spyware. Use software such as **Adaware** from LavaSoft (http://www.lavasoftusa.com) to detect and safely delete spyware your PC has accumulated.

14. **Disable file sharing.** Anyone can access your PC without your knowledge if file sharing is enabled. Disable file sharing by following the instructions at http://support.microsoft.com/kb/304040.

15. **Secure your router.** If you have a high-speed Internet connection at your home or office, it probably connects to the Internet through a device or software called a **router.** Routers are usually installed with a default password that's easy for a hacker to guess. Someone who wants to take over your PC can create a Web page containing a simple piece of malicious code, and then send you an e-mail directing you to it. When you view this page, the code attempts to change your router settings to point to a computer controlled by the hacker. From this point forward, everything you do online can be monitored. To guard, change the password on your router to one that can't easily be guessed. If you can't do this on your own, ask your ISP for assistance.

16. **Secure wireless networks.** In your home or office wireless network, prevent outsiders from using your wireless connection (and potentially engaging or illegal conduct online or monitoring your online activities) by changing the name of your network (the **Service Set Identifier** or **SSID**) from its default name to a name you assign. Set up some form of encryption—the most common forms are called **WEP** and **WPA**. WEP isn't as strong as WPA but is better than nothing and will deter most eavesdroppers. Finally, turn off **SSID broadcast**. This feature is useful in wireless hot spots, such as a coffee shop or airport, but not in a home or office environment.

Other wireless devices such as nanny cams and Web cams are also easily monitored, allowing strangers to look inside your home from up to one-quarter mile away. Use whatever security settings are available to prevent this type of surveillance.

17. **Avoid unsecured wireless networks.** At coffee shops, Internet cafes, airports, etc., it's often easy to tap into a wireless network. But many public access points aren't secure, and the traffic they carry isn't encrypted. Malicious users can use "sniffing" tools to obtain sensitive information such as passwords, bank account numbers, and credit card numbers in such locations. Protect yourself by subscribing to a **virtual private networking** (VPN) service through your ISP or an outside vendor. VPNs encrypt connections at the sending and receiving ends, and keep out traffic that's not encrypted. If a VPN is available to you, log onto it whenever you use a public wireless access point.

18. **Use portable storage devices securely.** You can purchase a USB drive that fits in your pocket or your keychain and that stores eight or more gigabytes of data—plenty of capacity for most users' data. USB "sticks" are particularly useful when you're traveling, especially if you're using a PC in an Internet café or other public location, or are traveling internationally with your laptop. It's possible to use a USB drive that includes a copy of your Web browser and e-mail reader. Your browsing records are stored on the USB, not on the PC in which you insert it. One product with this capability is **xB Browser**, from http://xerobank.com.

Warning: Never plug in a USB stick or other portable device in your PC if you're not 100% sure you can trust it. For instance, if someone at an Internet cafe plugs an iPod into your computer, it can be used to steal your passwords and critical files.

19. **Use a laptop screen.** If you use your laptop PC in public places, it's easy for others to view your screen. Use a laptop screen, such as the **3M Privacy Filter,** which prevents anyone looking at the screen from an angle from seeing anything on it.

20. **Sanitize your PC before disposing of it.** Use a program like Killdisk (http://www.killdisk.com) to wipe your old hard drive before you replace it or sell your old PC.

Obtain Insurance Privately

Applying for insurance means disclosing private facts. The lifeboat strategy for purchasing insurance means minimizing this disclosure insofar as you can so legally.

Life and health insurance. "I don't believe that anyone, in this day and age, should tell the truth—the stigma is too great."[498] This quote from Paul Fink, former head of the American Psychiatric Association, refers to forms you must complete to obtain life or health insurance. The fact is that if you disclose on the application that you have ever been treated for any psychiatric condition, alcoholism, etc., or have suffered from a major illness such as cancer, you're much less likely to be offered coverage. If you do receive it, you'll pay a hefty premium over people who have not suffered from such conditions—or who lied about it. In addition, once you're turned down for coverage or coverage is issued only conditionally, you must generally disclose this fact in all future insurance applications.

This isn't a recommendation to lie. You're legally obliged to truthfully answer all questions about your health on the application. If you don't, and you're later found out, the company might not be obligated to pay claims under the policy. In certain cases, you could also be prosecuted for fraud.

Assuming you do qualify, the good news is that you can generally obtain coverage without disclosing your SSN or residential address. Either leave the section asking for your SSN blank or insert your driver's license number there. Some applications for life and health insurance request a residential address; others don't. I've never encountered any problems listing the address of a mail drop rather than my residential address. Simply tell your agent that you never receive sensitive correspondence at your home due to problems with mail theft, and that you don't want confidential insurance information falling into the wrong hands.

If you've ever been seriously ill, or made a significant claim against a health or disability insurance company, a record of it probably resides at the Medical Information Bureau (Chapter 2). You can obtain a record of your MIB record without charge. Call MIB's toll-free phone number, 866-692-6901 or go to http://www.mib.com/html/request_your_record.html.

Vehicle insurance. The major privacy problem with vehicle insurance is the need to disclose where the vehicle is garaged or parked. Ordinarily, this will be your home; thus, your insurance application will contain your home address. This information can be disclosed to law enforcement officials or subpoenaed in a lawsuit. Private investigators or stalkers may also be able to obtain this information through pretexting.

The lifeboat strategy to deal with this problem is to purchase a vehicle in the name of a business entity such as a limited liability company (LLC). The vehicle should be the only asset the entity owns. If you set up the business entity in the manner I describe in Chapter 4, it will be difficult for anyone to connect that entity to you, thus preserving your privacy when you purchase insurance for it.

Homeowner's/renter's insurance. There's no way to avoid disclosing your home address on an application for homeowner's or renter's insurance, since the policy is written to insure property at a particular address. However, if you rent or own through a business entity such as a LLC, the policy will be written in its name, not your own.

Get a CLUE

If you make a claim against your vehicle or homeowner's insurance, your name will be entered into ChoicePoint's **Comprehensive Loss Underwriting Exchange** (CLUE) database. CLUE reports include detailed information about each claim you make, including the name of the insured person or entity, the property address, the Social Security number, or taxpayer ID number of the claimant, and the amount and reason for each claim. Even if you don't make a claim, merely inquiring about it may result in an entry in the CLUE database. Therefore, if you contact your insurance company or agent to discuss an actual loss, don't reveal your name or policy number.

When you apply for property or vehicle insurance, an insurance company will review your CLUE report to determine if you are a good risk. If the report shows that you habitually file claims, you may be refused coverage. This is where holding each property you own in a separate business entity can pay dividends. If you made an insurance claim against one property, it won't show up when you apply for insurance on another one.

You can obtain the CLUE report on any property you own by calling 866-527-2600 or online at http://www.choicetrust.com.

Slam the Door Shut on Medical Privacy Invasion

Chapter 2 discussed the many ways in which your medical privacy can be compromised. What if you don't want anyone, including the government, poking around in your medical records? Here are some lifeboat strategies to consider:

- **Pay currency for treatment or tests, and don't file insurance claims.** This is the single most important step you can take to protect medical privacy.
- **Ask your physicians to become "non-covered entities" under the Health Insurance Portability and Accountability Act (HIPPA).** To do this, physicians must file insurance claims only in paper form, not electronically, which may delay processing of claims. If your physicians refuse to become "non-covered entities," ask them to give you all copies of your medical records. Bring those records with you when you visit, or find a physician that has elected to become a non-covered entity. For more information, see http://www.aapsonline.org/confiden/advisory.htm.
- **Obtain treatment under an assumed name.** This isn't illegal if you don't intend to defraud anyone.
- **Discuss your concern for privacy with your physician.** Most physicians are aware of the eroding protection for medical records and are willing to help you protect your privacy. Sometimes, they'll agree not to note some subjects on your chart. Or they may keep a separate chart that doesn't go into a computer. Physicians will be most willing to take such steps if you're paying for your own treatment.
- **Purchase high-deductible insurance in conjunction with a Health Savings Account (HSA).**

Insurers issue such policies with less scrutiny than lower-deductible plans. To pay for claims that don't meet the deductible amount, open a HSA. Contributions to HSAs, like Individual Retirement Accounts, are tax deductible. And like an IRA, funds grow tax-free. For 2007, the maximum contribution for an eligible individual with self-only coverage is US$2,850, and the maximum contribution for family coverage is US$5,650. These limits are indexed for inflation.

- **Seek out physicians catering to patients that are uninsured or who have high insurance deductibles.** One such network is called **SimpleCare** (http://www.simplecare.com). It's a cash-based system and doesn't assign claims to insurance companies or Medicare. This reduces costs and increases patient privacy.
- **Ask health care providers not to share your records.** Such requests aren't legally binding, but the answer you receive will be informative of how the provider uses your medical information. A model letter to use for this purpose is posted at http://www.patientprivacyrights.org/site/PageServer?pagename=Right_To_Medical_Privacy_Statement.
- **If your condition requires a prescription, ask your physician for "professional samples."** Many pharmaceutical companies distribute drugs for use by medical professionals. Your physician may be able to give you the medication you need privately, rather than sending you to a pharmacist. An added bonus: You will ordinarily not be charged for professional samples. Don't transport prescription medication that doesn't contain your name on the container across a U.S. border. That's a violation of federal law and could lead to your arrest.
- **Beware free or low-cost "health screenings."** These are generally marketing efforts designed to find new patients. In many cases, medical records marketing companies buy the data. Find out what use will be made of the medical information collected on you—or use a pseudonym when you're screened.
- **Don't disclose your real name in online medical discussion groups**. When you sign up, use an anonymous e-mail address. In several cases, information revealed in an online discussion group has been made public through security breaches or theft, or been disclosed to insurance companies. Follow the suggestions for online privacy discussed earlier.
- **Don't use the "personal health record" (PHR) feature of your medical insurance plan, if it has one.** PHRs provide an online repository of your health and insurance claim history. The data you enter about your health history is owned by the insurer and can be shared for any purpose it deems necessary, unconstrained by any federal laws or regulations. With a PHR, you're essentially being encouraged to spy on yourself—and you have the right to refuse to do so.
- **Protect yourself against medical ID theft.** As I described in Chapter 2, medical ID theft is one of the fastest-growing forms of this crime. Protect yourself by asking your insurance company for a list of claims paid against your policy. If unauthorized claims exist, follow the procedures summarized earlier in this chapter to recover after you've been a victim of identity theft. In addition, obtain your MIB record and ask that it be corrected to delete any reports of claims you didn't make.
- **Obtain medical treatment in another country.** Medical treatment in most countries is less expensive than in the United States. In addition, you will often have more control over your care than you do domestically. For instance, in Mexico, you can order tests without a doctor's order and buy most medications without a prescription. For a listing of hospitals worldwide, see http://www.escapeartist.com/Offshore_Health_Care/Offshore_Health_Care.html.

Buy Your Vehicle Privately

In all 50 states, owning a vehicle and driving it on public highways is considered a privilege, not a right. All states require that vehicles be registered and that their operators obtain driver's licenses.

The lifeboat strategy to preserve vehicle privacy is to purchase a used car with currency. Don't buy it from a dealer who must report currency transactions over US$10,000 to the Treasury Department. Instead, purchase the vehicle from a private seller, who, in virtually all cases, will be delighted to receive currency.

In private sales, many buyers will ask that the seller leave the sales price entry on the title blank. Listing a lower amount than the actual sales price reduces sales tax, if any applies in the state in which you purchase the vehicle. However, doing so is illegal.

To obtain license plates, you'll need to register the car with your state's Department of Motor Vehicles. Register the vehicle under the name of a business entity created for that purpose—not in your own name. Use a mail drop address, not your residential address.

Keep Your Residential Address and SSN Off Your Driver's License

Most states require that you list your residential address on your application for a driver's license and that you notify the state Department of Motor Vehicles of your new address whenever you move.

However, it's not a good idea to list your residential address on your driver's license. If the license is stolen, the thief will know where you live. Another problem is that it's easy for private investigators to illegally obtain access to driver's license databases. If someone is bent on revenge, the last thing you want that person to have is your residential address.

Listing an alternative address may require some finesse, however. First, examine the application form: does it specifically ask for "residential address" or does it say "street address?" If "street address" is used, then you can list a mail drop address completely legally.

If the term "residential address" is used, ask the clerk how the state deals with individuals who just relocated to the state and who live in hotels designed for relatively long-term stays, such as "Residence Inns." (It might help if you can show the clerk your Residence Inn key.) Chances are (perhaps after consultation with a supervisor) you'll be advised to use this address, and to contact the Motor Vehicles Department when you eventually obtain a permanent address.

Other strategies are possible. I spoke to one person who claimed to have used the address of the local YMCA on his driver's license. Another person told me he didn't shower or shave for several days, then applied for a driver's license. He told the clerk that he was homeless, lived in his vehicle and received mail at his post office box. After checking with her supervisor, the license was issued with a post office box address.

The Real ID Act (Chapter 2) requires proof of a residential address to obtain a driver's license. It will be implemented over the next few years in all 50 states. It remains to be seen if the strategies listed in this section will remain relevant.

Federal law requires that states collect your Social Security number when you apply for or renew your driver's license. While many states use the SSN as a driver's license number, you can request an alternative number. State driver's license bureaus must grant this request. It may also be possible to obtain a driver's license without disclosing your SSN through "social engineering." When I applied for a driver's license, I told the clerk that I had a religious objection to disclosing my SSN for this purpose based on the biblical verse in Revelations 13:17 referencing "the mark of the beast." The clerk complied with my request, although she told me she was violating official procedure by issuing the license without obtaining my SSN.

International driver's licenses (IDLs) are scams—avoid them. International driving permits (IDPs) do exist, but they don't allow you to avoid paying traffic tickets, keep points off your driving record, or help you establish a new identify, as some promoters of IDLs claim. An IDP isn't a license in itself, but a booklet containing translations of the information found on your real driver's license into various languages. In the United States, the only organizations authorized by the State Department to sell IDPs are the American Automobile Association and the American Automobile Touring Alliance (through the National Automobile Club).

Don't Let Strangers Know Where You Live

The consequences of having the wrong person know your residential address can be personally or financially devastating—and occasionally, even deadly.

Many public databases may contain your residential address. If you'd prefer not to subject yourself and your family to surprise visits from robbers, government busybodies or other undesirables, not to mention the ever-increasing threat of identity theft, consider the following suggestions:

- **Don't disclose your residential address to anyone except for close friends and family members.** Make sure anyone living with you follows this precaution, too.
- **Rent, don't buy.** Home ownership records are now computerized in almost all states. At the click of a mouse, you can match the name of homeowners with addresses. If you purchase a home, title it in the name of a business entity or a land trust, as described later in this chapter. Any mortgage should be taken out in the name of the business entity, although it will likely be required to pay a higher interest rate.
- **Make your rental agreement in the name of a business entity.** Don't sign a lease if you don't have to. If you must, sign it in the name of a business entity. Have that entity make rental payments from its own bank account. This isn't a tax dodge—only a way to retrieve some of your lost privacy.
- **Never give out your SSN.** When landlords or utility companies ask for your SSN, it means they want to run a credit check. Their name and address will show up in your credit report, providing an easy-to-follow trail back to your residential address. Offer to pay a higher deposit instead of permitting a credit check.
- **Avoid utility payments.** Find a landlord who will let you just make one monthly payment that includes all utilities, including local phone service. Use pre-paid calling cards for long distance calls. If you must arrange for your own utility service, take out the service in the name of a business entity, not in your own name. Leave deposits as necessary.
- **Never have anything mailed or delivered to you at your residential address.** Instead, have correspondence sent to your post office box or mail drop.
- **Don't use a mainstream moving service.** Large moving companies maintain a nationwide customer database with "from" and "to" addresses noted. Private investigators regularly obtain access to these databases. Instead, rent a truck and hire "student movers" to assist you. The last time I moved, I drove to a local recreation area and paid two teenagers US$25 each for their assistance. Move valuable or fragile goods yourself and lock them in your vehicle until after the movers leave.

- **Don't answer the door when strangers knock.** Robbers (or worse) can come disguised as police, delivery personnel or even as clowns. If you haven't told anyone except close friends and family members where you live, no one else should come to your home looking for you.

How to Hide Currency and Other Valuables

You may have accumulated currency, jewelry, or other valuables you'd like to store in a secure location, in or out of your home. What are the best—and most private—options? This section answers those questions.

Safety Deposit Boxes Offer Near Zero Privacy

When you rent a safety deposit box, you'll be asked for your SSN. If you refuse, the bank may refuse to do business with you under its "know your customer" anti-laundering guidelines, and perhaps even file a Suspicious Activities Report (Chapter 2).

In many states, banks are required to monitor local obituary listings and seal any safety deposit boxes owned by a deceased resident. Heirs in most cases may not open the box without a representative from the state Tax Department present. To avoid having your heirs face this situation, rent the box in the name of a business entity or a trust. Since a business entity can't die, you'll ensure that your valuables are accessible to loved ones after your death.

You'll need to get a tax identification number for the business entity that sets up any kind of relationship with the bank. You're also likely to be asked to disclose the beneficial ownership of the entity to the bank. However, this information will be maintained in the bank's files—your connection to the entity won't be disclosed to anyone unless a specific inquiry is made to the bank by an authorized party (e.g., the IRS).

Some banks won't rent safety deposit boxes to persons or companies that don't hold accounts. If you must open an account, do so in the name of your business entity.

Don't jointly rent a safety deposit box with someone else. If that person is found liable in a judgment, a creditor may be able to legally seize all the assets in the box and force you to prove ownership of the portion of the contents belonging to you. Should the joint renter die, the box and contents may be sealed pending probate proceedings.

Thefts from safety deposit boxes aren't generally covered by insurance from the bank, except in the event of gross negligence. You'll need to obtain supplemental insurance on items you place in the box through a "valuable items" rider on your homeowner's or renter's insurance. This requires that you list the particular items that are covered by the policy for the insurance company's files. You'll also need to have these items appraised and send a copy of the appraisal to the insurance company.

It's common for a valuable items policy to be subpoenaed in collecting a judgment. The creditor then demands the items identified on the policy to be turned over to it. For this reason, I recommend keeping only documents in a safety deposit box. Keep your valuables at home, preferably in a fire-resistant floor safe or in a private vault.

If you do keep valuable items in a safety deposit box, consider the following lifeboat strategies to protect yourself from loss of these items.

- **Rent the smallest box available**. Try to get one at the top or bottom of the vault, as thieves target boxes at eye-level.
- **Keep your valuables in more than one safety deposit box.** If one vault is broken into, you will have access to some of your documents (or valuables) elsewhere.
- **Discard the envelope the keys to your safety deposit box came in with the name of the bank imprinted on it.** If someone steals the keys, the thief will only have access to a safety deposit box in an unknown bank.
- **Don't store currency in a safety deposit boxes**. U.S. law presumes all currency in a safety deposit box to be unreported income. The IRS may seize the currency and require you to prove that the money was earned legally, and all taxes paid. If the box contains more than US$10,000 in currency, you must complete a currency transaction report (Chapter 2).

Private Alternatives to Safety Deposit Boxes

One alternative to a safety deposit box is a private vault. Some are more secure than banks. Private vaults are more expensive than safety deposit boxes, but lower insurance costs may offset most if not all of the difference. In most cases, you won't need not disclose your SSN to rent storage space, although you will likely need to provide proof of identity. In addition, most private vaults don't monitor obituary listings, so it's unlikely the box will be sealed upon your death.

Four U.S. companies that provide private vault services are:

- **Zurich Depository Corporation** (http://www.zdcvault.com) with one location near New York City;
- **Fortress** (http://www.thefortress.com) with locations in New York City, Boston, and Miami;
- **Los Altos Vault & Safe** (http://www.losaltosvault.com) in Los Altos, California; and
- **24/7 Private Vaults** (http://www.24-7privatevaults.com) in Las Vegas, Nevada.

Most rental agreements for private vaults state that the company has no claim over the contents of your box. However, such a provision doesn't guarantee that you can easily retrieve your valuables if the firm shuts down or declares bankruptcy. Read the contract carefully to make certain that you're comfortable with whatever provisions are included to deal with this possibility.

Hiding Money at Home

Hiding money has a bad connotation. If you tell someone you're "hiding money," they'll probably think you're a tax evader or other criminal or perhaps even a terrorist.

Still, if your visible assets are seized or some natural or man-made disaster results in a serious breakdown in government authority and/or a suspension of trading on securities markets, wealth you've hidden away for a "rainy day" could be very useful.

There are two schools of thought regarding home concealment of valuables. One is that it's best to conceal valuables in inconspicuous locations around your home. The other is that valuables should be centrally deposited in a safe made resistant to opening or removal.

Every home is full of places where you can hide a lot of value—100 ounces of gold is only a double handful. If thieves come into your home, they won't want to spend much time looking for the goods. Anything you do to delay them will lessen the chances that they'll find anything valuable. Here are a few suggestions:

- **Baseboards.** By prying off a short section of baseboard that ends in a corner, ideally obscured by furniture, and boring a small hole in the wall behind it, you obtain a concealed and inconspicuous location to hide a roll or two of coins. Tap the baseboard back into place once you've completed this project using the original nails. Repair any scratches or gouges with putty, spackling or paint, taking care to match the existing finish as closely as possible.
- **Paneling.** The best choice is actual boards nailed to a wall. Choose an area behind furniture or in a corner, and make one of the boards removable, hollowing out a concealed area behind it. Attach hidden spring hinges (such as those made by **Soss** (http://www.soss.com) so that the board is held tightly against the wall when closed. Or the door may be designed to snap into place with cabinet fasteners.
- **Walls.** Since walls are hollow, they represent ideal hiding places. Choose a location behind a large, fixed object, such as a painting. Remove the fixed object and hollow out the space behind it between the vertical studs. Save the cut away plaster or wood. Hang a sack with your valuables in between the studs. Use cabinet fasteners or invisible hinges to replace the wood or plaster. Finally, replace the fixed object.
- **Light switch or electrical outlet.** This is one of the simplest hiding places available. Choose an inaccessible outlet behind furniture. After turning off the electricity, remove the faceplate and disconnect the electrical wires, removing the tape or wire nuts. Next, remove the metal box inside attached to the wall. This will provide access to the space inside the studs. Place your valuables in that space, make sure they won't interfere with the wiring, and then reattach the box, wiring, and faceplate.
- **Houseplants.** If you choose one houseplant out of many for concealment of valuables, chances for its detection are minimal. The best choice is a plant that requires little water, to spare your valuables from getting soaked. For a plant that you only water occasionally, a sealed plastic container may suffice, but otherwise, you'll need to build a sealed false bottom into the pot and drill a hole in it with a plastic tube inserted to carry water off from around your sealed container.
- **Coffee mug stash.** Buy an oversized coffee mug. Place your valuables in the bottom of the mug and insert a circular cardboard cutout on top of them. Fill the remainder of the mug with baking soda and place in your refrigerator. The mug will appear to be absorbing odors rather than hiding money or jewelry.
- **Book stash.** Choose a relatively thick book that you don't mind destroying (preferably with an extremely boring title) and cut out a square in the middle pages. Make sure that at least the first and last 20 pages or so are intact, and that you leave at least one inch on each side of your cut.
- **Closet stash.** Find a long-sleeve shirt, jacket or coat you never wear and sew one cuff shut. Drop in lightweight valuables, like cash, and hang the garment with the sewed-shut sleeve facing inwards.
- **Toothpaste tube stash.** Take an empty tube of toothpaste and cut off the flat end. Clean the inside with hot water and a dull knife. Place your valuables in the tube and fold the end down a few times. The result is what appears to be a tube of toothpaste that's been partially used.

Most of these suggestions are suitable for do-it-yourselfers, but if you're not able to do this work yourself, hire someone you trust to do it.

If you have a large home, you may be able to create a secret room or compartment that's revealed when you pull a hidden lever or pull a book from a bookshelf. One company that specializes in designing and installing secret rooms and compartments is Creative Home Engineering (http://www.hiddenpassageway.com).

Concealing your wealth throughout your home has potential drawbacks. One is fire, which can destroy even the most carefully concealed valuables. In addition, a thief equipped with a metal detector may be able to find precious metals hiding places, unless you've taken the precaution of creating fake stashes full of nails, screws or other metallic objects.

For these reasons, a fireproof safe may be a better alternative, protecting against fire as well as theft. The most secure way to install a safe is to set it in concrete in the floor. Install the safe so that its top is flush with the floor. Cover it with a rug or, even better, a false floor with a hidden hinge door built into it. One company that manufactures top-quality safes is **American Security Products** (http://www.amsecusa.com).

Safe dealers can provide instructions for installation. Most dealers also offer an installation service. The dealer may also be able to refer you to a specialist in "concealment construction" who will search your home for overlooked spots where they can build in a safe and conceal it so thoroughly that not even professionals will suspect it's there.

Hiding Money Outdoors

In a full-blown emergency, it's possible that banks will be closed, ATMs not functioning, and even private vaults shut down as a matter of "national security." In addition, under the emergency provisions you learned about in Chapter 2, at the stroke of the President's pen, the government has the authority to confiscate private property, including valuables in your own home.

While I'm not predicting this disaster scenario will ever unfold—and I certainly hope it doesn't—you may want consider creating an outdoor hiding place for your valuables. Here are instructions for construction of so-called "midnight gardener" containers suitable for burying your valuables:

To bury your valuables outside, you'll need several lengths of PVC pipe (available at any hardware store) sufficient to hold your coins. A foot of 6" diameter PVC pipe will hold about US$100 face value U.S. 90% silver coins. At the same time, for every container you plan to make, buy one round cap end and one screw-top end. Be sure to buy plenty of PVC pipe cement and Teflon sealing tape. If you don't have a hacksaw, you'll need that, too. If you've never worked with PVC, be sure to ask the hardware store sales clerk how to do it.

Cut the PVC pipe to a handy length, not more than 18". Prepare the surface of the end and the inside of the cap with steel wool, apply PVC cement, and stick the closed cap on one end. Prepare the surface of the other end, apply cement, and cement in place the screw-top closure. Let it sit 24 hours, and your midnight gardener capsule is ready to use.

Before you bury it, however, you'll want to drive out all the moisture (very important for silver). Turn your oven on to its lowest temperature ("Warm"), and place your midnight gardeners in the oven.

Leave them about 15 minutes, then take them out of the oven, put in your coins in, and screw down the closure. Be sure to put Teflon tape on the threads before you screw down the closure. Remember, PVC is plastic, and you only want to warm it enough to drive the moisture out of the air inside.

Now you are ready to bury your midnight gardener. But how will you remember where you buried it? Best to plant a bush over it, or measure an exact distance and direction from some landmark not likely to move, i.e., the corner of your house, a fence post, etc.

Bury it at least three feet down. Cover it with eighteen inches of dirt. Place some old scrap metal in the hole. A junk alternator is perfect. Then fill rest of the hole. If anyone with a metal detector searches your place, he will dig and find the alternator, and, you hope, give up.

The best security here is to buy six or eight old alternators, and bury them randomly all over your yard at different depths. Now the searcher is looking for a needle in a haystack. Obviously, the midnight gardener method of hiding gold and silver is not recommended for storing items you might need frequently or often.[499]

Even with these precautions, it's possible that the seals on your buried midnight gardeners will eventually break down. For this reason, consider carefully what you will store in the units. Cash breaks down easily and shouldn't be buried for long periods. Silver breaks down less easily but tarnishes badly. Gold is almost impervious to moisture; diamonds even more so. Hide your valuables in a dry climate, away from excesses of heat or cold. A cave may be appropriate in some areas.

To an untrained eye, midnight gardeners look a lot like pipe bombs. When transporting your midnight gardeners to their ultimate hiding place, keep them out of sight. You don't want to be stopped by police, only to have them see what appear to be pipe bombs sitting in the back seat of your vehicle!

22 Vital Steps to Protect Yourself from IRS Scrutiny

You can minimize confrontations with the IRS, as with other government agencies, if the information you submit doesn't stand out. Although the IRS audit rate for high-income taxpayers has fallen sharply in the past decade, the number of audits is once again rising. After falling from 200,000 in 1997 to 90,000 in 2001, the number of high-income persons (individuals earning more than US$100,000 annually) audited each year by the IRS rose to approximately 250,000 in 2006.[500]

Certain professions and situations frequently are prone to audits. If you have an annual income exceeding US$100,000, the odds of an audit increase. Other IRS audit targets include independent contractors, small businesses, professional pension plans, and anyone doing a substantial business in currency—owners of restaurants, movie theaters, etc. In addition, if you have financial interests outside the United States—particularly an offshore trust—the chances for audit rise sharply.

Consider the following strategies to reduce IRS hassles:

1. **File a tax return, declare your income, and pay whatever taxes you owe**. The expanding computerized auditing capability of the IRS makes it increasingly likely that individuals who don't file tax returns will be caught. Even taxpayers who have taxes withheld by their employer, and whose taxes are overpaid, are fined for not filing returns. Filing a return means that you'll get the overpayments back, so long as you claim them within three years.

2. **Keep records substantiating the income and deductions you claim on your tax returns and proof that you filed**. Thorough records are essential in proving that you're entitled to the deductions you claim and that your income is no greater than you have declared. Also, make certain that you have an explanation for any large deposits in bank or brokerage accounts that you have not declared as income. Ideally, you should be able to document every deposit in every account.

- Keep back-up documentation relating to your tax return, especially records of large deductions. Maintain all documentation relating to real estate ownership, investments and claims for a refund or credit based on bad debts or losses for at least six years after you file your tax return.
- Keep documents regarding the purchase or improvement of your home for at least six years after you sell it. If you deferred the tax on the gain from selling your old home by purchasing a new one, keep records relating to both residences permanently to establish your taxable basis in the new home.
- If you own securities, keep records showing purchase price, proceeds from sales and investment-related deductions for at least six years after you sell a particular security. Maintain a record of stock splits, dividends or any adjustments in basis (e.g., for investments in partnerships) to help determine your cost basis. Certificate numbers, number of shares and sales prices should be maintained.
- If you have a non-deductible IRA (Roth IRA), keep all records pertaining to that account as long as the IRA exists, including tax returns and/or IRS Forms 5498, 1099-R and W-2P.
- Keep tax returns permanently, along with a certified mail receipt proving you filed. The IRS can claim decades after a filing deadline that you never submitted a return for one or more years—and collect penalties and interest for the entire interval.

For more information on what tax-related information you should retain, and for how long, see http://www.iarfc.org/content_sub.asp?n=34.

3. **Know the rules for charitable deductions**. You may deduct charitable contributions only if you itemize deductions and contributed to qualified charitable organizations. You can't deduct a contribution, regardless of the amount, unless you have a bank record or written communication from the qualified organization confirming its receipt. Contributions of US$250 or more are deductible only if you obtain a written acknowledgment from the qualified organization. For more information on charitable contributions, refer to IRS Publication 526.[501]

4. **Send all correspondence to the IRS by certified mail, return receipt requested.** In addition to the Postal Service, the IRS accepts as proof of delivery a receipt from some private carriers for certain classes of service. Keep notarized copies of the documents you enclosed, along with a certified mail receipt,

Even with a certified mail return receipt, the IRS occasionally claims that the envelope for which the receipt was received was empty.[502] To avoid this problem, include in the certified mailing a cover letter stating that the tax return is enclosed with an extra copy of the cover letter and the tax return, along with a self-addressed stamped envelope. The cover letter should request the IRS to return a copy of the letter stamped "received" and the tax return in the enclosed envelope. This request won't always be complied with, but if it is, the IRS will have a very difficult time proving it didn't receive the tax return.

Don't hand-deliver documents to the IRS. In one case, when an individual hand-delivered a tax return to an IRS revenue agent, the agency ruled that the tax return was considered "not filed."[503]

5. **Meet IRS deadlines.** The IRS takes filing and payment deadlines seriously. Penalties and interest are imposed unless you apply and are granted a filing extension. For Form 1040, you can obtain an automatic six-month extension by filing Form 4868, which you can download at http://www.irs.gov/pub/irs-pdf/f4868.pdf. Filing Form 4868 prior to the annual April 15 filing deadline will avoid a late filing penalty, but unless you pay at least 90% of the tax due, there's a penalty for each month the tax isn't paid in full. This is in addition to the interest due on tax late tax payments.

6. **Have a professional prepare your return.** Testimony in 2006 before the U.S. Senate conclusively demonstrates that taxpayers who prepare their own return pay more in taxes across every income group. Use a CPA or other tax professional, not a tax preparer at a "chain" tax preparation service. According to the same GAO report, tax preparers at tax chains made significant errors in more than 50% of the returns they prepared.[504] If you prepare your own return, use software such as **TaxCut** (http://www.taxcut.com). While not perfect, tax software will insure that you don't make the type of mathematical errors that may lead to at least cursory IRS scrutiny of your return.

7. **Beware of tax shelters.** While many types of tax shelters exist, the ones in the IRS cross hairs involve "reportable transactions." Individuals who fail to disclose a reportable transaction to the IRS are subject to a US$10,000 penalty. Other non-reporting taxpayers are subject to a US$50,000 penalty

There are several types of reportable transactions. The most important categories are:

- **Listed transactions.** These are transactions specifically targeted as abusive by the IRS. An updated technical explanation and list of listed transactions is maintained at http://www.irs.gov/businesses/corporations/article/0,,id=97384,00.html.
- **Confidential transactions.** These are transactions where a tax advisor restricts you from disclosing the tax treatment or tax structure of a tax avoidance plan.
- **Contingent fee transactions.** In this arrangement, unless the IRS upholds the intended tax consequences of the transaction, you pay nothing to your advisor, or are entitled to a full or partial refund of the advisor's fees.
- **Loss transactions.** These are certain transactions resulting in a loss from gambling, theft, capital, worthless securities, casualty, disaster, insolvent financial institutions and several other categories.
- **Transactions involving a brief asset holding period.** This category includes many transactions that result in a tax credit exceeding US$250,000 if you hold the underlying asset 45 days or less.

8. **For aggressive tax positions, ask a tax attorney for an "opinion letter."** An opinion letter is a valuable tool in tax planning, because in general (although not in all cases),[505] you can use it to avoid most tax penalties, should the transaction in question later be challenged. The requirements of Circular 230 make opinion letters more expensive than they once were, and you should discuss the costs of such a letter with your advisors. If a transaction is for the principal purpose of reducing or avoiding federal taxes, and that transaction isn't consistent with the Tax Code and Congressional purposes behind that law, tax advisors must provide a formal tax opinion letter about every significant federal tax issue in the transaction.

9. **If you think something in your tax return could lead to an audit, prove its legitimacy in the return itself.** One way to do this is to submit Form 8275 with your return.[506] For 8275 is a disclosure statement that calls IRS attention to the item in question. Generally, if you fully disclose your position on the return itself, and explain to the IRS how you arrived at it, you can avoid being penalized. Deductions that arouse IRS scrutiny, and for which disclosure via Form 8275 may be appropriate, include moving expenses, medical expenses, charitable contributions, entertainment expenses and home office expenses.

10. **Make certain that income reported by third parties to the IRS matches the information reported on your tax return.** Banks, brokerages, barter services, and employers must report income, dividends, and salaries paid to the IRS, and send copies of the notification to you on Forms 1099 and W-2. Keep these copies and make certain this income is reflected on your tax return. If your records disagree with the information on these forms, ask the issuer to verify the numbers. If they still don't match with your records, and you're certain that you're right, file your tax return with the numbers you've calculated, along with a letter of explanation or with Form 8275.

11. **Make certain your return is internally consistent**. IRS auditors will examine your tax return for internal consistency prior to deciding whether a full-scale audit is worthwhile. For instance, if you make large deductions for medical insurance premiums, the IRS may look twice at deductions for medical expenses as well. The IRS also expects you to take certain deductions. If you're a self-employed salesperson, the IRS expects you to declare at least some travel and entertainment expenses. Not claiming a deduction might raise a red flag!

12. **Take the standard deduction unless itemizing your deductions will save you a significant amount of money**. Itemized returns are audited more frequently than non-itemized returns. Itemizing may also result in disclosure of information that you might prefer remain private.

13. **Make certain the IRS has your correct address**. Use Form 8822 for this purpose.[507] If you move, promptly notify the IRS of your new address. If the agency tries to contact you at a previous address after you have made a good-faith effort to notify it of your new address, it may not impose interest or penalties for the period for which notification of such interest or penalties is delayed due to its mistake.

Instructions for Form 1040 state that you should list a post office box address "only if the post office does not deliver to your home." However, many people list a post office box address or mail drop address on their tax returns. Due to the possibility of identity theft if you receive correspondence from the IRS in unlocked residential mailbox, using a post office box or mail drop address for this purpose only seems prudent, notwithstanding IRS instructions to the contrary.

14. **Try to deal with the same IRS representative at all times**. IRS agents are under no obligation to disclose their real name to you when you deal with them. Indeed, the use of pseudonyms is explicitly authorized in IRS regulations.[508] However, you should still try to get the identity of the individual to whom you're speaking, a phone number that will ring directly to that individual, and obtain that person's assistance every time you call. This gives you the name an employee who will be familiar with your situation.

15. **Get it in writing**. The IRS must cancel any portion of a penalty imposed on you due to erroneous written IRS advice. This applies to written responses to specific written requests and assumes you have provided the IRS with accurate information. However, the IRS is under no legal obligation to provide you with written advice. Asking for advice in writing isn't the same as requesting a **private letter ruling**. Such rulings, which provide the agency's opinion in regard to questions submitted on behalf of a taxpayer, are expensive to obtain and rarely granted. They are also applicable only to the particular taxpayer requesting the opinion and don't reflect official IRS policy.

16. **Don't participate in state tax amnesties**. Several states have recovered millions of dollars in delinquent state taxes by permitting taxpayers to pay what they owe without additional penalties. However, all records associated with state amnesties may be exchanged with the IRS, which has never declared a general amnesty for federal taxes.

17. **If you receive a check from the IRS that's clearly in error, return it.** The IRS often sends tax refunds to individuals not entitled to a refund. If the checks are cashed, the IRS can legally demand return of the money, plus interest. Like all correspondence with the IRS, send the check back by certified mail, return receipt requested.

18. **Don't assume the IRS will send refunds you're due.** Contact the agency if you haven't received your refund in a reasonable period; e.g., 90 days after it has been promised. The IRS takes only the most basic steps to find people to whom it owes money. After three years, the government can keep the money.

19. **Don't trust the IRS voluntary disclosure program.** For over a decade, the IRS has encouraged taxpayers who come forward to "voluntarily disclose" their non-filing status, and pay back taxes. In return, the IRS generally doesn't criminally prosecute these individuals for tax offenses. However, voluntary disclosure isn't official IRS policy. Voluntary disclosure also doesn't apply to non-tax criminal violations that might be uncovered by the IRS. The agency must refer any such violations it discovers for criminal prosecution. A better strategy in this situation is to approach a tax attorney. The attorney may be able to make an informal inquiry regarding your situation to the IRS and rely on the attorney-client privilege to avoid disclosing your identity to the IRS.

20. **Don't file your taxes electronically.** The IRS encourages taxpayers to file tax returns electronically, promising faster refunds. I don't recommend this practice for three reasons:

- An electronic return is much easier to audit than a paper return.
- Documents submitted electronically are much easier to monitor than documents submitted through the mail.
- The IRS has established partnerships with various companies to participate in electronic filing operations. These companies aren't permitted to monitor the contents of the tax returns they process, but it isn't clear that current security measures are strong enough to prevent them from doing so.[509]

21. **Don't respond to e-mails or telephone calls from someone who says they're from the IRS or an IRS-mandated collection agency.** Many taxpayers receive e-mails and telephone calls from fraudsters claiming to be collecting tax debts. E-mail scams that use the IRS logo to dupe victims into revealing passwords or PIN numbers are also common. The IRS doesn't communicate with taxpayers via e-mail, and has cancelled plans to use private contractors to collect debts on its behalf.

22. **Protect the privacy of your tax return.** Many lenders demand access to your tax return as a condition for credit. This is done on IRS Form 4506.[510] The return can be subpoenaed in a lawsuit and become part of the permanent public record. In the event of a judgment, it can be subpoenaed to aid in the collection of a debt. Compounding the problem is the manner in which many lenders use Form 4506. Because loans are often originated by one bank or broker and then sold to other financial entities, lenders frequently direct applicants to leave some parts of the form—such as the recipient and the date—blank.

Depending on how much you're borrowing and your financial status, you may be able to negotiate with the lender on filing Form 4506. If you can afford a higher down payment, you may be able to avoid submitting copies of your tax returns. Another way to possibly to avoid filing Form 4506 is to show your tax return to the lender, but not permit it to be copied. If a permanent record is required (as it almost always is), you might permit W-2 or 1099 records to be copied, but nothing more. Or provide a copy of your Form 1040, but none of the accompanying schedules. If you must file Form 4506, don't leave the recipient and date fields blank.

Protect Your Rights in a Tax Audit

Your chances of being audited by the IRS are greater under the following circumstances:

- Your itemized deductions exceed pre-defined IRS limits;
- You claim tax shelter investment losses on your tax return or have been involved in "reportable transactions;"
- You own or work in a business which receives substantial income in cash and/or tips;
- Your business expenses are large in relation to your income;

- Your tax return shows significant rental expenses;
- You have been audited previously and assessed for a tax deficiency;
- Your tax return shows complex transactions that aren't adequately explained;
- You are a major shareholder or partner in a partnership or corporation that is being audited;
- You claim large contributions to charities in relation to your income on your tax return; or
- An informant has contacted the IRS and claimed that you're engaged in tax evasion or tax fraud.

Some of these risk factors can be reduced. For instance, filing Form 8275 with your return to document large deductions, business expenses or complex transactions may provide the IRS with all the information it requires—thus avoiding an audit. As for informants, I refer you back to the beginning of this chapter to the #1 strategy for wealth and privacy preservation: keep your mouth shut!

Not all audits are the same. Your actions in an audit should relate to the type of audit you face.

Correspondence or letter audits. The simplest audits are conducted by letter. They indicate that an IRS computer has found a discrepancy on your tax return or that you have failed to make a payment on time, or at all. Letter audits don't mean you're being investigated for fraud or criminal tax evasion. They're merely notification that an IRS computer believes you have made an error, which may be in your favor. Since the IRS admits that nearly 50% of such letters are sent in error, examine their claims carefully before paying up.

If you believe the IRS position is wrong, write to the address listed on the letter and carefully document your position, sending copies of receipts, check stubs, etc. Do not send the IRS originals, as they may get lost in the mail or at the IRS. Send all correspondence certified mail, return receipt requested. Insist that the IRS clarify any unclear calculations. Also, request an abatement of all penalties and interest. When you act in good faith based on reasonable cause, the penalty may be abated. Your letter contesting a penalty must establish this.

Office audits. The IRS may ask you to come to a nearby IRS office and document items on your return. You may be able to send copies of the requested documentation and resolve the issue without actually meeting with an IRS auditor. Ask the agency to clarify exactly what it's looking for. Provide information only on those specific items, and nothing more.

Field audits. This type of audit is usually restricted to businesses and is conducted at your office. Field auditors are highly trained professionals specializing in forensic accounting. They may try to persuade you to grant unrestricted access to your business and its financial records. A professional tax advisor can help you avoid this type of probing and attempt to have the audit conducted outside your business to avoid disrupting it.

Criminal Investigation Division (CID) audits are conducted to investigate criminal tax fraud and for tax violations that can be prosecuted under the money laundering laws. If CID agents contact you, don't volunteer any information. Contact a criminal tax attorney immediately.

Lifestyle audits. If the IRS believes you are not reporting all your income, it may conduct a "lifestyle" audit to estimate your annual spending. It then computes how much income you would need before taxes in order to have sufficient after-tax income to support that lifestyle. If the income you've reported is substantially less than your spending indicates, you may be assessed for back taxes, penalties, and interest, and may face criminal charges. Once the IRS demonstrates that you're living beyond your reported income, the burden of proof shifts. In effect, you must now prove yourself innocent. You'll need to construct an "audit trail" to connect your total income to your bank deposits, your tax return, and your personal balance sheet. If you receive non-taxable income from gifts, inheritances, or loans, you must document those as well.

National Research Program (NRP) audits. These are the most intrusive audits of all. If your return is chosen for a NRP audit, you may be required to document every item and every deduction you've claimed. In certain classes of NRP audits, the IRS may seek to obtain much of this documentation from third parties, but if it's unable to do so, you'll be expected to provide it. Each year, the IRS carries out approximately 50,000 NRP audits.

IRS Publication 1, *Your Rights as a Taxpayer*, summarizes the examination, appeals, and collections process the IRS uses in an audit. [511] IRS Publication 556, *Examination of Returns, Appeal Rights and Claims for Refund*, discusses this process in detail. [512]

Your rights include:

- **The right to request a correspondence audit.** Correspondence audits force the IRS to make its demands in writing. They create an irrefutable record of what transpired. (Again, make certain to send all correspondence to the IRS by certified mail, return receipt requested.)
- **If the IRS refuses to accept a correspondence audit, you have the right to have the audit conducted at a convenient location.** The IRS shouldn't demand that you travel a long distance to be audited. However, I don't recommend that you invite the IRS into your home or office. A better location might be the office of your accountant or tax attorney.
- **The right to request a postponement of the audit to assemble your records.** The audit notice will generally provide at least two or three weeks notice. If this isn't sufficient time to prepare, ask for a temporary postponement. Rescheduling an audit also increases your odds of prevailing. The longer a case is open, the greater the pressure on the auditor to close it. Another idea: schedule the audit near the end of the month or on a Friday before a three-day weekend so that the auditor is against a deadline to complete it.
- **The right to request that the IRS isolate specific matters for the audit to address.** Frame your request in terms of the records the IRS wishes to examine. Ask what specific years and what specific items the agency wants justified. A request to bring "all your financial records" is an unreasonable demand and may be narrowed to specific years and/or items.
- **The right to be accompanied by an accountant or an attorney.** Most people represent themselves at an audit. For larger or more complex claims, ask your accountant or tax attorney to accompany you or even go in your place. Professional representation highly recommended where substantial monies are at stake. A tax attorney's service will likely be more expensive than those of an accountant, but the scope of "privileged communications" an attorney may legally refuse to divulge to the IRS is greater than an accountant's.[513]
- **The right to record the audit proceedings.** A tape recorder will put auditors on their best behavior! Professional videotaping is even better. The IRS requires that you notify it 10 days in advance of an audit if you intend to record the proceedings. Generally, it will want its own permanent record.
- **The right to bring witnesses.** A witness lessens the likelihood that an auditor might try to intimidate you.
- **The right to refuse to respond to an expanded inquiry.** This is where your insistence that the scope of the audit be narrowed can be beneficial. If you were told that the audit was to verify deductions for one year, but the auditor asks you to justify deductions for another year, you need not respond to this inquiry until you have time to gather your records.
- **The right not to extend the statute of limitations.** The general statute of limitations for a civil tax audit is three years from the due date or filing date of the return, whichever is later. Three

years after the filing date, the IRS must accept that return, unless you sign a waiver. Never sign such a waiver unless your tax advisor recommends that you do so. For significant under-reporting of income (25% or more), the statute of limitations is six years. There is also a six-year statute of limitations for tax-related crimes.

- **The right to break off the audit.** If an audit is going badly, you're confused by a question, need to obtain more information to support your position, or are merely afraid of revealing more information than you believe is prudent, you may request that it be halted. You may reschedule the audit and arrange for your tax advisor to represent you once it resumes.

- **The right to appeal.** If you disagree with an IRS auditor's position, you have the right to ask for a second opinion from a supervisor. If you still don't agree with the results, you can contact the IRS Appeals Office.

- **The right to request abatement of all penalties.** "Reasonable causes" for which penalties may be abated include ignorance of the law where difficult and complex issues are involved and there is no IRS guidance with respect to the issue; erroneous advice provided by a competent tax advisor; erroneous written advice from the IRS; and/or a bounced check due to an error by the IRS or a bank.

Negotiating and Litigating With the IRS

The IRS isn't omnipotent. Its employees have heavy workloads and its computer systems are themselves "overtaxed," despite multi-billion dollar investments. You can use these facts to your advantage in an audit.

IRS employees are under pressure to close cases. They're unlikely to force you to produce information you don't want to disclose, unless they believe that doing so will reveal substantial additional tax liabilities. This is because doing so will slow the case down.

For this reason, you can negotiate most IRS information requests. In the majority of cases, the worst that will happen if you refuse or are unable to provide documentation is any deduction relating to such documentation will be disallowed.

To save time, the IRS will often ask you to bring tax returns filed for the years before and after the year being examined. However, you're under no obligation to do so. Nor should you, since it gives the auditor many items to review that would otherwise not be available. You're required to provide only the information relating to the specific tax year listed in the audit notice. And the auditor may find it time consuming to obtain the returns from the IRS itself.

Generally, after an audit is complete, the auditor will tell you what he or she believes you owe the IRS. But this calculation isn't binding. A supervisor has the authority to overrule that determination. If your examination takes place in an IRS office, you can request an immediate meeting with the examiner's supervisor to explain your position. Except in **jeopardy assessments**, where the IRS believes that you're likely to begin dispersing your assets to avoid collection, the IRS can't begin seizing property at this stage.

If you and the supervisor can't come to an agreement in this manner, the examiner will write up your case explaining your position and the IRS position and forward the case for further processing.

At this stage, if you haven't already brought in a professional advisor to represent you before the IRS, you should consider doing so. You'll also need to make a decision whether to use the IRS **fast track mediation** service. Most cases that are not already before a court qualify for this process, which occurs at a conference with an appeals officer. You may represent yourself at the mediation session, or someone else can act as your representative.

You're under no legal obligation to agree to the settlement offer provided in fast track mediation, although you may wish to do so if it represents a substantial reduction from the original IRS demands. If you don't come to an agreement, within a few weeks, you'll receive a package with a letter (known as a **30-day letter**) notifying you of the amount the IRS has calculated that you owe and a copy of the examination report explaining the calculations. You generally have 30 days from the date of this letter to tell the IRS whether you accept the proposed changes. If you don't respond to the 30-day letter, or if you later don't reach an agreement with an appeals officer, the IRS will send you a 90-day letter, also known as a **notice of deficiency**.

You have 90 days (150 days if it is addressed to you outside the United States) to pay the assessment, or take the agency to court. There are two litigation options, either one of which may require you to retain a tax attorney:

1. **Tax Court.** If you can't pay the IRS assessment, you may petition the U.S. Tax Court for relief. Virtually every judge in the Tax Court is a former IRS tax attorney or Justice Department prosecutor. Even so, while more than 90% of cases are decided in favor of the IRS, it's often awarded a much smaller percentage of the dollar amount of alleged tax deficiencies.

2. **District Court.** To contest the assessment in a U.S. district court, you must pay it in full and sue to recover the money. In district court, the IRS gets about 85% of the dollars in litigation. For this reason, in the last 20 years, the popularity of the Tax Court to litigate tax disputes has mushroomed.

In any litigation with the IRS, you should obtain your **Individual Master File**, or IMF. An IMF exists on every U.S. taxpayer. It contains coded records of IRS assessments, correspondence, and a great deal of other valuable information, including the basis of any IRS assessment. You'll also want the corresponding document for businesses, the **BMF**, from the IRS well in advance of any litigation.

If the IRS won't release this information voluntarily, make a Freedom of Information Act (FOIA) inquiry to obtain your IMF. Make certain that you obtain Document 6209, which contains the codes you need to interpret the information on your IMF.[514] To learn more about filing FOIA requests with the IRS, see http://www.irs.gov/foia/index.html.

Many taxpayers request their IMF annually, or even more often. Some people avoid doing so because they believe that will make them a more likely target for audit. I'm unaware of any evidence suggesting this is the case. Since the IMF telegraphs future IRS audits, if you're going to be audited, the IMF will give you more time to prepare.

In some cases, income taxes can be discharged through bankruptcy. In general, taxes that were first due more than three years before the bankruptcy is filed, and for which a timely and non-fraudulent return was filed, can be discharged in full. However, the 2005 bankruptcy reform legislation (Chapter 4) makes it more difficult to discharge any type of debt in bankruptcy, including tax debts.

Keep Your Bank Records Private

Under federal "know your customer" rules (Chapter 2), banks are required to investigate account applicants to verify their identity, source of income, residential address, etc. Account application forms thus request information such as your occupation, your income, and the length of time at your job.

There's no legal obligation to answer the questions, but if you refuse to do so, the bank may not accept you as a depositor. Submitting false information on such forms is considered bank fraud: a criminal offense that can result in fines, imprisonment, and forfeiture of any funds relating to the crime—potentially, your entire account balance or the proceeds of any loans gained through the completion of such forms.

A growing trend requires bank customers to pose for photos or even provide fingerprints before opening checking accounts. Banks place your photo and/or fingerprint on each check as an anti-theft measure. Your bank probably won't mention that your image becomes its property, and may be sold to direct marketing companies, conveyed to law enforcement agencies, etc. Credit card companies have similar programs in place.

No SSN Required to Open Bank Account

There's no legal requirement that you provide your Social Security number when you open a bank account. While U.S. banks, brokers, credit unions, etc.—must **request** your SSN when you open an account, you're not required to disclose it. If you won't disclose your SSN, or don't have one, the bank has to maintain your name on a list that it must make available, on request, to the IRS.[515]

Because of the threat of identity theft, if you can open a bank account without disclosing your SSN, you should do so. However, most financial institutions won't open an account without it. There are exceptions, particularly in regions with large numbers of illegal immigrants. Many of these immigrants lack SSNs. For instance, Bank of America no longer requires a SSN to open an account in many of its branches in southern California.[516]

It's easiest to open a non-interest bearing account without a SSN. That's because banks are required to send the IRS a Form 1099 each year, reporting the interest your account earned during the year. Strictly speaking, the bank isn't required to list your SSN on Form 1099.[517] However, if you don't provide it, when the bank transmits Form 1099 to the IRS, it must prepare an affidavit attesting that the SSN was requested, but not provided. The bank must also withhold 31% of any income the account generates. Understandably, most banks don't want to deal with the time, expense, and potential liabilities involved in preparing such an affidavit and withholding the tax due.

If you open an account without a SSN, use it only for small accounts—certainly under US$5,000—to avoid the bank believing it has a legal duty to file a "Suspicious Activity Report" (SAR) documenting your refusal to provide a SSN.

10 Tips to Privatize and Secure Your Bank Records

To lower the profile of your bank account, and protect yourself from fraud, consider the following lifeboat strategies.

1. **Write personal checks only for ordinary, everyday expenses**. Don't write a personal check for any purchase that you'd rather keep private. Pay for such purchases with currency or a money order.

2. **Carry a minimal account balance.** Larger accounts merit investigation more often than smaller ones.

3. **Beware of suspicious transactions in your bank account.** Avoid the types of transactions listed in Chapter 2 as suspicious.

4. **Don't release more information than is required when you write a check.** If a merchant wants to record your driver's license number, ask him to write it in on a separate sheet of paper, not on the check itself. All major credit card companies now prohibit the once-common practice of requiring a credit card number to cash a check.

5. **Keep copies of your original cancelled checks.** This is more difficult than it once was, because banks are moving to a system of "paperless checking" where your original checks are destroyed. This practice eliminates forensic evidence such as fingerprints and handwriting, and makes it much more difficult to prove wrongdoing if someone forges a check from your account. A poor substitute to receiving the original cancelled checks back is to obtain copies of the checks, although you may pay as much as US$5 for each copy.

6. **Never have your home address or SSN imprinted on your checks.** This is an invitation to identity theft.

7. **Use an out-of-state bank.** This makes it harder for in-state creditors to attach your account. The out-of-state bank may ask you why you're not using a bank in your own state. A satisfactory answer may be that you're doing business in that state or will soon be moving there, and that you need a local account for that purpose.

8. **Keep your money in a strong bank.** A bank failure could lead to your account being frozen and any outstanding checks bouncing. In that event, you or your business might have to declare bankruptcy. Funds may be released for emergency use, but only on a case-by-case basis. Depositors in failed banks don't automatically get their money back from the Federal Deposit Insurance Commission (FDIC). Only deposits smaller than US$100,000 are covered. In addition, the FDIC must check IRS records to make certain depositors don't owe the government money, which is deducted from the refund. **Veribanc** is a financial safety rating service for U.S. banks. **WATS:** (800) 442-2657. **Link:** http://www.veribanc.com.

9. **Consider Internet banking.** Dozens of Internet banks such as **Everbank** (http://www.everbank.com) now exist. Since you open the account online or by mail, there's no need to meet a banker face-to-face, although e-banks must abide by the same anti-laundering requirements as regular banks. When banking online, be sure to apply the computer security safeguards summarized earlier in this chapter.

10. **Borrow money privately.** When you borrow money through a bank, you'll be asked for the purpose of the loan and generally required to complete a financial statement. Any substantial misstatement of facts on this document may be considered bank fraud. If you'd rather not disclose this much information, there are alternatives. An overdraft checking account is the simplest one. Just write a check payable to cash and redeem it at the teller window. A currency advance on a credit card is another alternative as is a home-equity loan. There's also the neighborhood pawnbroker: while interest rates may be exorbitant, to redeem your property, all that you need is the pawn ticket, along with currency to repay the loan.

The E-Money Alternative

Some futurists have predicted that privately issued e-currencies traded online will eventually replace government-issued currencies, making bank accounts, and banks themselves, largely obsolete.

163

In theory, e-currencies have much to offer. The biggest advantage is that consumers can choose to hold or do business in e-currencies that are backed by tangible assets rather than fiat money issued by a central bank. E-currencies can also enhance privacy. Residing on your hard drive, an Internet server, or a stored value card, e-currencies let you directly transfer value to someone else, without using a bank as an intermediary. This system architecture also lowers transaction costs.

The big disadvantage is the potential for fraud. E-currency systems provide security through encryption. If someone steals (or compels you to reveal) your private key (and in some systems a passphrase as well) and uses it to withdraw funds, the transaction will appear legitimate and you're liable for the loss. Your only recourse is to sue the company that defrauded you, if it hasn't disappeared into cyberspace.

In contrast, credit cards limit your liability for unauthorized activity to US$50. You can also "charge back" payments to merchants who fail to deliver the products or services you purchased. This isn't always possible in debit systems like e-currencies.

Another reason e-currencies haven't caught on is their potential for money laundering.[518] While most e-currency providers apply the same basic "know your customer" rules that apply to banks, the potential for stored value transactions to occur outside the banking system and thus outside the network of financial surveillance is of great concern to the FATF. In 2007, the Department of Justice indicted the operators of E-Gold (http://www.e-gold.com) on charges of money laundering, conspiracy, and operating an unlicensed money transmission business. E-gold may have been targeted because it permits the essentially anonymous transfer of money outside the banking system.[519]

A less private, but also less controversial e-currency system is **GoldMoney** (http://www.goldmoney.com). You can't open an anonymous account with GoldMoney, but the service has escaped the ire of law enforcement officials. You must provide the same basic identity documents to GoldMoney as you would to open a bank account. Your holdings are audited annually and 100%-backed by physical gold.

The Underground Banking System

Digital currencies promise a future where individuals can transfer value between one another without using a bank or other government-regulated institution as an intermediary. And one where the currency used can't be manipulated or debased by any government.

This development is of profound concern to world governments. Their most important concern, as always, is tax collection. Monitoring such transactions, much less collecting taxes on them, is difficult, if not impossible. This is one of the main reasons why governments want to end Internet anonymity and force Internet service providers worldwide to maintain customer logs, as discussed in Chapters 2.

But governments face an even larger threat—the fusion of these new forms of "digital money" with a much older worldwide network through which billions of dollars is transferred each year, outside the banking system. This is the world of *fei-ch'ien*—Chinese for "flying money."

Fei-ch'ien predates western banking by centuries. More than 1,200 years ago, growing trade between south China and the imperial capital created a need for a medium of exchange to avoid physically transporting copper, silk or other valuables. Similar requirements underscored the development of analogous exchange systems in India (**Hawala**) and Pakistan (**Hundi**).

Centuries later, flying money moves hundreds of billions of dollars each year, almost invisibly. It remains ethnically based: Chinese and other Asian communities are among its biggest users. It is particularly useful to individuals who don't have a bank account, but need to transfer funds internationally. According to Temple University Professor Nikos Passos, "it is an efficient, speedy and cheap way of moving money, often for very legitimate purposes."[520]

Here's a simple example: Hasan, a Pakistani laborer in Dubai, wants to send money to his wife Huriya in Karachi. Hasan can't afford a bank account, so he uses a *Hawalador* named Abbas to transfer the money. Abbas has a partner, Absalom, in Karachi. Hasan gives the money to Abbas and Abbas then sends an encrypted e-mail message to Absalom instructing him to deliver the funds, less a small fee, to Huriya. The transaction is completed in only a few minutes, in most cases at a much lower cost than if conducted through a bank.

Today, flying money brokers, often doing business as currency exchangers, can be found throughout the world. But the world's tax collectors are no longer sponsors. Despite its legitimate uses, both law enforcement agencies and independent researchers consider flying money a major source of tax evasion, currency exchange violations and money laundering—and have vowed to shut it down.[521] However, doing so presents a major challenge. According to police inspectors in Hong Kong:

The record keeping procedures of the underground banking system are nearly non-existent, with coded messages, chits, and simple telephone calls used to transfer money from one country to another. One Hong Kong police official stated that he once seized a piece of paper with the picture of an elephant on it that represented the collection receipt for US$3 million at a Hong Kong gold shop. The system, nonetheless, has the ability to transfer funds from one country to another in hours, provide complete anonymity, total security, convert gold or other items into currency and convert currencies.[522]

A report from the Financial Action Task Force, an anti-laundering consortium you'll learn more about in Chapter 6, acknowledges that this money transfer system "costs less than moving money through the banking system, operates 24 hours per day and is virtually completely reliable."[523] It also admits that in India, "up to 50% of the economy uses the *Hawala* system."

In response to the explosive growth of flying money networks worldwide, governments have tried to regulate it. U.S. law requires that "money transmitting services" be registered with the U.S. Treasury, or in the state in which they operate, and maintain detailed customer logs. Other countries, notably Dubai, home to one of the world's largest network of *Hawaladors*, have taken similar initiatives. Yet, this oldest form of monetary exchange remains alive and well.

Private Investments

Over the last 35 years, Congress has progressively restricted the ability for U.S. persons to invest privately. Laws like the Bank Secrecy Act, the Money Laundering Control Act, and the USA PATRIOT Act require banks and other financial institutions to report to adhere to stringent know-your-customer requirements, report to the IRS many types of income or gain, and monitor all customer activity for suspicious transactions.

This section outlines U.S. investments you can still make in relative privacy. As you'll learn in the section of this chapter dealing with international investments, there are many more options when you're dealing offshore.

Buy and Sell Precious Metals Privately

Under U.S. law, customer purchases of gold, silver, platinum or palladium need not be reported to any governmental authority. Dealers must report customer sales that equal or exceed minimum Commodity Futures Trading Commission certified contract sizes to the IRS on Form 1099-B:

- **Gold bars.** 1 kilogram (32.15 troy oz.), .995 fine or higher.
- **Silver bars.** 1,000 oz., .999 fine or higher.
- **Platinum bars.** 25 troy oz., .9995 fine or higher.
- **Palladium bars.** 100 troy oz., .9995 fine or higher.
- **1-oz. gold coins.** Maple leafs, Krugerrands and Mexican Onzas (but not U.S. Eagles). 25 coins.
- **Pre-1965 silver U.S. dimes, quarters, and half dollars.** US$1,000 face value (full bag). The bag need not be of a single denomination, i.e., a half bag of dimes and a half bag of quarters, transacted in a single transaction (or related transactions) would count as a single bag for reporting purposes.[524]

A dealer must notify the IRS if a customer appears to be deliberately structuring multiple sales under the reporting thresholds to avoid broker reporting. Multiple sales by a customer within a 24-hour period count as a single sale for reporting purposes. However, the reporting regulations apply only to individuals, or a business that is not a corporation, e.g., a sole proprietorship or partnership (including a limited liability partnership). If you sell your precious metals through a corporation, no reporting requirements apply.

Many precious metals dealers are subject to the anti-money-laundering provisions of the USA PATRIOT Act. Any company that buys and sells US$50,000 or more of "covered goods" from the public must have a written anti-money-laundering plan in effect and appoint an individual to monitor compliance with this policy. In this case, "covered goods" are precious metals items that derive 50% or more of their value from the precious metal content. Dealers aren't required to prepare Suspicious Activity Reports, although like all U.S. businesses, they must report currency transactions that exceed US$10,000 to the IRS.

You can buy and sell precious metals without triggering broker or currency reporting requirements by dealing with a fellow investor, either at a coin show or in a classified ad in publications such as *Coin World* or *Numismatic News*, which are available at any U.S. newsstand.

Collectibles: Low Profile Investments

Collectibles such as art, diamonds, antiques, stamps, and rare coins are more private than precious metals. No broker reporting requirements apply to either purchases or sales of collectibles. No reports must be sent to the IRS when you purchase or sell them, except for transactions that involve over US$10,000 in currency. While collectibles are sometimes difficult to sell and often subject to high dealer buy/sell spreads, they are usually not purchased purely as investments.

Collectibles are also valuable as private investments because they don't generate current income. No annual reports regarding interest or dividends are generated.

1. Numismatic coins. Rare or numismatic coins are among the most liquid collectible investments and subject to the smallest dealer mark-ups. However, prices are volatile. Many investors favor rare gold coins because they represent a form of tangible money directly backed by gold. For larger gold coins that have experienced significant wear on the surfaces, and thus are of lower value than like new or uncirculated coins, a significant percentage of the value of the coin comes from the value of the gold they contain.

Some investors purchase numismatic coins instead of gold because they believe that they believe in the event of a future confiscation of precious metals by the federal government, numismatic coins will be exempt. This belief is based on the terms of the emergency order President Franklin D. Roosevelt issued in 1933 that forced owners of privately owned gold to sell their holdings to the government. The directive specifically exempted "gold coins having recognized special value to collectors of rare and unusual coins."[525]

Should such an exemption again come into existence, which numismatic coins would be exempted? The 1985 legislation that authorized production of the coins now known as gold and silver Eagles stipulates that these coins are to be considered "numismatic items."[526] If you believe that numismatic coins would be exempt from a future gold (or silver) confiscation, you should consider purchasing the only coins specifically defined in U.S. law as "numismatic."[527]

I believe that fears of a future forced sale or confiscation of precious metals are overblown. President Roosevelt's 1933 emergency order was issued when the U.S. dollar was still backed by gold and both individual citizens and foreign central banks could exchange U.S. dollars for gold. Today, no holder of U.S. dollars is legally entitled to exchange their dollars for gold at the U.S. Treasury. Indeed, only a small minority of U.S. citizens own precious metals in any form. However, given the Treasury Department's assertion that it can confiscate any property under the Trading With the Enemy Act (Chapter 2), precious metals are hardly immune to government seizure.

From a privacy standpoint, uncertified coins (not pre-graded in plastic "slabs") are preferable, because they don't have a unique serial number assigned to them, as do "slabbed" coins. However, if you're new to coin collecting, and purchase coins with a market value significantly higher than the value of the bullion they contain, you'll probably want certified coins to guard against overgrading—although some certified coins are overgraded. The **Professional Coin Grading Service** (http://www.pcgs.com) and the **Numismatic Guaranty Corporation** (http://www.ngccoin.com) are the most widely accepted certification services.

The safest strategy to avoid overgrading is avoid purchasing uncertified coins graded MS-60 or higher, unless you're a grading expert. Coins of this quality are the most expensive and the ones where overgrading can inflate apparent value the most. On the other hand, in a bull market for numismatic coins, prices for coins graded MS-60 and higher (and especially MS-65 and higher) tend to rise the fastest.

The most private way to buy and sell rare coins or other collectibles is at a coin show or local coin shop. Pay with currency and don't leave your name. Buying and selling inexpensive coins in transactions under US$1,000 rarely poses a problem. However, coin and precious metals dealers are prime targets in the government's continuing crackdown on tax evasion and money laundering.

Diamonds. Diamonds are the world's most concentrated form of wealth. You can privately carry hundreds of thousands of dollars of value in a small envelope. Diamonds can also be transported quietly and legally and sold globally in most major cities.

Like rare coins, diamond prices fluctuate dramatically. And historically, the highest quality diamonds have performed the best. But unlike numismatic coins, there is little demand for lower grade diamonds from collectors. The key to successful investing in diamonds, as in any collectible, is grading. All diamonds should be purchased with an accompanying Gemological Institute of America (GIA) grading report or GIA origin of color report. An acceptable alternative is a grading certificate from the International Gemological Institute (IGI).

One buying strategy involves investing in colored diamonds, which are much rarer than white diamonds. However, high quality, artificially colored diamonds are now being produced.[528] While it's possible for experts to distinguish artificially colored diamonds from naturally colored ones, this may not always be the case, and could lead to declining values.

CHAPTER FOUR: PRESERVE WEALTH AND PROPERTY

Thus far, the focus of this book has been on maintaining privacy, both personal and financial. If you and your wealth don't show up in an investigator's database, you're not likely to become a target of a lawsuit or investigation.

However, this strategy won't always be successful. And for that reason, you should be aware of laws and techniques that can be used to protect and preserve wealth and property. This section presents a number of ideas to protect your wealth from lawsuits and other threats to your wealth.

No matter what strategies you employ to preserve your wealth, they should pass what I call the "debtor's exam" standard. A debtor's exam is a legal proceeding where, having lost a lawsuit, you're placed under oath and required to answer questions about the location of your assets. Failure to answer truthfully can result in perjury charges. If the creditor is the IRS or other government agency, more serious charges may be brought, such as obstruction of justice, fraud and (if affirmative steps have been taken to "hide money"), even money laundering.

The debtor's exam standard means that you must be prepared to answer questions about your asset protection plan truthfully, under oath, if circumstances ever make it necessary to do so. And, for reasons examined in this chapter, if the only reason you took a particular step or series of steps was to "hinder, delay or defraud" a creditor, those transactions can be legally unwound and you'll be obligated to pay off the judgment—and potentially, face incarceration if you can't.

Asset protection is serious business. Don't approach it lightly.

Whatever You Do, Don't Say "Asset Protection"

"Asset protection" has a negative connotation in the U.S. legal system. To many judges, anyone who makes their assets unavailable to meet the claims of a creditor is simply a deadbeat. To force "deadbeats" to pay their bills, judges have many legal tools available, including jailing a debtor for contempt of court. This last "remedy" isn't common, but there are several cases where it has been employed, most notably, in situations where a debtor or the debtor's legal advisors have made serious planning errors.

Fortunately, it's not necessary to go to jail to protect your assets. But, your plan must not be intended to "hinder, delay or defraud" creditors. If it is, any transfer of assets that makes your property more difficult to seize may be a voidable "fraudulent conveyance." It's best to make this determination after consultation with an experienced attorney.

If not asset protection, what should be the purpose of your plan? Let's say you want to form a business entity to operate a small business. You want the fewest hassles, both operationally and tax-wise, as possible. The solution, as I describe later in this chapter, is in many cases an entity called a limited liability company (LLC). LLCs have fewer "formalities" associated with them than the traditional choice for business ownership, a corporation. And, when properly formed and operated, they provide outstanding asset protection.

U.S. courts respect asset protection if it's done with "clean hands" and in conjunction with other legitimate purposes.

Use an Attorney to Oversee Your Asset Protection Plan

An attorney-client relationship is an important tool in preserving privacy and wealth.

You may not need an attorney if your estate and investments are relatively small. "Small" is a relative term and the amount of money you can protect on your own and will vary depending on where you live. Certainly, if your estate will be subject to inheritance taxes, you should involve an attorney in your planning, since the tax rules are exceedingly complex. (The individual estate tax exemption is US$2 million for 2007, increasing to US$3.5 million by 2009.)

If you operate your own business, you should use an attorney to help you avoid the many potential pitfalls. This is particularly true if others in your line of business tend to get sued, or if you hire employees.

The downside of using an attorney is that at least one additional person will know about your circumstances and plans. Attorneys require substantial disclosures from clients engaged in asset protection and estate planning. Otherwise, the attorney may be considered negligent and subject to civil and criminal penalties.

Attorneys must also be licensed. The licensing standards and practices may keep ethical standards higher than they would be otherwise, but these requirements also mean that the license can be withdrawn.

Finally, attorneys are "officers of the court." If you tell your attorney you're planning to commit a crime, the attorney must notify police. And attorneys are obligated to inform the IRS if their clients pay them more than US$10,000 in cash, although U.S. law doesn't require attorneys to report suspicious transactions.

Attorney-Client Privilege: Keep Your Planning Private

You as the client of an attorney generally have the right to refuse to disclose and to prevent others from disclosing all "confidential communications" between you and your attorney. This is known as the **attorney-client privilege**.

Attorney-client privilege exists to encourage you to make complete disclosure to your attorney without fear that the attorney will inform others. You as the client generally "hold" the privilege; the attorney may not to violate it without your consent or if so ordered by a court. You're in the strongest position to assert attorney-client privilege if you retain an attorney **before** discussing confidential matters. However, preliminary discussions with an attorney for the purposes of obtaining advice and representation are generally privileged, even if no attorney-client relationship results from that conversation.[529]

When you first approach an attorney, you should inform the attorney that you're considering legal representation in his or her professional capacity. All discussions, including those prior to your signing an engagement letter, should then be subject to attorney-client privilege. All attorneys should willingly agree to this condition, since maintaining the privilege is their ethical duty.

If your attorney delegates responsibilities to others, the privilege usually extends to these people. This delegation must generally occur within the scope of a written agreement to be enforceable.[530] The attorney's secretary and the non-attorney associates in the firm will ordinarily be included, as will individuals outside the firm working under the attorney's direction. In addition, individuals working under your direction who communicate with your attorney have those interactions protected by attorney-client privilege.[531]

In contrast, the privilege doesn't extend to work the attorney does at the direction of another person; i.e., an accountant. In addition, if an attorney is not acting in that legal capacity, but, e.g., to prepare tax returns, attorney-client privilege generally doesn't apply.[532]

You may inadvertently waive attorney-client privilege if you disclose information your attorney conveyed to you in confidence, or that you conveyed to your attorney.[533] The privilege is also waived if someone who isn't a client, employer or under contract to the attorney participates in a conversation between you and your attorney.[534]

An important requirement for attorney-client privilege to exist is that the communication was intended to be confidential.[535] Written communications to and from your attorney should always contain a statement stipulating that they are confidential and subject to attorney-client privilege.

Documents and other written materials produced for you by your attorney ("work product") are also privileged, if prepared "in anticipation of litigation."[536] So are the attorney's notes and working documents.[537] However, routine communications—notices of appointments, bills, payment records and other writings not directly related to the issue in which the attorney is representing you may not be privileged.[538]

If you have documents in your possession that your attorney needs to represent you effectively, make sure they're eventually returned. Such documents, unless prepared specifically for the purpose of communicating information to your attorney, aren't covered by attorney-client privilege.[539]

Important limitations on attorney-client privilege exist in the context of tax planning, if that planning involves anything construed by the IRS as a tax shelter. This is particularly true to a communication that relates to an "abusive tax shelter" that creates "the potential of criminal as well as civil liability on the taxpayer's part."[540]

Don't assume discussions with an attorney someone else is paying for are protected. If you're an employee in a corporation that becomes subject to a criminal investigation, the government may demand that the company waive attorney-client privilege with respect to its employees. It may also insist that the company pay for the legal representation of employees only if those employees cooperate with government investigators and waive their right to self-incrimination.[541] Moreover, if you agree to cooperate with in-house attorneys, and fail to tell them the truth, you may be subject to criminal prosecution.[542] The safest course is to hire your own attorney.

Attorneys, particularly those representing criminal defendants, may themselves become subject to criminal prosecution. Two former federal prosecutors advise attorneys that they may face "criminal liability [even] on the provision of routine legal services." In defending themselves in criminal cases, attorneys often may reveal information conveyed in confidence by their clients.[543]

Prosecutors have obtained criminal convictions against attorneys for:

- Efforts to facilitate financial transactions without filing required disclosure reports—both domestically[544] and internationally;[545]
- Providing erroneous advice regarding compliance and reporting requirements;[546]
- Advising clients on protecting assets prior to or during bankruptcy proceedings;[547] and
- Advising clients on how to comply with laws the client has violated without disclosing to the government the existence of such violations.[548]

To receive immunity from criminal prosecution and/or to obtain lucrative commissions, attorneys may become informants against their clients or other attorneys. The U.S. Department of Justice has "publicly defended using attorneys as informants as a 'perfectly valid' law enforcement tool."[549]

In light of these concerted attacks on attorney-client privilege, disclose only those facts to your attorney that are needed to assist you professionally. Don't try to strike up a friendship with your attorney. And, unless you're hiring a criminal defense attorney, don't say anything that would make an attorney believe that you're engaged in illegal activity.

Carefully review your attorney's engagement letter. It will be drafted to protect the attorney's interests, not yours. Look particularly for provisions that allow the attorney to sever the relationship with you or to testify against you. If necessary, ask a second attorney to review the contract.

How to Select and Use an Attorney

One of the most useful services attorneys provide is to prepare opinion letters putting their "blessing" on your legal planning. According to the U.S. Supreme Court, if in good faith you follow the written advice of an expert, you insulate yourself from future criminal or fraud charges that might otherwise be brought against you.[550] Still, you may be subject to civil sanctions. But, since attorneys are officers of the court, they write such letters at the risk of (potentially) being subject to civil and criminal sanctions or even losing their license.

Under U.S. law, for professional advisors to avoid possible criminal or fraud charges for their recommendations, they must demonstrate that there is "authoritative support" for their position. In reference to tax planning, attorneys must comply with detailed and in some cases ambiguous rules issued by the IRS. Circular 230, discussed in Chapter 2, substantially increases the penalties to which tax advisors may be subject if they violate these rules.

If you retain your attorney to prepare a written opinion, your engagement letter should stipulate that release of the letter doesn't waive the privilege in reference to other communication. Any other information you disclose in relation to your plan should be accompanied with such a statement.

Start Your Own Business and Take Back Your Privacy

Self-employment is one of the best ways to reclaim some personal and financial privacy. Self-employment is by its nature more private than working for an employer. You're responsible only to yourself. No background investigation is necessary in order to enter most types of business. If your business prospers, you reap the rewards of an owner, not an employee.

Of course, you'll still have to pay taxes on your income. Working for yourself also raises the likelihood of a tax audit, since the IRS believes that self-employed individuals do much of their business "off the books." You'll want to take the steps to audit-proof your tax return outlined in Chapter 3, along with following the recommendations in this section.

What type of business should you form? It should involve work you enjoy doing, that you're good at and that you're convinced can supplement (or replace) your existing income.

From a privacy standpoint, it's hard to beat the mail order business. You can operate it out of your home and conduct all transactions from your personal computer. You don't need to meet your customers face-to-face, and you can sell almost anything. A modern variation of the mail order business is to create a Web site that allows browsers to order your goods or services over the Internet.

While the classic dream of the entrepreneur is to turn a small company into another Ford Motor Co. or Apple Computer, there are advantages in staying small, even if your business becomes a roaring success. Small businesses maintain a much lower profile than large ones. In this age of frivolous litigation and constantly expanding government, staying small helps avoid the limelight.

As long as you don't hire employees, allow public access to your business, pollute the environment, or defraud your customers, your interactions with the government will be limited. Of course, you can't avoid interaction with the government altogether. For instance, many local governments will require purchase of a license if you're self-employed. There may be an exemption if you work out of your home or don't deal with the public. The license will cost you anywhere from US$10 to hundreds of dollars for every community in which your business operates. Most must be renewed annually.

Avoid purchasing a business license unless it's illegal not to do so. Businesses are one of the first sources of revenue that bureaucrats turn to when they need income, via business and occupation taxes. A license also makes you vulnerable to surprise inspections by bureaucrats administering programs ranging from zoning laws to building codes. If withdrawn, you may no longer be able to operate your business. Finally, a license is a public record and will be recorded in a variety of databases available to anyone with an Internet connection.

Using a fictitious name has its advantages from a privacy standpoint. For instance, you can have correspondence you'd rather keep private sent to "ABC Enterprises" rather than "John Smith." However, using a fictitious name will require that you register it with government authorities by filing a **fictitious name statement**, negating part of this advantage. In most counties, this information is published in local newspapers and is thus a matter of public record.

Dealings with the federal government usually aren't a major ordeal as long as you don't hire employees. You must file quarterly reports and tax payments with the IRS. Fortunately, this is the only federal agency with which most one-person businesses must deal.

Use Independent Contractors

If your self-employment venture is successful, you may find that you can't handle all the work yourself. Instead of hiring employees, turn first to members of your family for help. Keeping a business in the family lowers your profile and the risk of employee lawsuits, theft, etc. In addition, there may be significant tax advantages to such an arrangement.

If your business grows beyond the ability of you and your family to run, consider temporary help. This is particularly appropriate if you need the extra help only on a seasonal basis. Unskilled workers can often be hired out at minimum wage from local labor pools. Skilled workers can be found through temporary help agencies such as "Manpower," etc.

Using independent contractors rather than employees provides several significant benefits:

- **Unlike employees, independent contractors are business associates.** Absent a contractual obligation, you can end a business relationship any time at your sole discretion, without due process or right of appeal.
- **There is no need to withhold payroll taxes or union dues.** This is the responsibility of the independent contractor.
- **Any fringe benefits paid to employees—health insurance premiums, participation in a retirement plan, etc.—need not be extended to an independent contractor.**
- **Since you don't directly supervise independent contractors, they're generally accountable for their own actions.** Unlike employees, if the contractor commits an act that causes harm, even while performing work on your behalf, you're less likely to be held accountable than if an employee committed the act.

Unfortunately, the IRS considers independent contractors to be a threat to the tax withholding system (Chapter 2). Unless those working for you meet the following criteria, they are not considered independent contractors, but employees:

- They must have a regular place of business outside your office;
- They must work on their own time;
- In general, they must bill by the job, not by the hour, week or month; and
- They must not be working under your direct supervision or the supervision of another employee.

For more information on what factors the IRS considers in determining if a person is an independent contractor or employee, see http://www.irs.gov/businesses/small/article/0,,id=99921,00.html.

If you pay an independent contractor more than US$600 in any one year, you must file a Form 1099 with the IRS. You will need the independent contractor's Social Security or taxpayer ID number to do so.

Hire Employees as a Last Resort

Don't become an employer except as a last resort. Employers must comply with many federal, state, and local laws, regulations, and ordinances that don't apply to other businesses. If you fire an employee, you may have to pay unemployment benefits or even face a lawsuit for "wrongful discharge" or discrimination. Employers must also make payroll deductions to the IRS, and to state and possibly local tax authorities.

Under federal law, your business is criminally responsible for the actions of its employees taken within the scope of their employment. It makes no difference whether the employees' conduct violates official policy or contravenes explicit instructions.[551] It also makes no difference whether or not the business is organized as a corporation, since a corporation is a "legal person" with many of the rights—and responsibilities—of an individual. This includes being subject to criminal punishment. The most frequent offenses that may lead to corporate criminal liability are violations of federal mail fraud and wire fraud statutes. Surprisingly innocent activities may violate these laws, and even constitute a pattern of racketeering, as described in Chapter 2.

Further, money laundering and racketeering laws greatly expand the common-law concept of conspiracy. Your employees' conduct can cause your company to enter into a criminal conspiracy even if its officers, directors, and stockholders lack knowledge of it and had no intent to encourage it.[552]

If you must hire employees, conduct a thorough pre-employment investigation. The investigation should center on the applicant's credit and criminal history. Insist on a written employment contract that forbids any illegal activity, or contemplation of illegal activity, in the course of employment. Violations should subject the employee to termination. Have the signed contract notarized, which makes it admissible in court. Consult with your attorney to make certain your contract doesn't violate state or federal civil rights, disability or other statutes.

Explain to your employees your reason for taking these precautions. If you lose your business, your employees lose their jobs.

Protecting Your Business from "Legal Sharks"

If a business you own is sued, you'll be sued personally regardless of the legal form of the business. Sole proprietors and each member of a general partnership are personally liable for judgments that can't be covered by business assets.

Laws that prevent plaintiffs from holding officers and directors of corporations liable for damages may protect insulate you from personal liability, although not if the litigant can demonstrate you acted beyond your authority as officer or director (*ultra vires*), or that the corporation acted illegally.

Another common risk comes from claims arising from unrelated businesses; e.g., rental property. If you own rental property, and someone injured there obtains a judgment against you, the creditor can enforce the judgment against all your assets—not just the rental property. Any property you own jointly with someone else may also be at risk. A creditor may even make a claim against assets you have control over through a Power of Attorney—for an aged parent, for instance.

If your business has employees, train them not to do anything that might bring a legal claim against the company—therefore jeopardizing their employment. Supervisory personnel should be aware of the pitfalls of sexual harassment, hiring, firing, motivating, or disciplining other employees.

Another major source of liability in many businesses is breach of contract. For that reason, it's important to have a clear, written understanding with your customers as to the scope of your company's professional responsibilities.

When entering into contracts on behalf of your business, avoid giving a personal guarantee. Insist on a clause that limits the other party's damages to the assets of the business. A sample of such a paragraph for a corporation follows:

If a corporate party breaches this agreement, the non-breaching party agrees to look solely to the assets of the breaching corporation [partnership, LLC, etc.] in satisfaction of any damages incurred or judgment obtained as a result of the breach. The non-breaching party waives any claim it has against the breaching corporation to pierce the corporate veil, or to otherwise disregard the corporation. The shareholders, corporate officers, directors, employees, attorneys, agents and/or affiliates of the breaching party shall not be liable under or with respect to this Agreement. In a court proceeding to interpret or enforce this Agreement, each of the parties to this Agreement waives their right to a jury trial.[553]

Beware of overly aggressive marketing efforts that may well bring new business in the door, but at the potential risk of not being able to meet client expectations. Remember Rule #1 to avoid lawsuits: Don't make promises you can't keep (Chapter 3).

Try to isolate the most vulnerable portions of a business from its assets. For instance: If the business owns hazardous equipment or vehicles, can a separate company own those assets, and have the business lease them? If the equipment needs replaced, can it be leased from a leasing company?

Environmental risks pose virtually unlimited liability. One way to mitigate them is to use a legal entity separate from your existing business to purchase land that may have pre-existing environmental hazards. These hazards should be documented in a pre-sale survey. Have your business lease the property, with the lease clearly stipulating that your business isn't responsible for pre-existing environmental hazards. An attorney, of course, should carefully review such arrangements.

Carefully consider how to hold your ownership interest in any business. If you experience a judgment, the creditor has a right to your interest in a business up to the full amount of the judgment. Keeping your ownership interest below 50% means that a judgment won't force liquidation, but also means you lose control. Another option is to use a limited liability company or other limited liability entity to hold the stock or other indicia of ownership of the business. The more limited partners or members, the less susceptible the arrangement to challenge by creditors.

Money laundering and racketeering laws subject businesses engaging in any of nearly 300 "specified unlawful activities" to civil and criminal forfeiture (Chapter 2). You must be careful of the business conduct you condone by word, deed, or implication. If you let business partners know that you will ignore their illegal activities, from that point forward, the government may a hidden lien against your business under the relation-back doctrine. Anyone who discovers the illegal act is eligible for the generous informant awards forfeiture laws offer. Even the business partner whose illegal activity you consent to could eventually turn you in, and obtain a generous informant commission, along with immunity from prosecution.

Liability Insurance: Necessary, but NOT a Panacea

One of the foundations of asset protection is liability insurance. Depending on your business activities, you may need more than one kind of liability insurance. For instance, if you're a physician who has designed a new diagnostic instrument, and want to sell it, you'll need to consider not only malpractice insurance, but product liability coverage as well.

Make certain your coverage is adequate for reasonable and normal claims. Ask your agent to help identify risks and how much coverage you need. Ask employees and/or contractors for ideas that would reduce your business liability—and create a safer working environment for them, not to mention allowing them to keep their jobs.

Frequently overlooked risks include claims due to automobile accidents, director and officer liability, employment claims, pollution, personal guarantees, partnership liability, product liability, or even the insolvency of an insurance carrier. In some cases, you may decide to abandon certain lines of business that are not worth the risk or the cost of insurance. In others, you may decide to assume a part of the risk and to seek insurance for excess losses over what you can afford to lose.

The classic use of liability insurance is to pay for "tort" claims against you or your business. A "tort" is an injury against a person or property. The torts that are covered by liability insurance are "accidental" torts: injuries caused by automobile accidents, slips and falls on your property, unintended damage to property as a result of negligence, etc.

Purchasing liability insurance to cover these types of claims is important, particularly if your business is engaged in activities that are dangerous or hazardous. If you skimp on insurance, and don't have adequate financial reserves to meet claims that arise in the course of your business, a court may conclude that you deliberately undercapitalized your business—and hold you personally responsible for the damages. In addition, when considering asset transfers to a protected entity such as a limited liability company (LLC) or an irrevocable trust, having adequate insurance may insulate you from a claim by a creditor that the transfer was a "fraudulent conveyance."

Liability insurance doesn't cover against **intentional** torts, such as libel, slander, or harassment. Nor will it cover breach of contract or fraud claims. If you practice medicine or any other profession, you should be aware that many actions previously brought as malpractice suits are now couched in fraud or breach of contract terms and, thus, probably aren't covered by malpractice insurance.

Some other common exemptions and exclusions include:

- Punitive damages;
- Damages resulting from the violation of any law or regulation;
- Injuries caused by undocumented workers (aliens illegally working in the United States);
- Injuries resulting from athletic competition or any activity deemed "hazardous";
- Injuries resulting from intoxication or the use of any illegal drug; and
- Claims made after the policy lapses.

Liability insurance coverage is expensive. It's impossible to insure against every possible loss. A good way to control costs is to view liability insurance as protection against catastrophic losses—those that could potentially lead to bankruptcy. You can keep premiums down with high deductibles, co-insurance, and various exclusions. Higher deductibles also deter opportunistic litigants and their attorneys looking for a quick payoff.

In many liability insurance policies, your insurance carrier will pay the legal fees if you're sued. Since the cost of litigation can be substantial, this is a desirable option. You can also purchase a separate litigation expense policies. This type of policy only covers litigation expenses. It will not pay off a claim if you lose a lawsuit. However, a litigation expense policy can still be a valuable aid in inducing unreasonable litigants to settle. This is because many such policies give the issuing company the right to settle the claim within policy limits, meaning as legal expenses mount, the funds available for settlement shrink.

Insurance companies use a number of techniques to minimize losses from claims. Some of the most common reasons insurance companies deny claims altogether, or justify a lower payout, are:

- Claiming that the policy doesn't require what appears to be a covered loss to be covered;
- Alleging concealment, misrepresentation or fraud on the application for insurance;
- Asserting that you failed to report a covered loss in a timely manner; and
- Asserting that conditions for coverage in the policy (e.g., safety standards in your workplace) weren't met

Some insurance companies advertise low rates, often made possible by lax underwriting standards. But if you file a claim, the company will then audit your application and your business to try to find a way to deny coverage, or justify the smallest possible payout.

A frequently overlooked consideration in purchasing liability insurance is the financial health of the company issuing the policy. Several ratings services evaluate the financial health of insurance companies. The one that is the least popular with the insurance industry is Weiss Research (http://www.weissratings.com), perhaps because it has a history of downgrading some large companies before they became insolvent. Weiss Research is also the only rating service that purports to measure the ability of a company to survive a recession.

CPA Vernon Jacobs has written a comprehensive guide to liability insurance, entitled *Benefits and Pitfalls of Liability Insurance*. You can purchase it http://www.offshorepress.com.

Avoid Sole Proprietorships or General Partnerships

A **sole proprietorship** is the simplest way of conducting business. If you own a business in your own name, or under a trade name (e.g., John's Machine Shop), but haven't made the business a separate "entity," you have a sole proprietorship. Since there's no separate legal entity from "you," if the business fails, its creditors may seize your personal assets to satisfy business debts.

If you go into business with one or more persons, a **general partnership** exists. A general partnership is even more dangerous than a sole proprietorship. You're liable not only for your own actions, but for your partners' actions as well, under a legal concept called "joint and several liability." If one of your partners does something that makes the business experience a judgment, or forces it to declare bankruptcy, your personal assets can again be seized to satisfy the partnership's debts.

Limited Liability Companies: A Superior Business Entity for Asset Protection

Because of the threats to personal assets posed by doing business as a sole proprietor or general partnership, using a separate business entity is highly recommended. While corporations have traditionally used for this purpose, they're no longer the best solution to shield personal assets from business liabilities. A newer entity, the **limited liability company** (LLC), is a superior structure.

A LLC is a hybrid of a partnership and a corporation. Its owners, which are called **members**, are shielded from personal liability. LLC managers are also shielded from personal liability for the LLC's actions. LLCs are a relatively new legal entity in the United States, although similar entities have a long history in Europe. Since the first U.S. statute recognizing LLCs was adopted by Wyoming in 1977, all U.S. states have adopted similar legislation.

A 1988 IRS ruling stipulates that a Wyoming LLC is recognized as a partnership for federal income tax purposes, allowing profits and losses to flow through to the members in proportion to their ownership interest. [554] Unlike a corporation, there's no double taxation in a partnership or partnership-like entity such as a LLC. However, it's possible to have a LLC be taxed as a corporation.

LLCs are popular vehicles for foreign investments in the United States. Foreign owners pay no tax on the LLC's non-U.S. income. [555] In general, the IRS assumes a foreign member pays taxes in his own jurisdiction. In this way, foreigners can own a business entity in one of world's most "respectable" jurisdictions without being subject to U.S. income tax.

The Charging Order—a Powerful Asset Protection Tool

The principal reason LLCs are superior to corporations at protecting assets is because of a legal concept called the **charging order**.

Let's suppose that you own a 30% interest in a corporation that owns an apartment building. You (not the corporation) get sued personally and lose the lawsuit. Your creditor now has a judgment against you and is looking to seize whatever assets it can to satisfy it. The creditor can seize anything you own, other than what's called "exempt property" (discussed later in this chapter). Since you own the 30% interest in the form of corporate stock, you creditor simply forecloses against your interest in the corporation, forcing you to give up the stock.

In contrast, if you own the same 30% interest through a LLC, in most states, the judgment creditor won't be able to seize that interest. All the creditor will be able to get is a charging order issued by a judge. The charging order represents only a right to assets distributed by the LLC. It doesn't give a creditor the right to dissolve the LLC or to force the manager of the LLC to make a distribution.

The charging order concept often makes it possible to convince a creditor to settle on more reasonable terms than might otherwise be possible. In addition, a charging order can be a poisoned asset to a creditor, because the member's share of the income is considered the property of the creditor. Based on an IRS ruling, some attorneys believe that the creditor must pay taxes on that income even though it hasn't received any cash distributions.[556] The possibility that the creditor may have to pay these taxes makes the charging order a less-than-desirable remedy.

In theory, even with a charging order in place, a LLC can carry on its business and even enter into new ventures and business activities without being hindered by a creditor. Non-liable members can receive monies from the LLC as advances, loans, or other benefits not classified as a distribution. Liable members can receive these benefits as well, although a creditor may be able to attach them.

Charging orders also apply to some other types of partnerships that provide passive investors—although not necessarily managers—with limited liability. These include limited partnerships, limited liability partnerships, and limited liability limited partnerships. However, these entities aren't as flexible for business purposes as LLCs.

Limitations of the Charging Order

In practice, there are often practical difficulties to "waiting out" a creditor armed with a charging order. How will families or business associates dependent on income from their share of a LLC react when payments are suspended? If the debtor member owes a legitimate debt, how sympathetic will the remaining members be toward him?

Moreover, the intent of the charging order is to shield **non-debtor partners** in a partnership structure (e.g., a LLC) against unreasonable collection efforts by a debtor partner's creditors. The intent isn't to shield a debtor from creditors, although it may have that effect. The law and the courts don't look favorably on efforts by a debtor to "stiff" legitimate creditors.

In addition, a creditor may persuade judges to write a "tight" charging order, particularly if the creditor can demonstrate that the partnership's sole or primary purpose is to "hinder, delay, or defraud creditors." The order may prohibit loans, advances, or other transactions that are "distributions in disguise" or "deferred distributions" unless the creditor receives the debtor partner's share, up to the full amount of the debt owed.

A determined creditor may even seek a court order permitting the liable partner or member's interest to be foreclosed upon, with the proceeds awarded to the creditor. Or the creditor can petition the court to appoint it a substitute limited partner or member in place of the debtor-partner. It may even be possible for a creditor to foreclose against a LLC interest **without** the consent of the non-liable partners if the foreclosure won't cause a hardship to the LLC.[557]

LLCs or other partnership structures used primarily to hold family interests (e.g., **family limited partnerships** or **family LLCs**) are also vulnerable. According to *Trusts & Estates* magazine:

Where the partnership in question is a family limited partnership holding investment assets and perhaps even the family residence, it is difficult to argue that the partnership even has a real business that will be disrupted or that the interests of innocent, non-related third parties will be prejudiced.[558]

This was the situation in a 2005 *Ehmann* case. Here, a bankruptcy trustee won court approval to take control of a LLC of which the bankrupt debtor was a member.[559] In this case, the LLC interest was a purely passive one, with the entity used only to administer family assets with no significant business purpose. The central issue was whether federal bankruptcy law applied, or the more restrictive Arizona LLC statute. The court concluded that because the members of the LLC and the LLC itself had no reciprocal obligations to one another, the agreement couldn't be considered an "executory contract" under federal bankruptcy law, and the more restrictive Arizona law wouldn't apply. The property in the LLC therefore became subject to seizure under federal bankruptcy law.

Another risk arises if all members of LLC or other partnership structure become debtors of the same creditor. In this situation, all members are liable, and a court could conceivably disregard charging order restrictions. This might occur if a married couple that jointly own all the interest in a LLC incur a joint liability, such as an income tax debt assessed against a jointly filed income tax return. Another situation in which it could occur is if the non-liable spouse dies, and the liable spouse inherits the deceased spouse's limited partnership or membership interest.[560]

Single-Member LLCs Offer Anonymity, but Less Asset Protection

In most states, it's possible to form LLCs with only a single member. There are some striking privacy advantages of doing so. If you use a single-member LLC is used to hold just one investment, when that investment is sold, you don't need to transfer its title. The buyer can simply take possession of the LLC's articles of organization. Ordinarily, this creates no public record. Of course, the former LLC owner is obliged to pay taxes on the profits.

U.S. persons who own single-member LLCs also enjoy "stealth taxation." There's no need to obtain a taxpayer ID number, although you will need one if the LLC opens a bank account. Indeed, the name of the LLC need not show up on any tax return. The income it earns, if any, is listed on Schedule C of its your personal tax return along with any other sole proprietor income. In 1999, the IRS confirmed this tax treatment.[561]

However, single-member LLCs isn't as effective for asset protection as LLCs with more than one member. This is because the charging order concept may not apply to a partnership in which the debtor is the only participant. If there are no non-debtor members or partners to protect, a results-oriented judge might decide it's against "public policy" to restrict creditors to a charging order. In a 2003 case, a federal bankruptcy judge denied charging order protection for a single-member LLC and allowed a bankruptcy trustee to take possession of the LLC's assets to pay off the owner's creditors.[562] The judge applied Colorado law, which doesn't stipulate that a charging order is the exclusive remedy available for a creditor. For this reason, asset protection planners often recommend forming single-member LLCs in jurisdictions where the charging order is the exclusive remedy available.

Member-Managed Versus Manager-Managed LLCs

A LLC may be managed by its members (member-managed LLC) or by a non-member manager (manager-managed LLC). While the manager(s) of a LLC aren't personally liable for the LLC's debts, a manager-managed LLC may offer superior asset protection.

This would be true, for instance, if a bankruptcy trustee succeeds in obtaining a court order foreclosing against a debtor member's interest in the LLC. If the debtor member also serves as manager, the court could simply order the member-manager to make a mandatory distribution to the bankruptcy trustee. If the debtor member isn't the manager, but merely a passive investor, the bankruptcy trustee must obtain jurisdiction over the manager and issue a legally enforceable order for the manager to make a distribution. If the manager is in another state and especially another country (see Chapter 5's discussion of offshore LLCs), it may be impossible to enforce the court order.

This strategy may not be effective in a single-member LLC. The bankruptcy trustee might be able to obtain a court order requiring the debtor member to replace the manager with one appointed by the bankruptcy court. The new manager could then order the LLC's assets seized to satisfy the debtor member's creditors.

LLCs Can Save Estate Taxes, Too

LLCs and other partnership structures are widely used to reduce estate taxes. This is because membership interests can be gifted to family members or others, for less than the market value of the underlying assets—in many cases, 30% to 50% less. Such "valuation discounts" are available because a minority interest in an asset, such as an interest in a LLC, combined with restrictions on the transferability of such interests (which any standard LLC agreement will have) means that the combined interests are worth less than the underlying asset. A gifting strategy can increase the effective value of the U.S. estate tax exclusion by a corresponding percentage, although gifts are subject to the lifetime gift tax ceiling of US$1 million.

To use this strategy successfully, it's essential to obtain an **independent appraisal** of the assets placed into the LLC and a second independent appraisal of the value of the interests to be gifted after the partnership is formed. If you continue to use the gifted assets, this use must occur on an arm's length basis. In a 2003 case, the IRS denied valuation discounts to assets transferred into a limited partnership, based on a provision in the Tax Code that prohibits discounts or exclusions for transfers of assets with a retained interest.[563]

Strategies that experts suggest to insure valuation discounts in limited partnerships and LLCs are respected include:

- Not placing all assets into a family limited partnership or LLC;
- Retaining sufficient assets outside the partnership to provide for living expenses;
- Paying rent to the partnership for the use of personal assets, such as a residence or vehicle; and

- Avoiding control of the partnership by partners who are most vulnerable to lawsuits (e.g., a high-net worth partner)[564]

These same guidelines are valid with respect to ensuring that a LLC or limited partnership is respected so that creditors may not foreclose upon its assets.

Where to Form Your LLC

While Wyoming has the oldest LLC statute, New Mexico may be a lower-profile jurisdiction. In New Mexico, the only information required in the LLC Articles of Organization is the name of the company, the name and address of the resident agent and the duration of the entity. New Mexico also doesn't require listing the names of the LLC's members or managers.

However, New Mexico isn't the best choice if you're looking for asset protection. That's because New Mexico law doesn't prohibit foreclosure and forced liquidation of an LLC. The following states have LLC statutes that generally prohibit foreclosure and liquidation of LLC interests: Arizona, Arkansas, Connecticut, Delaware, Idaho, Illinois, Louisiana, Maryland, Minnesota, Nevada, Oklahoma, Rhode Island, and Virginia. Consider forming an LLC in one of these states, even if the business conducts its operations elsewhere. It may be necessary to register the out-of-state LLC in your home state if it does substantial business there. In some states, failure to register may result in your business not being legally recognized. A possible consequence of lack of legal recognition is your unlimited personal liability for the business's debts incurred in that state.

Certain states, including California, prohibit professionals, such as physicians, from operating their business as a LLC. If the entity can't be formed in a particular state, it won't be recognized if it's formed in another state, and then tries to do register in the first state.

A number of states, states, including California, New York, and Texas, levy a tax on LLCs. The tax can be based on revenue, profits, the number of owners, the LLC's capital, a combination of those factors, or a flat fee. Be certain to investigate if your LLC will be subject to this tax in the states where it's formed or conducts business.

Corporations: No Longer the Best Business Entity for Asset Protection

Corporations are the traditional way to limit personal liability in a business. And while the LLC is a superior entity for asset protection, a corporation is more suitable if free transferability of ownership interests—lacking in a LLC—is essential. This might be the case if you plan to take the corporation "public" and offer its shares on a securities exchange.

Corporations are generally viewed as being superior to LLCs in two other tax-related situations. However, in both cases, a LLC can be adapted to provide the same benefits:

1. **To avoid paying Social Security tax.** In most cases, the IRS considers you a sole proprietor if you own an unincorporated business by yourself. This classification includes a domestic LLC in which you're the only member. Sole proprietors must generally pay Social Security taxes on distributions from their unincorporated businesses.

The traditional solution for this dilemma is to form a domestic corporation and then file IRS Form 2553[565] to elect **subchapter S-corporation** status.[566] This corporate form is permitted for corporations with 75 or fewer shareholders, and enables the corporation to be taxed as if it were a LLC or other type of partnership. Distributions from an S-corporation aren't subject to Social Security tax. However, you can accomplish the same thing with a LLC and avoid Social Security tax plus obtain asset protection. Elect to have your LLC taxed as a corporation by filing IRS Form 8832.[567] Then file Form 2553 to elect to have it taxed as a S-corporation.

2. **To offer non-taxable fringe benefits**. A C corporation can provide more fringe benefits, tax-free to its owners, than a LLC. However, by filing Form 8832, your LLC can elect to be taxed as a corporation. Your LLC will be taxed as a C-corporation, and may offer its employees the same fringe benefits as any other C corporation. However, earnings of a C corporation are taxed twice; once at the corporation level, and again when dividends are paid to stockholders. For many small businesses, the ability to pay tax-free fringe benefits from a LLC generally won't outweigh the tax disadvantages associated with being taxed as a C corporation.

The "Corporate Veil" and How to Pierce It

*Author's Note: Feel free to skip this section if you've decided **not** to form a corporation. If you already own a business in the form of a corporation, or believe that a corporation would be a more suitable business entity than a LLC, you should review it to understand how to more effectively protect your ownership interests.*

A corporation has a separate legal personality from its owners, officers, and directors. This legal personality provides a **corporate veil** that may insulate officers and directors from corporate liabilities. The veil must be sustained by registering the corporation and following other statutory requirements imposed by the state. Shareholders of a corporation ordinarily aren't liable for its debts or other obligations unless they personally guarantee those debts or obligations, or serve as an officer, director, or in another managerial capacity. They may also become liable for a corporation's debts if state or federal law makes them responsible to pay the corporation's employment taxes, sales taxes or for worker's compensation claims.

The best way to avoid personal liability in a corporation is to hire officers and directors to run the business, and merely hold the corporation's stock. You as the majority shareholder retain the authority to replace these individuals and may take legal action against them if their actions damage the corporation.

Substantial corporate formalities must be followed to obtain asset protection for the corporation's officers and directors. These formalities require documenting all the corporation's business decisions and maintaining a paper trail separating the shareholders, managers, and directors from the corporation's assets and liabilities.

Litigants attempting to pierce the corporate veil will try to prove that these corporate formalities haven't been strictly followed. For instance, if your corporation neglects such details as shareholders' meetings, directors' meetings, or having directors approve important transactions, a court may pierce the veil and hold you personally liable for the corporation's debts. Even something as simple as neglecting to sign your name on official correspondence as an officer or director, could lead to a conclusion that corporate formalities weren't properly followed.

If you mingle corporate assets with your own, or use corporate assets to pay personal debts, a court may pierce the corporate veil as well. To prevent this result, document all situations where corporate assets are used to benefit yourself, or vice-versa. It's also important to document a business reason for every such arrangement in a corporate resolution. For instance, if you run a corporation out of a spare bedroom at home, the resolution could state that the business reason for this arrangement is to spare the corporation the added expense of renting an office.

The corporate veil is irrelevant if you do something that results in a judgment against you personally. In that event, you're responsible for paying the creditor out of your own personal assets. If you're the majority shareholder of a corporation, the creditor may be able to obtain a court order to seize your shares. Then the creditor can elect new officers and directors who may either dissolve the corporation or order it to pay your debt.

If you're an officer or director of a corporation, especially a large one, try to obtain "directors and officers" (D&O) liability insurance. D&O insurance is intended to reimburse a director or officer for costs incurred either in defending a civil suit and/or to indemnify them for any unfavorable judgment or settlement. Ask your D&O carrier whether the proceeds of the policy belong to the corporation, or to the officers and directors, if the corporation declares bankruptcy. Also, ask whether claims are paid out on a "first come, first served" basis. If they are, if the D&O policy pays off one officer or director, there might not be sufficient cover to pay off other offers and directors.[568]

D&O insurance is also important if you become a volunteer officer or director of a non-profit corporation. Since D&O coverage is expensive, and becoming more so, many non-profits can't afford it. The safest strategy is to simply be a volunteer—not an officer or director.

Where to Incorporate—Virtually Anonymously

For many years, **Delaware** has been the state of choice for incorporating. Many large corporations are chartered in Delaware because the state imposes no corporate income tax on companies not operating within the state. And because of the large number of major corporations chartered in Delaware, its courts are more experienced in the application of corporate law than courts in most other states.

A friendlier alternative for smaller corporations is **Nevada**, which has strict state laws preventing litigants from piercing the corporate veil. The corporation law effectively makes officers and directors immune from personal liability for their lawful activities. Nevada also has no state corporate tax, no tax on corporate shares, and no franchise tax.

Wyoming has advantages similar to Nevada, with no corporate income tax. In addition, the names of directors need not be listed in the Articles of Incorporation. The costs of running a corporation in Wyoming are also lower than in Delaware or Nevada.

In all three states, you only need a company name, an address where official notices can be sent, and signatures of your resident agent. Shareholders need not be identified in any public record. You can submit the forms by mail or through various online services such as http://www.incorp.com. Once you complete this simple process, you'll have a corporation that can conduct business and in most cases, open a bank account.

In recent years, the use of **shell corporations** headquartered in states like Delaware, Nevada, and Wyoming has become increasingly controversial. Shell corporations have no visible operations, no employees, and no assets. According to the U.S. Treasury's Financial Crimes Enforcement Network (Chapter 2), numerous U.S. shell corporations have been linked to terrorism and bank fraud investigations.[569] As a result, Congress is likely to enact legislation requiring states to gather and verify much more information before granting a corporate charter, much as banks and other financial institutions are required to comply with "know your customer" anti-laundering requirements before opening an account.

Wherever you incorporate, to maximize the protection of the corporate veil, maintain as many connections as possible to the state in which you're incorporated. Ideally, you should live in that state, have your corporate office there, and do business only with residents of that state. If it's not practical to live in that state, keep an office there, and make regular trips to visit it. Many incorporators provide **staffed office packages** that provide a more substantive connection to the state than a mere address at the incorporation service—although less than an office staffed with at least one employee. Finally, if you do business outside the state of incorporation, have contracts notarized in that state and include a stipulation in them that its law applies in any dispute.

Asset Protection Using Multiple LLCs or Corporations

Multiple entities can make it more difficult for a creditor to pierce the corporate veil (in a corporation) or charging order protection (in a LLC). In one arrangement, one LLC operates the business. A second owns all the equipment and office furniture, which is leased to the first. A third leases employees to the first. A fourth conducts all marketing. The first LLC signs contracts with the other three guaranteeing regular payments for these services. It also consents to a lien against its assets as security for such payments. If the first LLC is sued, all its assets are already pledged to the remaining LLCs.

A simpler strategy involves two LLCs. The first LLC operates a high-risk business. It borrows money from a second LLC based in another state. In return, the high-risk LLC pledges all its assets to the holding LLC. The holding LLC maintains a low profile and doesn't carry on independent business activities that might result in a lawsuit. If the high-risk business is sued, it can produce documents demonstrating that all of its assets are pledged to a LLC in another state.

Litigants often challenge multiple LLC strategies on the theory that they exist only to hinder, delay, or defraud legitimate creditors. They will try to convince the court that the structure should be ignored, giving the creditors claim to whatever entity holds assets that can satisfy a judgment. To avoid this result requires complete documentation of the arrangement along with a "paper trail" to demonstrate that the formalities of this arrangement are respected. Expert legal advice is essential to set up these arrangements.

Avoid Fraudulent Conveyance

Challenges to asset protection planning generally focus on the legitimacy of transfers into a legally protected contract or structure, rather than the contract or structure itself. If you owe money to someone, and instead of paying that person, convey the funds to a trust or other asset protection structure, that transfer can result in a **fraudulent conveyance** claim against you.

The Uniform Fraudulent Transfer Act (UFTA), the principles of which originate in the English Statute of Elizabeth (Chapter 5), has been placed into law in 41 states. In essence, the UFTA stipulates that if property is transferred to "hinder, delay, or defraud" an existing or known future obligation, the courts can void that transfer. If a creditor can demonstrate various **badges of fraud** associated with a transfer you make, the court may require you to demonstrate that the transfer was not intended to hinder, delay, or defraud the creditor. Badges of fraud include:

- Making the transfer to an insider;
- Retaining use or control of property;

- Concealing the transfer;
- Being sued or threatened with a lawsuit;
- Making a transfer of substantially all of your assets;
- Absconding;
- Removing or concealing assets;
- Not receiving reasonable value in return for the transferred assets;
- Becoming insolvent shortly after the transfer; or
- Making the transfer shortly before or shortly after a substantial debt was incurred.

One badge of fraud alone won't ordinarily demonstrate a fraudulent conveyance. Where several are present, however, the court may set aside the transfer and order you to pay the money owed. The court order may be reinforced with fines, foreclosures, seizure of substitute property, and occasionally, even criminal contempt citations; i.e., pay the creditor or go to jail.

A fraudulent conveyance hearing is a generally a civil proceeding, although a few states (including California) treat certain fraudulent conveyances as misdemeanors. Federal fraudulent conveyance statutes provide for more severe criminal sanctions for fraudulent transfers relating to bankruptcy fraud, tax fraud, bank fraud, money laundering, and the environment. Federal agencies also have more time to make fraudulent conveyance claims than private creditors can under state laws. For instance, the IRS may assess taxes, interest, and penalties for up to six years after an asset transfer if it alleges substantial underpayment of taxes or tax evasion. It has an additional 10 years to try to collect these obligations.

A transfer of assets that leaves you insolvent is a fraudulent conveyance with respect to known creditors. The definition of solvency, however, varies from state to state and under federal law. If you've left sufficient assets in an accessible form to pay all known creditors, a transfer generally won't be attacked as a fraudulent conveyance. **Exempt assets** that a creditor can't reasonably recover don't count, such as equity in a home protected by a state homestead statute; property owned by spouses as tenants in the entirety (which in states that recognize this form of ownership are protected from creditor claims); and qualified retirement plans. The legal protections for exempt assets are summarized later in this chapter.

Solvency may change with market conditions. For instance, most mortgages are secured by the property on which the mortgage is written. If you default on the mortgage payments, the lender has the right to seize substitute assets if it can't satisfy the loan balance in a foreclosure sale of the property. If you make all or most of these other assets unavailable when the home equity value is declining, or after the value has declined below the loan balance, and subsequently default on the mortgage, you would be insolvent. The lender could then potentially make a fraudulent conveyance claim.

The ideal position before transferring assets is to have no known creditors or debts, including student loans or other federal obligations. Should these retained assets have a variable market value, the safest strategy is to maintain a monetary cushion above their current value to avoid potential fraudulent conveyance claims.

A future creditor that you knew nothing about when you made an asset transfer generally can't make a successful fraudulent conveyance claim. However, in 2006, a federal appeals court ruled that transfers of assets intended to protect against a future unknown creditor violated the state of Washington's Uniform Fraudulent Transfers Act.[570] This case is more of an aberration than a restatement of the law. Outside Washington, U.S. state and federal courts generally require that a person have actual intent to "hinder, delay or defraud" a known or reasonably foreseen creditor to set aside a transfer as a fraudulent conveyance.[571]

It's critical that you obtain the advice of a qualified attorney when transferring assets into any of the contracts or structures discussed in this book. This is particularly true if you engage in offshore planning as described in Chapter 5.

The Amazing Trust and Its Many Uses

The idea of a trust is a simple one: you convey assets to someone else to administer on behalf of persons you name to benefit from those assets. The trust concept originated in English law and is more than 1,000 years old. This contributes to both its strength and ready acceptance by the courts.

All trusts require three participants: the **grantor** or **settlor** who establishes the trust and contributes assets to it; the **trustee** that administers it; and one or more **beneficiaries** who receive distributions from it. A fourth and optional participant is the **protector**; someone to watch over the trustee to protect the interests of the beneficiaries.

You may create a trust for virtually any purpose that isn't illegal or against public policy—a very broad category of choices. Indeed, a trust is one of the most flexible legal mechanisms recognized by law.

According to trust attorney Robert Miller:

Trusts can assist in the following (and still more) circumstances:

- *To make provision for someone under a legal disability (e.g. minority);*
- *To reduce substantially or eliminate death duties in respect of the settlor's assets;*
- *To the extent permitted by law and public policy, to protect assets against attacks by future, unknown creditors;*
- *To protect family assets from the extravagance or bankruptcy of a beneficiary (protective trusts);*
- *To lessen or eliminate probate formalities on the death of the settlor, while distributing assets in accordance with the settlor's wishes;*
- *To set aside both legally and physically, assets to be used in a flexible way in the future, thus as a financial planning tool for a family;*
- *To ensure the continuity of a family business;*
- *To provide for charitable institutions and for benevolent but non-charitable purposes (purpose trusts);*
- *In the context of commercial transactions where it is useful to separate legal and beneficial ownership;*
- *To avoid forced inheritance laws, thereby to maintain freedom to dispose of assets in a manner deemed desirable by the settlor rather than legislators;*
- *As a will-substitute, or supplement;*
- *To function as trading trusts and voting trusts;*
- *To hold life insurance policies;*
- *To segregate risk in commercial and individual situations;*
- *To protect assets from political, regulatory, exchange control or economic risk at home or abroad;*
- *To enable a family or business to conduct transactions with enhanced privacy and flexibility;*
- *In specialized investment applications: unit trusts, trusts for debenture holders;*
- *In accident and general insurance applications;*
- *In specific applications (e.g. restorative funds in mining operations); and*
- *To protect a reasonable level of assets from unreasonable awards.*[572]

Historically, the trust was the premier instrument in English common law devised to frustrate the collection of death duties, fines, and forfeitures. In recent years, in response to escalating risks to wealth, trust promoters have marketed **asset protection trusts** (APTs). Such trusts, usually organized in an offshore center with an English common law background, have special features discussed in Chapter 5. **Domestic** APTs may be formed in some states, but for reasons summarized in this chapter, may not be as effective as offshore APTs.

Revocable vs. Irrevocable Trusts

Trusts are often used to avoid probate. Using simple tax planning techniques, such as the **marital bypass trust** (otherwise known as a **credit shelter trust**), a married couple can double the value of the assets they can pass to their heirs without making the estate subject to U.S. estate tax.

Martial bypass trusts and other **living trusts** formed for estate planning purposes and to avoid probate are generally revocable (e.g., the assets aren't irrevocably conveyed by the grantor into the trust) and provide little asset protection. Since the grantor of a living trust usually serves as the trustee, the trust assets aren't legally separate from the grantor and are subject to creditor claims.

Irrevocable trusts provide much greater asset protection than revocable trusts. The greatest asset protection is in an irrevocable **spendthrift discretionary trust**. This is a trust that includes language giving the trustee wide latitude to avoid making distributions to beneficiaries if the distribution would go to a creditor, or where the trustee fears the distribution would be wasted by the beneficiary. To qualify for this protection:

- The trustee must not be required to distribute the assets to the beneficiary or beneficiaries at any particular time;
- Neither the beneficiary nor the grantor may have the right to withdraw the assets; and
- The grantor may not be a beneficiary of the trust.

Under both state and federal law, creditors can attach current or future distributions from a spendthrift trust in certain circumstances. The most common exception to the spendthrift rule is to enforce judgments or orders to support a trust beneficiary's child or current or former spouse.[573] In most cases, even "exception creditors" can't generally seize the assets in a valid spendthrift trust; they can only seize distributions from it. However, states that have adopted Section 504 of the **Uniform Trust Code** may permit a beneficiary's creditor to compel a distribution from a spendthrift trust for the benefit of a beneficiary's child, spouse, or former spouse.[574] Careful drafting and proper selection of the state in which to settle a discretionary trust may avoid this result.

It's possible to use an irrevocable trust in certain income deferral arrangements. The employee recognizes no income until payments are received. This kind of trust is called a **rabbi trust**, since the first IRS ruling approving this arrangement dealt with a rabbi. In this arrangement, trust assets remain subject to the claims of the employer's general creditors. A rabbi trust should therefore not be used without a careful assessment of your employer's legal and financial condition.

Another useful irrevocable trust is the **charitable remainder trust**. It's used primarily for estate tax and income tax purposes, but is also effective for asset protection. The trust removes a highly appreciated asset (e.g., shares in a business) from your estate, thus avoiding estate tax at your death and capital gains tax upon the sale of the asset. You're entitled to an income from the property contributed to the trust, and the assets contributed to the trust vest to a named charity at your death.

With a **secret trust**, which can be revocable or irrevocable, you make provision for a "hidden beneficiary" that you don't want named in your will or other document visible to outsiders. While historically, secret trusts have been used to make provision for illegitimate children or mistresses, they're also used for private donations to charities or educational institutions. You create a secret trust by making a bequest in your will to your lawyer or to a trusted friend. Instruct your lawyer or your friend beforehand to hold the money in trust for your intended beneficiary.

Two types of trusts used specifically to protect real property are the **qualified personal residence trust** and the **land trust**. A type of trust called an **intentionally defective grantor trust** can also be used for this purpose. These trusts are discussed later in this chapter.

Create a Family Legacy with a Dynasty Trust

A **dynasty trust** is an irrevocable spendthrift trust that is intended to have a very long life. Under the terms of most states' trust laws, a trust can survive 21 years beyond the death of the last beneficiary alive when the trust was written. A few states (e.g., South Dakota) and many offshore jurisdictions have abolished the **rule against perpetuities** that restricts the length of time a trust can exist. In these jurisdictions, a trust can literally last forever.

As with most other types of trusts, there are no tax savings when you create a dynasty trust. The trust income is also taxable. However, the trust assets can be free from all future federal gift and estate taxes, for as many generations as the trust exists. Since a dynasty trust normally has spendthrift provisions, its assets are sheltered not only from your creditors, but from creditors of succeeding generations.

A dynasty trust is often created as an **irrevocable life insurance trust** (ILIT). A life insurance policy funds the trust. At your death, the policy's death benefit pays any estate taxes due. Since the cash value of the policy and the death benefit will usually greatly exceed the premium paid for the policy, this is a powerful strategy to insure that the bulk of your estate passes to the next generation with estate taxes reduced.

Proper structuring of a dynasty trust requires substantial tax and estate planning expertise. There are many potential pitfalls, including the **generation-skipping transfer tax** (GSTT) to thwart the creation of large dynasty trusts. Be certain to retain a qualified legal practitioner to put this strategy into place.

Not Recommended: Domestic Asset Protection Trusts

In 1997, the states of **Alaska** and **Delaware** enacted legislation purporting to provide asset protection without adhering to all of the restrictions of a spendthrift trust. Several other states have now enacted similar legislation.

The most significant aspects of these laws provide for:

- **Self-settled trusts with spendthrift provisions.** In a self-settled trust, the person who creates the trust and transfers property to it is also a beneficiary. Under the laws of most states, a self-settled trust doesn't protect the grantor's beneficial interest in the income or principal of the trust from the grantor's creditors. However, an asset protection trust (APT) in states that have overridden the self-settled trust rule is purported to provide spendthrift protection to grantors who name themselves as beneficiaries.

- **Shortened statute of limitations.** Most states permit a transfer to a spendthrift trust to be challenged as a fraudulent conveyance for four to six years after the transfer take place. Domestic APT laws don't give creditors as much time to bring a fraudulent conveyance claim.
- **Restrictive fraudulent conveyance standards.** In states with domestic APT laws, it's more difficult for a creditor to prove that a transfer to the trust was intended to hinder, delay, or defraud the creditor.

To date, there have been no significant court cases testing the purported benefits of domestic APTs. However, according to asset protection attorney Jay Adkisson, such trusts suffer from at least five glaring defects:

Glaring Defect #1: A U.S. trustee can be compelled—by being thrown in jail for contempt—to do whatever the U.S. court wants. About as bad is the fact that the U.S. trustee is vulnerable to a civil lawsuit (trustee would rather give up your assets than his own), and is available to law enforcement authorities that could bring money laundering charges, etc., to coerce the trustee to cooperate. This defect alone guts the alleged protection of the domestic APT.

Glaring Defect #2: Full faith and credit. No matter which state you form the trust in, that state is required by the "full faith and credit" clause of the U.S. Constitution to recognize the judgment of any other state. This means that a creditor only has to take its judgment and register the judgment without having to retry the case (a very simple process, done every day by collection firms), and the creditor is back at your throat.

Glaring Defect #3: Attempts to "import" law or to make a "choice of law" in favor of the laws of Alaska, Delaware or Nevada will probably fail. Think you can get an Oklahoma judge to apply Alaska law in favor of an Oklahoma resident against an Oklahoma judgment held by an Oklahoma creditor involving Oklahoma property?

Glaring Defect #4: Federal courts will ignore. Because of the Supremacy Clause of the U.S. Constitution, federal courts are not necessarily bound by state law, which is really ugly considering that the nightmare cases are about as often federal cases, or worse, defenses against federal administrative actions.

Glaring Defect #5: No chance of secrecy. Because the trustee is in the U.S., the trustee will be subject to discovery order and subpoenas, and as each states applies its own procedure (as opposed to substantive law) without regard to the other states' procedure, and the federal courts follow their own procedure, it means that any secrecy protections of the laws of the state where the trust is formed, will be totally irrelevant and ineffective.[575]

Domestic APTs were created to tap the growing market for the offshore asset protection trusts described in Chapter 5. Offshore APTs largely overcome the "glaring defects" described above, although they must be carefully drafted and operated. Probably the only situation in which a domestic APT might be effective is if you live in a state that has adopted such a statute and keep all trust assets and business activities within that state to reduce the likelihood of a legal challenge in another state.

Avoid Defective Trusts

Trusts are very useful for asset protection and to reduce estate taxes, but they generally don't provide any income tax advantages during the lifetime of the grantor. Nonetheless, numerous promoters market so-called **constitutional, common-law,** or **contractual** trusts and claim such trusts can reduce or even eliminate your liability to pay tax. This isn't true, and if you rely on such claims as the basis for your tax planning, you're placing both your privacy and property at risk.

Typical red flags to look for to identify a defective trust include:

- A promise to reduce or eliminate taxes, including income tax, self-employment tax and estate tax;
- Claims that the trust may pay your personal expenses without tax consequences;
- Claims that you can transfer property into the trust and thereafter cease paying tax on any income or gain derived from the property;
- Use of backdated documents; or
- Lack of an independent trustee.

According to the *IRS Practitioner Letter*:

Currently, there are two prevalent fraudulent arrangements that are being promoted: The "domestic package" and the "foreign package." The domestic package involves a series of trusts that are formed in the United States, while the foreign trust packages are formed offshore and outside the jurisdiction of the United States. Further, trusts involved in the schemes are vertically layered with each trust distributing income to the next layer. The goal of this layered distribution of income is to fraudulently reduce taxable income to nominal amounts.[576]

For more information on what the IRS calls "abusive trust" schemes, see http://www.irs.gov/pub/irs-pdf/p2193.pdf.

The Promise and Pitfalls of Bankruptcy

If you don't have enough money to pay your debts, state and federal **bankruptcy laws** provide some relief. Once you file bankruptcy, creditors are **stayed** from trying to collect on your debts. That means no more harassing phone calls, threatening letters, lawsuits, or foreclosures. Bankruptcy **exemptions** also permit you to keep certain property, pursuant to state or federal law.

If you don't have an asset protection plan, bankruptcy may be the only option if you experience a judgment or unexpected expenses (e.g., medical bills not covered by health insurance). Because bankruptcy provides a way of delaying or reducing debt payments and in some cases wiping out debts altogether, the threat of bankruptcy can sometimes keep creditors at bay.

However, bankruptcy requires that you make full disclosure of your assets to a trustee appointed by the bankruptcy court. If you fail to make a full and truthful disclosure, you may not be entitled to a bankruptcy "discharge" and may even be prosecuted for bankruptcy fraud.

Bankruptcy is truly a last resort. A much better way to plan is to place your assets into legally protected forms, in particular, pensions and retirement plans, discussed later in this chapter. If you have substantial wealth, you should consider some of the offshore lifeboat investments discussed in Chapter 5.

Several different kinds of bankruptcy exist, each referring to a section of Title 11 of the U.S. Code. The most frequently used type is **Chapter 7** bankruptcy, which results in a complete settlement of all debts, except for certain debts that can't be discharged. Non-dischargeable debts under Chapter 7 include:

- Customs duties and most federal, state and county taxes;

- Credit obtained by fraud, concealment or false pretenses;
- Monies owed for luxury goods, cash advances, purchases on credit cards or other unsecured debt obtained within 60 days of a bankruptcy filing;
- Criminal fines or other court-ordered restitution for most criminal offenses;
- Alimony and child support;
- Liability or judgments for malicious injury to others;
- Student loans;
- Personal injuries caused to others as a result of operating a motor vehicle or other conveyance while intoxicated;
- Fraud or deception committed against depository institutions;
- Debt owed to a pension or profit sharing plan; and
- Debt resulting from a judgment pursuant to a securities law violation.

In other types of bankruptcies, debts are rescheduled and sometimes reduced, but not eliminated. A **Chapter 13** bankruptcy allows you to keep property that you might otherwise lose in a Chapter 7 bankruptcy, such as a mortgaged house or car. If you can't keep up the payments, it may be possible to convert the bankruptcy to a Chapter 7. A business can use a **Chapter 11** bankruptcy to continue operating while paying off a portion of its debts.

Debtors themselves begin most bankruptcy cases, in a **voluntary bankruptcy**. Your creditors can also initiate bankruptcy by filing a petition before a court asking you to be declared bankrupt. This is an **involuntary bankruptcy**.

While a bankruptcy requires you to turn over much of your property to a **bankruptcy trustee** for the benefit of your creditors, exemptions exist under both state and federal law. These exemptions may or may not apply to non-dischargeable debts. In some states, you can choose between the federal exemptions or the state exemptions. In others, you must use the state exemptions, which may (or may not) be more generous.

Federal exemptions as of 2007 include:

- Up to US$20,200 of equity in an owner-occupied home;
- Up to US$10,775 of the cash value of life insurance;
- Alimony or child support;
- Social security payments;
- Pension and retirement payments qualified under the ERISA statute;
- Up to US$1,095,000 of the aggregate value of assets in an Individual Retirement Plan
- Household goods with a value up to US$10,775;
- Property required for health needs;
- Jewelry up to a total value of US$1,350;
- A motor vehicle up to a total value of US$3,225;
- Personal injury compensation payments to US$20,200;
- Wrongful death payments;
- Unemployment compensation;
- Disability benefits;
- Veterans' benefits; and
- Professional books and equipment with a value up to US$2,025.[577]

Many states have higher limits for owner-occupied homesteads, life insurance, and annuities.

The interplay of federal and state bankruptcy exemptions with other laws is complex and, depending on your circumstances, can significantly strengthen—or weaken—your financial position. Don't file bankruptcy without first consulting an attorney who specializes in this area.

The 2005 Bankruptcy Reform Act places additional burden on debtors who seek refuge in bankruptcy:

- **Mandatory counseling**. Before declaring bankruptcy, you must consult with an accredited consumer credit counseling agency, at your expense. The counseling service will try to work out a repayment plan that satisfies your creditors. During this period, your bills keep accumulating.
- **Means testing**. If the combined gross income of your family is greater than the median family income in your state, you may be forced to file a Chapter 13 repayment plan where you repay a percentage of your debts over an extended period, rather than a Chapter 7 bankruptcy where your debts are eliminated.
- **Monthly expenses calibrated to IRS guidelines**. In a Chapter 13 filing, the bankruptcy court will require your spending to adhere to the **IRS National and Local Standard Expense Guidelines.** These guidelines mandate an essentially Spartan lifestyle and require you to eliminate all expenditures that the court considers excessive.

Another consequence of the 2005 law is that creditors may more easily force debtors into involuntary bankruptcy. This may allow creditors to reach assets that would otherwise be protected under state law, such as the equity in your home (see next section).[578]

Protecting Your Home

The equity in your home may be your most valuable asset. Yet, protecting it can present a difficult challenge.

Fortunately, there are techniques—some requiring only that you live in a particular state—that can essentially judgment-proof your home. Others require that you transfer ownership of your home to another entity; still others protect it by borrowing against the equity in your residence, sometimes in concert with an offshore entity.

This section explores these options and presents ideas to help you protect what is a notoriously difficult investment to shield from creditors.

Homestead Protections Vary Widely Between States

Most states have **homestead statutes** in effect to protect owner-occupants of dwellings from losing their home to creditors. Most such homestead statutes were enacted in the 1930s, and the limits have not risen with inflation, so the limits are generally very low—US$5,000-US$25,000 is typical.

A few states, such as New Jersey, have no homestead exemption. Other states protect your home from creditor claims with no limit to total value. States with no-dollar-limit homestead exemptions are Arkansas, Florida, Iowa, Minnesota, Oklahoma, South Dakota, and Texas.

Before passage of the 2005 Bankruptcy Reform Act, you could relocate to a state with an unlimited homestead exemption up to three months before filing bankruptcy. Then, you could use "non-exempt" assets that would otherwise be subject to creditor attachment to purchase a residence that became an "exempt asset."

The 2005 law significantly restricts such last minute planning. The value of any state homestead exemption is now limited to US$136,875 (2007, indexed for inflation) if you have owned the residence for fewer than 1,215 days (three years and four months) before filing for bankruptcy. In this situation, the equity in the homestead exceeding US$136,875 is subject to creditor claims. The exemption may be doubled for a joint filing by a husband and wife.[579] In states with an unlimited homestead exemption, this provision gives creditors an incentive to force debtors into involuntary bankruptcy.

Normally, the homestead exemption applies only to real estate you own in your name (or jointly owned with your spouse or in a few states, with an unmarried partner) and occupied as your principal residence. Some states protect only single-family homes and exclude duplexes, co-ops, apartments, or any other building where you occupy only a portion of the premises. Other states protect anything used as a dwelling, including boats, vehicles, and trailers.

The following obligations are generally excluded from protection:

- A mortgage on the home, including a home equity loan;
- Alimony or child support;
- Criminal fines and punitive damage awards;
- Damage awards in lawsuits for fraud, libel or slander;
- Federal tax claims,[580] although a few states grant homestead protection against state taxes; and
- Federal civil or criminal forfeiture proceedings.[581]

Free Asset Protection for Married Couples

Another form of protection for your home is available in about 20 states, mostly in the eastern and central United States, that recognize a form of common ownership of property, real or personal, tangible and intangible, by a husband and wife together. This form of ownership is known as **tenancy by the entireties.** Neither husband nor wife may sell any part of the property so held without the other's consent; each holds an indivisible half interest. The survivor of the marriage is entitled to the entire property.

Entireties ownership provides creditor protection for the entire homestead for an obligation created by one spouse. The property can't be divided without an end to the entireties estate or under a specific provision of state or federal law. In states that recognize entireties ownership, it's usually deemed to automatically exist at the time a husband and wife purchase a home.

To maximize the protection that entireties ownership provides, both spouses should never co-sign or guarantee the same obligation. In addition, if both spouses work in a family owned business, only one spouse should be an officer or director. Nor should both spouses pledge the value of the home for a loan. Doing so makes the equity in the property vulnerable to seizure.

In general, a creditor has no right to force the sale or division of the property against the wishes of the non-liable spouse.[582] However, a federal tax lien against one spouse may require the sale of entireties property, with half the proceeds used satisfy the lien.[583] Whether this is the result in a specific situation depends on the facts and circumstances of the case.

Another important exception may exist under federal bankruptcy law. In a Florida case, the court ruled that a bankruptcy trustee could liquidate a debtor's interest in alleged entireties property, for the benefit of creditors of only one spouse.[584] In this case, the entireties interest wasn't recorded properly, and the result may have differed in another factual situation.

Entireties ownership is also transitory. Death of the non-liable spouse, or divorce, ends all asset protection.

Further, entireties ownership can also make estate planning less effective. I've already described how a properly drafted marital bypass trust can double the estate tax exemption of a married couple. However, since title to entireties property passes directly to the surviving spouse, the marital bypass concept isn't applicable. For a valuable home, loss of this exemption could result in the needless payment of hundreds of thousands of dollars in estate tax.

One technique that deals with the possible death of the non-liable spouse is for each spouse to create a separate revocable living trust. Each trust holds an undivided half interest in the homestead. A creditor seeking to force the sale of the homestead for a debt incurred by one spouse will find that at most it is entitled to this undivided interest. This is an unmarketable asset since it would be virtually impossible to arrange a partition of the home satisfactory to the other owner. With proper planning (e.g., the trusts becoming irrevocable at incapacitation or death), it can also be an effective estate-planning tool. It's also effective in states that don't recognize entireties ownership.

How to Own Real Estate Anonymously

In some states, you can "anonymize" real estate holdings by taking title to them through a trust. This arrangement removes the names of beneficial owners of the trust from appearing on property ownership records. It generally employs a revocable trust (referred to as a **land trust** in some states). Mortgage lenders will generally finance property owned by a revocable trust. In some states, the trustee can be a corporation or LLC, shielding the identity of the individual who formed the trust.[585] There is generally no requirement to register the trust, although its property ownership will appear in public land records.

Land trusts are an excellent way to own property to preserve privacy. But unless the trust is irrevocable, your beneficial interest in the property may be subject to creditor claims.

If you take title to property in a trust, don't assume that homestead protection will apply without checking first. A Connecticut bankruptcy court has held that the homestead exemption in that state isn't effective if the home is held in a revocable trust.[586] In 2006, Florida revised its land trust statute to clarify that the homestead exemption applies to property in a land trust, after a Florida bankruptcy court ruled that it wasn't available under state law.[587]

An alternative to the land trust that achieves similar objectives is a **holding agreement**. This is a private contract between a holding company (typically, but not always, a title company) and the beneficial owner of the real property. The agreement itself is not usually recorded in public records, which will therefore reflect only the legal title-holder of the property; i.e., the title holding company.

Trusts Can Protect the Equity in Your Home

A land trust doesn't generally provide asset protection, although it can if it's irrevocable. However, conveying property into an irrevocable trust can have estate and gift tax consequences. If you live in the property, to obtain asset protection, you may need to pay market rental payments to the trust for the use of the house, with those payments potentially constituting taxable income.

One way to minimize the income tax bite while also protecting your home equity is to use an irrevocable trust called an **intentionally defective grantor trust** (IDGT). The trust is "defective" because you're treated as the owner of trust assets for income tax purposes, but not for estate tax purposes. Ordinarily, you wouldn't pay income tax on an irrevocable trust created for another person's benefit. But in an IDGT, the trust deed is modified to make you taxable on trust's income.

You sell your residence to the IDGT at its fair market value in exchange for an installment note and sign a lease with the IDGT to live in the residence. While you must pay the IDGT fair market rent for the use of the residence, the IDGT pays you an annual income from the installment note. You can't deduct the rental payments, but they're not considered income to the IDGT. Nor are the installment payments you receive taxable. If you've mortgaged the property, the IDGT can make the mortgage payments, which are deductible. If you wish to sell the property, the proceeds can be conveyed to you through an accelerated installment note payment.

You can also use an IDGT to remove highly appreciated assets, or assets with the potential for substantial appreciation, from your taxable estate. You may need to pay gift tax on the value of the assets when they're transferred, but at your death, the assets in the IDGT pass to your heirs, free of estate or gift tax. [588]

Another strategy to reduce the equity in your home is to mortgage it. An interest only mortgage avoids making more equity vulnerable as you pay down the loan. One strategy to protect the mortgage proceeds is to place the money into an irrevocable spendthrift trust. The trustee can invest the funds conveyed to earn enough income to recoup most or perhaps all of the mortgage interest. However, the trust can't give you a legally enforceable right to demand that it make mortgage payments. If it does, a court could order you to demand a payment to pay off a creditor. Instead, the trust should give you the right to request the trustee to make mortgage payments. And the trustee can grant that request if there are no judgments pending against you. Many variations on this strategy are possible.

Mortgages from commercial lenders are commonly issued for 80% of the equity in a residence. The remaining 20% can be protected if you're willing to pay a higher interest rate. However, this 20% won't generally be attractive to creditors, because at a court-ordered auction, the home generally won't sell for its full value. State homestead laws may also protect this remaining equity.

Again, it's essential to use a qualified legal professional to set up these arrangements. But the payoff is very strong protection for your home equity.

Make the Same Assets Work Twice to Protect Your Property

If you or your business own multiple properties, consider a strategy involving multiple entities that pledge one another's assets to each other. This strategy is called **cross-collateralization**.

Assume you own two limited liability companies (LLCs), which in turn own property you want to protect from judgments. LLC #1 receives a loan from LLC #2, secured by LLC #1's property. LLC #2 receives a loan from LLC #1, using the loan proceeds LLC #1 previously received from LLC #2, providing LLC #1 with a lien on the property of LLC #2. If LLC #1 experiences a judgment, LLC #2's property lien is superior to the creditor's claim, leaving the creditor with an unenforceable judgment. Thus, without needing to go to an external source for funding the loan, the property in both LLCs is protected from creditors.

This simple example would not be difficult for a sophisticated creditor to penetrate. However, cross-collateralization arrangements typically involve three or more entities, one or more of which may be domiciled offshore. It's also important that the loans have a legitimate business purpose. If they do, it will be difficult for a creditor to prevail in a fraudulent conveyance claim. Crafting such a structure is a job for an experienced asset protection planner.

Asset Protection with Annuities and Life Insurance

Only minimal protection exists under federal bankruptcy laws for life insurance and annuity contracts, but laws in some states exempt certain insurance products from creditor claims.

An **annuity** is a contract where an insurance company or other guarantor agrees to make a series of payments to someone for the rest of their life, their joint lives (e.g., husband and wife) or for a fixed number of years in exchange for a single premium. The contract may also provide for a guarantee of enough payments to be at least equal to the amount that paid for the contract.

Annuities can be **immediate**, in which case you receive payments immediately after paying a premium, or **deferred**, in which case payments are deferred for a specified number of years. In a **fixed annuity**, payments are guaranteed to be of a certain size for the duration of the contract. In a **variable annuity**, some or all of the funds are invested in securities. The value of the annuity and thus the size of the payments vary depending on the performance of the underlying investments.

Income earned within an annuity is tax deferred until you cash in the contract or receive payments from it. The income component of the payments is subject to ordinary income tax rates: a maximum federal rate of 35%, plus applicable state income tax. This is in contrast to the top federal rate of 15% on long-term capital gains. There is a 10% penalty tax on most withdrawals from an annuity before you reach age 59-1/2. Consequently, an annuity is most beneficial for the portion of your portfolio that generates ordinary income rather than long-term gains.

Annuities are usually purchased for income during life, rather than to pass assets on to your heirs. To the extent that an annuity policy guarantees a minimum payment in the event of your death, that payment will be an asset of your estate. For this reason, an annuity isn't a tax-efficient way to pass assets on to your heirs.

In contrast, **life insurance** provides a guaranteed death benefit to your loved ones or a named charity. In addition to its asset protection advantages in some states, life insurance enjoys uniquely preferential treatment under the U.S. Tax Code:

- **All earnings accumulate free of taxes until withdrawal.** There's no tax on the appreciation in value or accumulation of income of the investment account maintained within a life insurance policy.
- **The death benefit can pass to beneficiaries tax-free.**
- **Tax-free loans are possible.** Generally, policyholders may withdrawal up to 90% of the balance of their investment accounts as a loan. These loans need not be repaid and are deducted from the proceeds at death.
- **Tax-free exchanges are possible.** Among other planning possibilities, the Tax Code permits the tax-free exchange of a life insurance policy for an annuity contract. Therefore, it's possible to purchase a life insurance contract to protect your loved ones against financial problems if you die prematurely, and later, convert it into an annuity to provide a lifetime income stream for yourself.

- **With proper structuring, the proceeds can flow to beneficiaries free of both estate and generation-skipping taxes.** As discussed earlier in this chapter, this is possible using a life insurance policy in conjunction with a life insurance trust.

There are three main types of life insurance:

- **Whole life insurance** provides for a level premium, and a cash value guaranteed by an insurance company. Gains within the policy are tax-deferred.
- **Universal life insurance** offers the potential for higher returns. Instead of a guaranteed cash value, there a separate cash account established by the insurer. Interest is paid into the cash account at a minimum rate guaranteed by the company, but payments may be higher than the minimum.
- **Variable life insurance** is similar to universal life insurance, except that the cash account may consist of a securities portfolio. As with a variable annuity, the value of the account is determined by the performance of investments within it.

Almost every state protects the death benefit of an insurance policy from creditors where a spouse or child is the beneficiary. However, the policy's cash value may not be exempt. Similarly, stocks or other investments purchased through life insurance and annuity policies may not be protected from creditors. Life insurance under a group policy may enjoy greater protection than a policy you own.

In most states, for an annuity to be protected, it must be payable to someone other than the contract owner. And even if a creditor can't get at the assets in an annuity during the deferral period, it may be able to attach the payments, once they begin. Whatever protection exists may also not extend to alimony or child support, criminal fines, punitive damages, or federal tax claims, among other possible exemptions.

There are substantial advantages to owing life insurance and annuity policies issued under the laws of some offshore jurisdictions. Chapter 5 describes these advantages.

Protecting Your Retirement Plan

In view of the significant asset protection afforded pension and retirement plans under U.S. law, an important lifeboat strategy is to use them for "nest egg" assets you can't afford to lose.

Assets in an employer-sponsored retirement plan (defined benefit plans and defined contribution plans) are protected from creditor claims under the federal ERISA law.[589] In 1992, the Supreme Court held that all "ERISA-qualified" retirement plans are protected from creditor claims in bankruptcy.[590]

Many other types of retirement plans are not ERISA-qualified, including IRAs and simplified employee pension (SEP) plans. However, the 2005 Bankruptcy Reform Act exempts from creditor attachment IRAs and other non-ERISA-qualified retirement plans or contracts similar to those plans covered by ERIS. For IRAs, these plans are protected up US$1 million maximum value.

You must declare bankruptcy to gain this protection. That means creditors can seize property that isn't exempt under bankruptcy laws. For instance, a personal residence that would otherwise be protected under a state's homestead laws may be seized in a bankruptcy proceeding if you've owned it for fewer than 1,215 days, unless your equity in it doesn't exceed specified limits (for 2007, US$136,875). Further, spousal and child support claims aren't exempted; nor are claims from the IRS.[591] IRAs may also be seized in criminal forfeiture cases.[592]

An innocent spouse living in a community property state[593] may also lose his or her community property interest in an ERISA-qualified plan to non-exempt creditors.[594]

CHAPTER FIVE: THE OFFSHORE ADVANTAGE

The fundamental strategy this book recommends is to create "lifeboats" of privacy and wealth. At least some of those lifeboats should be outside your domestic jurisdiction.

Creating offshore lifeboats may require overcoming some preconceptions about investing outside your own country, especially if you live in the United States. Indeed, the U.S. media is filled with stories equating "offshore investing" with "tax evasion," "money laundering" and "terrorism."[595]

Don't believe the anti-offshore hype. As this chapter demonstrates, there are many legitimate reasons to "go offshore." Moreover, the vast majority of funds held in offshore centers are placed there by individuals and businesses engaged in lawful investment or commerce. A 1994 study from the United Nations estimated that money laundering accounted for less than 10% of the activity in offshore centers.[596] Given the global crackdown on money laundering since 1994, the percentage today is probably even lower.

However, the United States, along with non-governmental organizations such as the Organization for Economic Cooperation and Development (OECD) and the Financial Action Task Force (FATF), have forced offshore jurisdictions to enact—and enforce—stringent anti-laundering and information exchange laws. While the advantages of investing offshore remain compelling, there are now fewer opportunities for tax savings or financial privacy (at least from governments). Moreover, fees for offshore services have risen sharply to offset the costs of enforcing stricter money laundering laws.

At the same time, penalties for violations of U.S. tax, financial reporting, and money laundering laws have become increasingly severe. **The bottom line:** Don't invest or do business offshore without a thorough understanding of the legal and tax consequences, as discussed in this chapter.

Defining "Offshore"

What is "offshore?" The definition depends on your frame of reference. Offshore is anywhere other than your domestic jurisdiction or its possessions. To a Canadian, the United States is an "offshore" jurisdiction, and vice versa.

Offshore jurisdictions are often defined in terms of their tax advantages. From this perspective, offshore jurisdictions have a very long history. In the fourth century B.C., the Romans built what may have been history's first tax haven: a tax-free shipping port at Delos that diverted traffic from Rhodes, where ships were charged a 2% tax.[597]

Today, offshore centers are generally thought of as jurisdictions that have enacted laws and administrative policies designed to attract certain types of investments and business entities. Entities commonly formed in offshore financial centers include:

- International holding companies;
- International finance companies;
- License owning or royalty routing companies;
- Sales, purchase and international trading companies;
- Management and service companies;
- Captive insurance companies;
- Ship registration companies;

- Operational headquarters companies;
- International business companies; and
- Asset protection trusts.

The size of the offshore industry is staggering. A 2005 study estimated that high net-worth individuals hold at least US$11.5 trillion offshore.[598] These private funds are held primarily in offshore banks, trusts, and mutual funds. To this figure must be added trillions of dollars more in captive insurance companies, shipping companies, and the foreign subsidiaries of multinational corporations.

There is no comprehensive list of jurisdictions considered to be offshore centers. Any jurisdiction that seeks to attract foreign capital by enacting tax, regulatory or other fiscal advantages into law can be considered an offshore center, or in more pejorative terms, a "tax haven." Under this definition, more than 100 countries are tax havens, including many high-tax countries: Austria, Denmark, France, Ireland, Luxembourg, the Netherlands, the United Kingdom and the United States, along with jurisdictions better known as offshore centers such as Bermuda, the Cayman Islands and Switzerland.

The Case for Offshore Investing

Despite ongoing efforts to eliminate the tax advantages of offshore investing, substantial non-tax advantages remain for U.S. persons who make offshore investments. They include:

- Access to investment and business opportunities not available in the United States;
- Protection from the falling U.S. dollar;
- Reduced portfolio risk;
- Protection from professional liability and other claims;
- Increased privacy; and
- Investment continuity in the event of disruptions in U.S. markets.

Access to investment and business opportunities. While the United States has by far the world's largest securities markets, more than half of the world's stock investment opportunities, as measured by capitalization, are in other countries. The economies of China, India, and Central Europe, among other countries and regions, are growing much faster than the United States.

Non-U.S. exchanges already trade securities of:

- 9 of the 10 largest metals and mining companies;
- 8 of the 10 largest electronic equipment and instruments companies;
- 7 of the 10 largest automobile companies;
- 7 of the 10 largest household durables companies; and
- 7 of the 10 largest telecommunications companies.

In many cases, it's not possible to purchase non-U.S. securities through a U.S. broker. While Americans can participate in foreign markets by purchasing securities traded on U.S. exchanges known as **American Depository Receipts** (ADRs), only a few thousand foreign securities are listed, representing the largest and most liquid shares in the most developed foreign markets. Additional foreign shares are traded in the over-the-counter (OTC) market, but ADRs and OTC shares are typically less liquid and have higher buy-sell spreads than shares traded on local exchanges.

Securities of most foreign companies, especially smaller ones, are available only on the local market. Some U.S. brokers can execute trades in these securities, but brokers are forbidden by SEC rules to discuss any security not listed on a U.S. exchange with their clients. There are exceptions for high net worth clients under the SEC's Regulation S, but offshore securities issuers must avoid "directed selling efforts" which requires registration and compliance with a myriad of U.S. securities laws.[599]

Protection from the falling U.S. dollar. Offshore investing provides valuable exposure to foreign currencies. This is important because in recent decades, the U.S. dollar has lost value in relation to stronger currencies. For instance, in 1970, a U.S. dollar purchased approximately 4.5 Swiss francs. By 2007, the dollar purchased less than 1.2 Swiss francs, representing a loss in value of more than 70%. While U.S. investors can purchase foreign currencies through a few domestic banks, offshore banks generally offer higher yields and lower minimums.

Reduced portfolio risk. Investment portfolios that are globally diversified carry significantly less long-term risk than those that aren't. While foreign stock markets often mirror performance of the U.S. market, long-term correlations are relatively low, thus reducing risk compared to a portfolio of all U.S. stocks.[600]

Protection from professional liability and other claims. Domestic strategies and structures to avoid lawsuits aren't always effective against the expanding theories of liability in U.S. courts. The prudent use of offshore centers enhances your ability to protect assets from judgments, civil forfeiture, business failure, divorce, foreign exchange controls, repressive legislation, or political instability. It largely avoids the sophisticated U.S. asset-tracking network, which permits investigators to easily identify the unencumbered assets of a potential defendant.

It's also much more difficult for a successful litigant to collect against offshore assets. No country automatically enforces U.S. civil judgments, and many countries don't enforce them at all. Nor is there any bilateral treaty or multilateral convention in force between the United States and any other country on reciprocal recognition and enforcement of judgments.

The legal systems of most countries discourage frivolous litigation. Outside the United States, the loser must generally pay the winner's legal bills, courts can't award punitive damages in civil disputes, and lawyers are forbidden to accept contingency fees, or may accept them only in restricted circumstances. A litigant may even be forced to post a bond to cover the expenses of the defendant should the defendant prevail in court. Because such rules aren't enforced in the United States, there is a widespread perception abroad that U.S. litigation is "out of control."

Increased privacy. The United States is one of the few nations lacking a federal statute that protects bank or securities accounts from disclosure except under defined circumstances.[601] In contrast, dozens of countries recognize the principle of bank secrecy.[602] Many disclosures that would be illegal in other countries, either under international agreements such as the European Privacy Directive,[603] or under national laws guaranteeing bank secrecy, as in Switzerland, are commonplace in the United States.

Bank secrecy generally extends to investments from foreign investors, although international agreements may require greater disclosure, as described in Chapters 6 and 7.

Investment continuity. The attacks of Sept. 11, 2001 demonstrated the vulnerability of the U.S. financial infrastructure. U.S. securities markets were closed for four days after the attack. During this time, investors with strictly U.S. bank or brokerage accounts could not trade securities. But U.S. investors with foreign accounts could trade foreign securities on foreign exchanges.

While this disruption of the U.S. securities markets did not lead to widespread investor panic, there's no assurance that a future attack on the U.S. financial infrastructure wouldn't lead to a longer suspension of trading. The lifeboat strategy for U.S. investors is to maintain "nest egg" positions in politically neutral offshore havens that are unlikely terrorist targets.

Your Offshore Bank Account

The most basic strategy for offshore investment is to open a foreign bank account.

There are immense practical privacy and asset protection advantages to an offshore bank account. Since the money is offshore, it becomes virtually invisible to domestic information brokers and private investigators. If someone is sizing you up for a lawsuit, assets you hold offshore won't show up without some digging.

Even if a creditor discovers your offshore assets, those monies ordinarily won't be retrievable without a judgment. In that event, a U.S. court can order you to repatriate any offshore assets that you control. Failure to comply may lead to a civil or criminal contempt citation.[604] However, in some offshore centers, such as Switzerland, such an order may not be honored if the bank knows or believes the request is being made under duress.

How to Choose the Right Offshore Bank

Most offshore banks specialize in one of the following areas:

1. Taking money on deposit and lending it to businesses (commercial banks);
2. Taking money on deposit and lending it to private individuals (savings and loans); or
3. Buying and holding investments for private individuals (private banks)

Find a bank that specializes in the activity you plan to be engaging in the most. If you need to deal in more than one category, you may need more than one bank. Although larger banks may be able to take care of all your needs, by dealing with specialized banks, you will usually get better service and may save money in fees and commissions.

If you're merely looking to establish a small offshore nest egg, and don't plan to actively trade your account, your best option may be to open a small account at a commercial bank. Fees are lower at most commercial banks than at the "private banks" I'll discuss later in this chapter. If you're doing business offshore and need commercial banking services, find an offshore commercial bank that specializes in business financing, multiple currency dealings, and merchant payment solutions.

If you're an active investor and plan to purchase securities globally, you'll want to use a private bank. However, you may not be eligible for all the bank's services unless you have several hundred thousand dollars to invest—sometimes more. As a rule, open trading accounts in the region(s) where you intend to trade regularly. For instance, if you plan to trade European stocks, open a euro account at a European bank. This can save you money, since you won't need to pay foreign exchange fees when purchasing euro-denominated securities.

You can find the names of offshore private banks at http://www.escapeartist.com/offshore3/banks.htm. Check the financial strength of any bank at http://www.fitchratings.com.

Four Ways to Avoid Offshore Investment Restrictions

U.S.-resident investors will experience a bias throughout the offshore world, and that bias is increasing. The bias isn't aimed at individual Americans, but is a consequence of the extraordinary risks offshore banks assume when they deal with U.S. residents.

Many U.S. laws extend U.S. legal authority to foreign countries or assets (**extraterritorial jurisdiction**). Among the most important U.S. laws with extraterritorial effect are:

- **The USA PATRIOT Act.** As discussed in Chapter 2, this law permits the U.S. government to confiscate the U.S. assets of foreign banks, without convicting, much less accusing, the bank, or any of its depositors of a crime.
- **Qualified intermediary rules.** Tax rules enforced by the IRS impose a draconian 30%-31% withholding tax on both income and **gross sales proceeds** for U.S. securities owned by foreign banks. The tax can only be avoided if the foreign banks enter into one-sided **qualified intermediary** agreements with the IRS to enforce U.S. tax laws.[605]
- **Securities laws.** Laws enforced by the U.S. Securities and Exchange Commission prohibit the marketing of non-U.S. registered securities, which include the vast majority of securities trading outside the United States. The SEC has an extraordinarily expansive definition of what constitutes "marketing." As a result, some offshore banks no longer permit U.S. residents to purchase foreign securities, even if those orders are unsolicited.

There are several ways to legally avoid these restrictions:

1. **Have a legal residence outside the United States.** Offshore banks are more willing to accommodate non-resident U.S. citizens than those living in the United States. If you're a U.S. citizen with a legal residence outside the United States, investment restrictions offshore banks impose on U.S. residents won't apply. You'll need to prove that you're legally resident offshore; e.g., in the form of an official identity card or residence visa and possibly a driver's license and/or utility bill with a non-U.S. address.

2. **Conduct transactions in person.** Most offshore banks place fewer restrictions on instructions conveyed by a U.S. resident in a personal visit than those originating in the United States. You may also be able to arrange that after you leave, certain trades will occur automatically, depending on market conditions.

3. **Have the portfolio managed by your bank or an independent portfolio manager.** Once you sign a portfolio management mandate, investment instructions will no longer originate in the United States. Most offshore banks impose fewer investment restrictions on such portfolios.

4. **Invest through non-U.S. insurance or annuity policy, or an offshore entity such as an offshore corporation, offshore limited liability company, or offshore trust.** These contracts and entities often eliminate offshore investment restrictions, but have significant tax and reporting consequences described later in this chapter.

Current Accounts: Your Offshore Banking Foundation

A **current account** is the foundation of the business relationship between a foreign bank and its customers. From your current account, you can make investments into many other types of investments, with interest, dividends, and capital gains credited back to the account.

In some countries (like Austria), the minimum investments for current accounts at commercial banks are very low—less than US$150—and the accounts earn no or a very low interest. Private banks, which specialize in portfolio management, generally have much higher minimums—US$100,000 and up.

A very small account isn't practical, though, because of the fees charged by most foreign banks. Expect to pay at least US$50 in fees annually, even for the smallest account with minimal activity.

You can carry out account transactions in writing, in person, over the phone or, in some cases, via e-mail or the Internet. With a sufficiently large deposit, and after establishing an account for a minimum period—usually ranging from one to six months—you can obtain a bank debit card to draw against monies in your account.

Funds you hold in a current account are generally considered an asset on the bank's balance sheet and available to creditors (including you as a depositor) in the event of the bank's insolvency. If you purchase securities in your account, which aren't part of the bank's balance sheet, these investments belong to you alone, and aren't available to creditors if the bank declares bankruptcy.

Savings Accounts: Good for Small Investors

Most foreign banks offer savings accounts. One option is a **demand account**, in which your money is available without providing the bank advance notice. If you don't need instant access to your funds, higher interest rates are available by providing one month or even three months advance notice. If you need the money before the notice period has expired, an early withdrawal fee is imposed.

The interest rate on savings accounts may be only a little higher than that available in current accounts. Slightly higher rates may be available for longer commitment periods. The interest rate also depends on the currency you choose and the amount you invest.

Savings accounts are ideal if you simply want to put a little money offshore in a foreign currency account, especially if the investment is too small to qualify for purchase of CDs, which often have minimums of US$10,000 or more. But like a current account, funds in a savings account are an asset on the bank's balance sheet and available to creditors in the event of the bank's insolvency.

Profits from Investments in Foreign Currency CDs

One of the best ways to invest in foreign currencies is through CDs. They're available for periods as short as a week to 12 months or longer. As with U.S. CDs, you earn more interest for a larger investment or for a longer commitment. If you redeem your CD early, you may forfeit part or all of your interest earnings and pay a penalty.

The interest rate paid on CDs varies depending on the credit quality of the issuer and the currency in which the CD is denominated. The rates tend to be slightly lower than the prevailing inter-bank rates published in financial tables in *The Wall Street Journal*, the *Financial Times,* and other sources.

When your CD matures, you have several options. You may roll it over; most foreign banks will take automatic rollover instructions, which will be followed until you send the bank fresh instructions. Or you can instruct the bank to rollover only the same face value of the CD and deposit the interest into your regular account.

Another option is to tell the bank to purchase securities, precious metals, or other investments with the proceeds. You can also switch currencies, although you'll pay up to 2% in foreign exchange spreads and commissions—sometimes more.

As with any time deposit, there are penalties if you need the funds before maturity. The worst that can generally happen is that you forfeit most or all of the interest on the CD and pay a cancellation fee—typically no more than the equivalent of US$50.

CDs may or may not be considered an asset on the bank's balance sheet. If they are, the assets will be available to creditors in the event of the bank's insolvency.

Buy and Sell Precious Metals Offshore

Precious metals—gold, silver, platinum, and palladium—are an excellent hedge against the long-term decline of the dollar. Indeed, since 2000, as the U.S. dollar has fallen more than 25% against the currencies of America's largest trading partners, the price of gold has nearly tripled.

Offshore banks offer a range of precious metals purchase and custody options similar to those available for securities, including limit and stop orders. It may or may not be possible to purchase and sell precious metals free of local tax, so be sure to ask.

Buy or Sell any Security in the World

Many offshore banks offer all the services you would expect from a full-service stockbroker—and you may purchase any security in the world, not those just listed on a domestic exchange. The purchase price, less applicable commissions, is debited from your current account and credited to a **custodial account** maintained by the bank. SEC roadblocks are no longer relevant, because the offshore bank purchases the securities in its name, not yours. And, like a domestic securities broker, you may issue limit and stop orders. It's also possible to generate additional income from your securities holdings by writing options or employing other strategies.

Interest and dividend payments from foreign securities may be subject to withholding tax in that country. Such payments may often be reclaimed under a tax treaty between the United States and whatever jurisdiction has imposed it.

There's one securities market you may want to avoid if you have a foreign account: the United States. The IRS requires offshore banks that hold U.S. correspondent accounts (Chapter 2) to execute "qualified intermediary" (QI) agreements. These agreements are intended to identify U.S. persons trading U.S. securities without paying tax on income or gains from such trades. QI agreements may require offshore banks to prohibit transactions in foreign securities if trading instructions originate in the United States. The agreements may also prohibit the offshore bank from making its buy/sell recommendations available to U.S. persons. Fortunately, by doing business with an offshore bank that has minimal contacts with the United States, you can often avoid these restrictions.

Foreign Bonds Give You Four Opportunities to Profit

One of the most popular ways to invest in a foreign bank account is to purchase bonds. Trading fees are lower for bonds than for other securities, and if you're a U.S.-resident investor, there are fewer restrictions on purchasing foreign bonds than purchasing foreign stocks and (especially) offshore funds.

Without accounting for fees, taxes and commissions, the total return that a bond denominated in a foreign currency provides has four different components:

1. **Interest payments.** As with bonds denominated in your domestic currency, you earn interest, which is a fixed return regardless of what happens to market interest rates after you buy. During times of high interest rates, you can lock in high yields.

2. **Interest rates.** If interest rates drop after you buy the bond, its market value rises. If interest rates rise, bond prices will drop and you will face a capital loss if you sell before maturity. The further in the future the maturity date for the bond, the faster it will gain (or lose) value when interest rates change.

3. **Credit rating.** Should the bond issuer's credit rating be upgraded, the value of the bond may increase. If the credit rating is downgraded, however, its value is likely to fall.

4. **Foreign exchange.** If the currency in which the bonds are denominated changes in value relative to your domestic currency, your returns vary accordingly.

Tens of thousands of bonds are available worldwide, from issuers with credit quality ranging from AAA to junk. Euro-denominated bonds issued by EU governments or corporations are a popular choice, with interest rates varying according to the credit quality of the issuer. The EU has made it easy to purchase or sell bonds listed on EU exchanges through an account with a EU bank. Commissions may be lower on such purchases than on purchases outside the EU, and you save on foreign exchange fees.

Bonds from smaller and emerging markets offer higher interest rates. Yields are higher because there are greater risks in emerging market currencies than in mainstream currencies such as the euro or dollar. When you buy bonds, don't base your buying decision on the highest interest rates you can obtain. Instead, look at the prospects for the currency the bond is denominated in, and of course, the credit quality of the issuer. Most offshore banks let you borrow against the value of any bond, either to help pay for it or to leverage your investment. Keep in mind the obvious: if the interest rate you'll pay for the privilege will effectively wipe out the interest return you will receive on the bond, then there is no advantage.

The following chart gives a few examples of the wide range of bonds that your offshore bank can purchase for you, in all major currencies:

Currency	Name	Country
CAD (Canadian dollar)	4.25% Rabobank 1/5/09	Netherlands
EUR (euro)	6.25% Prosieben 5/15/09	Germany
EUR (euro)	11.0% Brazil 4/2/10	Brazil
ISK (Icelandic krona)	7.25% Rikisbref 5/17/13	Iceland
NOK (Norwegian krone)	5.5% Norway S468 5/15/09	Norway
TRY (Turkish new lira)	13% European Investment Bank 3/23/08	Turkey

Purchasing Stocks Through an Offshore Bank

Tens of thousands of stocks are available worldwide, from every conceivable market and issuer. Minimum purchases for bonds are low at most offshore banks, in some cases €1,000 or less. However, minimum purchases tend to be higher for stocks than for bonds.

Without accounting for fees, taxes and commissions, the total return that a stock denominated in a foreign currency has three different components:

1. **Dividends.** As with bonds denominated in your domestic currency, you earn whatever dividends, if any, paid by the issuer. However, unlike repayment of interest on a bond, the issuer of stock doesn't generally guarantee dividend payments.

2. **Market value.** If the market perceives that the company issuing the stock has good business prospects, its value may increase. Should the company's profits fall, or its prospects seem less bright, its value may fall.

3. **Foreign exchange.** If the currency in which the stock is denominated changes in value relative to your domestic currency, returns vary accordingly.

As with bonds, stocks denominated in euros and traded on EU exchanges are popular investment choices at offshore banks. Stocks from smaller and emerging markets, particularly in Asia and Eastern Europe, are also popular. These fast growing economies may offer greater opportunities than more developed markets. Yet, share prices and the value of the currency in which the shares are denominated are volatile.

Buying stocks means making an indirect bet on the direction of interest rates. When interest rates rise, stock prices generally fall. This is because companies encounter higher borrowing costs, resulting in lower profits. Investors who perceive interest rates are rising may reorient their portfolios toward short-term bonds and CDs, both of which have little interest rate risk.

As with bonds, most offshore banks let you borrow against the value of any stock, either to help pay for it or to leverage your investment. The percentage of value permitted as a loan is less for stocks than for bonds, since stocks are perceived to be higher risk investments.

Overcoming U.S. Tax Traps in Offshore Funds

WARNING: U.S. citizens and residents should avoid purchasing offshore funds without considering the potentially adverse tax consequences.

For purchases of U.S. mutual fund, income or gain is reported to the IRS on Form 1099. Since offshore funds and unit trusts don't file Form 1099, the IRS requires investors to determine their share of the income and pay tax on it. This isn't always easy to do. And if it's not possible to make the necessary calculations, using IRS-approved methods, the IRS imposes punitive taxes and interest payments on whatever taxes you defer.

The U.S. Tax Code (I.R.C. §1291-1297) refers to offshore funds organized as corporations as **passive foreign investment companies (PFICs).** A PFIC is any foreign corporation that earns at least 75% of its income through "passive" investments (interest, dividends, passive rents, royalties, capital gains, commodity gains, and currency gains) OR that holds 50% or more of the average value of its assets for the generation of passive income. Since most offshore funds are organized this way, the overwhelming majority of them are PFICs.

You'd think the IRS would make it easy to avoid deferring income or gain in a PFIC. But that's not possible unless the PFIC qualifies under one of two sets of rules.

1. U.S. investors may pay taxes at **ordinary income tax rates** on their income or gain each year in offshore funds that are **qualified electing funds (QEFs)**. However, QEF status is available only to funds willing to submit to SEC jurisdiction and to comply with U.S. accounting standards. The overwhelming majority of offshore funds aren't willing to do so for the sake of U.S. shareholders. As a result, very few offshore funds qualify as QEFs.

2. **The mark-to-market rules** apply to closed-end funds traded on a qualifying securities exchange. Under these rules, U.S. investors again pay tax at ordinary income tax rates on income or gain from the fund during the year. A long list of requirements must be met

for this exception to apply, but many off-shore funds traded on major securities exchanges appear to qualify. However, no official list of approved countries or exchanges exists.

If an offshore fund doesn't qualify under either the QEF or mark-to-market rules, it is deemed a "Section 1291 Fund," after the section of the U.S. Tax Code describing its unique tax treatment. At first glance, treatment as Section 1291 Fund seems ideal because you're not generally required to pay any income tax until you sell, other than income tax at your marginal rate on any income or capital gains actually distributed to shareholders). However, the results are anything but ideal:

- When tax is paid, all income and gains are taxed at the highest ordinary income rate bracket that applies (presently 35%), not your actual tax bracket;
- All losses are non-deductible;
- You must calculate gains as if they were made evenly, for each year that you held the fund; and
- An interest charge applies for each year tax was deferred on these gains.

For offshore funds held for many years, the tax and interest due can easily exceed the total gain. However, the law provides that the tax and interest charge shall not exceed the amount of the distribution.

Most offshore banks aren't familiar with these rules. U.S. investors in offshore funds who don't report and pay tax on income or gain each year will generally come under the PFIC rules, and can wind up owing huge amounts of interest to the IRS for the "privilege" of deferring taxes due.

U.S. investors in PFICs must also complete IRS **Form 8621** each year in which they generate income or gain from an offshore fund, and report it as ordinary income on their tax return. This form is relatively easy to complete for offshore funds that qualify for QEF or mark-to-market treatment. But for Section 1291 funds, you'll likely require an accountant familiar with the PFIC rules to complete the form.

The chart below gives a few examples of the wide range of stocks that your offshore bank can purchase for you, in all major currencies:

Currency	Name	Country
AUD (Australian dollars)	Westpac	Australia
CHF (Swiss franc)	Roche Holding AG-Genuss	Switzerland
EUR (euro)	Deutsche Telekom AG-Reg	Germany
EUR (euro)	France Telecom SA	France
GBP (British pound)	Vodafone Group PLC	U.K.
JPY (Japanese yen)	Nippon Telegraph & Telephone Corp.	Japan

Offshore Funds Open a World of Opportunity

Mutual funds are pooled securities funds. More than 55,000 mutual funds exist worldwide, but only about 11,500 are U.S.-registered. Due to the SEC registration requirements, most offshore fund issuers prohibit U.S. persons from becoming shareholders.

As with other types of securities, offshore banks have started to restrict the ability of U.S.-resident investors to purchase offshore funds, although as I described earlier in this chapter, there are ways to avoid these restrictions.

Without accounting for fees, taxes and commissions, the total return that an offshore fund provides has three different components:

Distributions. You earn whatever distributions are paid by the companies whose securities the offshore fund holds. **Distributing** offshore funds pay out this income to fund investors. **Non-distributing** or **roll-up** funds don't pay out this income, but adjust the share price upward to account for it.

Market value. If the market perceives that the investments in the fund are increasing in value, the share price of the fund will increase, and vice versa. **Closed-end funds** trade on securities exchanges and the market sets the share price. That price may represent a premium or discount to the net asset value (NAV) of the underlying assets. In **open-end funds**, issuers control the market and buy or sell interests based on the fund's NAV.

Foreign exchange. In a fund denominated in a foreign currency, if that currency changes in value relative to your domestic currency, your returns vary accordingly.

One profit strategy is to purchase closed-end funds with big discounts to NAV, hoping that this discount will eventually narrow. These discounts may be larger on foreign exchanges than on U.S. exchanges for similar funds holding similar assets. Of course, there's no guarantee that discounts won't widen, instead of narrowing.

Most offshore banks let you borrow against the value of any fund. The percentage of value permitted as a loan is about the same as for a stock.

Offshore Banks Hold Your Investments in "Safe Custody"

When you purchase securities or precious metals through your foreign account, the bank will establish a custodial account to hold them. The securities or metals are held in the bank's name, for credit to your account. Increasingly, for securities, certificates are not issued in paper form—they exist only electronically.

As custodian, the bank collects dividends, coupon payments and, if the security has a maturity date, the value of its principal when it matures. These payments are all credited to your account. Custodial fees are deducted based (usually) on the market value of your securities or metals. For large holdings, you may be able to negotiate a flat fee for assets held in the bank's custody.

Most banks will allow you to maintain your securities or metals in **collective custody** or **individual custody**. In both types of custody, your

Three Ways U.S. Investors Can Safely Buy Offshore Funds

There are three ways U.S. investors can avoid the draconian PFIC regulations:

1. Purchase offshore funds through IRAs and other types of pension or profit-sharing plans. Income or gain within a retirement plan isn't taxed until it's paid out to the beneficiary, at which time it's taxed as ordinary income. There's no provision in the U.S. Tax Code for income or gain from offshore funds to be taxed any differently, offering a convenient way to avoid the PFIC rules.

As long as the retirement plan is administered according to U.S. law, there's no prohibition against a retirement plan owning offshore funds. This is true of both **"qualified"** plans under the 1974 ERISA law and **"non-qualified"** plans (e.g., IRAs and SEPs).

For this strategy to work, you must have: 1) a self-directed plan; and 2) a U.S. custodian willing to purchase offshore funds or other "non-traditional" investments. Determining whether a non-self-directed plan can be made self-directed requires an inquiry to the plan administrator. If it can be made self-directed, make sure that no tax is triggered upon a "rollover" to a self-directed plan.

Next, you need to find a U.S. custodian willing to purchase offshore funds or other "non-traditional" investments. While no law prohibits U.S. custodians from holding foreign investments and offshore funds in particular in U.S. retirement plans, few are willing to do so.

2. Purchase offshore funds through an offshore variable annuity. Under U.S. tax law, a variable annuity serves as a tax-deferred "wrapper" for an underlying investment account. Income or gain in the account isn't taxed until it's actually distributed to the beneficiary. Again, there's nothing in the U.S. Tax Code subjecting offshore funds held within a variable annuity to a different standard. As with any other investment wrapped in a tax-qualified variable annuity, income or gains from offshore funds is tax-deferred

210

until you receive it, without the PFIC interest charges.

U.S. insurance companies generally aren't willing to issue variable annuities permitting the purchase of offshore funds. But numerous offshore insurance companies offer IRS tax-compliant variable annuities that routinely hold offshore funds in their investment accounts. Minimum policy sizes for this strategy start around US$50,000. Due to state and federal insurance licensing and securities laws, it may be necessary to travel to the country where the annuity contract is issued to put it into force.

3. Purchase offshore funds through an offshore life insurance policy. A life insurance policy provides the advantages of a variable annuity and more: the death benefit received by beneficiaries is not subject to income tax. The policy can be structured to make the death benefit free of estate and generation-skipping taxes as well (Chapter 4).

A few U.S. life insurance companies will issue "private placement" policies to high net worth clients that permit the purchase of offshore funds. Very high minimums (US$5 million or more) are the norm. Offshore, the minimums for this strategy are much lower (typically US$500,000). Again, you may need to sign the insurance contract in the country where it's put into force.

WARNING: For a foreign variable annuity or life insurance contract to be "qualified" for U.S. tax purposes, stringent IRS requirements must be followed. The U.S. policyholder may not make investment decisions, although it's possible to request that a particular advisor or investment strategy be followed. Consult with a qualified international tax advisor to confirm that any policy offered by an offshore insurance company is U.S. tax compliant.

If you're interested in implementing one or more of these strategies, please contact The Nestmann Group for more information. We can assist U.S. persons in setting up tax-compliant offshore structures to purchase offshore funds and other international investments.

securities holdings are segregated from the bank's assets and are not available to meet claims by the bank's creditors.

Collective custody is most common. For most securities, it means the bank holds your position in **book entry** form on a computer and doesn't maintain physical possession. If it does maintain physical possession, your holdings aren't segregated from alike and interchangeable securities of other investors.

Individual custody means that the bank takes physical possession of your securities and holds them in a segregated account. There will be a certificate placed in the bank's vault with your name on it. This process requires more work for the bank, so individual custody costs more than collective custody.

For precious metals, in most cases your offshore bank will establish a **claim account** with **unallocated** storage. The bank buys a "specific but undivided" amount of gold on your behalf. **Allocated** or **custodial** storage is safer in the event of the bank's insolvency. The bank purchases a "specific and divided" quantity of precious metals that are segregated from the bank's assets.

The legal status of the metals in this situation is similar to securities in a custodial account and the metals aren't of the bank's balance sheet. Again, this means that the bank's general creditors can't seize the metals.

Managed Accounts: You Set the Rules

If you have the equivalent of US$300,000 or more to invest (more in some cases), you qualify for the services of an offshore portfolio manager.

Why not use a domestic portfolio manager? By using an advisor outside your own country, you may gain enhanced market and investment knowledge regarding along with additional asset protection and privacy.

Traditionally, offshore portfolio management was the province of "private bankers" working at a few dozen banks in Switzerland. The term "private banking" encompasses a range of financial services made available to individuals with significant amounts of money to invest, centering on portfolio management. But private banking is a growth business—there are more wealthy individuals now than ever before—and today, almost every major bank has a private banking department.

A private banker can tailor a portfolio according to your wishes. Within the portfolio, the bank can arrange for a mix of investments according to your risk preference: conservative, aggressive, or in-between.

Most private bankers are conservative. They're unlikely to make any rash promises about how rich you will become by letting them manage your money. If you press them, they are apt to say that their prime role is to preserve your assets. Profits are important, but a secondary concern.

Private bankers provide individualized services to their clients. The relationship may even extend to personal touches such as picking you up when you come to "visit their money," sending Christmas and birthday gifts to your family, etc.

While the minimum investments for offshore portfolio management are relatively high, the published minimums are often negotiable. If you have significant future earnings potential, yet don't meet the published investment minimum, you'll likely be given some leeway.

A typical portfolio management fee is 1% annually, plus commissions and custody fees. Some banks adjust this fee downward for larger portfolios. Lower fees may apply to a portfolio consisting primarily of bonds.

An alternative to portfolio management through an offshore bank is to use an independent asset manager. While independent asset managers will ordinarily execute trades through a bank, they are not bank employees.

Perhaps the biggest advantage of using an independent portfolio manager is direct access to the individuals who own and operate the company. Another advantage is continuity. The owner-operators of independent portfolio management firms are relatively stable. In contrast, there may be considerable turnover in portfolio managers at a bank's private banking division.

Independent asset managers also don't face the same pressures as private bankers to follow a model portfolio set by the bank or to include the bank's own securities and in-house mutual funds in their clients' portfolios. These securities may not necessarily be the highest-potential investments in their re-spective categories. Further, since the compensation of independent portfolio managers comes primarily from management fees, rather than commissions, they are under little pressure to generate commission income by turning over the investments frequently.

Multi-Currency Strategies

You can use several advanced strategies to potentially increase your profits from an offshore bank account. One is to borrow money in one or two low-interest-rate currencies and investing the loan pro-ceeds in a spread of investments in a high-interest-rate currency. This is a variation of the famous "carry trade" used for decades by currency traders. It can dramatically increase profit potential to your portfolio, although if the lending currencies gain value against the invested currencies, losses can mount quickly.

The private banking departments of many foreign banks are familiar with this strategy. Each bank has its lending policy. Many banks lend account-holders up to 50% of assets they hold at the bank as gold, mutual funds, shares and lower quality bonds, and up to 80% on CDs.

The key to success is spotting distortions where one currency is oversold and has a high interest rate and another is overbought and has a low interest rate. Borrow the low interest rate currency. Convert it into the high interest rate currency. You earn the difference between the low loan rate and high deposit rate.

For instance, it's been possible for nearly a decade to borrow Japanese yen at 1%-2% and reinvest the proceeds in much higher yielding currencies. If the respective values of the lending and invested currencies doesn't change, a 5% interest rate differential combined with 5:1 leverage (80% of funds invested borrowed) can result in a 25% annual return, before fees.

There are significant risks to this strategy. The worst risk is if lending currencies appreciate sharply against the invested currencies. If interest rates rise in the invested currencies, the capital value of the bonds could fall. Maintaining the portfolio in CDs or bonds with short maturities can reduce this risk. Risks are further reduced if the portfolio is diversified across several different currencies.

Transferring Ownership at Death Without Probate

It's important to consider what will happen to your offshore account at your death. The lifeboat strategy is to name a beneficiary or beneficiaries on your account application. The beneficiaries may be your spouse or partner, your children, your business partners, a trust or a company. If you don't name a beneficiary, once individuals named in your will learn of the account and try to claim it, they may be required to go through a foreign probate proceeding to claim it. This can be a lengthy and expensive process, and is unnecessary if you prepare in advance.

In most countries, your beneficiaries need not be made aware of that designation, and you can change your mind if you divorce, remarry; find a new partner, etc. However, it's important that beneficiaries be notified of the existence of your account at your death so that they can make a claim. This is their responsibility—the bank may not be permitted to contact them.

One way to notify them is to leave sealed envelopes with your attorney, with instructions to mail the envelopes to your beneficiaries upon your death. At that point, the beneficiaries can contact the bank and claim the assets.

In most countries, all that is necessary is for a beneficiary to claim the account is to produce a certified copy of your death certificate. Ordinarily, no probate formalities or local taxes are necessary, but check with the bank to find out what requirements apply.

Why It Costs More to Bank Offshore—and How to Reduce Fees and Commissions

Fees charged by offshore banks are higher than those charged by U.S. banks; sometimes much higher. One reason fees are higher is that unlike the United States, banks in most other countries aren't permitted to release client data for marketing purposes. Fees are usually negotiable, though, especially for large accounts. Here's a rundown of some of the fees you'll encounter:

Account package fees. At minimum, you can expect to pay a quarterly fee for maintaining whatever account package you choose. Private banks may charge an administrative fee based on assets deposited, generally around 0.25% annually. Some banks will waive this fee if the account generates sufficient fees or commissions in securities trades or other transactions.

Statement fees. Offshore banks charge for producing account statements, although you may be able to eliminate this fee if the bank doesn't mail you statements. In banks that provide online account access, your statement can be viewed and printed online at no charge. Commercial banks operating offshore may permit you to print account statements at bank kiosks in the countries in which they have branches.

Foreign exchange fees. There may or may not be a commission due when converting one currency to another currency. However, the bank will take a cut of the buy/sell spread to generate income from the transaction. Depending on the market, the currency, and the amount converted, this can range from 1%-3%.

Debit card fees. If you have a debit card to draw against the account, you'll pay an annual fee—typically, US$50-$100. To save on foreign exchange fees, maintain the account in the same currency as the one in which you'll take withdrawals.

Securities commissions. Buying and selling securities offshore is expensive. Except for the smallest trades (where minimum fees apply), fixed commissions per trade don't exist. Instead, fees are generally imposed as a percentage of the transaction. These fees can range from 0.25%-2% of the trade. Lower commissions apply for bonds. Commissions may also be reduced for trades placed online. Larger offshore banks are direct issuers of many types of securities. If you purchase securities (especially bonds) for your account directly from the issuing bank, you may reduce commissions and custody fees. For stocks, you can save on commissions by limiting purchases to blue chip issues you're prepared to hold for an extended period. Bonds held to maturity avoid paying a commission upon sale.

Offshore funds commissions. Offshore funds are more expensive to buy than individual securities. Many funds impose a 3%-5% (sometimes higher) front-end load. You can cut these fees by purchasing no-load funds, although most offshore banks will charge a 1%-2% commission to execute the transaction. Your bank may also offer its own offshore funds, a strategy that may result in commission savings. Another way to save on commissions is to buy exchange-traded funds listed on offshore exchanges. Commissions are about the same as those for stocks (0.25%-2%).

Precious metals commissions. Commissions on precious metals purchases range from 0.5%-1.0%, with higher commissions applying for less commonly traded coins or bars. There's also a larger buy/sell spread for precious metals than for stocks or bonds. Even the most liquid forms of gold (e.g., commonly traded 1-ounce gold coins such as the U.S. Eagle or Canadian Maple Leaf) sell for 2% or more above the prevailing spot price and are repurchased for 2% or more below the spot price. Spreads are smaller for larger purchases and may be reduced on the buy or sell side depending on market sentiment. You can eliminate commissions if you purchase coins yourself from the bank or a coin dealer and store them in your safety deposit box or a private vault. The bank's only source of profit is the spread.

Custodial fees. Safekeeping fees for securities or precious metals held by offshore banks are generally based on the market value of those assets. Fees are negotiable for larger customers. The fees range from 0.2%-1.5% per annum, depending on the asset and the type of custody used. For securities, typical custodial fees are 0.25% per annum for collective custody, 0.5% per annum for individual custody. You can reduce these fees by taking possession of the securities, if they're available in certificate form, and keeping the certificates in a safety deposit box or private vault. This strategy is appropriate only for securities that you anticipate holding for an extended period and that don't issue regular dividends. For precious metals, custody fees are slightly higher; around 0.5% per annum for collective custody, 0.75% per annum for individual custody. Fees for silver may be higher than for gold, platinum, or palladium. You can eliminate these fees by taking delivery of your metals and storing them securely yourself.

Using Bank Secrecy Effectively

For the reasons summarized earlier in this chapter, a bank or other financial account in a foreign country offers considerable privacy advantages, even if that country has no bank secrecy laws in effect. Bank secrecy laws reinforce this protection.

Bank secrecy is never absolute, and in recent years, exceptions to secrecy have expanded. Your financial information won't necessarily remain secret in the event of a criminal or tax fraud investigation. Although bank secrecy may be lifted in such an inquiry, other requests for information are routinely turned away.

Apart from the desire to avoid needless disclosure of your financial affairs to potential thieves or litigants, bank secrecy has an important role in protecting depositors from totalitarian governments. People living in jurisdictions with bank secrecy laws know this well, because of history.

In **Switzerland**, bank secrecy has been a tradition for more than 200 years. When Adolf Hitler assumed power in neighboring Germany in 1933, many prominent Jews had their property targeted for confiscation by the Gestapo. Many Jews responded to these threats by moving their assets out of Germany, mainly into Switzerland. The Gestapo followed and began making inquiries at Swiss banks about their Jewish depositors, often through bribery or subterfuge. A bank employee might be asked to credit a small deposit to the account of "Mr. Josef Silverburg from Hamburg." If the deposit was accepted, this was considered proof that the individual had a foreign bank account. Eventually, Nazi Germany made it a capital offense for a German national to have a foreign bank account. In response, in 1935, Switzerland enacted a bank secrecy law, backed by stiff criminal penalties.

Bank secrecy should therefore be viewed not as a shield to criminal activity, but as an essential element to protect wealth against the most threatening predator of wealth: government. However, governments have many tools available to pry open "secret" foreign bank accounts.

These tools are most fully developed in the United States. For instance, the U.S. Supreme Court has upheld a procedure through which a U.S. court can issue an order directing you, under penalty of imprisonment for contempt of court, to sign a "consent directive." This directive provides legal authority to a foreign bank to turn over your account records to the IRS.[606] You'll learn more about how the U.S. government combats what it considers "abuses" of foreign bank secrecy later in this chapter.

The Numbered Account: More Secrecy, but not Anonymous

You can obtain an additional layer of secrecy with a **numbered account.** Here, you conduct all transactions by account number and password, and only a handful of people at the bank know your identity. All transactions are carried out in the name of your pseudonym or number plus a password, not your real name. Bank statements show only your pseudonym or number.

The main benefit of a numbered account is that it avoids the possibility that a bank employee might be coerced or bribed by an outside party to reveal information about your account. These tech-

215

niques are well known to kidnappers, extortionists, and tax collectors. Another advantage is that bank statements won't actually contain your name. No one can prove with a stolen bank statement that the account actually belongs to you.

The operating costs of a numbered account are often several times higher than a regular account. Only you can decide if the privacy advantages are worth the additional costs.

It was once possible in Switzerland, Liechtenstein, Austria, and a number of other countries for individuals to open **anonymous** bank accounts. However, these accounts have now been eliminated or severely restricted. While a few banks in politically unstable jurisdictions still offer anonymous accounts, in these countries, foreign exchange controls or outright confiscation could occur almost overnight.

Offshore Banks Must Follow "Know Your Customer" Rules

Money laundering laws offshore are just as strict as in the United States, sometimes even stricter. When you open an account with an offshore bank, you'll be expected to verify your identity and the source of funds. You'll need to provide a copy of your passport, a bank reference, and (at some banks) a utility bill that verifies your residential address. You may also be required to provide a statement attesting to the source of the funds you're depositing.

Documentation you may be asked to complete includes:

A detailed application form. This includes your name, address and information on where you want account statements mailed (unless you want the bank to hold all correspondence); what type of account you wish to open; which currency you wish to invest in; and if you want a debit card. If you're opening a securities account, the bank will want to know how to handle orders (at market or with a limit price). If you're opening a precious metals account, you'll need to specify which metals you wish to purchase, and in what form (bars or coins), etc.

For a corporate account, you'll probably need to include an extract from the official company register showing the company to be in good standing; a notarized corporate resolution conferring the authority for the account to be opened; and the names of authorized signatories. Some banks may also require you to include a copy of the articles of incorporation (for a corporation), the articles of association (for a limited liability company) or (in the case of trusts) the trust deed, or an extract from it. You may also need to provide the bank with details about the beneficial owners of the corporation or LLC, or the beneficiaries of the trust.

Investor profile. Depending on the type of account opened (but particularly if you're seeking portfolio management services), the bank will ask that you specify your investment objectives, investment experience, and the investment approach you prefer (aggressive, conservative or balanced). You may also be asked to complete a risk tolerance assessment.

Introduction letter. Each bank will have its own version of this form, which the account officer must complete to satisfy due diligence requirements. To complete it, the bank will ask you, among other things, to verify the source of funds, the purpose of the account, etc.

These requirements also have a consumer protection purpose. For instance, if you want to make high-risk trades in options or financial derivatives, your bank will want make certain that you're familiar with securities trading. If you lose money and the bank can't produce a signed document that you were aware of the risk involved, the bank may be fined.

Funding and Repatriating Foreign Investments

WARNING: Moving money internationally leaves a paper trail; it isn't private. Any attempt to disguise the source of funds transferred internationally can be construed as money laundering and result in forfeiture of those monies, along with criminal prosecution. Moving funds through multiple accounts in different countries could also be construed as an attempt to hide the source of the funds. Sudden or unexplained money movements may arouse suspicion, especially if they don't appear to have a business purpose. In many countries, banks are required to report their suspicion of illegal activity to authorities.

Wire transfers. Sending funds internationally via a wire transfer is the fastest and safest way to fund foreign investments. Wire transfers are safer than checks and your account is credited more quickly. U.S. banks must maintain detailed records of wire transfers that exceed US$3,000. Proposed regulations would require them to report all international wire transfers to the U.S. Treasury.[607]

If you plan to transfer funds by wire, ask for wiring instructions. All offshore banks maintain correspondent relationships with banks in other countries, particularly in the United States. It may not be necessary to send the funds directly to the foreign bank; they may instead be directed to an intermediary account in your own country.

Personal or business checks. Most offshore banks will accept a check made payable to the institution. Such a check will eventually "disappear" in the sense that the trail ages (although banks in every country keep records of cleared checks). The disadvantage is that it takes a long time for a check written to a bank in another country to clear, and there may be substantial fees incurred.

Avoid using endorsed third-party checks to fund an offshore account. This is a check payable to you that you transfer to someone else by endorsing it as, "pay to the order of" [a new payee]. Most offshore banks no longer accept endorsed third-party checks, and U.S. banks have been alerted using them may be considered a "suspicious transaction."[608]

IRAs and pension plans. One frequently overlooked source of funding for international investments is a U.S. individual retirement account (IRA) or qualified pension plan. This achieves several benefits, including decreased visibility of the plan assets, asset protection, and access to many non-U.S. investments—the same advantages you would achieve for any offshore investment.

There are no laws restricting the investment of retirement or pension assets offshore. There must be an approved U.S. trustee, but that is true for any pension plan regardless of the funds' location. With IRAs, no short selling, commodity or options trading is permitted. However, the plan can purchase almost any other offshore fund or security. Foreign annuity policies and precious metals are also eligible for IRAs.

In practice, the most significant difficulty associated with this strategy is finding a U.S. trustee willing to make offshore investments. The Nestmann Group, Ltd. can assist in finding a cooperative trustee.

If you require access to your offshore assets, the same methods used to fund foreign investments may also be used to reclaim them. For current accounts, no notice is required to withdraw your funds.

Savings accounts, CDs and other investments may require a 30-day or longer written notice before you can withdraw funds.

Checks and wire transfers. It's usually not a good idea to have an offshore bank send you a check directly, particularly if it's denominated in a foreign currency. You won't be able to cash it easily, and you'll have to wait one month or even longer for it to clear. A better solution is to ask the bank to have its U.S. correspondent bank issue you a check. You'll receive a check from a U.S. bank, denominated in U.S. dollars, making it much less time-consuming to gain access to your funds. You can also arrange for the bank to wire funds to your account. This results in your account being credited almost immediately, although the fees may be higher than for issuing a check.

Debit cards. Most offshore banks offer debit cards. You can use them like any other debit card for cash withdrawals or to purchase goods and services. When you apply for the debit card, make it clear that you intend to use the card outside the country where it's issued. This will insure that you receive a debit card with a VISA or Master Card imprint which can be used anywhere in the world.

Transactions with a foreign debit card are more private than transactions with a U.S. one. Your purchase records won't be available for warrantless inspection by police and in most countries, the card issuer won't be permitted to create a financial profile of your purchases and sell it to direct marketing companies, a perfectly legal practice in the United States.

Use of a foreign debit card will **not** avoid IRS scrutiny. The IRS is reviewing hundreds of millions of debit card transactions drawn on foreign banks in an effort to reveal previously unreported offshore accounts held by Americans (Chapter 6).

Not recommended: "unsecured" offshore credit cards. Most offshore financial institutions don't issue unsecured credit cards. But dozens of fraudulent unsecured cards are promoted on the Internet. You're required to pay an application fee of several hundred dollars and provide extensive background information. In almost all cases, your money disappears and you never receive a card. Increasingly, these scams are tied in to identity theft rings.

Back-to-back loans. It may be possible to structure a loan in which your funds are used as collateral for the bank to make a loan to you. If the transaction is properly structured, it will be difficult to discover that the collateral for the loan is an offshore deposit. Don't try to fool the IRS with this strategy. For tax purposes, the IRS looks behind the transaction to the ultimate lender and the ultimate borrower.

The Dangers of Moving Currency Internationally

In most offshore jurisdictions, funding accounts with currency (cash) is now discouraged and in some cases prohibited. While most offshore banks permit currency withdrawals, an increasing number discourage them. Higher fees and foreign exchange commissions may apply than for withdrawals by check, debit card or wire transfer. Foreign banks also discourage and may prohibit funding an account with money orders or traveler's checks, except (possibly) from known customers.

The Bank Secrecy Act (Chapter 2) requires anyone who conveys more than US$10,000 in currency or "monetary instruments" across a U.S. border to make a declaration on FinCEN Form 105. Structuring a single transaction over US$10,000 into smaller related transactions, each under US$10,000, is illegal.

According to the instructions for Form 105, a monetary instrument is:

(1) Coin or currency of the United States or of any other country, (2) traveler's checks in any form, (3) negotiable instruments (including checks, promissory notes, and money orders) in bearer form, endorsed without restriction, made out to a fictitious payee, or otherwise in such form that title thereto passes upon delivery, (4) incomplete instruments (including checks, promissory notes, and money orders) that are signed but on which the name of the payee has been omitted, and (5) securities or stock in bearer form or otherwise in such form that title thereto passes upon delivery. Monetary instruments do not include (i) checks or money orders made payable to the order of a named person which have not been endorsed or which bear restrictive endorsements, (ii) warehouse receipts, or (iii) bills of lading.

Note that money orders and traveler's checks are considered monetary instruments for purposes of Form 105. U.S. issuers of money orders must also maintain the names, addresses, and Social Security numbers of individuals who purchase more than US$3,000 of money orders or traveler's checks at one time or in a series of "related" transactions (Chapter 2).

Several different penalties may apply to individuals who fail to file Form 105 when filing is required. Forfeiture of the currency or other monetary instruments is virtually automatic.[609] Civil and criminal penalties may apply for willful failure to file Form 105.

U.S. Reporting Requirements for Offshore Accounts

The Bank Secrecy Act requires U.S. citizens and permanent residents to report signatory or "other" authority over all foreign accounts that in aggregate exceed US$10,000.[610]

There are two parts to this reporting regime:

(1) You must acknowledge foreign accounts each year on Schedule B of your federal income tax return; and
(2) You must file Form TD F 90-22.1 (the "foreign bank account reporting" or "FBAR" form) with the U.S. Treasury Department.[611] Information requested on the FBAR form includes how many foreign accounts you hold, their maximum value, the name of the financial institution where the accounts are held, the account numbers, etc.

The FBAR form isn't part of your tax return and can therefore be shared with state, local, or foreign law enforcement agencies. The form isn't generally available to prospective plaintiffs or lawyers who are trying to decide whether to take a case on a contingency fee basis. However, it can be demanded in a deposition or in the event of bankruptcy.

FBAR filing requirements may also be triggered if you're a shareholder, officer, or director of a foreign corporation; a partner in a foreign partnership; or a grantor or beneficiary of foreign trust, and the entity has an offshore account or accounts in its name. Policy owners of a foreign variable annuity or life insurance contract (discussed later in this chapter) may also be required to adhere to these reporting requirements.

The lifeboat strategy is to comply with this reporting regimen. By far the most common investigation of U.S. persons with offshore interests is for failure to file the FBAR form.

Keep in mind that the currency in which the account is denominated can rapidly change value. If you wish to legally avoid reporting the existence of the account, keep the account balance far enough below the US$10,000 ceiling so that an increase in currency value can be absorbed under the limit.

Penalties for non-compliance with these reporting requirements are severe. The civil penalty for negligent failure to file the FBAR form can be as much as US$10,000. The IRS can waive the penalty if there was reasonable cause for the delay and the account was properly reported later. An exception may also apply if any income from the account was properly reported on your income tax returns.[612] Civil and criminal penalties may also apply. If the violation is part of a pattern of criminal activity, the fine and/or prison term may be doubled.[613] Prosecution under the tax perjury and tax fraud statutes (Chapter 2) is also possible.

Even if you file the FBAR form, but falsely declare on Schedule B that you don't have a foreign bank account, you can be fined or prosecuted.[614] You must file Schedule B to report foreign accounts even if you earn less than US$1,500/year in interest and dividends, the ordinary filing threshold for this form.

In 2003, in an effort to raise the FBAR compliance rate, the Financial Crimes Enforcement Network (FinCEN) delegated enforcement authority for the FBAR to the IRS. Unlike FinCEN, the IRS has direct authority to enforce and collect civil penalties for non-compliance with the FBAR filing requirements. This initiative, combined with an ongoing IRS probe into offshore tax evasion described in Chapter 6, will likely lead to increased civil and criminal penalties against U.S. persons holding unreported offshore accounts.[615]

WARNING: If you have unreported foreign bank accounts, seek immediate legal counsel from a criminal tax attorney. Working with the attorney, it may be possible to file the appropriate information returns and avoid both civil penalties and criminal prosecution.

What's Reportable?

Instructions for Treasury Form TD F 90-22.1 read, in part:

Who Must File This Report. Each United States person, who has a financial interest in or signature authority, or other authority over any financial accounts, including bank, securities or other types of financial accounts in a foreign country if the aggregate value of these financial accounts exceeds US$10,000 at any time during the calendar year, must report that relationship each calendar year by filing Form 90-22.1 with the Department of the Treasury on or before June 30, of the succeeding year...

Financial account. Generally includes any bank, securities, securities, derivatives, or other financial instruments accounts. Such accounts generally also encompass any accounts in which the assets are held in a commingled fund, and the account owner holds an equity interest in the fund. The term also means any savings, demand, checking, deposit, time deposit, or any other account with a financial institution or other person engaged in the business of a financial institution...

Financial interest. A financial interest in a bank, securities or other financial account in a foreign country means an interest described in either of the following two paragraphs:

1) A U.S. person has a financial interest in each account for which such person is the owner of record or has legal title, whether the account is maintained for his or her own benefit or for the benefit of others including non-U.S. persons. If an account is maintained in the name of two persons jointly, or if several persons each own a partial interest in an account, each of these U.S. persons has a financial interest in that account.

(2) A U.S. person has a financial interest in each bank, securities or other financial account in a foreign country for which the owner of record or holder of legal title is (a) a person acting as an agent, nominee, attorney, or in some other capacity on behalf of the U.S. person; (b) a corporation in which the U.S. person owns directly or indirectly more than 50% of the total value of the shares of stock; (c) a partnership in which the U.S. person owns an interest in more than 50% of the profits (distributive share of income); or (d) a trust in which the U.S. person either has a present beneficial interest in more than 50% of the assets or from which such person receives more than 50% of the current income.

Signature or Other Authority Over an Account. A person has signature authority over an account if such person can control the disposition of money or other property in it by delivery of a document containing his or her signature (or his or her signature and that of one or more other persons) to the bank or other person with whom the account is maintained. Other authority exists in a person who can exercise comparable power over an account by direct communication to the bank or other person which whom the account is maintained, either orally or by some other means.

Some offshore promoters claim that if you don't have signature authority over an account, it need not be reported. This isn't correct. For instance, if a debit card is connected to the account, and you have the ability to use the debit card to withdraw money from it, even absent signatory authority over the account, you clearly have "other authority" over it.[616]

Not only foreign bank accounts, but also other "bank-like" relationships with foreign parties are reportable. For instance, various "digital gold" services now permit users to make financial transactions over the Internet in gold-backed accounts. Several of these services are organized outside the United States. While digital gold services clearly aren't banks, they do carry out "bank-like" functions. For that reason, the safest course of action would be to report such accounts via the FBAR.

The need to report "bank-like" relationships is reinforced in one of the rare reported criminal prosecutions for failure to file a FBAR. In the 1980s, U.S. intelligence agencies set up an offshore company for a key operative in a top secret CIA operation. A Swiss firm managed the company, providing both financial and management services. The Swiss company wasn't chartered as a bank, but made disbursements from the account at the operative's direction. A few years later, the operative was convicted for failing to report the relationship as a foreign account. A federal appeals court upheld the conviction, reasoning that the defendant used the Swiss firm to make transactions typically made through a bank, thereby making the relationship reportable as a foreign account.[617]

Four Non-Reportable Offshore Investments

The reporting rules suggest several possible exceptions:

1. **Securities purchased directly from an offshore bank**. A securities account is a reportable account. But if you purchase securities from an offshore bank, without opening an account, and keep the certificates in your safety deposit box, the reporting requirements don't appear to be triggered. There are practical difficulties to this approach, including the need to clip coupons (bonds) or receive dividends (stocks), and arrange to receive this income yourself, rather than have the custodial department of your offshore bank do so.

2. **Real estate**. Direct ownership of real property (including timeshare arrangements) in a foreign country doesn't constitute a foreign account. But you're required to report income from your real estate holdings, wherever they're located.

3. **Safekeeping arrangements**. Valuables purchased outside the United States and placed directly into a non-U.S. private vault don't appear to trigger the reporting requirements.

4. **Warehouse receipts and similar instruments.** Certificates that represent ownership of a specified quantity of precious metals or other commodity, stored outside the United States, may not be reportable. A certificate should provide for "allocated" or "non-fungible" storage to qualify. This means you own specific barrels, bars, coins, etc. that are stored in your name and not available to meet other claims of the warehouse company. Commodities held in non-allocated, pooled, or fungible form may be reportable.

Your Offshore Trust

An offshore bank account gives you the freedom to direct your investments, as you wish, with few limitations. With other types of offshore relationships and structures, however, you must give up some of this freedom. Why might you wish to do so? Mainly to obtain other benefits: enhanced asset protection, privacy, and/or tax advantages. Offshore trusts are a prime example.

The primary limitation to the domestic trusts discussed in Chapter 4 is that you must give up all rights to the assets you place in trust to obtain asset protection. A long line of case law stipulates that such **self-settled trusts** can be invaded for the benefit of your creditors.

The only effective way that you can both benefit from a trust and protect the assets you place into it is to use an **offshore asset protection trust** (OAPT) structure. An OAPT can serve as a shield for your business and personal assets, deflecting would-be creditors, litigation, and potential financial liabilities. When a creditor realizes that you have transferred your assets to an offshore OAPT, the result will often be a quick, cost-effective settlement in your favor.

The cost of creating an OAPT can exceed US$15,000, plus several thousand dollars in annual maintenance and compliance fees. Unless the total assets to be shielded justify such costs, an OAPT may not be practical. As a rule of thumb, you should have a net worth of US$5 million or more to justify the set up and ongoing maintenance costs of an OAPT. For individuals in high-risk professions or businesses, these costs may be partially or even entirely made up by a corresponding reduction in professional liability insurance.

The Cook Islands was the first jurisdiction to enact OAPT laws, followed by Nevis, the Turks & Caicos Islands, St. Lucia, Gibraltar, etc.

Benefits of Offshore Trusts

OAPTs have numerous advantages over domestic trusts. These include:

- Non-recognition of U.S or other foreign judgments;
- Short statute of limitations for challenges;
- Enhanced asset protection;
- Enhanced privacy;
- Investment flexibility; and
- Tax planning opportunities.

Non-recognition of foreign judgments. A creditor seeking to collect a judgment against an OAPT must in most cases re-litigate the original claim in local courts after hiring local lawyers. The legal complexity and cost of such an international collection effort is likely to stop all but the most determined adversaries.

Section 13D of the Cook Islands International Trusts Act provides:

Foreign judgments not enforceable—Notwithstanding—
(a) The provisions of any treaty;
(b) The provisions of any statute;
(c) Any rule of law, or equity;

To the contrary, no proceedings for or in relation to the enforcement or recognition of a judgment obtained in a jurisdiction other than the Cook Islands against either—
(d) An international trust;
(e) A settlor of an international trust;
(f) A trustee of an international trust;
(g) A protector of an international trust;
(h) A beneficiary of an international trust;
(i) A person appointed or instructed in accordance with the express or implied provisions of an instrument or disposition to exercise a function or undertake any act matter or thing in connection with an international trust; or
(j) Property of either an international trust or of a trustee or a beneficiary thereof; shall be entertained by any Court in the Cook Islands if—
(k) that judgment is based upon the application of any law inconsistent with the provisions of this Act;
(l) that judgment relates to a matter or particular aspect that is governed by the law of the Cook Islands.

Similar provisions are found in the laws of numerous other offshore jurisdictions.

Enhanced asset protection. Many OAPT jurisdictions require an elevated level of proof to establish a fraudulent transfer. For example, the statutes in both the Cook Islands and St. Kitts & Nevis require proof "beyond a reasonable doubt" that a transfer was fraudulent for a creditor to prevail in a fraudulent conveyance claim. If a local court finds a transfer fraudulent, it will generally be set it aside only to the extent necessary to satisfy actual damages (**not** punitive damages) suffered by a particular creditor. Each creditor must bring a separate action in the local court.

Attorneys in most OAPT jurisdictions can't accept cases on a contingency basis. If a creditor wishes to pursue litigation, it must be prepared to pay the lawyer out of its own pocket, usually in advance. Further, the "loser pays" rule generally applies—the prevailing party in litigation is entitled to recover the costs of legal representation from the loser.

Some OAPT jurisdictions even require a plaintiff-creditor to post a bond to guarantee the payment of costs that the court may charge against the creditor if he is unsuccessful. St. Kitts & Nevis law provides:

Every creditor before bringing any action or proceeding against any trust property shall first deposit with the Minister a bond in the sum of 25,000 dollars from a financial institution in the Federation, for securing the payment of all costs as may become payable by the creditor in the event of the creditor not succeeding in such action or proceeding against the trust property.[618]

What happens if the law in the jurisdiction you select for your offshore trust is weakened? Many OAPTs deal with this possibility using a clause permitting the trustee to change the jurisdiction and thus the governing law of the trust. The use of dynasty trusts combined with possible changes in the geopolitical landscape make a such a **flee clause** worth considering.

Enhanced privacy. An OAPT can provide far greater privacy and confidentiality than a domestic trust. Since all records are offshore, nothing shows up in a domestic search. In most OAPT jurisdictions, little information about a trust is registered with the government. The trust agreement and the parties involved don't generally need to be disclosed. In most cases, the only public record is a registry of the trust's name, date of creation, and the name of the local trustee. Additional information can be released in limited circumstances (e.g., in a money laundering investigation) or by the order of a local court.

Investment flexibility. An OAPT can purchase many offshore securities that are difficult for U.S. persons to purchase directly, including offshore funds. But for the reasons summarized earlier in this chapter, OAPTs should not generally purchase offshore mutual funds unless the interests are held in a tax-deferred vehicle such as a life insurance policy.

Tax planning opportunities. In most cases, an OAPT is considered a **grantor trust** for U.S. tax purposes. All income, gains, losses, deductions, and credits are taxable to the grantor (i.e., the person funding the trust) and reportable on the grantor's individual tax return. The same investments that can be used to reduce taxes in a domestic trust can be used to reduce tax liabilities in an OAPT —e.g., cash value life insurance, municipal bonds, etc.

When the grantor of a grantor trust dies, the OAPT becomes part of the resulting estate for estate tax purposes. However, an OAPT can also serve the same traditional estate planning goals achieved by domestic strategies. These include using bypass trusts (Chapter 4) to maximize estate tax exemptions for a married couple; employing the trust to maximize gift tax exemptions; and providing for the needs of a surviving spouse.

Structuring an Offshore Trust

The structure of an OAPT is similar to a domestic U.S. trust. The grantor creates the OAPT and transfers assets to it, which are administered according to the terms of the trust deed by a trustee on behalf for named beneficiaries.

Protecting assets that can't be relocated to a foreign trust, such as real estate or assets used in a domestic business, can be problematic. Simply transferring title to real estate or a business located within the United States to a foreign trust may provide less-than-optimum protection since the assets themselves remain within easy reach of domestic creditors and courts.

A common structure designed to address this problem uses a U.S. limited partnership (or LLC) in conjunction with an OAPT. Often, the trust grantors, typically a husband and wife, serve as general partners of the limited partnership (or managing members of the LLC). The foreign trustee holds a super-majority, typically 99%, of the partnership or membership interest. Typically, the foreign trustee has the right to liquidate the domestic structure in the event of duress (e.g., a lawsuit or threatened lawsuit against the settlor or beneficiary of the OAPT). However, if this power exists, the estate planning opportunity for valuation discounts on gifts of minority interests (Chapter 4) will disappear.[619]

Attempting to use this strategy at a time of financial crisis could potentially backfire and lead to a contempt citation based on a theory that the entire structure is a sham. It could also bring the OAPT within the jurisdiction of the U.S. courts, if a judge uses the transfer as evidence to justify a finding the OAPT is "doing business" in the United States. Still, because of the complexity of bringing suit against an OAPT, combined with the division of ownership and limited liability of a limited partnership or LLC, most adversaries will think twice before challenging the structure.

Another benefit of this split form of ownership is where the OAPT holds a significant amount of securities. While some offshore banks are reluctant to open an account in the name of a trust, this limitation is overcome if the portfolio is owned by another entity. From a U.S. tax perspective, this split ownership doesn't result in any tax reduction or avoidance. In virtually all cases, all income earned by the entity is still taxable to the grantor.

Another common structure uses an OAPT to hold title to an offshore insurance policy. This combination has tremendous asset protection and tax advantages, as discussed later in this chapter.

Your Most Crucial Decision: Choosing a Trustee and Protector

To provide asset protection, a trust must have an independent trustee who isn't legally obligated to follow the grantor's wishes. While trustees and trust companies are strictly regulated in most offshore jurisdictions, you should not cede this authority over your wealth lightly.

Some offshore jurisdictions permit the grantor to serve as the OAPT trustee. This isn't recommended, as it may lead to claims by creditors that the trust is a mere "alter ego" of the grantor. In one case, a grantor who served as trustee of "his" OAPT until after he was sued was jailed until he ordered the new trustee to repatriate the assets of the trust.[620]

The trustee's first duty is to the beneficiaries of the trust. While it's possible, and often recommended, for you as the grantor to provide the trustee with a "letter of wishes" setting out your preferences for how the trust is to be managed, such a letter is not legally binding.

Use a corporate trustee, rather than an individual trustee. A corporate trustee will have additional staff available in the event of the incapacity or retirement of any single employee. The trustee you select should have substantial experience in the local market and employ trust experts with respected professional affiliations (e.g., Society of Trust and Estate Practitioners). It should have no connections to your home jurisdiction that might subject it to pressure from your domestic court system. In most OAPT jurisdictions, you can hire a local attorney or investigator to learn if the trust company has been involved in litigation.

In many cases, your professional advisor—the attorney who sets up your OAPT—will have a recommended trustee. There's no reason not to accept your advisor's recommendation, so long as it's made on the basis of the factors summarized above.

Most offshore jurisdictions allow the appointment of a trust **protector**. This neutral party oversees the operation of the OAPT to insure its objectives are met and the law is followed. The protector's role is to step in the event of unforeseen circumstances that could adversely affect the beneficiaries. Often the trust grantor has the right to name the protector, but this authority should be discussed with your professional advisors.[621]

The most important power of the protector is the right to replace the foreign trustee, with or without cause. The protector also may have the authority to:

- Change the jurisdiction of the trust;
- Appoint an investment adviser to manage assets;
- Obtain information from the trustee about any aspect of the trust;
- Petition courts for redress;
- Co-sign accounts with the trustee;
- Veto decisions of the trustee, particularly in relation to investment decisions or the distribution of income and assets;
- React to changes in the circumstances of the beneficiaries. For example, if a beneficiary becomes experiences a judgment, the trust protector could instruct the trustee to delay distributions to that individual; and
- Terminate the trust for good cause. For example, if a trust is set up primarily for estate tax reasons, and because of repeal or increased exemptions it no longer provides tax savings, the trust protector could distribute all the property to the beneficiaries and terminate the trust.

Since the protector oversees the trustee, the protector should be independent of the trustee. However, it's important that the trustee and protector are comfortable working together. Typically, the grantor will name a trusted friend, relative, accountant or attorney as the protector. Professional trust protector services are also available.

If the grantor, a beneficiary, or a person closely related to them, can control the trustee in the role of a trust protector, a U.S. court may find the grantor retained the power to repatriate the assets. For instance, if you name yourself as protector, a domestic court might order you to exercise your authority to name a substitute trustee that could then authorize the repatriation of trust assets. For that reason, you should avoid naming yourself, your spouse, or any trust beneficiary as protector of your offshore trust.

The protector should also not be permitted to become the trustee after removing a trustee. This eliminates any possibility that the protector would be tempted to step into the trustee's shoes and assume legal ownership of the trust assets.

Legal Challenges to Offshore Trusts

An OAPT must be carefully constructed to effectively protect your assets. Unless all legal requirements are observed, you run the risk of having a court declare the trust invalid.

In most cases, ordinary, non-governmental creditors won't be able to take any action against you or your offshore trust until they obtain a judgment. This is a consequence of a 1999 Supreme Court decision, in which it ruled "an unsecured creditor suing to collect a debt isn't entitled to preliminary injunctive relief to prevent the debtor's dissipation of assets prior to judgment."[622]

Once a judgment is in place, in a few cases, U.S. courts have invalidated OAPT structures. These cases, far from invalidating the OAPT concept, provide a road map for insuring that assets committed to an OAPT remain safe.

The most famous of these cases dealt with a Nevada couple, the Andersons, who operated a telemarketing venture that the Federal Trade Commission (FTC) attacked as a Ponzi scheme. The FTC alleged the trust existed only to shelter the income from the Anderson's illegal scheme. The agency sued the Andersons in federal court and obtained a US$20 million judgment. When the Andersons claimed that they couldn't pay the judgment, the FTC obtained a court order requiring the couple to repatriate US$8 million in assets from a Cook Islands offshore trust. When the Andersons failed to obey this order, the court jailed the couple for civil contempt. A federal appeals court affirmed this decision.[623]

This decision led to a sensational article in *The Wall Street Journal* (July 12, 1999) with the headline "U.S. Appeals Court Says Trusts Can't Be Used to Protect Assets." However, this headline failed to convey the whole story. Like many other offshore jurisdictions, Cook Islands law stipulates that local trustees are not bound by the orders of a foreign court. Indeed, they are forbidden from returning assets held in trust under such circumstances.

After six months in jail, the Andersons eventually convinced the court that they had made a *bona fide*—but ultimately unsuccessful—effort to repatriate the trust assets, and were released. In the end, the Cook Islands trustee settled the case with the FTC with a US$1.2 million payout from the Anderson's trust.

In many ways, this case is a worst-case scenario for an OAPT due to serious defects in the trust. The Andersons' most important error was to name themselves as both co-trustees and co-protectors of the trust, a position they gave up only when their trial began. But even with this serious defect, and the extraordinary circumstances of this case, their OAPT still protected the bulk of the assets entrusted to it. Indeed, in virtually all cases where such a worst-case scenario developed, creditors settled for substantially less than would have been received had a domestic asset protection solution been utilized.[624]

One tool available to prevent a domestic court from compelling you to repatriate the assets in an OAPT is an **anti-duress clause**. This clause directs the foreign trustee to ignore any order or instructions given under duress. The purpose of an anti-duress clause is to protect you as the grantor against coercive orders of a U.S. court and possible exposure to contempt charges. Such a clause permits you to assert what is called the **impossibility defense** and claim truthfully that you are unable to comply with the U.S. court's demand.

According to asset protection attorney Howard Rosen:

The U.S. Supreme Court in [two cases][625] has held that a person cannot be held in contempt for failing to do that which is not within his power to do—unless he created the impossibility. The settlor-debtor should not be deemed to create the impossibility where the trust containing a properly constructed duress provision has been established far in advance of the origination of the creditor's claim.[626]

Some asset protection attorneys believe that an anti-duress clause creates an impossibility to comply with the order of a U.S. court, and that this could lead in turn to a contempt citation. However, in virtually every case involving an OAPT in which a court issued a contempt citation, the debtor took extraordinary measures—well beyond a mere anti-duress clause—to create the impossibility of repatriating assets.

Because of the effectiveness of the OAPT concept, the vast majority of disputes involving offshore trusts are quietly settled out of court, without reaching a judge. Creditors realize that judgments against OAPTs simply aren't collectable. Lawyers working on a contingency basis won't waste their time pursuing someone who is essentially judgment-proof.

There are, however, a few recommended precautions to guard against the possibility of a contempt citation in the event of a court challenge to your OAPT:

- Avoid naming yourself, your spouse, or any trust beneficiary as trustee or protector of your off-shore trust;
- The OAPT grantor and beneficiaries shouldn't have direct access to any part of the trust assets. Such access (e.g., by a debit card from which withdrawals from the trust principle can be made) support a sham argument;
- Don't convey all or even most of your assets to an OAPT;
- Hold and invest all trust assets outside the United States;
- Make certain that you're solvent at the time you convey assets into an OAPT, keeping in mind the definition of "solvency" discussed in Chapter 4;
- Don't use an OAPT to hide assets from any creditor or from the U.S. government;
- Make certain that all required IRS reporting requirements are followed;
- Don't retain the power to manage the trust; and
- Use both a trustee and a trust protector with no financial or organizational connection to the United States.

Another challenge to OAPTs—and all self-settled trusts—is the 2005 Bankruptcy Reform Act (Chapter 4). Under its provisions, a bankruptcy trustee may void any transfer to a self-settled trust made within 10 years of a bankruptcy declaration if the debtor is a beneficiary and the debtor made the transfer with an **actual intent** to hinder, delay or defraud a current or future creditor. While the burden of proof to demonstrate actual intent is relatively high, where numerous "badges of fraud" are present, this burden would likely be met. A silver lining in this law is that an OAPT formed more than 10 years prior to a bankruptcy filing is likely survive even a finding of "actual intent."[627]

What about attacks against foreign trusts in a trust jurisdiction's local courts? These are less common, but do occur. In a 1991 case, a judge in Jersey (part of the Channel Islands off the coast of England) ruled that a trust grantor had exercised nearly complete control over trust assets, to the exclusion of the trustee. Therefore, the court concluded that the assets were never placed in trust, but remained a part of the grantor's estate. As result, the assets passed to heirs under the probate laws in the grantor's home country, rather than as stipulated in the trust.[628] Successful challenges to OAPTs have also been made in the Cook Islands, discussed in Chapter 7.

U.S. Tax and Reporting Requirements for Offshore Trusts

Most offshore trusts do **not** result in any tax reduction or tax avoidance to the offshore grantor. Income from the trust is taxed as if it was earned directly by the grantor.[629]

The IRS believes many U.S. taxpayers use offshore trusts to evade taxes. Congress has responded with increasingly burdensome reporting and disclosure requirements.[630] An offshore trust must appoint a limited U.S. agent to receive and respond to IRS inquiries and requests. The trust grantor is liable to civil and criminal penalties if these requirements aren't met.

An offshore trust with a U.S. grantor must also apply for a U.S. taxpayer ID number and submit IRS Forms 3520 and 3520-A. Form 3520-A is an annual report that requires financial information about the trust. The trustee of a foreign trust with any U.S. grantors, or the grantor, must file it. Form 3520 is filed only when there are certain transactions in the foreign trust such as loans, distributions, or new contributions to the trust. These forms are among the most complex of any published by the IRS.

Information returns for any foreign entities or accounts owned by the trust must be filed. In addition to Forms 3520 and 3520-A, these forms may include:

- Form 720 for premiums paid to foreign insurance companies, unless payment of excise tax is waived under a tax treaty. If excise tax is waived, Form 8833 must be filed;
- Form 926 for transfers of property to a controlled foreign corporation;
- Form 1041 to report the income and expenses of a grantor trust. If the trust earns U.S. source income, it must file Form 1040NR annually;
- Form 5471 annually for a controlled foreign corporation;
- Form 8621 to report income from or dispositions of a foreign mutual fund;
- Form 8832 to elect to have a foreign entity disregarded for U.S. tax purposes;
- Form 8858 annually for a disregarded entity;
- Form 8865 annually for a controlled foreign partnership;
- Form TDF 90-22.1 annually for a foreign bank, securities, or "other financial account" owned by a foreign trust or other entity over which the OAPT grantor has signature or "other" authority. [631]

Penalties for failure to file these forms are draconian. Failure to file a timely or accurate Form 3520 may result in a penalty of 35% of the gross value of any property transferred to a foreign trust. An offshore trust with a U.S. grantor that fails to file required annual reports on trust activities and income subjects the grantor to a penalty of 5% of the trust's assets treated as owned by the U.S. person. Comparable penalties apply for failure to file any of the other required disclosure forms.

The Many Benefits of Offshore Variable Annuities

A variable annuity contract issued in the United States is generally protected from the claims of the **insurance company's** creditors. However, the same protection isn't always present with respect to the **policy owner's** creditors. In many U.S. states, a policy owner can be required by court order to liquidate the annuity policy and secure any cash value for the benefit of judgment creditors.

Even in states where there are restrictions on creditors' rights to an annuity contract, creditors can simply wait until the policy matures and then demand the receipt of the annuity payments. What's more, if you relocate from a state with excellent protection for annuities to one with less stringent provisions, you may lose the legal protection that previously applied.

In contrast, if you purchase a foreign variable annuity contract, foreign law will govern the contract. By selecting the appropriate jurisdiction, you can achieve a much higher degree of asset protection.

Offshore variable annuities provide numerous other advantages:

- Asset protection for a lower cost than offshore trusts;
- Significantly increased privacy in comparison to domestic annuities;
- Tax-deferred access to offshore securities markets;
- Avoidance of possible foreign exchange controls;
- Lower regulatory expenses;
- Avoidance of state and federal taxes on insurance companies and policies;
- Lower marketing and distribution costs than U.S. companies; and
- Tax planning for U.S. citizens or long-term residents considering expatriation

Affordable, non-Controversial Asset Protection and Privacy

Outside the United States, variable annuity policies may include provisions similar to the spendthrift provision in a trust, which prohibits the beneficiary from assigning a future benefit to a creditor or making an assignment in exchange for some immediate benefit. In some countries, annuity contracts are additionally protected from creditor claims if the policy has a beneficiary other than the policy owner.

Another asset protection advantage is that it's difficult to sustain a fraudulent conveyance argument (Chapter 4) against a person who purchases a variable annuity. This is because you take back value (the promise of future payments) in exchange for your investment.

Annuity contracts are less controversial than other methods of asset protection, especially offshore trusts. In light of the handful of unfavorable court decisions relating to offshore trusts discussed in previously in this chapter, purchasing an offshore variable annuity may be regarded as more acceptable by judges skeptical of offshore asset protection arrangements.

Although U.S. annuity contracts aren't recorded or registered in any government database, policyholder and beneficiary information is included in the database of the insurance company. If you're required to disclose the existence of the annuity contract and the name of the insurance company, a plaintiff (or judgment creditor) can secure complete details about the policy from the U.S. insurance company. There are also few restrictions on how domestic insurance companies may use the information in their databases. For instance, they can compile a list of annuity contract owners and/or beneficiaries and rent this information to other companies

In contrast, even if the existence of an offshore annuity contract is disclosed during a deposition or by court order, most offshore insurance companies will not disclose any details about the policy to any U.S. creditor or in response to a U.S. court order. An exception may apply if the applicable country has a treaty (such as a mutual legal assistance treaty, discussed in Chapter 6) with the United States to permit an exchange of information. This exception won't apply with respect to civil litigation or non-government creditors. Foreign insurance companies also don't engage in the widespread U.S. business practice of renting the customers' names and addresses (with extensive demographic information) to anyone.

Lower Costs than Offshore Trusts

Offshore variable annuities offer affordable asset protection. Especially for annuities not held within some type of offshore structure, there are generally no fees associated with their purchase, and investment minimums are as low as US$50,000. Depending on the size of the contract and its terms, ongoing expenses can range up to 3% annually. There may also be a front-end load as high as 6%. This load, if imposed, is generally payable over an extended period (typically, five years, or 1.2% per year).

The largest expense associated with the purchase of an offshore variable annuity may be the need to travel to a foreign country to purchase the contract. Many foreign insurance companies require the insured to sign the documents and to make the premium payments outside the United States.

In contrast, the cost of creating an OAPT can exceed US$15,000, plus several thousand dollars in annual maintenance and compliance fees. Since an OAPT doesn't generally offer tax deferral for a U.S. investor, one of the only ways to achieve this goal is to have the OAPT invest its assets in an annuity contract that meets the IRS requirements for a tax-deferred annuity. Further, there are substantial compliance costs for a foreign trust that don't apply to an annuity contract.

Tax-Deferred Access to Offshore Securities Markets

An offshore variable annuity is one of the few ways that U.S. investors can participate in foreign securities markets without suffering adverse tax consequences or substantially higher costs. This is particularly true with respect to offshore mutual funds. Nor are investments in an offshore variable annuity subject to the IRS qualified intermediary requirements summarized earlier in this chapter.

NOTE: Unlike domestic fixed annuities, **offshore** fixed annuities have no tax benefits and don't permit the tax-free compounding of income generated within the policy.

Avoidance of Foreign Exchange Controls

Virtually every U.S. annuity policy is denominated in U.S. dollars. In contrast, foreign insurance companies frequently permit premium payments, withdrawals, borrowings, and death benefits in different currencies. Indeed, within some variable annuities, it's possible to switch the currencies targeted by the policy. This is easiest and most practical with a portfolio of bonds.

The ability to select the underlying currency of an offshore variable annuity is valuable protection against the sinking U.S. dollar. Yet, there's another important benefit. Historically, many countries—including Great Britain and France in the 1970s—have instituted foreign exchange controls prohibiting residents from exporting their national currencies. This policy persists today in countries such as Zimbabwe and Venezuela, where governments periodically revalue the national currency, prohibit its export, or force persons holding foreign currencies to exchange them for virtually worthless domestic currency. [632]

One solution that has proven effective for dealing with this threat is a variable annuity denominated in a foreign currency. Historically, most countries have exempted annuities from foreign exchange controls, regardless of the currency in which they are denominated, because they are classified as retirement or pension accounts, rather than investments.

The United States has never imposed foreign exchange controls. It has imposed currency controls on two occasions: in 1933 (when President Franklin Roosevelt forced owners of gold and silver to sell their holdings to the government) and in 1971 (when President Nixon suspended the right of foreign central banks to exchange dollars for gold). For most U.S. persons, the thought of the dollar becoming worthless is unthinkable. Yet, what would you do if, in reaction to some future catastrophe the U.S. dollar lost a substantial portion of its value in relation to other currencies, virtually overnight? Or, if consumer prices began rising 20% or more annually? In similar scenarios, dozens of countries have imposed foreign exchange controls.

Lower Taxes, Regulatory Costs, and Commissions

Most U.S. states impose a tax on the gross premiums received by U.S. insurance companies for policies sold to residents of each state. The cost of this tax is simply added to the fees paid by the customer. While this tax varies from state to state, it's generally 2% to 3% of the gross premiums paid for the policy. U.S. insurance companies are also subject to a "deferred acquisition cost" tax, which doesn't allow insurers to deduct actual expenses incurred in writing new contracts. These taxes put U.S. insurance companies at a significant disadvantage compared to companies located in countries that don't impose a corporate income tax, such as the Isle of Man or the Bahamas, or a low corporate income tax, such as Switzerland.

Variable annuities issued by U.S. insurers are among the most highly regulated financial instruments, as they're overseen not only by the insurance departments and securities departments of all 50 states but also by the SEC. All these agencies require extensive disclosure of information about the product and the company. The rules and regulations in each agency are different and sometimes conflict with each other.

In contrast, most foreign insurance companies are subject to regulation by only one agency so long as their products are purchased within their jurisdiction. This is a major factor in the lower administrative cost of policies issued in foreign jurisdictions versus those issued in the United States.

Finally, most U.S. insurance companies have a multi-level commission marketing system that substantially adds to the cost of coverage. In some cases, commissions amount to as much as 15% of the policy premium. Offshore insurance companies rarely use this kind of multi-layered commission system. While commissions exist offshore, they are generally lower and thus, there are substantially less expenses to be absorbed from the premiums collected.

Tax Planning for Expatriation

The United States is the only country that imposes significant income and estate taxes on the worldwide income and assets of every citizen, even those living outside its territorial boundaries. As discussed later in this chapter, giving up U.S. citizenship is the only way to potentially eliminate this liability.

The U.S. Congress has enacted a series of "anti-expatriation" laws to frustrate the ability of wealthy citizens to lower their tax liability by giving up U.S. residence and citizenship. Taxes are imposed for a period of 10 years after expatriation on the net combined amount of U.S. source income and income "effectively connected" with a U.S. trade or business, along with a few other types of property.[633] However, the rules do NOT apply to investments in offshore annuities. Therefore, an offshore annuity may offer a way for prospective U.S. expatriates to accumulate tax-deferred savings that will not be subject to future U.S. income taxes after expatriating.

The Amazing Private Annuity

Until 2006, it was possible to transfer highly appreciated assets to a **private annuity** (also called a **contract annuity**) and legally defer tax on the gains. This is no longer possible.[634] However, private annuities still provide a flexible solution for many types of offshore planning, although they're typically financed with after-tax funds.

A private annuity is an arrangement in which you (the "annuitant") transfer property to another person or company (the "obligor") in exchange for the obligor's **unsecured** promise to make periodic payments to you for the remainder of your life. When you die, the annuity payments stop. But the obligor receives the remaining property, free of estate tax.

In a simple private annuity arrangement, the obligor may be your adult children. If your children don't have sufficient independent income to make these payments, they can sell or borrow against the property to generate cash to make the payments. It's also possible to have the obligor be an offshore company set up for the sole purpose of issuing a private annuity contract. The obligor can't be in the business of selling annuities, so it can't be an insurance company.

More sophisticated private annuity arrangements can serve as a fiscal "kernel" to set up additional entities and possibly purchase assets to be transferred into the structure, with annuity payments deferred for years, if not decades. Such **international deferred private variable annuity** (IDPVA) arrangements exist only for your benefit, or the benefit of anyone else you choose—your spouse, children, etc.

It may be possible for the annuity company to place a portion of the underlying account values in a foreign corporation or other entity that operates an ongoing international business, with all profits tax-deferred. Many other types of investments are possible, including private hedge funds, pre-IPO investments, real estate lending, venture capital, or acquisition of operational businesses. At your death, the assets held within the IDPVA can pass free of both income and estate taxes to your heirs, provided the structure includes a life insurance component.

The annuity company can also capitalize an **intellectual property and critical information** (IPCI) company, where intellectual property can be purchased and brought into the company and licensed back out. International licenses for copyrights, trademarks, patents, public appearances, etc., can all be handled by this structure. This can be a particularly effective structure for a U.S. person who wishes to license intellectual property abroad and legally defer tax on the income it generates until payments from the IDPVA begin.

Private annuity and in particular IDPVA arrangements must in all cases be custom-tailored. The Nestmann Group, Ltd. has considerable experience in this area. Contact us for more information.

Compliance with U.S. Tax Law

It's important to insure that any offshore variable annuity you purchase be designed to qualify as a variable annuity under the U.S. Tax Code.[635] Investments in non-compliant annuity contracts are taxed as if the annuity didn't exist.

This is particularly onerous if the annuity invests in offshore funds. In that event, you might not only be subject to back taxes, interest and penalties, but an additional interest charge imposed for the "privilege" of deferring tax for the time you owned the offshore funds, as discussed earlier in this chapter. The only way that an offshore variable annuity (or offshore life insurance policy) can safely hold offshore funds is if the funds are available **only** through the insurance company and not otherwise available to the public.[636]

Another precaution is to insure that the annuity policy doesn't permit you to control the investments within the policy. It's permissible to request the insurance company to invest your funds aggressively, conservatively, or in a balanced portfolio, but you can't order the investment manager to purchase specific investments. Similarly, while it's permissible to request a specific investment manager to oversee the annuity portfolio, you can't assign the manager directly—the insurance company must do so.

To avoid a costly dispute with the IRS, seek a written opinion from a U.S. tax lawyer or tax accountant as to whether the variable annuity is tax-qualified under U.S. law. Sometimes the insurance company or one of its agents will get a written opinion from a U.S. law firm or accounting firm. Other companies leave it to the investor to get an opinion from a U.S. tax professional.

U.S. law requires a one-time acknowledgement to the IRS of the purchase of a foreign insurance contract, including an offshore variable annuity, and payment of a 1% excise tax on IRS Form 720. The excise tax may be waived under a tax treaty. If you rely on a tax treaty to avoid paying the excise tax, you must notify the IRS by filing IRS Form 8833.[637] This requirement doesn't apply to a private annuity, since it's not issued by an insurance annuity.

Some insurance brokers claim that a foreign variable annuity isn't a reportable "foreign financial account" as discussed earlier in this chapter. However, in the opinion of the U.S. Treasury Department, it

233

is reportable. According to Elizabeth B. Witzgall, Senior Bank Secrecy Act Analyst at the Treasury Department:

The position of the Department of the Treasury is that premium payments for insurance policies with cash surrender value or other investment features constitute "deposits" within the meaning of Form 90-22.1. Therefore, if a life insurance policy is a 'whole life' or other type of policy with investment value, then it is an 'other financial account' subject to reporting.[638]

Most offshore variable annuity policies have investment features and a cash surrender value, and can be accessed through policy loans or partial withdrawals. While Witzgall's statement isn't an official Treasury pronouncement, it indicates that U.S. authorities realize that numerous U.S. persons are purchasing offshore life insurance products. Reporting an offshore variable annuity or offshore life insurance policy as a foreign account is the wisest course to avoid potential problems.

Tax Disadvantages of Variable Annuities

From a U.S. perspective, there are some tax disadvantages to consider with any annuity, whether issued by a domestic or offshore insurance company. One disadvantage is that income from an annuity, less the original amount invested, is generally taxed as ordinary income, not as a long-term capital gain or qualified dividend. (This disadvantage may or may not exist for a private annuity, depending on how it's configured.) For this reason, annuities make the most sense, tax-wise, to hold income-producing assets such as bonds.

For long holding periods (generally 15 years or more), the advantage of tax-free compounding may outweigh the disadvantage of eventually paying tax at regular income tax rates (up to 35% for 2007 federal tax, plus whatever state tax, if any, that applies) on capital gains or dividends generated inside an annuity. If your income is relatively low when you begin receiving annuity payments, the disadvantage of paying income tax on these payments will not be as large as if your income is relatively high. Finally, if the main reason you're considering an offshore variable insurance annuity is asset protection, this tax disadvantage may not be a significant factor in your planning.

Another disadvantage is that if you purchase a variable insurance annuity with a death benefit, the recipients of that benefit are subject to income tax on the unrealized gains within the policy and, should your estate be sufficiently large, estate tax as well. You can avoid this outcome by combining the annuity in an offshore life insurance policy, as discussed in the following section.

The Unique Benefits of Offshore Life Insurance

As described in Chapter 4, life insurance enjoys uniquely preferential treatment under U.S. tax law:

- All earnings accumulate free of taxes until withdrawal;
- The death benefit can pass to beneficiaries tax-free;
- Tax-free loans are possible;
- Tax-free exchanges are possible; and
- With proper structuring, the proceeds can flow to beneficiaries free of both estate and generation-skipping taxes.

Only life insurance can claim these five advantages. Essentially, you avoid tax on portfolio income and transactions in exchange for the cost of insurance; approximately 1-3% per year.

The most flexible life insurance policies are the variable universal life insurance (VUL) policies discussed in Chapter 4. VUL policies written by U.S. carriers can offer all of these benefits. However, VUL policies written by non-U.S. companies offer the same competitive advantages in comparison with U.S. policies as offshore variable annuities, namely affordable, non-controversial asset protection; greater privacy; tax-deferred access to offshore securities markets; potential avoidance of foreign exchange controls; lower taxes, regulatory costs, and distribution costs; and tax planning for expatriation

For wealthy persons, another benefit of offshore VUL is that much larger policies are available offshore than in the United States. This is mainly due to the fact that the world's largest reinsurers are located outside the United States. Especially for large policies, insurance companies often contract with reinsurers to help pay death benefits upon the death of the insured person.

Because VUL is, in fact, life insurance, someone generally has to be in sufficiently good health to be insurable. However, the person insured in a VUL policy doesn't necessarily need to be the person investing in the policy. For instance, if you're 70 years old and in poor health, and are therefore a poor actuarial risk for life insurance purposes, it may be possible to make the insured person or persons your spouse, your children, grandchildren, etc. For larger policies, it may be possible to craft a structure that itself issues a life insurance policy without evidence of the policyholder's insurability.

Leave "Assembly Line" Insurance Policies Behind

U.S. insurance companies design products to appeal to a broad market and then market those products to millions of prospects. Foreign insurance companies are much more willing to custom-tailor a policy to your specific needs—especially if you can invest US$2 million or more in a single policy.

The most innovative offshore insurance products tend to be variable life insurance contracts, known as **private placement variable universal life** (PPVUL) policies. As with international deferred private variable annuity arrangements, it may be possible for the investment manager of the PPVUL policy to place a portion of the underlying account values in a foreign corporation or other entity that operates an ongoing international business, with all profits accumulating free of tax. If income during life is required, the policy can own an IPDVA company, which issues an annuity for your benefit, the benefit of your spouse and children, etc.

It's also possible for the contract to be written to protect against foreign exchange controls. For instance, if a central bank prohibits withdrawals from bank accounts, the contract may permit premiums to be paid in other ways—for instance, with shares of stock. However, such innovations may affect the tax treatment of the policy. It may also be possible to customize the insurance contract to direct the carrier to consider such items as duress before deciding whether to release money to a policyholder who, e.g., is being ordered by a U.S. court to repatriate assets.

Initial fees for such a structure are approximately 2%-3% of premium dollars contributed. Total annual costs exclusive of asset management fees are typically 1%-3%.

Offshore life insurance policies are worth considering if you're seeking a flexible, tax-advantaged, and comprehensive estate plan providing tax efficiency and access to a wide selection of international asset management options. Since it requires expert tax advice to set up properly, and requires ongoing maintenance to insure tax compliance, it's most cost effective if you can invest US$1 million or more in the policy.

Configuring Your Offshore Life Insurance Policy

PPVUL policies are generally held through an irrevocable trust. While there are many possible variations, a simple PPVUL structure involves a married couple setting up an irrevocable offshore trust for the benefit of their children. This arrangement is classified as a **foreign non-grantor trust**. The trust has no taxable owner for U.S. income tax purposes and generally has no U.S. beneficiaries until one year after the death of the grantor.

After contributing US$1 million or more to the trust, the trustee purchases a PPVUL policy from an offshore insurance company. A small portion of this contribution is used to fund the cost of insurance, with the balance is placed in an investment account. That account is then invested with one or more investment managers recommended by the policyholder, but ultimately approved by the insurance company.

On the death of the insured person or persons (if more than one person is insured), the assets in the PPVUL policy pass to the irrevocable life insurance trust free of income and estate taxes. It's possible to avoid generation-skipping taxes if the trust grantor files a gift tax return at the time the trust is funded, and elects to allocate his or her generation-skipping transfer tax exemption to the gift.

While trusts are the primary legal arrangement for owning a PPVUL policy, a limited partnership or a LLC may also be used for this purpose. This can provide greater flexibility and offers additional tax planning options. It may also be possible to have an insurance limited partnership or LLC funded by monies in an Individual Retirement Account. In this way, the PPVUL policy may be acquired using pre-tax dollars.

In some situations, an individual who wishes to purchase a PPVUL policy is in poor health and doesn't qualify for life insurance. In this situation, it's possible to set up an IPDVA, and have the IPDVA form an offshore insurance company to create a policy on the policyholder's life. No evidence of insurability is necessary in this situation. Again, the proceeds of the PPVUL go to the beneficiaries tax-free upon the death of the insured.

Compliance with U.S. Tax Law

The tax benefits of PPVUL policies haven't been lost to the IRS. It isn't surprising that the agency isn't pleased with a planning technique that simultaneously eliminates federal estate taxes, creates a situation where no U.S. person is subject to tax upon transfer of the assets to the beneficiaries, and facilitates tax-free offshore investment.

In an attempt to limit these benefits, IRS regulations issued in 2005 end tax deferral for insurance policies which purchase interests in hedge funds set up as private limited partnerships. To qualify for tax deferral, insurance companies must set up their own hedge funds, so that investors can purchase interests only through insurance contracts.[639]

Numerous other requirements must be met for a PPVUL policy to achieve the tax benefits described in this section.[640] For instance, the Tax Code requires that the death benefit under a PPVUL policy satisfy various rules that guarantee that the insurance protection meets certain minimum requirements at the inception of the policy and for subsequent years. These rules are complex and require the use of an insurance actuary.

The underlying accounts of a PPVUL policy must also comply with IRS diversification requirements, and the policy owner may not directly appoint or control the investment advisor in any direct way. Non-binding requests are permissible, although the investment advisor or manager must at all times control the disposition of investments.

To deal successfully with these challenges, it's essential to consult a qualified international tax planner when constructing an international insurance structure.

As with offshore variable annuities, no U.S. law explicitly requires that the existence of an offshore variable life insurance contract be disclosed to the IRS. However, if you have direct or constructive ownership, of an offshore life insurance policy that contains securities, the safest stance is to report it as a "foreign account" as discussed earlier in this chapter. In addition, the use of a foreign trust or other offshore entity to hold the life insurance contract is reportable as discussed later in this chapter.

The Nestmann Group, Ltd. can assist with the design and implementation of PPVUL policies. Contact us for more information.

The Right Way to Use Offshore Business Entities

How might an offshore business entity—most commonly an **international business company (IBC)** or an **offshore limited liability company (OLLC)** benefit you? Here are a few of the most common ways they're used:

- **To hold an investment portfolio producing passive income.** Increasingly, offshore banks won't open accounts in the name of U.S. residents. This is a consequence of laws like the USA PATRIOT Act, overreaching U.S. securities and tax laws, etc. But, in most cases, they'll open an account in the name of an offshore business entity. It's generally not possible, though, for U.S. persons to defer tax on income from passive investments using an offshore structure with the exception of a variable annuity or life insurance policy.
- **For asset protection purposes.** The charging order concept protects ownership interests in some offshore business entities, notably OLLCs (Chapter 4). This concept, combined with the difficulty of litigating in an unfamiliar legal environment, is a powerful deterrent to litigation.
- **To achieve greater privacy.** It's virtually impossible for someone to identify you as an owner of a properly organized offshore business entity, unless you're required by law or legal process to disclose your interest.
- **To operate an offshore business.** Offshore business entities can be used to operate businesses ranging from Web sites to hotels and everything in-between.
- **To own real estate.** Some countries prohibit foreigners from owning real estate at all, or restrict them to certain areas. Other countries subject real estate owned by foreigners to probate proceedings at the owner's death. Owning foreign property through an offshore business entity may avoid these problems. An additional benefit is that when you sell the property, you can simply sell the company to the buyer. This may avoid capital gains and inheritance tax in the foreign jurisdiction (although not the United States).
- **In conjunction with other structures or contracts.** As described earlier in this chapter, offshore business entities are often used in conjunction with offshore trusts, offshore insurance policies, etc.

IBCs Are a Tax Minefield for U.S. Persons

International business companies (IBC) are the most commonly used entities for these purposes. In most offshore jurisdictions, there's no requirement that accounts be audited, and meetings can be held anywhere in the world, if they're held at all. The IBC's directors or officers need not be resident in the jurisdiction where it's formed. Generally, no information on beneficial owners or managers is publicly available. Most countries with IBC legislation are in low or no-tax jurisdictions and income from the IBC, particularly if earned outside the country of formation, isn't taxed there.

However, for U.S. residents doing business overseas, IBCs usually aren't a good choice unless they're owned by an offshore annuity, offshore life insurance policy, or tax-deferred pension or retirement plan. This is due to the unfavorable tax treatment imposed on the IBC's U.S. shareholders. In virtually all cases in which U.S. shareholders use an IBC to hold assets that generate passive income, they become entangled in a complex web of rules designed to prevent U.S.-based multi-national corporations from diverting profits into foreign subsidiaries where they can be tax deferred indefinitely.

These **controlled foreign corporation** (CFC) rules[641] are among the most complex in the U.S. Tax Code. Here's a highly simplified summary:

If U.S. shareholders own 50% or more of the shares in a foreign corporation (e.g., an IBC), by vote or value, the foreign corporation is classified as a CFC. U.S. shareholders are defined as U.S. natural persons, partnerships, corporations, trusts, and estates that own, respectively, 10% or greater interests in the foreign corporation.

If you're a U.S. shareholder in a CFC, and it generates what the IRS calls "subpart F" income,[642] you can't defer tax on that income, even if it's not distributed as a dividend.[643] Subpart F income includes passive investment income, income from personal service contracts, income from transactions with related U.S. persons or entities, and income from certain industries such as insurance, banking, mining and others. Naturally, various exceptions apply to many of these general rules.

If that's not enough, if you're foreign corporation is classified as a CFC:

- The 15% income tax rate on capital gains and dividends isn't available;
- Losses on investments can't be allocated against gains until the IBC is liquidated;
- Any investments in the United States may result in double taxation;
- The basis of the stock does not step-up to its fair market value at the death of a shareholder for estate tax purposes; and
- Complex reporting requirements also apply.

It's possible to avoid this unfavorable tax treatment by electing to be taxed on your proportionate share of the subpart F income of a CFC in which you hold shares, as if you were a domestic corporation.[644] This also allows you to claim a credit for foreign taxes paid by the CFC in which you're a shareholder. When the dividend is actually paid, it's generally taxed at the 15% rate imposed on dividends from domestic corporations. This produces a result similar to a taxable dividend paid from a domestic corporation that has paid corporate tax on its income, and then distributed as after-tax income to shareholders as a dividend. However, this still results in double taxation.

With an IBC, you also won't receive much more asset protection than you would with a corporation chartered in a U.S. state (Chapter 4). While IBCs are unquestionably less visible than domestic corporations, if you suffer a judgment, a creditor can simply seize your IBC stock, and even liquidate it (assuming you own more than 50% of the shares).

Offshore LLCs are Usually Better for Americans than IBCs

For these reasons, OLLCs are often a better choice for U.S. residents doing business offshore. An OLLC doesn't suffer the unfavorable U.S. tax treatment of an IBC. Domestic LLCs are taxed by default as partnerships (if there are multiple owners) or disregarded entities (if there is one owner) under U.S. tax rules. The foreign rules are a little different; you must make an affirmative choice to have an OLLC taxed as a disregarded entity. You do this by filing Form 8832 and check the box to make the election for disregarded entity status. In both cases, the profits or losses of the OLLC "flow through" to the individual owners (members) in proportion to their ownership interests. However, an OLLC won't avoid the potentially disastrous tax problems awaiting U.S. persons who purchase most offshore mutual funds through a non-tax deferred entity.

OLLCs can also be used as estate planning tools in the same manner as domestic LLCs or domestic limited partnerships. If the OLLC is properly structured, membership interests should be discounted for estate and gift tax purposes for lack of marketability and lack of control.

OLLCs can also provide a significant degree of asset protection—much more than an IBC— against the debts of the owners. This is the result of the charging order concept, which generally prohibits creditors from seizing a debtor's interest in a LLC. Attorney Christopher Riser explains why an OLLC provides greater protection than a domestic LLC:

A creditor of a member of a U.S. LLC with a U.S. manager may be able to obtain a court order forcing the manager to make distributions which, combined with a charging order, will satisfy the member's judgment debt. The creditor of a member of an offshore LLC with a non-U.S. manager in most cases will not be able to obtain jurisdiction over the non-U.S. manager. Even if an order were issued by a U.S. court, the non-U.S. manager could not be forced to comply unless and until a successful action was brought in the non-U.S. manager's jurisdiction.[645]

The greatest asset protection is provided if the OLLC has more than one member, is managed by a non-U.S. resident manager, and holds all of its assets outside the United States. That makes it virtually impossible for a U.S. court to obtain jurisdiction over the offshore OLLC's management, or any of its investments. As long as the OLLC's operating agreement is drafted correctly, all managing parties will be outside U.S. jurisdiction and thus not subject to a U.S. court order.

To mitigate the risk that a creditor could obtain a court ruling ordering the U.S. members of the OLLC to replace the offshore manager with a domestic manager, the OLLC's membership interest can be owned by an irrevocable offshore asset protection trust. If the OAPT trustee is offshore, it won't come under U.S. jurisdiction, thus preventing replacement of the OLLC manager.

There are a few situations, however, where a foreign corporation may be a more suitable entity than an OLLC, with respect to its U.S. owners:

- **If an offshore entity is used to purchase real estate in a country where a LLC isn't recognized, or not recognized as an independent entity.** This would potentially subject the property to a probate proceeding upon the death of one of the members of the LLC.
- **In a holding company situation, where the relevant foreign legislation requires the use of a corporation.**

- **If free transferability of ownership interests—lacking in a LLC—is essential.** This might be the case, e.g., if the entity might be publicly traded in the future.

Planning a Tax-Advantaged Offshore Business

A major thrust of the CFC rules is to prevent U.S. shareholders in foreign businesses from deferring tax on passive income—interest, dividends, rents, royalties, and capital gains. Therefore, even if you are the only shareholder in a CFC, you may be able to avoid current taxation if it generates "active" income in a genuine offshore business—a restaurant, hotel, manufacturing facility, etc. In this situation, the business profits would generally need to be reinvested in expanding production, upgrading manufacturing capacity, etc., rather than being invested in a portfolio of passive assets.

Traditionally, a foreign corporation would be used in this situation. However, if asset protection is a concern, it may be possible to use an offshore LLC to operate the foreign business by filing Form 8832 and electing to have the LLC taxed as a foreign corporation.

To achieve tax deferral on this income, the business must be managed from outside the United States. If you live in the United States, your participation should be limited to being a passive investor in the business. According to tax attorney Richard Duke and CPA Vernon Jacobs:

> If a U.S. person, or persons, controls a corporation domiciled and operating in a foreign country and if that CFC has business profits from buying and selling personal property to and from unrelated persons, the profits of the foreign corporation are not subject to U.S income tax and the U.S. shareholders are not taxed until the income is repatriated to the U.S. shareholder(s) in the form of dividends, compensation or from the sale of the stock. Within some strict limits, the profits of the foreign corporation can be invested in passive assets without generating a current tax. If the profits are reinvested in other trade or business activities that do not produce 'subpart F' income, then the tax deferral can continue for an extended time...

> To have any hope of being able to avoid U.S. taxes on profits from a foreign corporation, the corporation must not be an IBC. It must have a standard corporate charter. It must have an office that is a permanent establishment in that country. It needs employees to do all of the tasks necessary to produce a product or service, to market that product or service and to handle all of the ancillary accounting and administrative tasks. It must be a self-sustaining operation. If the foreign corporation is a CFC, the U.S. owners must not engage in any significant management or operational activities while physically within the United States.[646]

Another strategy to avoid current taxation on an offshore business is to use the definition of "controlled foreign corporation" to your advantage. A CFC is a foreign corporation in which one more U.S. shareholders own more than 50% of it. Therefore, if your foreign business has non-U.S. partners that collectively own 50% or more of the foreign corporation, its earnings won't generally be subject to the CFC provisions.

Another strategy to avoid CFC status is to take advantage of the IRS definition of "U.S. shareholders." Only shareholders that own (directly or indirectly) 10% or more of the foreign corporation's stock are included in the "more than 50%" ownership test. For instance, a foreign corporation with 11 shareholders from the United States, each with equal shares of 9.09% of its stock, isn't a CFC, because the IRS doesn't consider any of the shareholders to be "U.S. shareholders." However, you can't simply list family members or business associates as "shareholders" and think that you can secretly control their interest in the corporation. IRS attribution and constructive ownership rules result in these interests being combined with yours.

Even if you avoid CFC status, your profits won't necessarily stay tax deferred forever. Unless you reinvest the profits in growing your offshore business, the foreign corporation may eventually come up against another one of the IRS's anti-deferral tools: the passive foreign investment company (PFIC) regime, described earlier in this chapter. The PFIC problem arises as income or gain from the foreign corporation accumulates in bank or securities accounts. Once 50% of the foreign corporation's assets are held for the production of passive income, or 75% of its income derives from passive sources, it's deemed to be a PFIC. One small consolation is that the CFC and PFIC regimes don't apply simultaneously; if a foreign corporation is subject to CFC provisions, it's not subject to the PFIC rules on the same income, and vice-versa.[647]

There are complex techniques to minimize the impact of these provisions, but planning is **much** simpler if:

- The business is managed outside the United States;
- You reinvest the profits from your business into other business ventures, rather than placing them into investments that generate passive income;
- To the extent the business holds passive assets, they're placed in non-interest-bearing investments;
- The foreign corporation itself develops any intellectual property, such as copyrights or patents, from which it generates income, or buys them from a non-U.S. source. If you assign a foreign corporation the rights to intangible assets from the United States, this must be done in an arm's-length transaction, which will produce taxable income;
- You hire a competent professional to determine, in advance, the likely tax consequences of your offshore business venture.

Reporting Obligations for U.S. Persons Using Offshore Business Entities

The IRS imposes significant reporting obligations for U.S. persons who form and operate offshore business entities.

For **offshore corporations**, the transfer of assets to the entity is reportable on IRS Form 926. If you acquire or dispose of more than a 10% interest in the offshore corporation (by vote or value), or add to your interest in the offshore corporation to reach the 10% threshold, you must make a one-time filing of Form 5471. If the offshore corporation is a CFC, and you have a 10% or greater interest in it, you must file the form annually.

Form 5471 is complex and requires a great deal more detail than an ordinary U.S. corporate tax return. It requires the use of U.S. **Generally Accepted Accounting Principles** (GAAP) in certain parts of the return. GAAP is a set of rules for the measurement of income and net worth in the financial statements of a business. Trying to reconcile records based on foreign country GAAP and U.S. GAAP is a job for an accountant familiar with both sets of rules.

For offshore LLCs, the reporting varies depending on how you elect to have the entity taxed. If you file Form 8832 electing to have the LLC taxed as a disregarded entity, you'll need to make an annual information filing via Form 8858 to disclose a summary of its income, expenses, assets, and liabilities.

Form 8858 is filed with your income tax return. Income from a disregarded entity is reported on Schedule C of Form 1040.

If you elect via Form 8832 to have your offshore LLC taxed as a partnership, you may be required to file Form 8865. If you acquire or dispose of more than a 10% interest in the LLC (by vote or value), or add to your interest in the LLC to reach the 10% threshold, you must file IRS Form 8865. If U.S. persons own 50% or more of the offshore LLC, and you have a 10% or greater interest in it, you must file the form annually. In the event you elect to have the LLC taxed as an offshore corporation, and you meet the ownership thresholds summarized earlier in this section, you must file Form 5471.

For any foreign business entity, if you have signature or "other" authority over the IBC's bank account, you must file Treasury Form TD F 90-22.1 each year and separately acknowledge this authority each year on Schedule B of Form 1040.

All these forms are available at http://www.irs.gov/formspubs/lists/0,,id=97817,00.html.

Penalties for non-compliance with these reporting requirements are draconian. For instance, a civil penalty of up to US$50,000 applies for failing to file Forms 5471, 8858, or 8865. Criminal penalties may be imposed in aggravated circumstances.

You'll find it difficult to prepare some of these forms without the assistance of a knowledgeable accountant, particularly Form 5471 or Form 8865. Typical fees to prepare these forms will range from US$3,000 a year for a very small business to as much as US$15,000 a year for a medium size business.

Bearer Shares are a Minefield for U.S. Taxpayers

Spend a few minutes searching for information on the Internet about "asset protection" or "privacy" and you'll see dozens of links pop up touting "bearer share" corporations in a handful of offshore jurisdictions, as providing practical anonymity, bulletproof asset protection, and (in some cases) even a way to supposedly avoid tax claims. Unfortunately, these claims have little if any credence.

In jurisdictions that permit the issuance of bearer shares, a stock certificate need not state the name of the person to whom the certificate is issued. Instead, the certificate can be made out simply to the "bearer." This individual can exercise the rights of a shareholder of the corporation.

A company that issues bearer shares has no shareholder list or register for those shares. The identity of the shareholders is impossible to determine. And because the shares can be transferred simply by handing them to another person, ownership can be conveyed much more simply and privately than with registered securities.

However, these purported advantages aren't nearly as great as they might appear at first blush. Indeed, bearer shares have many traps, and if you're subject to U.S. income, gift, estate or capital gains taxes, or U.S. securities laws, you should generally avoid them.

Advocates of bearer shares claim that by conveying your shares to a trusted friend or relative, you can state under oath that you don't own them. However, if discovered by the IRS, the gratuitous transfer of bearer shares will trigger a gift tax of up to 45% (2007 rates) on their fair market value. Gift tax is again triggered when the friend or relative later returns the shares.

By arguing that a transfer to another party was a transfer in trust for safekeeping, you may avoid a gift tax assessment. However, by making this argument you could hardly claim that you're not the actual owner of the shares. This defeats any asset protection purpose for which you transferred the bearer shares in the first place.

Finally, if this transfer occurs after litigation has begun or settled adversely, it may be considered a fraudulent transfer, and invalidated by the courts, as discussed in Chapter 4.

If the IRS discovers you've formed a bearer share company, and you've used it to evade taxes, it's also possible prosecutors could argue that you're using "sophisticated means" to defraud the government, thereby elevating a tax evasion prosecution into a tax fraud case involving money laundering, which carries much harsher penalties (Chapter 2).

Owners of bearer shares may also violate securities laws when they transfer the shares to another person. If the shares aren't registered with the Securities and Exchange Commission, or issued under one of the SEC's exceptions to registration, they're not freely transferable. Anyone who sells unregistered bearer shares in the U.S. will be guilty of civil and possibly criminal securities violations unless the sale qualifies for such an exception.[648]

There are also safety issues to consider with bearer shares. What if you lose your bearer shares, someone finds them, and then tries the vote the shares in your place? Lost shares can be replaced (assuming you know about the loss), but the process can be time-consuming and expensive.

Finally, bearer shares are becoming obsolete. In 2007, Wyoming and Nevada abolished bearer shares, ending their status as the last two U.S. states to permit their use. Most offshore jurisdictions have banned them as well. While bearer shares are more frequently used offshore, many jurisdictions allow them to be used only if "immobilized"; i.e., held by a custodian.[649]

Is "Captive" Insurance for You?

Many U.S. businesses find it difficult or impossible to obtain liability insurance at a reasonable price. This has led to an explosive growth in "captive" insurance: an insurance company formed to insure the risks of an operating business, or group of businesses.

The arrangement is "captive" because the insurance company is generally dedicated to the insurance needs of the business or group—although captives are free to underwrite the risks of other related or unrelated businesses. Premiums for a captive are usually lower than commercial coverage due to the absence of the costs of marketing, sales, and agent commissions, and because premiums reflect the experience of a particular corporation or group, rather than general market experience.

The captive concept dates back more than 300 years to syndicates formed to insure marine risks or to underwrite the risks of a particular community or association. Growth of the industry began in the 1950s when large U.S. corporations began to establish offshore captives. It accelerated in the 1980s and 1990s in response to the increasing reluctance of U.S. insurance companies to write liability coverage, given new theories of liability enforced with huge damage awards. Captives now account for more than 10% of all commercial insurance premiums collected worldwide. In the United States, captives were responsible for over US$9 billion in premiums in 2005.[650]

In recent years, it has become practical for smaller businesses to form captives by purchasing an interest in an already-formed captive. So-called "rent a captives" make it practical for businesses with annual insurance costs under US$100,000 to benefit from the captive concept.

Some of the top jurisdictions for captive insurance include Bermuda, the Cayman Islands, Guernsey, Luxembourg, Barbados, the British Virgin Islands, Ireland, and the Isle of Man. A number of U.S. states have also enacted captive legislation. Vermont is the leading U.S. captive jurisdiction.

Apart from obtaining coverage at more affordable rates, captive insurance also provides:

- Direct access to the reinsurance market, thus potentially providing coverage for risks not available through conventional insurance; e.g., nuclear risk, supertankers and labor stoppages;
- More effective claim management;
- Coverage more precisely tailored to a company's needs;
- Increased control and liquidity. Premiums paid the captive insurer are available for investment by the parent or associated companies;
- Increased investment options without restrictions by the U.S. Securities and Exchange Commission; and
- An independent profit center, if the captive acts as an insurer for other companies.

Substantial tax benefits are possible as well. The most significant tax benefit is that premiums paid by a business for insurance are tax deductible when paid. Deductibility requires that the insurance arrangements are *bona fide*, adequately shift and distribute risks, and that the parent, the captive and the insured company or companies are separate entities for legal and tax purposes.[651]

Setting up a captive insurance company is a major undertaking that you should pursue only with expert tax advice. There are many pitfalls for the unwary.

Live Offshore and Earn Up to US$171,400, Tax-Free

If you're a permanent resident of the United States, you must pay taxes on your worldwide income. This isn't uncommon—most other high-tax countries have similar laws. But the United States is the world's only major country that taxes its citizens and not just its permanent residents. U.S. citizens are taxed on their income wherever they live or generate income.

Fortunately, the Internal Revenue Code contains an escape clause that allows you to earn up to US$85,700/year tax-free (2007) if you're working outside the United States. If your spouse accompanies you overseas, you can double this exemption and jointly earn up to US$171,400, free of U.S. tax obligations. You can exclude tax on additional income used to pay for your housing expenses. In most cases, the maximum exclusion for housing is limited to 30% of the applicable exemption, or US$28,233 annually.[652] These exclusions are indexed upward each year to keep pace with inflation. Fringe benefits that are non-taxable to a U.S.-based employee are also non-taxable overseas. Your employer can pay for your health insurance, or contribute to a retirement plan, with no additional tax liability.

You must qualify under one of two tests to be eligible for this **foreign earned income exclusion** (FEIE): the **bona fide residence test** or the **physical presence test**:

- **Bona fide residence test.** If you have established legal residence in another country for an uninterrupted period of at least one year, you qualify under this test.

- **Physical presence test.** You qualify under this test if you're physically present in a foreign country or countries for at least 330 full days during any period of 12 consecutive months.

Under either test, you must prove that you have a new **tax home** outside the United States; i.e., a jurisdiction that can tax your income on the basis of residence or other ties. There is no requirement that you live in a country that actually imposes an income tax. You must also file a U.S. tax return every year you wish to take advantage of the FEIE, along with IRS Form 2555.[653]

The FEIE provides no exclusion for **unearned** income—rents, royalties, interest, dividends, etc. You also remain subject to capital gains tax and estate tax. And while U.S. Social Security and Medicare taxes don't generally apply to wages for services performed outside of the United States, if you're self-employed or work for an "American employer,"[654] you'll be subject to Social Security and Medicare tax on the same proportion of your earned income as you would in the United States. You also may be subject to these taxes if you work in a country with which the United States has signed a **totalization agreement.**[655]

While you can take either a tax credit or a deduction for income taxes imposed on you by a foreign country, you can't credit or deduct foreign income taxes on income exempt from tax under the FEIE or the foreign housing exclusion. If the taxes are higher in a foreign country than what you would pay on the same income in the United States, you can only take a credit for the equivalent tax you would pay in the United States.

For more details about the FEIE, see IRS Publication 54, *Tax Guide for U.S. Citizens and Resident Aliens Abroad.*[656]

Even if You "Live Nowhere," You May Still Owe Tax

Do you want to become a PT? (To the uninitiated, a "previous taxpayer," "perpetual tourist," etc.)

I did, when I first read "W.G. Hill's" (not his real name) now-classic book, *PT.*[657] This libertarian manifesto claimed that you can live tax-free, out of reach of Big Brother, by "living nowhere." The essential elements of this purported tax-reduction strategy involve moving out of whatever high-tax jurisdiction in which you currently reside in and then roaming the world, never staying in one place long enough to become subject to its government's taxing authority.

You also have no real home, must give up most of your possessions, and be prepared to instantly move from wherever you have made your temporary resting place at the first sign of trouble from the tax authorities. Harry Schultz, who coined the term "PT," recommends "keeping a packed suitcase."

Unfortunately, the PT strategy in most cases will not eliminate tax liability. Virtually all high-tax countries require that you acquire a new "tax home" before they give up their taxing rights. For estate tax purposes, you must also establish a new **domicile**, or permanent home, a concept I'll explore later in this chapter.

For U.S. citizens, merely acquiring a new tax home and domicile isn't sufficient to eliminate tax liability. You must also give up your U.S. citizenship, for reasons summarized in the next section.

Expatriation—the Ultimate Estate Plan

Since the United States taxes its citizens and not just its permanent residents, the only way for a U.S. citizen to eliminate U.S. tax liability is to acquire legal residence and citizenship in another country and subsequently give up U.S. citizenship.

Thousands of wealthy Americans have done exactly that and substantially reduced (and with proper planning, eliminated) their U.S. tax liability. Such "tax exiles" include Michael Dingman, chairman of Abex and a Ford Motor Co. director; Campbell Soup heir John Dorrance III; former Star-Kist Foods Chairman Joseph Bogdanovich; and Kenneth Dart, an heir to Dart Container and the US$1 billion Dart family fortune.

The mechanics of expatriation are relatively simple. U.S. citizens or green-card holders are subject to U.S. taxation until they give notice of their "expatriating act" or termination of residence and file IRS Form 8854. U.S. citizens give notice of an expatriating act by either renouncing their citizenship before a U.S. diplomatic or consular officer, or by submitting a signed statement affirming their relinquishment of citizenship with the documentation required under the Immigration and Nationality Act. Green-card holders give notice of termination of U.S. residence by completing Form I-407 before a U.S. diplomatic or consular officer or immigration official.[658]

U.S. citizens who don't have a passport from another country may not give up their U.S. citizenship. This prohibition is due to U.S. policy not to permit its nationals to become "stateless persons."[659]

Expatriation is politically unpopular. As a result, anti-expatriation rules penalizing U.S. citizens and long-term residents who give up their citizenship or residence for tax avoidance reasons have been in effect for decades. First imposed in the 1960s, the rules were tightened in 1996 and again in 2004.

Currently, the U.S. Tax Code imposes income, gift, and estate taxes for 10 years after an individual gives up their U.S. citizenship in any "tax-motivated" expatriation. Also covered are permanent resident aliens who have resided in the United States for any eight of the preceding 15 years. This alternative tax regime applies to individuals who:

- Have a global net worth exceeding US$2 million; and/or
- Have an average annual net income tax liability for the five preceding years ending before the date of the loss of U.S. citizenship or residence exceeding US$124,000 (as adjusted for inflation after 2004—US$136,000 in 2007); and/or
- Fail to certify under penalties of perjury that they have complied with all U.S. federal tax obligations for the preceding five years or fail to submit evidence of compliance as required by regulation.

Only certain dual citizens and minors with few ties to the United States are exempted from these requirements.[660]

Generally, expatriates covered by the alternative tax regime must pay income tax for the 10-year period at rates applicable to U.S. citizens. The rules apply to the net combined amount of U.S. source income and income "effectively connected" with a U.S. trade or business. While careful planning is essential for an individual considering expatriation, it's relatively easy to avoid U.S. taxes for the 10 years after giving up U.S. citizenship, should you be subject to the alternative tax regime. The most important precaution is to avoid U.S. source income—although U.S. source income under the anti-expatriation regime has a wider scope than elsewhere in the Tax Code.[661] It's also possible to avoid tax on gains from certain types of U.S. assets by postponing their sale until after the 10-year period has elapsed.

Former U.S. citizens and long-term residents who wish to avoid estate tax on their global estate must also establish a new domicile. Your domicile is your permanent home—the country to which you eventually intend to return. It can be different from your country of actual residence. To change domicile, you must first change residence and subsequently take steps to indicate that you intend to stay in that country permanently. Steps you can take to establish a new domicile include purchasing property, obtaining a driver's license, setting up a business or purchasing a burial plot in that country.[662]

Expatriating Americans subject to the alternative tax regime must also:

- **File Form 8854 annually for 10 years after expatriation.** This form requires submission of an annual balance sheet and income statement, among other information.
- **Spend only 30 days annually in the United States, if they were U.S.-resident prior to expatriation.** Otherwise, they are subject to U.S. tax on their worldwide income, gifts, and estate for that year. Other non-resident aliens may spend up to six months per year in the United States without suffering this consequence, although repeat visitors may stay no more than an average of 120 days annually to avoid being taxed as U.S. permanent residents.[663] After 10 years, the rules applicable to other non-resident aliens apply.
- **Risk being categorized as an "excluded person" and denied a visa to re-enter the United States.**[664] Other categories of excluded persons include narcotics traffickers and terrorists. This authority extends only to former citizens, not former green-card holders. This provision not been enforced since enactment in 1996.

Because the anti-expatriation rules aren't difficult to circumvent, there have been periodic calls to make them stricter. The proposal most often repeated is for an **exit tax:** any expatriate with a net worth above a certain threshold would be subject to a tax on unrealized gains, to be paid at the time of expatriation. The idea for an exit tax first surfaced in 1995 and is brought up again in almost every congressional session. It appears inevitable that some kind of exit tax will eventually become law.

Recent exit tax proposals would replace the existing rules with a tax on all unrealized gains worldwide at their fair market value. The gains would be calculated mark-to-market; i.e., the difference between the market value at the time of expatriation and the value at acquisition. Payment would be due within 90 days of relinquishing U.S. citizenship or long-term residence. The first US$600,000 of gains would be excluded (US$1.2 million in the case of married individuals filing a joint return, both of whom relinquish citizenship or terminate long-term residence). These thresholds would be adjusted annually to account for inflation.[665] The punitive nature of this proposal is underscored by the fact that the tax will generate only an estimated US$444 million for the 10-year period after enactment.[666]

Under the proposed legislation, it would be possible for former U.S. citizens or long-term residents to defer payment of the mark-to-market tax by paying an interest charge on the amount deferred. Alternatively, they could make an irrevocable election to continue to be taxed as U.S. citizens with respect to any income or gain generated by the property they owned at the time of expatriation. The property would continue to be subject to U.S. gift, estate, and generation-skipping transfer taxes.

The proposal modifies the immigration rules that deny tax-motivated expatriates entry into the United States by removing the requirement that the expatriation be tax-motivated. Instead, any former citizen would be denied entry if not in full compliance with U.S. tax obligations.

Is expatriation for you? The decision to give up U.S. citizenship is a serious one. It's a step you should take only after consulting with your family and professional advisors. But it's the only way that U.S. citizens and long-term residents can eliminate U.S. tax liability on their non-U.S. income, wherever they live. And it's a tax avoidance option that may eventually be foreclosed by Congress.

The Nestmann Group offers a report analyzing the proposed U.S. exit tax and its potential impact on wealthy U.S. citizens and long-residents. For more information, see http://www.nestmann.com/catalog/product_info.php?cPath=21&products_id=43.

The Best Ways to Obtain Alternative Citizenship and Passport

Expatriation from the United States requires that you obtain another citizenship, passport, and residence. The most economical way to do so is to take advantage of your ancestry, your spouse's ancestry, or your religious affiliation.

Having a second passport and dual citizenship has numerous non-tax benefits. It can expand your travel possibilities, reduce your profile to terrorists, give you the right to reside in other countries, and give you a way to cross international borders if your primary passport is lost or stolen.

The most valuable passports are from countries that don't tax non-resident citizens on their worldwide income or impose exit taxes on long-term residents and on whose passport visa-free travel is available to many countries.

Almost every country has a program offering citizenship or passports to individuals with a family history in that nation. In Ireland, for instance, persons with at least one Irish-born grandparent qualify for Irish citizenship and passport. Many countries allow spouses of citizens to apply for citizenship and passport, usually after a specified period of residence. In Austria, for instance, the ordinary 10-year period of residence necessary to qualify for a passport and citizenship is reduced to six years if you're married to an Austrian citizen. Your religion may also be a viable route to alternative citizenship. For instance, Jews who immigrate to Israel are entitled to Israeli citizenship and passport. Since Israel has compulsory military service, taking out Israeli citizenship may not be prudent for parents of teenagers and young adults.

If you don't qualify based on these factors, in most countries, you can acquire citizenship following a period of prolonged residence. Among other countries, Australia, Canada, Gibraltar, New Zealand, the United Kingdom and the United States exchange residence rights for internal domestic investment. Eligibility can also depend on age, education, life skills, health, and other criteria. In most cases, after continued residence for three to ten years, you can apply for citizenship and passport.

A handful of countries offer "instant" citizenship in return for an economic contribution. The Commonwealth of Dominica, the Federation of St. Kitts & Nevis, and Austria are the only countries with an official, legally mandated, citizenship-through-investment program.

- **Commonwealth of Dominica.** Under this country's economic citizenship program, you may acquire citizenship and passport in return for a cash contribution of US$75,000. A US$100,000 contribution entitles you, your spouse, and two minor children to citizenship. Legal, due diligence, and processing fees add approximately US$30,000 to the cost. Dominican passport holders can travel without a visa, or obtain a visa upon entry, to nearly 90 countries and territories. Travel to the United States, however, requires a visa.

- **Federation of St. Kitts & Nevis.** Applicants for economic citizenship must invest US$350,000 in an approved real estate project. In addition, applicants must pay a registration fee of US$35,000 for a main applicant and US$15,000 for each spouse and dependent child under 18. Alternatively, applicants may contribute to the Sugar Industry Diversification Foundation. The cost for a single applicant under this option is US$200,000, or US$250,000 for an applicant with up to three dependants, and there is no registration fee. Legal, due diligence, and processing fees add a minimum of US$10,000 to the cost. St. Kitts & Nevis passport holders can travel without a visa, or obtain a visa upon entry, to more than 90 countries, but not to the United States.

- **Austria.** It may be possible to obtain "instant" Austrian citizenship and passport after making a substantial investment in Austria. Only a handful of persons gain citizenship in this manner every year. However, this program is politically unpopular and it is increasingly difficult to obtain citizenship under this option. The Austrian program is fundamentally different from that of Dominica and St. & Nevis, in that you must make your investment first and then apply for citizenship. You don't get your money back if citizenship isn't granted. Generally, you must invest at least US$4 million to have a reasonable chance at qualifying, and pay additional legal fees of at least US$500,000 for the main applicant, and a minimum of US$70,000 per dependent (spouse and children under 18).

In all three of these economic citizenship programs, applicants must pass a strict vetting process that includes a comprehensive criminal background check.

An Internet search will reveal many companies offering to sell passports from countries that don't legally sanctioned economic citizenship programs. In recent years, passports from Costa Rica, Nicaragua, the Dominican Republic, Ireland, Lithuania, and other countries have been offered. All these offers are either scams or involve illegally purchased or stolen documents. Securing a passport on this basis, through fraudulent misrepresentation, either directly or through an agent is clearly illegal. Your passport could be revoked at any time and you could be subject to arrest and/or deportation.

The Nestmann Group, Ltd. can assist individuals seeking alternative citizenship and tax-advantaged residence. Please contact us for more information.

Tax-Advantaged Alternative Residence

Once you give up residence in whatever high-tax country in which you live (or, in the case of the United States, both citizenship and residence), you can either in any other country where you can obtain a residence permit or possess a passport. The lifeboat strategy is to coordinate your selected citizenship and residence in such a way as to maximize privacy, wealth preservation, and travel options, while minimizing taxes and other government obligations.

This isn't as difficult as you might think. Many countries don't impose income taxes at all, or only tax income generated from sources within that country. Countries with this system of taxation include Belize, Costa Rica, Panama, and (for non-domiciled persons only) the United Kingdom. In Switzerland, you can negotiate with local authorities to pay a flat tax each year.

The United Kingdom has one of the most attractive regimes for wealthy persons who wish to live in a highly civilized country, but pay minimal tax. To benefit from the U.K.'s **non-domiciled resident** tax regime, you must earn the bulk of your income outside the United Kingdom. You must also have a non-U.K. domicile; a "permanent" home country to which you eventually intend to return.[667] It's easy to prove non-U.K. domicile if you weren't born in the United Kingdom and have never lived there for an extended length of time. Finally, you must qualify for U.K. residence, but this isn't generally difficult if you are wealthy and don't have a criminal record.[668]

Non-domiciled U.K. residents are taxed only on their U.K. source income, non-U.K. income remitted to the United Kingdom and capital gains on non-U.K. assets remitted to the United Kingdom. At death, inheritance tax is due only on U.K. assets. Tax on U.K. source income, remitted assets and estates is assessed at approximately 40%, but can often be reduced well below this level. Indeed, with careful planning, you can pay near-zero income tax on remittances and no tax on non U.K.-source income not remitted to the United Kingdom.

The U.K. non-domiciled residence scheme has attracted more than 100,000 immigrants. They include some of the U.K.'s wealthiest inhabitants, a fact which has led to considerable political resentment. The European Union has also placed considerable pressure on the U.K. government to end or restrict the program.[669] However, I don't foresee any significant changes in this scheme in the foreseeable future due to the enormous economic contributions non-domiciled residents make to the U.K. economy, even without paying large sums in income tax.

Avoid Offshore Scams

I've already discussed a few offshore scams, notably the fraudulent trust, tax, and passport schemes being peddled to unsuspecting victims. Yet, these scams merely scratch the surface. By far the most prevalent scams promise offshore investors unbelievably high investment returns. Many international investors seem to expect these returns as normal. Indeed, in a survey by *Offshore Business News:*

- 22% of respondents expected annual profits of 100% or higher;
- 32% of respondents expected returns of at least 50%; and
- 42% of respondents expected returns of at least 25%.

These expectations are unrealistic, particularly when accompanied by a "guarantee," but demonstrate why international investors are such easy prey for scam artists. This section summarizes some of these scams and presents suggestions to avoid them.

Bank Debenture/Prime Bank Scams

In this type of scam, you're offered the chance to participate in a supposedly lucrative international investment that promoters tell you was formerly available only to wealthy investors, multinational corporations and international banks. Promoters promise gains of 10% or more monthly and try to persuade you to "shelter" your earnings in an offshore corporation or offshore trust.

One scheme involves trading of so-called **bank credit instruments (debentures)**, also known as known as deferred payments, delayed payments, or stand-by credits. Promoters also use terms like "bank purchase orders," "promissory bank notes," or "bank debenture instruments" and claim to be operating under guidelines from the International Chamber of Commerce. However, the ICC warns that no such guidelines exist.

Here's an example of a slick bank debenture scheme that "guaranteed" a 10% per month return on investment. Quoting from a now-defunct Web site:

What is a Bank Debenture Trading Program?

Also referred to as a secured asset management program, this is an investment vehicle commonly used by the very wealthy where the principal investment is fully secured by a bank endorsed guarantee. The principal is managed and invested to give a guaranteed high return to the investor on a periodic basis. There is no risk of losing the investor's principal investment.

This investment opportunity involves the purchase and sale of bank debentures within the international market in controlled trading programs. The program allows the investor to place his funds through an established program management firm working directly with a major trading bank.

The investment funds are secured by a bank-endorsed guarantee by the banking institution at the time the funds are deposited. The investor is designated as the beneficiary of the guarantee unless otherwise instructed by the investor. The guarantee is issued to secure the investor's principal for the contract period. This guarantee will be bank endorsed with the bank seal, two authorized senior officers' signatures, and will guarantee that the funds will be on deposit in the bank during the contract period and will be returned fully to the investor at the end of the contract term.

After sending payment to a company in Panama, the company operating this Web site claimed that it would set up a bank account for you in an unspecified European country. Here, it wrote:

SECRECY is the watchword rigidly enforced by the European banker, always eager to protect his client from all unauthorized and prying inquiries from any source.

Profits were supposedly "paid monthly directly into the members' offshore bank account which then may be accessed from anywhere in the world with an ATM card." You also earned extra money if you convinced others to invest.

Sound convincing? Bank guarantees and debentures do exist. A debenture is simply a long-term unsecured debt instrument, backed only by the general credit and earnings history of a company. Banks routinely issue debentures and write guarantees on those debentures. But no legitimate bank will issue a debenture promising a higher rate of interest than it needs to pay, and no bank could possibly guarantee a debenture promising returns of 10% per month or more without quickly going insolvent. A typical interest rate for a legitimate debenture issue is 5-15% per **year**, not per month.

Another tip-off to the scam is the promise that your offshore account will be protected "from all unauthorized and prying inquiries from any source." Any implication that secrecy would apply an investigation from "any source"—even U.S. federal investigators alleging money laundering by terrorists—is highly questionable.

An Autopsy of a Phony Offshore Bank

Dozens of offshore banks promote themselves on the Internet as delivering returns of 10% or more monthly. It appears to be as simple as sending in your deposit, then waiting for the returns to begin piling up.

Unfortunately, the reality is somewhat different. Just ask any of the thousands of depositors who lost nearly US$500 million in the First International Bank of Grenada (FIBG). The essential facts are as follows: Gilbert Allen Ziegler came to Grenada from Oregon, after declaring bankruptcy in 1994. With no banking experience, no identifiable assets, and a passport issued by a non-existent country (the so-called "Dominion of Melchizedek"), Ziegler obtained a banking license in Grenada, apparently with the aid of corrupt local officials. Grenadian banking regulators permitted Ziegler to capitalize the bank on the strength of a jeweler's supposed US$17 million appraisal of a single ruby. Ziegler possessed only a photograph of the ruby and wasn't able to prove that he owned it.

Ziegler proceeded to create a Web site and marketing materials that promised a "guaranteed" annual interest rate of up to 300%. To assure depositors that their investments were safe, FIBG claimed that an independent deposit insurance company insured them. However, when FIBG went belly-up in 2001, the company supposedly insuring these deposits never made good on them.

FIBG went into liquidation in Grenada in 2001, after being exposed as a fraud. In 2004, Ziegler and a number of his associates were arraigned in U.S. federal court on multiple counts of mail fraud, wire fraud, conspiracy, and money laundering. While Ziegler died of a heart attack in 2005, four of his associates were sentenced to prison terms in 2007.[670]

The lesson of FIBG is simple: if something sounds too good to be true, it probably isn't true. Unfortunately, this lesson has yet to be learned by many investors.

You Get What You Pay For

For sheer chutzpah, few offshore promoters can match the record of Marc Matthew Harris. After having his Florida CPA license suspended in 1990, Harris relocated to Panama where he formed an international financial services company. At prices much lower than what competing firms were charging, The Harris Organization provided everything from trust services and company formations, to offshore mutual funds and annuities, to offshore insurance company and bank formations. Harris also offered tax advisory services, and claimed to have devised proprietary schemes to create enormous paper losses for U.S. companies, while moving millions of dollars offshore to be controlled by the business owner.

The beginning of the end for Harris came in 1998, when an investigative newsletter accused his organization of being insolvent, stealing clients' funds, operating a Ponzi scheme and money laundering.[671] Harris sued for libel in U.S. federal court, but lost. Over the next four years, investors filed a steady stream of lawsuits against Harris, and federal prosecutors began building a case against him. In 2001, Harris left Panama for Nicaragua, but he was arrested there in 2002 and deported to the United States. In 2003, a federal jury found Harris guilty on 16 counts of fraud, tax evasion, and money laundering. Harris was sentenced to 17 years in prison and ordered to pay fines and restitution totaling US$26 million.

One remarkable aspect of the Harris odyssey was the naïveté demonstrated by certain of Harris' clients. Investigative journalist David Marchant explains:

In 2000, I was contacted by the Reverend Albert Jackson, head of the U.S.-based "Church of the Oversoul." Jackson claimed to have invested US$230,000 of church members' funds with The Harris Organization in October 1999. When he requested a US$15,000 redemption two months later to support humanitarian projects, he was told that no money was available. Oversoul has unsuccessfully sought to redeem its investment ever since.

Jackson contacted me for assistance after learning that my company and I had won a libel trial in Miami after The Harris Organization sued over an article we published making serious allegations against Harris.

What I found remarkable during my correspondence with Jackson was his admission that he had been aware that a judgment had been entered in favor of [my company] before he had invested the US$230,000. Nor did he obtain a copy of the judgment prior to investing.

If he had, he would have read Judge Michael Moore's comments that The Harris Organization's 1997 audited financial statement was "of questionable validity," that the group had prior involvement in "fraudulent and criminal activity" and that it had a "continuing association with persons and entities that had been involved in or advocated criminal activity." And that "from the time he published the initial article to the present, Marchant had evidence which provided persuasive support for the truth of each of the allegations at issue." These "allegations at issue" included one that Harris was insolvent.[672]

Due Diligence: The Key to Avoiding Offshore Scams

No matter where you invest or do business, onshore or offshore, appearances can be deceiving. There is no substitute for due diligence. Here are a few precautions:

- Only deal with licensed companies. Make inquiries to ensure that all licenses claimed are valid and in good standing.
- Inquire about the qualifications of the management, especially their professional credentials and experience.
- Ask for references if you have not already received a recommendation from a reliable source.
- Don't make the mistake of settling for the least expensive service provider. Costs are important, but experience, professionalism, and integrity are factors that are more important.
- Don't ask for tax advice from offshore professionals. Instead, consult with tax experts in your own country to insure that the structure or investments you're contemplating are tax-compliant.

CHAPTER SIX: INTERNATIONAL TAX, EVIDENCE GATHERING AND FORFEITURE INITIATIVES

For decades, governments have tried to discourage offshore investments. The earliest anti-offshore efforts date from the 1920s, when tax authorities in Europe sought to slow down the flow of capital to Liechtenstein, which in 1926 enacted the world's first "tax haven" legislation. U.S. efforts to discourage offshore dealings date from 1937, when it enacted legislation designed to curtail the tax-free accumulation of profits overseas by U.S. companies.[673]

These efforts often led to unintended consequences. Perhaps the most spectacular example was the U.S. Revenue Act of 1962,[674] which imposed an **interest equalization tax**. This was a 15% tax on interest received from foreign borrowers, designed to restrict foreign debt issues sold into the United States market. Its effect was to drive dollar-based financing activity to offshore jurisdictions. Then, in an effort to reign in offshore financing, in 1965, the U.S. Office of Foreign Direct Investment issued regulations requiring U.S. persons investing abroad to borrow money abroad. That initiative backfired as well, and led to a huge growth in the development of offshore banking to provide the necessary financing.[675]

Such anti-offshore initiatives continue. In 2006, the U.S. Senate held hearings on "Tax Havens and Offshore Abuses." Witnesses testified as to the immense harm that offshore investments cause the U.S. economy. A lengthy report issued in conjunction with these hearings claimed that Americans evade as much as US$70 billion in U.S. taxes annually using offshore tax schemes.[676]

U.S. International Tax, Evidence Gathering and Forfeiture Initiatives

Many nations have ratified agreements with the United States that establish rules to retrieve evidence in civil, criminal, and tax collection cases. These agreements obligate the signatories to exchange documents and, in some cases, restrain and/or forfeit assets under mutually agreed conditions.

Not all foreign countries willingly enter into these agreements. The United States has sought through legal, diplomatic, and occasionally military pressure to force offshore centers to disclose information that would otherwise be legally protected.

The United States applies criminal and civil sanctions to activities that in many other countries are legal or at worst subject to minor penalties. Many countries restrict or even prohibit cooperation in international criminal investigations where **dual criminality** is lacking; i.e., the activity in question is not a criminal offense in that country. However, U.S. law provides a variety of coercive tools to obtain information in such situations.

An Imbalanced "Balancing Test"

The *Restatement (Third) of Foreign Relations Law* lists rules for a "balancing test" U.S. courts should follow in applying domestic laws coercively against foreign persons or entities.[677] In reality, this balancing test is badly imbalanced. Virtually no situation exists in which the interests of a foreign country in enforcing its law outweigh the interests of the United States in requiring disclosure.[678]

One of the most important ways the United States exerts its legal authority outside its territorial boundaries is through constantly expanding theories of **jurisdiction**: i.e., the legal authority of a court, or a government, over a person or property. Jurisdiction over persons is *in personam*; i.e., "against the person." Jurisdiction over property is *in rem*; i.e., "against the thing."

In most countries, jurisdiction is based on physical presence. Persons or property physically present within the territory over which a court has legal authority are subject to its jurisdiction. However, the United States takes a much more expansive view of its jurisdiction that most other countries.[679] Under U.S. law, a court may establish *in personam* jurisdiction based on a person's:

- Physical presence within the court's jurisdiction;
- Consent or implied consent to jurisdiction;
- Domicile; i.e., a person's permanent home;[680]
- Contacts,[681] even minimal contacts;[682]
- Intentionally obtaining benefits;[683]
- Having an "effect" in the territorial jurisdiction of the court;[684] and
- Engaging in an activity in a foreign country that violates U.S. law.

If you meet **any** of these tests, a U.S. court can exercise *in personam* jurisdiction over you. Unless you follow its orders, you can be cited for contempt—and potentially jailed. For instance, U.S. persons may not refuse to release to the government foreign records or foreign property under their control.[685] A U.S. court may compel a foreign entity with a U.S. office or branch to release such records or property, even if the items demanded are not in its possession. If refused, the U.S. office or branch, and/or its officers, managers, and directors, may be held in contempt of court, fined, and/or imprisoned.[686]

This authority has the potential to impose contradictory legal duties on a foreign bank or other institution if such disclosure is prohibited under that institution's domestic law. However, under the "balancing test," U.S. courts have imposed sanctions even when non-compliance is based upon a foreign court order not to produce the requested documents.[687]

Even in purely civil cases, U.S. courts take an expansive view of their jurisdiction over foreign entities. For instance, in 2000, a U. S. district court in Florida ruled that it had jurisdiction over an offshore bank, despite the fact that bank was headquartered in a foreign country and had no U.S. subsidiaries. Among the factors leading to this conclusion:

- The bank had used the Florida court system to sue a Florida resident;
- Bank officers visited Florida, spent money, and then claimed the expenditures as business expenses for tax purposes;
- The bank maintained a mailing address in Florida; and
- The bank "engages in routine bank services such as mailing of checks and wiring funds into Florida."[688]

The United States also asserts its jurisdiction through trade sanctions against numerous countries. For instance, U.S. law prohibits virtually any dealings with or in Cuba by not only U.S. companies, but also their foreign subsidiaries.[689] The U.S. Treasury Office of Foreign Assets Control (Chapter 2) enforces these laws. In response to, some countries have enacted **blocking statutes** that prohibit local companies from complying with the coercive U.S. measures.[690] Again, foreign subsidiaries of U.S. companies, or U.S. subsidiaries of foreign companies, must deal with conflicting legal requirements. If they fail to comply with U.S. laws, they risk sanctions in the United States; if they comply, they risk violating a blocking statute.

U.S. Courts Can Enforce Foreign Tax Obligations

A long-established principal of international law is that governments won't enforce foreign tax claims in their courts. The theory, known as the **revenue rule**, was succinctly summarized by a court in Jersey (Channel Islands): "Just as one State cannot send its police force into another State, so also it cannot send its tax-gatherers."[691]

In its own collection efforts, the United States has for decades used **tax treaties** and **tax information exchange agreements** to bypass the revenue rule. These agreements, which can be used coercively, are discussed later in this chapter. More recently, the United States has modified its longstanding prohibition against the enforcement of foreign tax obligations through U.S. courts.[692] In the 2005 *Pasquantino* case, the Supreme Court held that a "plot to defraud a foreign government of tax revenues" could constitute a wire fraud violation under U.S. law.[693] Given this reality, one tax lawyer postulates the following scenario:

Imagine that you walk into work tomorrow and find a criminal indictment sitting on your desk. The indictment alleges that recent actions by your company violated the wire fraud statute and that you, as the CEO, are criminally liable. According to the government, your company used the U.S. telephone system to place calls between New York and California for the purpose of defrauding the Chinese government... Specifically, the [indictment] contends that your company defrauded China by not paying taxes due under a Chinese revenue law. While this hypothetical may seem absurd at first, the Supreme Court's recent decision in Pasquantino vs. United States makes this very situation all too realistic.[694]

Based on this decision, it appears that a U.S. court may apply the revenue rule only if concludes that enforcement of a foreign tax law would pose an "unmanageable complexity." This standard makes it virtually impossible to apply the revenue rule as a bar to domestic criminal prosecution based upon conduct alleged to defraud tax authorities in another country.

Can You Trust Your Offshore Bank to Keep its Secrets from the IRS?

The United States doesn't always need to use treaties or coercive court orders to gather evidence overseas. Sometimes the evidence is disclosed "voluntarily," even in the face of foreign laws prohibiting such disclosure.

In the early 1990s, U.S. prosecutors bought money-laundering charges against John Mathewson, the former director of Guardian Bank and Trust in the Cayman Islands. To avoid a lengthy prison sentence, Mathewson turned over Guardian's customer database to federal investigators. The database contained the names, addresses, and account information of people who had opened "secret" bank accounts at Guardian—over 1,500 in all.

Once the IRS had the opportunity to examine the database, it announced that Mathewson's assistance was "the most important... in the history of tax haven prosecutions." A wave of tax evasion and money laundering cases followed against U.S. persons who had established accounts at Guardian without reporting the accounts, or the income they generated, to the IRS.[695]

Mathewson also described what he claimed were popular schemes used to evade taxes offshore. One frequently used method, according to Mathewson, was for Guardian to form an international business company (Chapter 5) for a U.S. customer. The customer would then deposit untaxed monies into account. To allow the customer to repatriate the funds, Guardian often issued the customer a debit card tied to the account.

To investigate this activity, in 2000, the IRS began petitioning U.S. federal courts to issue **John Doe summonses** against credit/debit card issuers and related businesses. In a John Doe summons, the IRS doesn't know the identity of the taxpayer(s) under investigation.[696] The IRS uses such summonses to examine the financial transactions of persons who are not under investigation, but who may potentially be involved in tax evasion, tax fraud, or money laundering.[697]

The IRS served John Doe summonses on MasterCard, Visa, and American Express with respect to accounts held by U.S. taxpayers in more than 30 jurisdictions. Because many of the accounts were held in corporate names, or couldn't otherwise be associated with U.S. persons, the IRS followed this effort up with John Doe summonses on over 40 hotels, airlines, and car-rental companies. Subsequently, the IRS received court approval to serve John Doe summonses on processors of credit card information, including PayPal.[698]

These efforts were not as fruitful for the IRS as the original Mathewson investigation. Based largely on estimates Mathewson provided, the IRS published an estimate that as many as two million Americans held unreported foreign accounts. But in subsequent testimony before Congress, the IRS admitted it had evidence against only about 80,000 taxpayers with allegedly unreported offshore accounts.[699]

Amnesty ... or Not?

Once it became clear that its offshore credit card project would not be as fruitful as originally believed, the IRS announced a limited amnesty for individuals who participated in offshore arrangements not properly reflected on their tax returns. The amnesty ended April 15, 2003.

This amnesty, which the IRS called the **Offshore Voluntary Compliance Initiative** (OVCI) didn't forgive payment of delinquent taxes. Instead, if a taxpayer met certain requirements, the IRS promised not to impose civil and criminal penalties. But all back taxes and interest still applied. The most important condition for participation in the OVCI program was for taxpayers to provide complete information about any person or entity that had promoted the offshore tax evasion scheme in which they had been involved. With this information, the IRS began targeting those promoting such schemes.

The OVCI program was far more successful than the credit card program. In 2004, the IRS reported it had yielded over $170 million in taxes, interest, and penalties. More importantly, it resulted in the creation of a detailed database on offshore tax evasion schemes, and the identities of those promoting them.[700] Subsequently, the IRS shut down numerous promoters engaged in what the IRS believed to be tax evasion schemes and seized their client lists.[701]

Turning Offshore Banks Into IRS Agents

IRS regulations came into effect in 2001 requiring offshore banks to identify the beneficial owners of their clients who purchase U.S. securities.[702] Otherwise, all income and **gross sales proceeds** are subject to a 31% withholding tax. To avoid the 31% withholding tax, the offshore bank must sign an agreement with the IRS and become a "qualified intermediary." The QI bank must:

- Assign a "U.S. withholding agent" to withhold appropriate amounts of tax depending on the status of the individual account-holder.

- Provide the name and address of every U.S. investor holding a position in the correspondent account to the U.S. withholding agent via Form W-9. Otherwise, the 31% withholding tax applies.
- Agree to have the IRS or a third party (e.g., an accounting firm) conduct periodic audits of the bank's adherence to "know your customer rules" and other aspects of the QI agreement.[703]

Each QI agreement is different. Some foreign banks have signed more restrictive QI agreements that require Form W-9 to be filed for any U.S.-resident client who purchases any security, U.S. or non-U.S., when investment instructions originate in the United States. In cases where obligating a client to sign such a statement would violate a foreign bank secrecy statute, the bank may prohibit a U.S.-resident customer from purchasing any security, U.S. or non-U.S. The same policies may extend to corporate accounts in which a U.S. person has direct or indirect ownership. With offshore trusts, the IRS requires Form W-9 when the trust has a U.S. grantor and opens a foreign account that purchases any securities.[704]

Foreign banks need not disclose the identities of non-U.S. investors in custodial accounts to the IRS. However, non-U.S. depositors must complete Form W8BEN to certify non-U.S. status. Otherwise, all income and **gross sales proceeds** are subject to a 30% withholding tax. Similarly, a non-U.S. company or trust operating a non-U.S. account with no U.S. beneficial owners must file IRS Form W8BEN when it purchases U.S. securities. This form certifies its non-U.S. status.

To avoid the QI regime, U.S. resident investors can make investments in foreign shares, bonds, and offshore funds, to the extent the foreign bank's QI agreement permits these investments. In addition, assets held by U.S. residents in offshore variable annuities and offshore variable life insurance contracts aren't subject to the QI requirements.

Sneaky Treaty Tricks

Except under the circumstances noted earlier in this chapter, U.S. courts have no authority over persons or companies in other countries. Therefore, a U.S. litigant, prosecutor, or administrative agency wishing to serve notice or gather evidence in another country must obtain cooperation in that country in order to do so.

However, in recent decades, the United States has ratified treaties that entitle U.S. investigators to gather evidence, seize property, and even conduct undercover investigations in other countries. In some cases, these treaties appear to be designed for one purpose—e.g., to avoid double taxation—but are used for another purpose—e.g., to collect taxes. In other cases, the treaties, once ratified by the U.S. Senate in one form, are amended through unratified "executive agreements" to make them more coercive. In all cases, the net effect is to reduce the burden of proof that U.S. investigators would otherwise be required to meet to gather evidence gather abroad.

Letters Rogatory: The Slow Road to Evidence Gathering

The legal process of **letters rogatory** is the oldest and most cumbersome process of obtaining cooperation from a court in another country in gathering evidence, freezing assets, effecting service of process, or apprehending a fugitive. Letters rogatory is a formal request from a court in one country to "the appropriate judicial authorities" in another country requesting such assistance.[705]

Foreign countries answer letters rogatory in accordance with their own laws and regulations. Absent a specific treaty obligation, the granting of a request for judicial assistance by the foreign court is based on the concept of **comity**. According to *Black's Law Dictionary*, this is:

The recognition which one nation allows within its territory to the legislation, executive or judicial acts of another nation, having due regard both to international duty and convenience and to the rights of its own citizens or of other persons who are not under the protection of its laws.

The letters rogatory process requires obtaining two court orders—one in the United States and a second in a foreign country. In addition, many such requests must be made through diplomatic channels. Due to the cost and time required for to complete this process, U.S. tax and law enforcement authorities have long sought streamlined procedures to gather information.

Using Tax Treaties to Enforce U.S. Tax Laws

Cross-border transactions often trigger overlapping income taxation by the two countries involved. **Double taxation conventions,** commonly known as **tax treaties**, are designed to avoid or at least minimize double taxation. However, they have another, less publicized function: to help enforce domestic tax laws.

All tax treaties have a similar format and call for various categories of income to be "distributed" for tax purposes between the source country (i.e., where the income is earned) and the country in which the taxpayer is resident. Alternatively, the source country may tax the income and the residence country credits the tax paid against whatever domestic income tax is due.

For instance, it's common for royalty income to be taxed in the source country, via a withholding tax. Such income may be taxed again by the taxpayer's residence country, resulting in double taxation. A tax treaty may avoid this result. Absent a tax treaty, the residence country can avoid double taxation by applying a unilateral tax credit. The United States uses both tax treaties and tax credits to help U.S. taxpayers avoid double taxation.

Residents of low-tax countries that invest in high-tax countries are at a disadvantage if no tax treaty exists to reduce withholding rates. For instance, the United States withholds tax at a 30% rate on many types of income earned by a non-U.S. resident. If a non-U.S. resident resides in a country with a tax treaty with the United States, that rate can be reduced substantially, sometimes to zero.

Tax treaties are based on a model treaty prepared by the Organization for Economic Cooperation and Development (OECD). Like the International Law Enforcement Telecommunications Seminar described in Chapter 2, the OECD sets "minimum standards" for treaties and other agreements. While developing standardized mechanisms for tax authorities to avoid double taxation facilitates global commerce, in making this effort, the OECD, in common with other non-governmental organizations, undermines constitutional and international human rights law. This process again illustrates the trend of policy laundering introduced in Chapter 2—using international agreements to overrule domestic legislation protecting wealth and privacy.

The OECD model treaty is regularly updated, most recently in 2005.[706] Each successive model provides tax authorities greater powers to retrieve financial information from the other signatory. While the OECD model is not legally binding, most tax treaties follow it as they are created or revised.

In older tax treaties, information is exchanged only when a resident of either signatory country claims a benefit under the treaty. The only information exchanged is to insure that the individual making the claim is entitled to make it and to verify the amount withheld. The 2005 model treaty significantly expands the information exchange requirements. Article 26 of the 2005 model creates an obligation for signatories to exchange any information that is "foreseeably relevant" to the correct application of a tax treaty as well as "for purposes of the administration and enforcement of domestic tax laws." Ownership information and information held by banks, financial institutions, nominees, agents and fiduciaries may be exchanged. The revised Article 26 also stipulates that **all taxes**—not just taxes covered in the treaty itself—are covered by this obligation. It also states that domestic bank secrecy rules don't limit the obligation to exchange information.

All U.S. tax treaties are available online at http://www.irs.gov/businesses/international/article/0,,id=96739,00.html.

Offshore "Fishing Expeditions" Unleashed

Fishing expedition: A colloquial, informal legal term often encountered in the United States and other similar legal systems ... to cynically refer to the prosecution's attempt to undertake more intrusive searches of a defendant's premises, person, or possessions when (in the defense's view) there is insufficient probable cause to carry out such a search.

— Wikipedia (2007)

Beginning in the 1980s, the United States began terminating tax treaties with countries imposing little or no income tax. This was done purportedly to prevent U.S. taxpayers from abusing the tax treaty by setting up holding companies in places like the Netherlands Antilles to substantially reduce their effective tax rate on U.S.-source income. The IRS alleged that U.S. citizens masquerading as foreign persons owned many of these holding companies.[707]

In place of tax treaties, the United States began pressuring low-tax jurisdictions to ratify a new type of treaty called a **tax information exchange agreement** (TIEA). In a TIEA, signatories exchange data relating to beneficial ownership of trusts and corporations, along with bank-deposit information. Since the treaties are considered "executive agreements," they don't require U.S. Senate ratification.

Many low-tax countries resisted signing TIEAs, because they would receive nothing in return. Although TIEAs provide for exchange of tax information on a reciprocal basis, most low-tax countries have no use for such data. Nor do TIEAs give residents of low-tax countries any of the benefits typically provided in tax treaties, such as reduced withholding taxes—although in a handful of countries, including Mexico and Barbados, both ordinary tax treaties and TIEAs are in effect.

Realizing the one-sided nature of TIEAs, the U.S. Congress enacted the Caribbean Basin Initiative of 1983. This program establishes favorable tariff arrangements for the exports of countries that sign TIEAs with the United States. The law also gives U.S. corporations the ability to write off expenses incurred at conventions held in countries that have ratified a TIEA. These incentives, combined with U.S. diplomatic "clout," have led more than 20 countries to ratify TIEAs.

As with tax treaties, TIEAs are based on a "model treaty," the provisions of which constantly expand to encompass greater information exchange. The U.S. model TIEA originated in the Caribbean Basin Initiative, but the TIEA concept attracted many other OECD members. Eventually, the OECD's Committee on Fiscal Affairs published a model TIEA. Like the OECD model tax treaty, the model TIEA isn't legally binding, but is generally followed. A key provision of the model TIEA is Article V, which obligates the requested party, to the extent permitted by its domestic laws, to:

...obtain original and unedited books, papers, and records, and other tangible property, including, but not limited to information held by banks, other financial institutions, and any person, including

nominees and trustees, acting in an agency or fiduciary capacity, ...[and] ... information regarding the ownership of companies, partnerships, trust, foundations and other persons, ownership information on all such persons in an ownership chain.

Both the U.S. and OECD model TIEAs state that any information "foreseeably relevant or material to tax administration and enforcement with respect to the person identified" for investigation must be turned over to the requested state. U.S. courts have interpreted this authority as permitting TIEA information requests "even if the United States has no tax interest and no claim for U.S. taxes are potentially due and owing."[708] "Fishing expeditions" into offshore accounts are explicitly permitted. The potential for abuse is obvious.

As of June 2007, the United States had TIEAs in effect with Antigua & Barbuda, Aruba, the Bahamas, Barbados, Bermuda, the British Virgin Islands, the Cayman Islands, Costa Rica, Dominica, Dominican Republic, Grenada, Guernsey, Guyana, Honduras, the Isle of Man, Jersey, the Marshall Islands, Mexico, Netherlands Antilles, Peru, St. Lucia, and Trinidad & Tobago. A TIEA with Brazil has been signed, but is not yet in effect.

Sharing the Plunder with MLATs

Mutual legal assistance treaties (MLATs) provide for the exchange of financial and other records in the investigation of suspected criminal activities. They may also provide for extradition of criminal suspects and for "equitable sharing" of forfeited property. MLATs originated due to the perceived need of U.S. prosecutors to bypass the lengthy letters rogatory process and lift foreign bank secrecy laws in criminal investigations. The first MLAT, with Switzerland, came into effect in 1977.[709] This MLAT, and future MLATs, generally override foreign bank secrecy or other confidentiality statutes.

While the U.S. Senate must ratify MLATs, they may be amended by an exchange of diplomatic notes. Such amendments can make far-reaching changes in the agreement. For instance, 1993 amendments to the U.S.-Swiss MLAT provide for the enforcement of U.S. civil forfeitures and implement an "asset sharing agreement" with the Swiss government. The two countries have subsequently shared billions of dollars in confiscated assets.[710]

The MLAT between the United States and the United Kingdom with respect to the Cayman Islands, a U.K. overseas territory, is typical for those in effect with offshore centers.[711] The agreement covers all crimes recognized by both countries punishable by more than one year in prison. It also covers offenses that are illegal in the United States, but not in the Cayman Islands, including racketeering, insider trading and bribery of foreign officials. Pure tax offenses are excluded, but not if committed in conjunction with other crimes.

MLATs often give governments procedural advantages that are lacking in domestic law. For instance, MLATs typically don't require a judicial or administrative finding of probable cause to be invoked. **Reasonable suspicion**—not much more than a hunch—is sufficient. According to one commentator, "In effect, MLATs reduce the requisite burden of proof for a warrant for international evidence-gathering."[712]

Subjects of MLAT requests may also lack the right to challenge disclosure in the courts of the requesting state.[713] A person seeking to block the improper release of information must seek redress in that country's courts.[714] But most MLATs deny this option to investigative targets, leaving them with no redress to contest disclosure in the courts of either jurisdiction. MLAT targets also lack standing (i.e., the right to litigate) to challenge the admission of documents gathered under the MLAT, even if they're prosecuted for a crime not covered by the applicable MLAT. U.S. courts have concluded lack of standing exists even when evidence to support the MLAT request is fabricated.[715]

Nor may investigative targets use MLATs in their defense, even after indictment. The U.S. Department of Justice justifies this position by observing that MLAT targets are usually customers of the financial institutions from which evidence is sought. Therefore, the defendants already have access to the evidence. However, MLATs permit a much greater variety of evidence to be gathered than mere account statements. They also contain procedural rules that permit foreign testimony and other evidence to be gathered and used against the target. MLATs prohibit investigative targets from using these expedited evidence-gathering procedures. Subjects of MLAT inquiries must use the much slower letters rogatory process. While evidence that would exonerate the defendant is supposed to be turned over to the defendant's attorney, prosecutors on some occasions have ignored this obligation.

Nor can a defendant object to evidence gathering if the government neglects to follow the procedures set forth in the treaty. U.S. courts concluded long ago that individuals lack standing in asserting violations of treaties.[716] Individuals may use treaties on their own behalf only if the agreement explicitly implicitly provides this right.[717]

Finally, with MLATs, evidence gathered in one signatory country may be used against a defendant in the other signatory country, even if that evidence wouldn't have otherwise been admissible. The U.S.-Canada MLAT is a case in point. In Canada, witnesses can be compelled to answer self-incriminating questions, but that evidence cannot be used against them in subsequent criminal proceedings. In the United States, individuals being questioned can refuse to answer on grounds of self-incrimination, but if they answer, the responses can be used against them. The interplay of these rules means that a Canadian court can compel someone to answer questions in a MLAT inquiry, and those answers can later be used against that person in a U.S. criminal proceeding.[718]

A new trend in MLATs is to provide for "special investigative techniques." The U.S.-German MLAT permits authorities in one country, at the request of the other country, to execute wiretap orders, conduct undercover investigations, and engage in any other form of assistance not prohibited by the laws of the requested state.[719]

As with tax treaties and TIEAs, many other countries have followed the U.S. lead and constructed their own network of MLATs. Many of these agreements are based on model MLATs prepared by the United Nations or the G-8 group of industrialized countries.[720]

As of May 1, 2007, the United States had MLATs in effect with Anguilla, Antigua & Barbuda, Argentina, Australia, Austria, the Bahamas, Barbados, Belgium, Belize, Brazil, British Virgin Islands, Canada, Cayman Islands, Cyprus, Czech Republic, Dominica, Egypt, Estonia, European Union, France, Greece, Grenada, Hong Kong, Hungary, India, Israel, Italy, Jamaica, Japan, Latvia, Liechtenstein, Lithuania, Luxembourg, Mexico, Montserrat, Morocco, Netherlands, Nigeria, Panama, Philippines, Poland, Romania, Russia, Spain, St. Kitts & Nevis, St. Lucia, St. Vincent & the Grenadines, South Africa, South Korea, Switzerland, Thailand, Trinidad & Tobago, Turkey, Turks & Caicos Islands, Ukraine, United Kingdom, and Uruguay. MLATs with Colombia, Denmark, Finland, Germany, Ireland, India, Malaysia, Portugal, Slovenia, Sweden, Venezuela have been signed, but aren't in force.

Individuals doing business in jurisdictions that have signed MLATs with the United States should presume that U.S. criminal law is enforced there, whether or not that jurisdiction has enacted corresponding laws. In most cases, dual criminality is **not** required.

Global Tax Collection Initiatives

While the tax burden in most countries grew rapidly in the decades following World War II, that trend is now reversing. Some governments—particularly in Eastern Europe—have imposed flat tax systems with significantly lower marginal tax rates.[721] In every country where tax rates have been reduced, economic growth has followed, and tax revenues have increased. This paradoxical result is due to two factors: higher compliance rates and greater economic activity, both spurred by lower tax rates.[722]

However, not all governments welcome this growing phenomenon of tax competition. Indeed, high-tax governments are conducting a coordinated strategy to end what they call "harmful" tax practices.

When is Competition Harmful?

In 1998, the OECD's Committee on Fiscal Affairs released a report outlining what it perceived as a dangerous trend: more and more countries were reducing taxes and providing fiscal incentives for residence and investment.[723] This trend toward what the OECD called "harmful tax competition" was dangerous, according to the Committee on Fiscal Affairs, because it had the potential to reduce tax revenues in nations that didn't wish to engage in tax competition.

To help fight harmful tax competition, the report proposed that low tax countries be required to dismantle bank secrecy to the extent that it applied to foreign tax investigations. It also called for sanctions against jurisdictions engaging in harmful tax practices, including termination of tax treaties, ending tax credits, and imposing extra domestic reporting requirements for people or entities doing business in those countries.

The report ignored the fact that many OECD jurisdictions are themselves tax havens: notably, Luxembourg, Switzerland, the United Kingdom, and the United States (the world's largest tax haven for non-U.S. resident investors). As international tax lawyer Marshall Langer explains:

Most OECD member countries are guilty of tax competition that is much more harmful than that of which the OECD is complaining. It does not surprise people when I tell them that the most important tax haven in the world is an island. They are surprised, however, when I tell them that the name of the island is Manhattan, in the United States...

The 1998 OECD Report on harmful tax competition set forth four key factors for identifying and assessing harmful preferential tax regimes. Applying these factors to some of the U.S. regimes for taxing nonresidents, the United States is clearly such a regime:

- ***The United States imposes no tax on relevant income.*** *The United States taxes its residents, citizens and domestic corporations but exempts all nonresident aliens and foreign corporations on interest paid by banks, savings and loan associations and insurance companies. It does the same with respect to portfolio interest and most capital gains.*
- ***The U.S. regime is "ring fenced."*** *Residents, citizens, and domestic corporations are excluded from taking advantage of these benefits.*
- ***There is a lack of transparency.*** *Most U.S. residents are completely unaware that foreigners enjoy these benefits. Although the U.S. government does not advertise the existence of these benefits to foreigners, banks and brokerage houses see to it that any foreigner who needs to know does know all about them.*

263

- *There is a lack of effective exchange of information.* With one exception, the United States does not provide information concerning those who benefit from these regimes to its tax treaty partners. The IRS does not even collect information about most of the income and gains arising from them. It will try to get information in response to a specific request by a tax treaty partner but only if that country can tell the IRS where to look. It cannot do even that for a country that does not have a tax treaty or Tax Information Exchange Agreement with the United States.[724]

The OCED escalated its fight against harmful tax practices in 2000, when it identified 35 so-called "uncooperative tax havens" and outlined a series of sanctions to be imposed against them unless they agreed to rewrite their tax and financial privacy laws according to OECD specifications.[725] The OECD's own tax havens were conspicuously absent from this blacklist. The report gave the 35 jurisdictions until 2001 to sign compliance agreements with the OECD that would obligate each one to bring its tax regime into line with "international standards" set by the OECD.

A few blacklisted jurisdictions immediately capitulated to OECD demands. Overseas territories of OECD members made the most sweeping commitments. Their colonial masters forced them to adopt the OECD mandate with only minor changes. The U.K. overseas territory of the Cayman Islands, for instance, agreed to relax its financial secrecy laws to permit inspections of bank account records by foreign tax authorities, in any tax investigation (administrative, civil or criminal). Cayman law now provides for assistance to any "overseas regulatory authority" in carrying out tax-related "civil and administrative investigations and proceedings." Other amendments beef up "know your customer" requirements for Cayman banks and impose penalties for failure to report suspicious transactions.[726]

The harmful tax initiative stalled in 2001, when the United States announced that it would not support it out of respect for other nations' rights to determine their own tax system.[727] With the defection of the United States, the consensus that allowed the OECD's anti-offshore vendetta to progress ended. The OECD subsequently agreed to end efforts to prohibit non-OECD countries from offering special tax breaks to foreign companies and investors. An even more important concession was its announcement that it was no longer demanding the right for tax authorities to conduct wholesale fishing expeditions into offshore accounts.[728]

With these concessions in place, most low-tax jurisdictions signed agreements with the OECD agreeing to exchange tax information in restricted circumstances. Many of these jurisdictions agreed to exchange information under the OECD framework only if all OECD countries made similar concessions—a condition that Luxembourg, Switzerland, and the United States refused. Most low-tax jurisdictions that imposed such conditions were nonetheless removed from the blacklist.

A handful of jurisdictions refused to make any concessions to the OECD and remain on its unco-operative tax haven blacklist: Andorra, Liechtenstein, and Monaco.[729]

The harmful tax initiative has achieved some of its objectives, but the long-term goal of giving tax authorities in high-tax countries unrestricted access to banking and other financial records in low-tax countries has foundered. As long as the United States opposes this thrust of the OECD's campaign against tax competition, it is unlikely to succeed.

EU Tells Savers to Invest Outside Europe

The European Union is a group of 27 European nations, including France, Germany, Italy, and the United Kingdom.[730] It's also home to some of the world's highest tax rates.

EU governments have long sought a mechanism to automatically exchange tax information globally and thus collect taxes on trillions of dollars allegedly invested by their residents in countries that prohibit exchange of information between tax authorities. However, since EU members Austria and Luxembourg have strict bank secrecy laws, internal opposition stymied these efforts. In addition, two major offshore centers with strict bank secrecy laws—Switzerland and Liechtenstein—border EU countries, although neither jurisdiction is a EU member.

In 2003, a compromise measure came into effect: the **EU Savings Tax Directive**.[731] While most member states began sharing information in 2005, Austria, Belgium, and Luxembourg impose a withholding tax on the earnings of EU residents and hand back 75% of the proceeds to their countries of origin. The withholding tax started at 15% in 2005, rose to 20% in 2007 and will increase to 35% in 2010.[732] Crucially for the plan, both Switzerland and Liechtenstein agreed to participate.

The plan has serious flaws—the worst of which is that neither the United States nor Asian offshore centers have agreed to participate. This means that EU depositors seeking to avoid the withholding tax merely have to transfer funds outside the EU, Switzerland, or Liechtenstein. This is precisely what has occurred. Billions of dollars of capital have left Europe.[733] In addition, since the directive only covers interest payments, it's easy for EU depositors to switch to dividend paying shares or real estate—neither of which is covered by the directive—to preserve financial privacy.

It comes as little surprise that the plan hasn't raised nearly as much revenue as anticipated. Switzerland—by far the largest recipient of offshore investments from EU residents of any country complying with the directive—collected the equivalent of only US$440 million in 2006.[734] This is less than one-fourth of what EU tax authorities had hoped to collect from this initiative.

Are You Ready for the Global IRS?

In 2001, the United Nations endorsed expanded efforts to use tax policies as a tool to redistribute wealth and income. The U.N.'s "High-Level Panel on Financing for Development" published a report that proposed the following initiatives:

- **International Tax Organization.** This agency would help countries tax income earned outside their borders, and "take a lead role in restraining tax competition."
- **Global taxation.** The report proposed a tax on all international currency transactions, the so-called Tobin tax. This tax, according to the report, would generate as much as US$400 billion each year. It also proposed a worldwide energy tax, calculated so that each type of fuel (oil, gas, coal, etc) would be taxed in accordance with its contribution to greenhouse gases
- **Taxation of emigrants.** The report suggested that governments should have the permanent right to tax individuals who exercise their right to emigrate from their homeland. The International Tax Organization would enforce this proposal.
- **Global information exchange.** The report recommended that national governments be required to collect private financial data on individual taxpayers and share it with other governments to prevent harmful tax competition.[735]

In 2006, the United Nations renewed its call to impose global taxes in a report that proposed taxation of air transport and airline tickets, currency transactions, carbon emissions (gasoline) and arms sales.[736]

While the International Tax Organization is not yet a reality, one initiative along these lines that has come into place is a global computer database listing abusive tax shelters and their promoters. In

2004, revenue authorities in the United Kingdom, Britain, the United States, Canada, and Australia formed the Joint International Tax Shelter Information Center (JITSIC) to share detailed information on allegedly fraudulent tax schemes. In 2007, the IRS reported that the JITSIC had successfully dismantled at least three abusive tax shelters, including one that would have resulted in a tax loss exceeding US$100,000,000.[737]

"Dirty Money" and the Global Effort to Confiscate It

International agreements to combat money laundering and forfeit the proceeds of crime are strikingly similar to those in place to collect taxes; namely, to end bank secrecy and increase the ability of governments to seize assets across borders. This is hardly a surprise, as the same actors are involved, albeit with different names. For instance, the lead role in the global war on money laundering is the Financial Action Task Force (FATF), operating out of OECD headquarters. The FATF operates from the same playbook as well, issuing supposedly non-binding recommendations that are subsequently enacted into law by individual countries.

Efforts by the FATF and other organizations to encourage greater asset forfeiture are frustrated by substantial differences between national legal systems. Many countries view civil forfeiture laws as enforced in the United States as repugnant to human rights. However, these barriers are breaking down, to the detriment of both privacy and wealth preservation.

Globalizing Asset Forfeiture

After the United States enacted its first money laundering law in 1986 (Chapter 2), it moved quickly to globalize the "War on Money Laundering." One of its first initiatives was to create a multinational group that could apply behind-the-scenes pressure against countries reluctant to enact U.S.-style money laundering laws, due to concerns about human rights or protecting their own sovereignty. In 1989, spearheaded by U.S. efforts, the G-7 Group of industrialized nations[738] created the Financial Action Task Force.

In common with the OECD, neither the G-7—essentially a club for the world's wealthiest nations—nor the FATF have the legal capacity to enact treaties or to make law. Nonetheless, the G-7 gave the FATF the responsibility to create a global anti-laundering plan. In 1990, the FATF released a report containing 40 recommendations for global anti-laundering enforcement. Not surprisingly, the suggestions mirrored measures already in effect in the United States.[739] They included:

- Making money laundering a criminal offense in connection with all serious crimes;
- Setting aside bank secrecy in money laundering investigations;
- Providing for the forfeiture of laundered proceeds of crime;
- Creating financial intelligence units in all countries;
- Imposing both monetary and civil penalties for laundering offenses;
- Voiding contracts where parties knew or should have known that the contract would make it more difficult to forfeit laundered proceeds;
- Imposing a global "know your customer" burden on all financial institutions;
- Requiring financial institutions to report suspicious transactions to law enforcement authorities;
- Imposing a global currency transaction reporting system;
- Studying measures to detect or monitor currency crossing national borders;
- Monitoring currency flows globally;

- Encouraging governments to automatically provide information on suspicious transactions to other governments and inter-governmental organizations;
- Monitoring electronic money movements, particularly international wire transfers; and
- Coordinating the confiscation and forfeiture of tainted assets, including the payment of commissions to informants and inter-governmental organizations.

More recent FATF recommendations include:

- Abolishing anonymous bank accounts worldwide;
- Imposing stricter licensing requirements for non-bank financial institutions;
- Initiating anti-laundering sting operations globally;
- Requiring greater transparency in electronic money movements;
- Removing the "fiscal exemption" to anti-laundering laws that in some countries exempt tax evasion and other fiscal offenses from their coverage;
- Reversing the burden of proof in laundering cases so that accused launderers must prove their assets came from a legitimate source, or risk having them confiscated; and
- Expanding mandatory suspicious activities reporting to all businesses and professions.[740]

After Sept. 11, 2001, the FATF shifted its emphasis to focus on anti-terrorist initiatives. In addition to recommending that all nations criminalize the financing of terrorism, terrorist acts and terrorist organizations, the FATF began an orchestrated attack on alternative remittance systems; methods of moving money outside the banking system.[741]

FATF Blacklist Targets Offshore Jurisdictions

Throughout the 1990s, the FATF found that its "soft law" recommendations were not being adopted as quickly as had hoped. To prod recalcitrant countries into bringing its recommendations into law, in 1999, the FATF announced that it was preparing a "blacklist" of non-cooperative countries and territories and encouraged FATF member countries to apply financial sanctions against those jurisdictions.

In 2000, the FATF released its first blacklist, four days prior to the publication of the OECD's tax haven blacklist.[742] There's little doubt that the release of the lists was orchestrated to make the maximum impact on the affected jurisdictions. Blacklisted countries were given one year to amend their laws to comply with FATF demands, or face severe sanctions, including the possibility of being cut off from the global electronic wire transfer system.[743]

Some FATF members immediately imposed sanctions against blacklisted countries. In the United States, the Financial Crimes Enforcement Network issued advisories recommending that U.S. banks "give enhanced scrutiny to all financial transactions originating in or routed to or through [blacklisted jurisdictions], or involving entities organized or domiciled, or persons maintaining accounts [there]."[744] Numerous banks simply curtailed doing business with blacklisted jurisdictions or began filing a suspicious transaction report on any transaction involving a blacklisted country. The effect was to introduce delays and added costs to such transactions. Offshore business in the affected jurisdictions dropped precipitously.

Of any blacklisted nation, the tiny Pacific island of **Nauru** suffered perhaps the most severe sanctions. Many banks blocked all dollar-denominated transactions involving Nauru. Even after Nauru abolished offshore banking, due to its lack of diplomatic clout, it remained on the FATF's blacklist until 2006.

What, exactly, did the FATF demand to avoid blacklisting? Let's begin with the FATF's definition of money laundering:

> ... [T]he processing of ... criminal proceeds to disguise their illegal origin. Illegal arms sales, smuggling and the activities of organized crime, including for example drug trafficking and prostitution rings, can generate huge sums. Embezzlement, insider trading, bribery and computer fraud schemes can also ... create the incentive to "legitimize" the ill-gotten gains through money laundering.[745]

None of these offenses, other than embezzlement and computer fraud, has an identifiable victim. The remaining crimes are consensual, in which a willing buyer and willing seller make a contract that the state criminalizes. From the FATF's viewpoint, money laundering consists almost exclusively of crimes against the state, not against individual victims.

Tax evasion isn't included in this list—but only because the FATF's parent organization is the OECD, whose campaign against harmful tax competition demands an end to offshore tax advantages. Nor is it really absent—the FATF condemns "restrictive practices in international co-operation against money laundering ... on the grounds that such transactions may relate to tax matters."[746]

Most offshore centers have limited financial resources. Many of them cannot effectively enforce the anti-laundering laws the FATF has insisted they enact, much less staff the financial intelligence units they're obligated to form to evaluate suspicious transactions and liaise with anti-laundering units in other countries. This is particularly true since these laws have in many cases led to substantial investment outflows. Moreover, the FATF's parent organization, the OECD, is simultaneously asking them to dismantle their tax and fiscal incentives.[747]

Ironically, the combined impact of the OECD harmful tax initiative and the FATF anti-laundering efforts could actually encourage lawlessness and terrorism in the targeted countries. This is particularly true in isolated island jurisdictions, where smuggling has been a traditional source of income for centuries.

Another unintended result of these blacklists has been an increased reliance of offshore centers on funding from international aid agencies such as the World Bank and International Monetary Fund.[748] These funds come mainly from taxpayers in OECD countries, who also guarantee any loans made to offshore centers. OECD/FATF bureaucrats are supposedly protecting these same taxpayers from harmful tax competition and money laundering.

No countries remain on the FATF blacklist. Perhaps this is because the FATF now realizes that the real centers for money laundering are OECD/FATF members, not the politically powerless offshore jurisdictions these organizations are targeting. This point was confirmed in 2002, in a study by the prestigious Society of Trust and Estate Practitioners. The study concluded that while the FATF is targeting offshore jurisdictions for ever-greater anti-laundering compliance burdens, corporate domiciles such as Delaware and Nevada are excused from compliance with rules to regulate service providers and track beneficial ownership.[749]

Policing for Profit Goes Global

Another important FATF initiative is the creation of a global anti-laundering network of national financial intelligence units (FIUs) similar to FinCEN in the United States, called the **Egmont Group**. This network now consists more than 100 FIUs, many of them funded by the proceeds from forfeited assets.[750]

The NSA's ECHELON initiative (Chapter 2) demonstrates how a surveillance network created to gather military intelligence might be used against political opponents or civil liberties groups. Egmont Group FIUs could be used for similar purposes. Indeed, since these agencies are generally created along the lines of FinCEN, and are thus exempt from any public disclosure of their activities, there are few legal remedies to prevent such a result.

A worldwide network of FIUs funded with forfeited assets creates a global network of bounty hunters with ever-expanding authority to seize suspect assets. Seizures of narcotics, gambling equipment, nuclear materials, child pornography, and other illegal commodities generate no revenues for law enforcement. But, in an increasing number of countries, seizing agencies keep up to 100% of the seized proceeds of such commodities, along with all property "involved in" such transactions. Some of this bounty is now shared with FIUs.

It is inconceivable that a global network of FIUs operating under these incentives, with continuous input from intelligence sources such as ECHELON, won't be used for political purposes, private gain or be vulnerable to penetration by hackers. Certainly, drug kingpins would pay dearly for access to FIU databases. The information FIUs have on their assets and laundering techniques, not to mention those of their competitors, would be extremely valuable.

These concerns aren't merely theoretical. In 2002, the Chief Justice of the Cayman Islands accused the head of the island's FIU of wiretapping his telephone and destroying evidence that may have proven the innocence of a bank accused of money laundering. These actions were taken, the judge ruled, "upon the direction of an agency of the U.K. Government." The chief justice did not name the agency, but it is widely believed to be MI-6, the British equivalent of the CIA.[751]

An investigation revealed that the unnamed U.K. agency had monitored telecommunications in the Caymans since at least the mid-1990s, perhaps even longer. This was done through a switch secretly installed by Cable & Wireless, which holds a monopoly on telecommunications in the Caymans. This company also provides telecommunications services to several other U.K. overseas territories.

Since FIUs are expected to generate revenues beyond their operating costs, corruption in the Cayman FIU may be only the first of many similar scandals to come.

Before Hiring a Lawyer, Hire a Lawyer

FATF recommendations were taken especially seriously in Europe. And in response, in 1991, the European Commission, the governing body of what is now the European Union, adopted the EU Laundering Directive.[752]

Building upon the FATF's 40 recommendations, this directive obligates EU members to enact and enforce a number of criminal offenses connected with drugs and money laundering in general. Among other requirements, the directive forces financial institutions to identify all customers when beginning a business relationship. Non-account holders who engage in a single transaction or linked transactions that exceed €15,000 must also be identified. EU financial institutions must also report suspicious activities to authorities, even where the transaction is below the reporting threshold.

In 2001, the European Commission reached agreement with its member states for a second Laundering Directive, with the following provisions:

- Making the proceeds of all serious crimes illegal.
- Extending customer identification suspicious activity reporting requirements to many non-financial activities and professions. These include insurance companies, accountants and auditors, real estate agents, notaries, dealers in high value goods such as precious stones and metals or works of art, auctioneers, transporters of funds, casinos, and attorneys.
- Improving coordination between FIUs in the EU by amending laws prohibiting cross-border data exchange between law enforcement authorities. A key objective of this requirement is to increase cross-border asset forfeiture.
- Amending national laws to permit **value confiscation** related to the value of the proceeds from crime as opposed to "less efficient" **property confiscation** relating to the proceeds themselves.

EU countries have now placed the provisions of this second directive into their domestic law.

In 2005, the European Parliament approved a third directive intended to amend and consolidate the previous two laundering directives.[753] All EU members must put the following measures into effect in their domestic law:

- Make it a laundering offense to use legally acquired money to finance terrorism;
- Oblige financial institutions to identify the beneficial owner of all legal entities with which they are conducting business;
- Expand the definition of "financial institution" to include all trades and businesses which accept cash payments of more than €15,000; and
- Prohibit institutions and persons covered by the directive from disclosing to customers or third parties the fact that information about specific transactions or accounts has been conveyed to authorities.

The third directive will have an extraordinary impact on the formation of trusts in the United Kingdom and Ireland, since lawyers are required to obtain proof of identity from any person who is a 10% or greater beneficiary of a trust. This proposal is likely to lead to family conflicts if a beneficiary discovers that he or she is receiving less money than other beneficiaries. It would eliminate or seriously restrict the widespread practice of creating "secret trusts" for the benefit of mistresses, illegitimate children, etc. Since funds in trusts make up a large proportion of the more than US$600 billion invested by private investors in the United Kingdom, when the directive comes into full effect, much of this business could go elsewhere.[754]

The revised directives also affect attorneys practicing in the EU. They must inform authorities if they have a "serious suspicion" that a client is involved in money laundering, without telling the client they have done so. In EU countries in which tax evasion is a laundering offense, lawyers who suspect their clients of tax evasion are subject to the same requirements. Lawyers who fail to abide by the requirements can be convicted of money laundering, fined, stripped of their law licenses, and imprisoned.

A tax attorney who asked to remain anonymous, and who is licensed to practice law in both the United States and the United Kingdom, pointed out the following problem to me:

Let's say that a U.S. client flies to London to meet me. While there, the client informs me that he has committed criminal tax fraud. Under U.K. law, I am obliged to inform the U.K.'s National Criminal Information Service of this disclosure. But under U.S. law, which does not require such disclosure, I would be violating attorney-client privilege if I obey the U.K. law. I could be sued by my client and potentially disbarred from practicing law in the United States.

Another attorney from Liechtenstein put it more succinctly: "When in Europe, consult your lawyer first before dealing with another lawyer."

Legal Unification in Common Law

More than two billion people live in jurisdictions that were once colonies of the United Kingdom. One consequence of colonization has been the spread of English common law throughout the world. More than 50 current or former U.K. colonies have inherited English law. This list includes dozens of offshore financial centers.[755]

In these jurisdictions, laws, regulations, financial systems, and judicial systems are interrelated. This insures a predictable legal, financial, and regulatory background for international trade and business, as English law is widely respected. However, there are important practical consequences to consider in this "legal contagion," since legislation, regulations, and court decisions in one jurisdiction may apply in other jurisdictions, unless dealt with by statute.

The Crown: More than a Legal Artifact

The most important unifying factor in offshore centers with a common law background is the **Crown**. Its most visible symbol is the reigning Windsor monarch (currently Queen Elizabeth). But the legal heritage created by this "Crown in common law" has been far more enduring.

When English explorers colonized a new region of the world, they did so in the name of the Crown. As time progressed, the Crown—in this guise the bureaucracy set up to administer the colony—set up an elected parliament and legal system, and tried to adapt them to the local population.

While the English colonial legacy was in some cases brutal, it often brought considerable benefits. Some of the most important benefits were the common law courts, which often replaced tribal or religious courts. Common law was often recognized for providing fairer results in disputes than the legal system it replaced. Because of its virtues, and the zeal of the English colonizers, common law spread throughout the world.

Yet, the legal tradition of the Crown originates from a time when a hereditary monarch granted government and law to its subjects under an inherent, prerogative authority. Neither the legislature nor the courts exist independently of the executive. The executive appoints all judges and ministers of government, including the prime minister. It introduces and must assent to all legislation

In those jurisdictions that remain U.K. colonies (now called **overseas territories)**, the powers of the Crown apply as strongly today as they did when the colonies were established. The reigning Windsor monarch, acting through the governor of the overseas territory, can issue an **order in council** under the monarch's **royal prerogative** with the effect of binding legislation in that territory.

Orders in council are rarely issued under the royal prerogative, but in 2004, the U.K. Foreign Office forced its overseas territories (with the exception of Bermuda) to enact legislation in which it agreed to enforce the EU Savings Tax Directive (discussed earlier in this chapter). The Foreign Office informed each overseas territory that if their local parliament refused to enact the legislation, the U.K. government would bring it into existence, over the heads of the elected legislature.[756] All the territories so informed complied with the demands.

Most jurisdictions that retain English common law are no longer U.K. colonies. The 1926 **Statute of Westminster** provides a blueprint for colonies to achieve independence and enter into **Commonwealth** status. (The Commonwealth is a group of 53 countries that exist in a loose association, bound by the legal heritage of English common law and allegiance to the reigning Windsor monarch.) However, "independence" in a Westminster constitution has a very different meaning than in the sense Americans understand. Such constitutions:

- Call for English common law to be inherited (i.e., all applicable U.K. legislation as of a particular date as well as decisions of the English courts).
- Provide for executive authority to be vested in the executive branch of each particular jurisdiction, with no separation of powers.
- Allow the executive to enter into treaties without the consent of the local legislature.

With the Statute of Westminster, a single Crown embodied in a ruling English monarch devolved to multiple Crowns embodied in Westminster constitutions, united in the Commonwealth. The basic legal structure remained the same; in particular, a high degree of centralized executive authority over all areas of government. Under the Westminster framework, Queen Elizabeth is today the head of state in 16 of the 53 members of the Commonwealth. In those 16 countries, she must sign all legislation enacted by the local legislature for it to come into effect, although that role has been relegated to a legal formality. In the remaining Commonwealth member nations, her title is "Head of the Commonwealth."

Practical Consequences of Legal Unification

There are numerous practical consequences to consider due to legislation, regulations, and court decisions in one common law jurisdiction possibly applying in other common law jurisdictions.

Judicial independence. Westminster Constitutions often preserve a right of appeal to the highest common law court, the Judicial Committee of the Privy Council in London, an organ of the English House of Lords. In this manner, laws enacted by an elected national parliament can be overridden in London. This authority is most frequently invoked in criminal cases, but also applies in non-criminal matters.[757]

An important initiative toward true independence in numerous Westminster jurisdictions occurred in 2001, when the Caribbean Community (CARICOM) established the **Caribbean Court of Justice** (CCJ), a judicial tribunal intended to serve as the court of final appeal for the region. For a number of CARICOM members, the CCJ replaced the Privy Council as the court of final appeal. The CCJ now hears appeals from the following common-law jurisdictions: Antigua & Barbuda, Barbados, Belize, Dominica, Grenada, Guyana, Jamaica, St. Kitts & Nevis, St. Lucia, Trinidad & Tobago, and St. Vincent & The Grenadines.

Bank secrecy. In common law, decisions of the English courts may have the same effect as parliamentary legislation and be enforced throughout the Commonwealth. The legal status of bank secrecy in common law countries is an example. English law requires bankers and other financial professionals to adhere to a "duty of confidentiality" with respect to their customers. This duty is not set out in a 1924 decision of the English Court of Appeal: the *Tournier* case.[758]

There are significant exceptions to the banker's duty of confidentiality. *Tournier* gives banks discretion to release information under four broad sets of circumstances:

- When disclosure is under compulsion of law;

- When there is a duty to the public to disclose;
- When the interests of the bank require disclosure; or
- When the disclosure is made by the express or implied consent of the customer.

Jurisdictions in which *Tournier* is the legal foundation for bank secrecy include the offshore centers of the Bahamas, the British Virgin Islands, the Cayman Islands, Gibraltar, Hong Kong, Ireland, the Isle of Man, Singapore, and in any other country in which a national court draws upon *Tournier* as precedent.[759]

Even where a common law jurisdiction enacts a statute that appears to override a decision of the English courts, that law may not have the intended effect. In the case of *Tournier*, this was made plain by a 1991 decision of the Cayman Court of Appeal. The decision interpreted the Caymans' Confidential Relationships (Preservation) Act, which sets forth criminal penalties for violations of bank secrecy, in the following manner:

The ... [Confidential Relationships (Preservation) Act] ... relied on the common law principle that a duty of confidentiality did not exist where there was disclosure under compulsion of law and it recognized that the circumstances under which this compulsion might be exerted could ... be changed without derogation from the principle. Consequently, any breach of confidentiality ... could only derive from the common law position with respect to the limits and qualifications of the contractual duty of secrecy implied in relation to banker and customer ... The appellants never had a right to confidentiality in respect of information required in criminal proceedings.[760]

Injunctive relief. Another example of the power of the English courts to mold legal policy throughout the Commonwealth comes in the form of the **Mareva injunction.** This injunction, devised in 1975 by the English Court of Appeal, permits persons or companies who believe they have been defrauded to obtain a global asset freeze order against the alleged perpetrator.[761] If the order is granted, people or institutions holding assets for the defendant, such as banks, are obliged to freeze them. Failure to do so may be punished as contempt of court.

Typically, a Mareva injunction is granted prior to trial in hearings the defendant is not entitled to participate in (*ex parte*), and may not know about at all. A Mareva injunction issued by a judge in London will be enforced in Jamaica, the Bahamas, or any other common law country in which a court decides to adopt this coercive legal remedy.[762]

Unlike the vast majority of jurisdictions with a common law background, U.S. courts have declined to make the Mareva injunction part of U.S. law.[763]

Inherited legislation. The Statute of Elizabeth (1571) stipulates that transfers of property may be voided if a creditor presents a valid claim to that property. This is the basis of the common law concept of **fraudulent conveyance.** While the Statute of Elizabeth was repealed in 1926, its principles may still apply in jurisdictions that inherited English common law.

The Statute of Elizabeth voids all property transfers made with the intention of delaying or hindering any creditor. A court may set aside the transfer and order the assets paid to the creditor. "Intent to defraud" is interpreted broadly and has been held to mean merely depriving creditors of timely recourse to property. Nor is there a limitation period for actions brought under it; indeed, the Statute of Elizabeth has been held to apply to **future unknown** creditors.[764]

The Statute of Elizabeth is most problematic in relation to transfers made gratuitously; i.e., without consideration being paid for use of the property. This issue frequently arises in the context of trusts.

Most common law jurisdictions have dealt with the Statute of Elizabeth issue with relation to trusts either by repealing it or modifying it to not apply to future unknown creditors. Other innovations may include requiring creditors to prove a fraudulent conveyance "beyond a reasonable doubt" (rather than the usual standard in civil court of "balance of the probabilities") and instilling a time limit for bringing claims against the trust, ranging from an immediate cut-off of all possible claims against the trust settlement (Belize) to six years (e.g., the Cayman Islands).

CHAPTER SEVEN: CHOOSING THE RIGHT OFFSHORE JURISDICTION(S)

There is no "best" offshore jurisdiction. The choice depends on your objectives. Finding a reliable and trustworthy offshore bank, investment advisor, or trustee is often more important than choosing a "perfect" jurisdiction(s) for your offshore dealings.

Choosing the right offshore jurisdiction first requires that you define what you want to accomplish, and what offshore structure (if any) is required to accomplish it. This determination should ideally be made with the aid of a knowledgeable attorney.

Don't choose an offshore jurisdiction solely on the basis of its "black-letter law." What actually happens in the legal system may be quite different from what's written in the law books. Moreover, even the strongest law won't do you any good if your offshore assets are lost or stolen. If they are, you'll be at the mercy of an unfamiliar legal system. That's what makes choosing the right offshore "partners" so important.

Seven Criteria for Choosing the Right Offshore Jurisdiction

Once you and your attorney decide what's required to accomplish your objectives, the next step is to choose the jurisdiction(s) that recognizes the concepts and entities your plan requires, and enforces their rights in its legal system. Here are seven factors to consider:

1. Will the jurisdiction honor foreign judgments against assets transferred to a bank account or legal entity? There may be exceptions if the assets are derived from fraud or other criminal activity, but otherwise, the assets should be protected unless legal action is successfully pursued in the local courts.

2. Are the "fraudulent conveyance" rules reasonable? Common law jurisdictions should have amended or repealed the English Statute of Elizabeth to reduce the time creditors can challenge a transfer to trust or other asset protection structure to a reasonable period—certainly no more than six years. Jurisdictions that didn't inherit English law should set out clearly under what circumstances a transfer can be invalidated under the relevant fraudulent conveyance or unjust enrichment statutes.

3. How strong are the asset protection and privacy laws? Considerations here include how high a burden of proof creditors must overcome in the local courts to obtain a judgment against a trust or other entity formed in the jurisdiction and whether financial secrecy legislation is in effect. U.S. courts often hold negative views of offshore jurisdictions with strong asset protection and privacy laws. On the other hand, assets in a jurisdiction with weak or non-existing asset protection or secrecy laws may be vulnerable to attachment.

4. What legal "back doors" are in effect permitting governments to seize assets or compel disclosure without resorting to normal legal channels? Tax information exchange agreements (TIEAs), mutual legal assistance treaties (MLATs), and to a lesser extent, tax treaties (Chapter 6), should all be examined in this regard. If the jurisdiction is a dependency or has other legal connections to a larger country, it may also be subject to the dictates of that country's government or its courts.

5. How politically and economically stable is the jurisdiction? Nigeria and Zimbabwe inherited English law, but you probably wouldn't want to form a trust in either country, even if they enacted favorable trust laws. A more relevant case: Belize, which arguably has the world's strongest OAPT law, had its political stability shaken in 2005 when widespread civil disturbances broke out.

6. How well developed is the legal and financial infrastructure? Numerous offshore jurisdictions are remote islands with few banks, trustees, and lawyers to choose from. A limited custodial infrastructure may require that trust assets to be placed in custody elsewhere. If the assets must be maintained and managed outside the jurisdiction in which a structure is formed, it may be desirable to keep those assets in a jurisdiction that has robust asset protection laws; e.g., Switzerland or Liechtenstein. Cayman Islands attorney Anthony Travers observes:

The attack will come from the jurisdiction in which the assets are situate and the more excessive the local legislation, for example the Cook Islands or the Bahamas model, the less likely are the courts of any such jurisdiction in which the assets are situate to apply the laws of the offshore jurisdiction in question.[765]

7. Does the jurisdiction impose taxes on the offshore income of non-resident investors? Most offshore jurisdictions qualify on this count, or impose tax only on domestic income of offshore trusts, companies, bank accounts, etc.

The bottom line: There is no "best" jurisdiction for investing or doing business offshore. Depending on your specific objectives, many different ones may be suitable—or not.

Common Law Offshore Jurisdictions

Common law jurisdictions have legal systems inherited from English law. Trusts originated in English law, and therefore, the most frequently used jurisdictions for trusts have a common law background. Common law jurisdictions also provide superior protection for partnerships under the charging order concept (Chapter 4). Many jurisdictions that offer innovative offshore insurance contracts also have a common law background.

Belize: Strong Asset Protection Laws

Belize is a small country in Central American, just south of the Yucatan Peninsula, with a population of approximately 300,000. The former colony of British Honduras, Belize became independent in 1981.

The constitution of Belize follows the principles laid down in the Statute of Westminster. Executive authority is vested in the Crown. The head of state is the reigning Windsor monarch, who must approve all legislation enacted by the local legislature. Since 2005, the court of final appeal has been the Caribbean Court of Justice (CCJ), rather than the Privy Council in London.

Belize is a rapidly growing offshore center. Offshore companies, trusts, mutual funds, and most other forms of business organizations are generally exempt from all taxes. The largest offshore sectors are banking, captive insurance, mutual fund management, and trust administration. Belize also has stringent financial secrecy laws.

The Belize Trust Act, dating from 1992, is arguably the world's strongest. The law not only repeals the Statute of Elizabeth in relation to international trusts, but also permits individuals creating a trust to maintain control and/or be a beneficiary without invalidating the instrument. A Belize court doesn't have the authority to set aside or vary a Belizean trust under any circumstances. This specifically includes any claim against the trust resulting from the order of a foreign court regarding marriage or divorce, or succession or claims by creditors in bankruptcy. This protection takes effect **immediately** upon settlement (funding) of the trust. These departures from the common law of trusts are not in accordance with trust laws in most other jurisdictions. For that reason, these provisions may not be enforceable outside Belize.

Belize also seeks to attract wealthy retirees. To be designated a **Qualified Retired Person** and be eligible for Belize residence, you must receive a monthly income of not less than US$2,000 through a pension or annuity generated outside Belize.

Since offshore legislation was first drawn up in 1991, Belize has resisted pressures from the OECD, FATF, the EU, and the United States to weaken its protective laws and enforce foreign tax obligations. While a U.S.-Belize MLAT is in effect,[766] Belize has refused to buckle to U.S. pressure to ratify a TIEA. Belize's courts have also repeatedly stood up to the U.S. government.[767]

Belize was among the 35 nations that appeared on the OECD's harmful tax competition blacklist issued in 2000 (Chapter 6). Shortly thereafter, Belize signed a commitment letter that led to its removal from the blacklist. Belize committed to exchange tax information with other governments, but only if all OECD member nations were subject to the same requirements.[768] Such a "level playing field" is a long way off, since many OECD countries, notably the United States, have refused to commit to the same standards.

Largely because of its stringent anti-money laundering laws and strict enforcement, Belize escaped being placed on the FATF "dirty money" blacklist.

Despite the success of its offshore industry and a rapidly growing tourism market, Belize faces grave economic challenges. More than one-third of its population lives in poverty, and in 2005, riots broke out in its capital city, resulting in widespread looting. During this period, Belize also suffered a total collapse of its telecommunications infrastructure.[769] Belize also suffers from high unemployment and is subject to periodic devastation by tropical storms. A long simmering border dispute with Guatemala remains unresolved.

But Belize's largest challenge is its unsustainable level of foreign debt, which has led to a sharp drop in credit ratings for Belize government bonds.[770] Donor agencies such as the International Monetary Fund are demanding that Belize carry out a comprehensive program of tax reform, which may require cooperation with foreign tax authorities and weakening bank secrecy laws.[771]

Belize is worth considering as a relatively low-cost center for offshore banking, offshore trust administration, or permanent residence. However, concerns about its political stability and its ability to defend its offshore industry in the face of pressure from donor nations are likely to persist.

Bermuda: Leading Captive Insurance Center

The U.K. overseas territory of Bermuda is a group of islands located 600 miles east of the North Carolina coast. Bermuda has a population approximately 66,000 and enjoys the highest per-capita income in the world.[772] The islands have an enviable combination of economic prosperity, political stability, a predictable legal climate, and no income tax, capital gains tax, value added tax, sales tax, use tax, or wealth tax. The reigning Windsor monarch is the head of state and is represented by a governor, and the court of final appeal for all legal disputes is the Privy Council in London.

Bermuda is best known as an offshore center for business. Its insurance, investment fund, and trust management sectors are particularly well developed, and it boasts a substantial financial infrastructure, including numerous international law and accounting firms.

The Bermuda captive insurance sector is the world's largest. More than 1,600 insurance companies with assets exceeding US$100 billion are domiciled there.[773] Several reinsurance companies relocated to Bermuda following the attacks of September 11, 2001 and again after Hurricane Katrina struck the Caribbean and the United States in 2005, contributing to the expansion of an already robust international business sector.

Bermuda's company and trust laws are not as protective as legislation in many competing jurisdictions. For instance, a transfer to a Bermuda trust may be contested for up to six years after it's made. Competing jurisdictions generally have a shorter statute of limitations, and one (Belize) provides no opportunity for creditors to claim property in a properly settled trust.

No financial privacy exists in Bermuda beyond that provided in common law under the *Tournier* decision. Bermuda has agreed, in response to OECD demands, to open the books of local banks, trust companies, and insurers to foreign tax authorities in both criminal tax inquiries (in 2004) and in civil and administrative inquiries (in 2006).[774] As a result, it was not included on the OECD's tax haven blacklist or the FATF's blacklist of uncooperative jurisdictions in the global war on money laundering. Bermuda has also ratified TIEAs with the United States[775] and several other countries.

As a U.K overseas territory, Bermuda is subject to the dictates of the U.K. Parliament and the U.K. Foreign Office. However, the U.K. authorities have generally not interfered in the operation of its offshore sector, as they consider Bermuda to be a well-regulated jurisdiction. In particular, while most other U.K. overseas territories are subject to the EU Savings Tax Directive, it hasn't been extended to Bermuda.[776]

In 2007, a scandal emerged in Bermuda after a local newspaper reported that the prime minister, while serving in another ministry, obtained US$150,000 of publicly funded renovation on his home.[777] The allegations are serious, but are likely to pass without doing serious damage to Bermuda's reputation.

Bermuda is worth considering for captive insurance and trust administration, particularly for larger companies and estates. Costs are substantially higher, however, than in most competing jurisdictions.

Cayman Islands: Capitulation to U.S., EU Tax Demands

The Cayman Islands are a U.K. overseas territory located in the Caribbean between Cuba and Central America, 500 miles southeast of Miami, with a population of approximately 45,000. A classic "tax haven" jurisdiction, the Caymans impose no income tax, capital gains tax, value added tax, sales tax, use tax, or wealth tax.

The Caymans are the world's largest offshore banking center with more than 350 banks and deposits exceeding US$1 trillion, although substantial deposits have been lost in recent years. Captive insurance and trust administration are also major contributors to the Cayman economy. The Caymans have recently emerged as a leading jurisdiction for hedge funds and for the development of securitized financing.

Like many other offshore centers, the Caymans were in 2000 named to the OECD's harmful tax blacklist. It was removed only after promising to end all "harmful tax practices" identified by the OECD and to begin exchanging information with tax authorities in OECD countries, in both civil and criminal tax matters.[778]

In addition, the Caymans have suffered from a reputation as a money-laundering haven, as illustrated by the 1993 movie, *The Firm*. Perceived abuses of strict Cayman bank secrecy laws led to its placement on the FATF money-laundering blacklist in 2000, although it was removed after it instituted strict anti-laundering legislation and established a financial intelligence unit. As discussed in Chapter 6, this office has been enmeshed in scandal almost since its creation.

Pressure from the United States has led to ratification of both a MLAT[779] and TIEA.[780] The U.S.-Cayman TIEA provides assistance to U.S. tax authorities in both civil and criminal investigations.

While its U.K. connection gives the Caymans political stability, like all U.K. overseas territories, must follow the dictates of the U.K. Parliament and Foreign Office. In 2003, the U.K. government forced the Caymans to participate in the European Savings Tax Directive. The Caymans now impose a with-holding tax on interest payments to residents of the European Union.

In 2004, the Caymans suffered a devastating blow from Hurricane Ivan. While most Cayman banks and insurance companies moved records to other jurisdictions to insure business continuity, the hurricane still led to disruptions and inconvenience for some clients.

Individuals and businesses seeking a stable, zero-tax and well-regulated jurisdiction with a deep financial infrastructure will find the Caymans appealing, particularly in offshore banking, captive insurance, and trust administration. But the Caymans can no longer be considered a secrecy haven, and remain vulnerable to the legal dictates of the United Kingdom.

Cook Islands: Birthplace of Offshore Asset Protection Trusts

The Cook Islands are a group of 15 islands located in the south Pacific with the largest island, Rarotonga, approximately 2,000 miles northeast of New Zealand. Most of the approximately 21,000 in-habitants are Polynesian and speak the local language, although those Polynesians engaged in the commercial sector are largely fluent in English.

The Cooks have a constitution that follows the Westminster model. The head of state is the reigning Windsor monarch and the court of final appeal is the Privy Council. However, the Cooks have a unique political status in that they are an "associated state" of New Zealand. While independent in local governance, New Zealand is responsible for the defense and conduct of the foreign affairs of the islands.

The Cook Islands' efforts to develop an offshore industry date from 1981, when it enacted one of the first international business company (IBC) laws. Among other innovations, this act exempts IBCs from income, corporation, gift, withholding, estate, asset inheritance, succession, and stamp taxes.

However, its most notable legislation is in the area of offshore asset protection. The International Trusts Act 1984 as amended established what was then the world's strongest offshore asset protection trust (OAPT) law. This law repeals the Statute of Elizabeth and imposes much stricter conditions for a creditor to prevail in a fraudulent conveyance claim. The statute of limitations for a fraudulent conveyance challenge is two years from the date of the originating cause of action, and the creditor must bring legal action in the Cook Islands courts within one year from the date of an alleged fraudulent transfer.

To recover assets from an OAPT, a creditor must prove "beyond a reasonable doubt" that a trust was established or a transfer made to it "with principal intent to defraud that creditor" and that the trust's establishment or funding left "the settlor insolvent or without property by which that creditor's claim (if successful) could have been satisfied." If this burden is met, the Cook Islands' courts will enforce actual damages only, not punitive damages. In another departure from the common law of trusts, the act permits individuals creating a trust to serve as a trustee and name themselves as beneficiaries.

The International Trusts Act has been subject to numerous challenges. In 1995, the Cook Islands High Court ordered a worldwide Mareva Injunction to be enforced against assets in a Cook Islands OAPT after the two-year statute of limitations had expired.[781] To avoid this result in future cases, in 1996, the legislature amended the act to make it clear that that the relevant cause of action for the purposes of the limitation periods in the act is the creditor's earliest possible cause of action.

In 1999, the High Court issued another Mareva Injunction against one-half the assets (US$2 million) a physician had conveyed irrevocably to a Cook Islands trust, even though the trust was established well beyond the two-year limitation period.[782] Concurrently, the Supreme Court of New York ordered the physician to convey to his ex-wife US$2 million in assets retained in the United States.[783] The Cook Islands High Court based its decision on its conclusion that the physician funded the trust in part with assets that didn't legally belong to him, and that the two-year limitation period therefore wouldn't apply.

Despite these successful challenges to Cook Islands OAPTs, many U.S. advisors continue to recommend them because the law has been thoroughly tested, and its most important loopholes closed. Another advantage is that the Cook Islands has resisted attempts to force it to ratify a MLAT or TIEA with the United States.

The OECD named the Cook Islands to its harmful tax competition blacklist in 2000. Removal occurred once the Cooks signed a commitment letter in which it agreed to exchange tax information with other governments, but only if all OECD member nations were subject to the same requirements.[784] Also in 2000, the FATF placed the Cook Islands on its money-laundering blacklist in 2000. After the government made extensive amendments to anti-laundering laws, including the creation of a financial intelligence unit, and the extension of suspicious activity reporting requirements to 26 different types of businesses,[785] the FATF removed the Cooks from its blacklist in 2004.

Isolation from foreign markets, lack of natural resources, periodic devastation from typhoons, and inadequate infrastructure all hinder the Cook Islands' economic development. However, its biggest challenge is its immense external debt. In 1996, the Cook Islands declared bankruptcy, brought on in part by the corrupt actions of local officials. In response, the government dismissed more than half of public employees and slashed the salaries of those that remained by more than 50%. It also sold many of its public assets and closed all overseas diplomatic posts except for the one in New Zealand. Subsequent reforms, including the sale of state assets, the strengthening of economic management, the rebirth of a tourist industry, and a debt restructuring agreement, have rekindled investment and growth.[786]

Some practitioners consider the Cook Islands to be a "notorious" jurisdiction due to the perceived excesses of its OAPT legislation. Its external debt position is also problematic, as is the lack of a sophisticated financial infrastructure. However, its battle-tested OAPT law, lack of information exchange agreements, together with its political stability, make the Cook Islands worth considering.

Nevis: State-of-the-Art LLC Law and Economic Citizenship

Nevis is an independent island jurisdiction located in the Caribbean between Puerto Rico and the South American coast. It's one half of the Confederation of St. Kitts & Nevis. The two islands have a total population of approximately 40,000 inhabitants. The constitution of St. Kitts & Nevis is based on the Westminster model, but the court of final appeal is the Caribbean Court of Justice (CCJ), rather than the Privy Council.

Under the constitution adopted when St. Kitts & Nevis became independent in 1983, both islands have their own legislative assembly. Nevis began its evolution into an offshore center a year later, with IBC legislation, followed shortly by LLC and international trusts ordinances. These entities are excluded from income, corporation, gift, withholding, estate, asset inheritance, succession, and stamp taxes in Nevis. Today, Nevis is home to 50 trust and company service providers and more than 15,000 offshore corporations. In 1985, the St. Kitts & Nevis Confidential Relationship Act was enacted, imposing mandatory criminal penalties for persons who disclose private banking and financial records to foreign authorities.

Nevis is perhaps the best jurisdiction for non-U.S. LLCs because it provides that the charging order is the exclusive remedy available to a creditor against a member (Chapter 5). The Nevis international trusts ordinance is modeled on the Cook Islands' legislation. It forbids the enforcement of foreign judgments, while permitting the trust grantor be a beneficiary of a trust and retain asset protection. As with the Cook Islands, these departures from the common law of trusts may not be enforced outside Nevis.

In 2000, Nevis found itself on both the OECD's blacklist of uncooperative tax havens and the FATF's money laundering blacklist. The OECD removed Nevis from its blacklist after the government signed a commitment letter in which it agreed to enter into TIEAs with OECD members dealing with both civil and criminal tax investigations.[787] However, to date, Nevis has not ratified any TIEAs. The FATF removed Nevis from its blacklist after the St. Kitts & Nevis federation upgraded its anti-money laundering legislation. Among other initiatives, the amended law imposed suspicious activities reporting requirements and established a financial intelligence unit.

St. Kitts & Nevis has signed tax treaties with Denmark, Norway, Sweden, Switzerland, and the United Kingdom. A tax treaty with the United States is limited to social security benefits. In 1998, St. Kitts & Nevis signed a MLAT with the United States. The agreement facilitates information exchange in investigations of money laundering, drug trafficking, and most other criminal acts, but not tax evasion—only tax fraud.[788]

Both St. Kitts & Nevis face substantial economic challenges. Tourism revenues are the chief source of revenue, now that sugar exports from St. Kitts have ceased. In recent years, the government has held discussions with donor nations and the International Monetary Fund to devise a strategy to bring down the federation's excessively high levels of public debt. Strategies suggested by the IMF include the adoption of a value-added tax and the privatization of the electricity industry.[789]

Another challenge is the continuing rivalry between the two islands. In 1996, Nevis announced that it wished to secede from its federation with St. Kitts. Although the Nevis Assembly passed a resolution to secede, the measure failed to gather the required two-thirds super-majority vote in a subsequent public referendum. Relations have been further strained by competing offshore regimes, with Nevis being far more successful than St. Kitts in drawing offshore business.

Despite these ongoing challenges, Nevis remains a first-rate offshore jurisdiction, particularly for LLCs and OAPTs. The St. Kitts & Nevis citizenship-by-investment program (Chapter 5) is also the oldest still in existence, and well respected internationally.

Civil Law Offshore Jurisdictions

The term **civil law** refers to legal systems derived from Roman law. The first modern descendant of the Roman legal tradition was the French **Napoleonic Code** of 1804. Throughout the 19th and early 20th centuries, other legal codes derived from Roman law were enacted throughout Western Europe. Colonization and cultural ties led to the implementation of civil law systems in most of South and Central America, and much of Africa.

The origin of the common law came from a body of legal decisions by judges. Even today, common law judges not only interpret the law, but also make it through their decisions. In contrast, in a civil law system, judicial authority is more restricted. The duty of the judge is to apply the law as enacted. Judicial interpretation is limited to interpreting ambiguous provisions of the law. Judges may draw upon previous decisions to guide deliberations, but the interpretation of previous decisions as binding precedent is more restricted in civil law than in common law.

Each civil law legal system stands alone. The application of a court decision in one country in another country isn't possible in civil law. For instance, the decision of the English courts establishing a Mareva injunction quickly spread to other common law legal systems. This phenomenon isn't possible in civil law legal systems.

There are other differences between civil law and common law legal systems to consider:

- **Civil law has many unfamiliar features to an individual accustomed to dealing with a common law legal system.** Contracts written in civil law jurisdictions tend to be short. A contract covers only what the law doesn't mandate, while in common law, contracts cover much more, since they have to allow for as little judicial interpretation as possible.
- **Civil law jurisdictions are generally non-English speaking countries.** Language differences can lead to misinterpretation and misunderstandings. In the event of a legal dispute, documents will generally need to be translated into the local language.
- **Civil law is not well suited to trusts.** While some civil law jurisdictions recognize the trust concept, or have ratified international treaties promising to recognize it, civil law courts are ill suited to adjudicate disputes involving trusts. If your planning requires the use of a trust, it's generally best to form it in a common law jurisdiction.
- **Civil law recognizes the concept of *forced heirship*.** This doctrine provides that the bulk of an individual's property must pass on death to that person's descendants immediately and unconditionally, regardless of intent. Careful planning can often overcome this result. However, where this is the individual's intent, forced heirship may avoid creditor claims in an estate settlement, including claims from foreign governments.

Largely in response to demands from the United States, OCED, and FATF, all civil law jurisdictions have enacted money laundering statutes and laws establishing a duty for financial institutions to "know their customers" and in many cases, report suspicious activities by them. Many civil law jurisdictions have also ratified treaties with the United States that provide, among other provisions, for the enforcement of U.S. civil forfeiture orders.

Austria: Bank Secrecy of Constitutional Rank

Austria is an independent republic in central Europe, bordering the Czech Republic, Germany, Hungary, Italy, Liechtenstein, Slovenia, Slovakia, and Switzerland. It has a population of about eight million and ranks among the 10 richest countries in the world on a per-capita basis. The largest city is Vienna and the national language is German, although English is widely spoken.

Austria is wealthier and more industrialized than most common law offshore centers, which are largely dependent on tourism and revenue from their offshore sector. No body of law exists in Austria setting up an offshore sector to attract non-Austrian investors or creating instruments and investments available only to non-residents. This lowers Austria's profile as an international financial center.

Austria's bank secrecy law is of constitutional rank and may be abolished only after a national referendum. Banking records may not be released without a court order, which may be issued only in a criminal investigation or under an Austrian treaty obligation. The routine disclosures of confidential banking information by banks in the United States to direct marketing companies, credit bureaus, private investigators etc. would be considered criminal offenses in Austria.

Apart from secrecy, Austria provides significant opportunities for non-resident depositors. Interest and dividends are generally free of Austrian tax, and where they are not, payments can be reclaimed a wide network of tax treaties, including one with the United States. For businesses, Austria's tax treaty network, combined with recent amendments to its tax law, make it one of the most attractive jurisdictions in Europe for holding companies. However, for local companies and legal residents, Austrian taxes are relatively high.

In the absence of a treaty, Austria will enforce foreign judgments when **reciprocity** exists; i.e., if the other country would enforce judgments of a similar nature from their courts.[790] However, in practice, Austria doesn't enforce U.S. civil judgments.

Austria joined the European Union in 1995 and is now subject to various EU "harmonization" initiatives, including the EU Laundering Directive (Chapter 6).

Since Austria isn't a tax haven, it never appeared on the OECD's harmful tax competition blacklist. While there is ongoing pressure within the EU for Austria to open bank account or other financial records to inspection by foreign tax authorities, under the EU Savings Tax Directive, Austria applies a withholding tax to interest on savings accounts maintained by EU nationals, rather than disclosing account information.[791]

In 2000, the FATF briefly placed Austria on its money-laundering blacklist. It was removed once the government eliminated the opportunity for anonymous banking transitions via passbook savings, or *Sparbuch* accounts.

The U.S.-Austria tax treaty[792] applies to all taxes. While the primary intent of this treaty is to avoid double taxation, a memorandum of understanding attached to it authorizes U.S. authorities to obtain access to Austrian bank account information in investigations regarding tax fraud. There is no TIEA in effect.

The U.S.-Austria MLAT[793] calls for assistance in connection with the investigation and prosecution of "penal offenses" which are within the jurisdiction of the requesting state. There is no requirement that the offense be a crime in both countries. Nor is there any restriction of assistance in "fiscal" matters relating to taxation or customs matters. However, in the absence of dual criminality, the MLAT permits Austria to turn down requests that under Austrian law require a court order for search and seizure or other coercive measures. In practice, since tax evasion isn't a crime, but a civil offense in Austria, information on suspected tax evasion that doesn't involve tax fraud isn't exchanged under the MLAT.

Austrian civil law adheres to the principles that no punishment can occur without a conviction for a crime articulated in law; that the punishment must be strictly proportional to the severity of the crime; and that "punishment" can't occur outside the "penal monopoly" of the state.[794] Among other consequences, this means that the U.S. procedure of civil forfeiture isn't part of Austrian law. However, the U.S.-Austria MLAT permits U.S. civil forfeitures to be enforced in Austria pending the outcome of an accompanying criminal proceeding.

In summary, Austria is a stable and prosperous country with a well-developed financial infrastructure. It's particularly well suited for investors seeking a relatively low profile international banking center with strict bank secrecy laws.

The Nestmann Group has published a special report on Austria. To learn more, see http://www.nestmann.com/catalog/product_info.php?cPath=21&products_id=45.

Liechtenstein: Birthplace of the Offshore Industry

The Principality of Liechtenstein is a tiny alpine enclave, surrounded by Austria and Switzerland with a population of approximately 35,000. It has entered into a customs union with Switzerland and uses the Swiss franc as its currency. However, its legal system is separate from that of Switzerland. Unlike most common law offshore centers, Liechtenstein has a highly diversified industrial economy and is one of the world's wealthiest countries. German is the official language, although English is widely spoken.

In 1926, Liechtenstein ratified the **Law on Persons and Companies**, or **PGR** (the German acronym).[795] This statute created several unique entities including the *Anstalt* ("establishment") and the *Stiftung* ("foundation"). The PGR was the world's first statute designed to attract offshore capital and Liechtenstein is thus the birthplace of the offshore financial industry. The PGR also provides a statutory framework for the recognition of trusts, making Liechtenstein one of the only countries with a civil law background to do so.

Bank secrecy is a longstanding legal obligation in Liechtenstein and may be lifted only by order of a local court, in accordance with Liechtenstein law. Its provisions are similar to those in effect in Austria, although the law is not of constitutional rank. Tax evasion is not considered a crime.

With the exception of certain judgments from Switzerland and Austria, Liechtenstein doesn't recognize civil judgments from other countries.[796] All foreign judgments must be re-litigated in Liechtenstein courts, which don't enforce punitive damages.

While Liechtenstein recognizes the trust concept, a more frequent tool to preserve family wealth is the *Familienstiftung* or family foundation without commercial objectives. In recent years, Panama and other civil law countries have also passed foundation statutes. These laws, while possessing admirable asset protection features, are largely untested.

A Liechtenstein *Stiftung* is a fund endowed for a specific purpose or purposes. Unlike a trust, the *Stiftung* may hold both legal and beneficial title to assets in its own name. The *Familienstiftung*, which may not engage in commercial activities, is the preferred structure. Although the *Familienstiftung* cannot be established for business purposes, it can own assets (such as active companies) that generate profits.

It isn't possible to own a *Stiftung*. However, the founder can influence its management to a greater degree than a trust settlor. And unlike a trust, the members of the foundation council, the ruling body, can be changed without affecting the title to assets held by the *Stiftung*, under whatever circumstances are defined in the bylaws. In a trust, changing the trustee requires changing the legal ownership of the underlying assets. From a practical standpoint, this can be difficult.

A Liechtenstein *Stiftung* can offer exceptionally strong asset protection, assuming that the founder doesn't have the ability to comply with a court order to repatriate the assets conveyed to it. If set up correctly, assets conveyed to a *Stiftung* can't be seized, attached, or otherwise used to satisfy the obligations of either the founder or the beneficiaries. The founder of a *Stiftung* may appoint a protector to oversee the foundation council. Similarly, after the death of the founder, a *Stiftung*, like an OAPT, can be designed to avoid probate, reduce estate tax, and insure that property is passed to named beneficiaries.

A *Stiftung* begins its existence when entered into the public register. However, a *Familienstiftung* only needs to deposit the foundation deed—which should contain only the attorney's name—with the public register. Both the founder's identity and the names of beneficiaries may be kept secret.

Because the *Stiftung* concept isn't part of common law, its judicial and tax treatment can be problematic. Despite promises to the contrary by some promoters, a *Stiftung* generally has no U.S. income tax advantages, unless set up for charitable purposes. However, it can own tax-advantaged investments such as life insurance policies or annuities.

Proper drafting of the *Stiftung* is crucial to avoid unforeseen tax problems for U.S. persons, who should avoid "off-the-shelf" foundation documents sold by promoters. For a U.S. founder, the most advantageous tax treatment will be to elect to have the *Stiftung* taxed as a foreign grantor trust (Chapter 5). To achieve this result, the formation documents and bylaws must be carefully drafted to avoid the possibility that the entity will be taxed as a foreign corporation, with potentially disastrous tax consequences. The founder of a *Stiftung* and any U.S. beneficiaries that receive distributions, loans, or marketable securities from it, must also make substantial disclosures to the IRS.

A lower cost alternative to a *Stiftung* that provides excellent asset protection is a Liechtenstein variable annuity (Chapter 5). Under Liechtenstein law, if the beneficiary designation is **irrevocable**, the beneficiaries become the policy owners if there is a claim against the initial policy owner, or if that person declares bankruptcy. The beneficiary designation may be **revocable** if the beneficiary is the spouse or a descendent (child, grandchild, etc.) of the policy owner without endangering this asset protected status. The unmarried partner (opposite sex or same sex) of a policy owner may be a revocable beneficiary.

Variable annuities aren't as flexible as a *Stiftung*, however, and aren't generally effective estate planning vehicles. For estate planning purposes, a Liechtenstein private placement variable universal life insurance policy (Chapter 5) may be a better choice.

Liechtenstein's prosperity has historically made it less susceptible to political pressure than less affluent common law offshore centers. However, in 2000, the OECD placed Liechtenstein on its list of countries purported to engage in harmful tax competition and the FATF placed Liechtenstein on its money-laundering blacklist. At the same time, the EU applied pressure to Liechtenstein to participate in the EU Savings Tax Directive.

Responding to the OECD initiative, Liechtenstein refused to cooperate with foreign tax authorities unless all other jurisdictions do the same, and thus remains on the OECD tax haven blacklist.[797] In 2005, Liechtenstein agreed to participate in the EU Savings Tax Directive by applying a withholding tax to interest on savings accounts maintained by EU nationals.[798] However, it has only one tax treaty in effect (with Austria).[799]

In response to its blacklisting by the FATF, Liechtenstein amended its laws so that attorneys and other intermediaries could no longer make anonymous client introductions to banks. It established a financial intelligence unit and expanded the grounds under which assistance would be provided in foreign criminal investigations. These efforts led to its removal from the FATF blacklist.[800] Liechtenstein has also ratified the EU Anti-Laundering Convention and defines money laundering as dealing with the proceeds of "any serious crime." However, judicial assistance is provided only where dual criminality exists, except as mandated under a treaty obligation. A Liechtenstein court reviews all such requests before assistance is rendered. Judicial assistance is excluded for tax and fiscal offenses.

While Liechtenstein generally doesn't recognize the concept of civil forfeiture, the U.S.-Liechtenstein MLAT mandates the enforcement of a civil forfeiture order accompanying a criminal conviction.[801]

Liechtenstein is a high-cost jurisdiction for offshore services. Bank account minimums are high and legal, fiduciary and other financial services are some of the most expensive in the world. Nonetheless, Liechtenstein's substantial financial infrastructure and well-tested laws for foundations and insurance policies provide outstanding opportunities for asset protection and estate planning.

Panama: Low-Cost Financial Center with Residence Incentives

The Republic of Panama lies at the southern tip of Central America, between Colombia and Costa Rica. The population is approximately 3.2 million.

While Panama is best known for its namesake canal, it has a long history as an offshore center. Its offshore laws date back to 1927, when it enacted a corporation statute (*Sociedad Anonima*) based on Delaware law. Today, there are more than 120,000 corporations in Panama formed under this law, most of which trade or hold assets externally. Along with Liechtenstein, Panama may thus be considered the world's oldest offshore center.

Earnings of Panamanian SAs outside of Panama are not subject to Panamanian tax. They can enter into any business arrangement, and don't require accounts or annual returns. Directors and officers need not reside in Panama. Beneficial ownership need only be declared to the service provider and banker, and bearer shares are allowed.

An important drawback of Panamanian SAs is that they're not eligible for treatment as partnerships or disregarded entities for U.S. tax purposes (Chapter 5).[802] Panamanian SAs are always taxed as foreign corporations. The appropriate Panamanian entity to use if partnership or disregarded entity tax treatment is required is a *Sociedad de Responsadilidad Limitada* (SRL). A SRL is roughly equivalent of a limited liability partnership in the United States. However, the names of the partners in an SRL must be listed in the Public Registry along with details of the amount of capital committed and paid in (in cash or kind) by each of them.

Panama is popular for estate planning, particularly among wealthy Central and South American clients. Panamanian foundations are generally used for this purpose, although Panama also recognizes trusts. In 1995, Panama enacted a private foundation statute modeled after the one in effect in Liechtenstein. The Panamanian private foundation is a flexible estate-planning alternative, with significantly lower costs than Liechtenstein. Creditors have a right to challenge an asset transfer to a Panamanian foundation within three years from the date the assets claimed are given to the foundation. While there are minor differences between the Panamanian and Liechtenstein statutes, the comments earlier in this chapter in reference to Liechtenstein foundations generally apply to Panamanian foundations.

Panama's financial secrecy statute covers banks and other financial institutions along with other financial professionals and public servants entrusted with client information. These individuals may not divulge information to unauthorized persons, except in the case of serious crimes. Unauthorized disclosure can result in fines up to US$100,000 and imprisonment.

A unique feature of Panama's financial system is that since 1904, the U.S. dollar has been Panama's official currency. This has been an important stabilizing factor for Panama's economy, because it reduces exchange rate risks. Panama has never had a sustained banking crisis and the stability of the dollar has led to low interest rates in comparison with its neighbors. However, a dollarized economy poses risks for Panama if the value of the dollar continues to fall. It also means that many financial transactions in Panama are tied to the U.S. clearing system—and therefore are subject to U.S. jurisdiction under laws such as the USA PATRIOT Act (Chapter 2).

Panama adheres to a system of **territorial taxation**, which means that only income within Panama is taxed, either to businesses or residents. There are no tax treaties in effect, which maximizes privacy, but minimizes planning opportunities for Panamanian residents or companies investing in or doing business in high-tax jurisdictions.

Banking and shipping are Panama's two main offshore industries. Panama's banks focus on the South and Central American markets, although European investment is growing in importance, due in part to the enactment of the EU Savings Tax Directive and the subsequent flow of funds out of Europe. Substantial investments in Panama are also being made by China.

Most banks have low deposit minimums and fees are generally lower than in Switzerland or Liechtenstein. However, Panamanian banks are reluctant to deal with U.S. citizens. It's usually necessary to use an intermediary to open an account. In addition, private banking services aren't as well developed as in Austria, Liechtenstein, or Switzerland.

In 2000, Panama found itself on both the FATF money-laundering blacklist and the OECD harmful tax competition blacklist. Panama enacted money laundering legislation in line with FATF recommendations and was removed from the FATF blacklist a year later. The new law covers all crimes and requires all banks and other financial professionals to establish "know your customer" programs. However, Panama refused to capitulate to the OECD without a "level playing field" that would also require the United States and other OECD tax havens to abide by the same rules. Its agreement to enforce OECD mandates under these conditions was sufficient for it to be removed from the harmful tax blacklist.[803]

Panama's relationship with the United States has been a stormy one. While a MLAT between the two countries is in effect, Panama has steadfastly refused to enter into negotiations for a TIEA. This is in marked contrast to the capitulation of regional rivals, notably the Bahamas and the Cayman Islands.

Panama is a popular residence haven. Living costs are low, and the local amenities, while not up to U.S. standards, are very good. There are no taxes on offshore income. The two most popular ways to obtain Panamanian residence are the *pensionado* visa and the "person of means" visa. The *pensionado* visa requires that you must be over 50 and receive a pension of at least US$500 a month from a verifiable private or government source. A "person of means" visa requires that you invest at least US$200,000 in a two-year fixed-term deposit in a national bank CD and/or property in Panama.

In summary, Panama is suited to individuals interested in forming a family foundation with lower costs than Liechtenstein. Panamanian banks are worth considering if you receive an introduction from a local service provider and don't require top-flight private banking services, and the *pensionado* program is among the best in the world.

Switzerland: The World's Most Trusted Asset Haven

Switzerland, a mountainous confederation of 26 cantons (states) in the heart of Europe, has a population of approximately seven million. One of the world's oldest countries, the Swiss confederation has existed since 1291.

Switzerland is the world's quintessential offshore haven. Drawn by its policy of permanent neutrality, a rock-solid national currency (the Swiss franc), and an offshore banking tradition dating back to the 1700s, it's estimated that one-third of the world's private wealth resides in Swiss banks. Switzerland, however, is not a tax haven. While taxes on personal income and corporate profits are lower than most other countries in Europe, there is no general exemption for offshore income.

The most important investment opportunities in Switzerland are in private banking and portfolio management. Switzerland's insurance law provides excellent asset protection opportunities in a similar manner to that of Liechtenstein. For businesses, Switzerland is a popular jurisdiction for holding companies due to its extensive network of tax treaties. Switzerland is also a residence haven for wealthy individuals, who may negotiate flat tax arrangements with individual Swiss cantons.

The Swiss tradition of bank secrecy dates from 1713, when the canton of Geneva enacted an ordinance that prohibited bankers from divulging any information about their clients' transactions, except with the expressed agreement of the cantonal council. The federal Swiss bank secrecy law, enacted in 1935, punishes violations of bank secrecy with fines up to 50,000 Swiss francs and six months in prison. Contrary to popular opinion, Switzerland has never permitted totally anonymous bank accounts. However, until 1990, an attorney or other nominee could open an account in which the beneficial owner's identity wasn't revealed to the bank.

In 1998, a strict money laundering law took effect requiring bankers and other financial professionals to report suspicious transactions to police and heightened "know your customer" obligations. Banks must pay particular attention to currency transactions that exceed 25,000 Swiss francs or an equivalent amount in a foreign currency.

Switzerland's secrecy laws and steadfast refusal to exchange information with tax authorities in other countries have long complicated its international relations. To deflect EU criticism of Swiss bank secrecy laws, Switzerland agreed to enforce the EU Savings Tax Directive and now imposes a withholding tax on the interest earnings of EU residents.

Along with Luxembourg, Switzerland was one of only two OECD members that in 1999 refused to sign on to the OECD's "harmful tax" initiative. Switzerland narrowly missed being placed on the FATF's money laundering blacklist in 2000. However, its diplomatic clout, combined with continuing refinements of its money laundering laws and willingness to cooperate with foreign authorities in criminal investigations, kept it off the list.

Switzerland may grant legal assistance in criminal matters to all jurisdictions that request it, even if a treaty isn't in place. It has entered into many treaties that permit information release under the dual criminality principle. [804] For instance, the U.S.-Switzerland MLAT, which came into effect in 1977, has been used to investigate alleged criminal activity, and in many cases, to confiscate assets allegedly derived from crime.

Switzerland is an attractive residential haven for wealthy individuals. To qualify, you must not be a Swiss citizen or engage in any substantial economic activity in Switzerland. Typically, you negotiate with the canton in which residence is planned through a Swiss intermediary. The negotiated tax is based on expenditures, rather than income. It may be tied to the rental value of your accommodations in Switzerland, or a multiple of your deemed expenses. The minimum tax you can expect to pay annually is around 100,000 francs.

Switzerland remains a first-class financial haven. The professionalism of its banks and portfolio managers is first-rate, and its insurance industry provides excellent opportunities for asset protection. And for wealthy individuals seeking a low-tax residence with top-flight amenities, Switzerland is worth considering.

HOW TO BUILD YOUR OWN LIFEBOAT STRATEGY

An important strategy stressed throughout this report is to build private and secure refuges for your wealth—refuges that I call "lifeboats."

The Nestmann Group, Ltd. can assist you in creating such lifeboats. After analyzing your special needs, you benefit from personal introductions to qualified legal and financial service providers in the United States and offshore. Their specialties include:

- International tax planning;
- Private banking;
- Securities trading;
- Hedge funds;
- Pension plans and Individual Retirement Accounts;
- Portfolio management;
- Life insurance and annuities;
- Charitable giving;
- Real estate;
- Precious metals purchase and safe custody (bullion, semi-numismatic coins and warehouse certificates)
- Trusts and trustees;
- Tax-advantaged residence;
- Alternative citizenship and passports;
- Company formation and management; and
- Collectibles (colored diamonds, rare coins, etc.)

Recommended service providers are certified for their expertise by relevant professional organizations and, where applicable, licensed by the jurisdiction in which they conduct business.

For details on becoming a client of The Nestmann Group, contact:

The Nestmann Group, Ltd.
2303 N. 44th St. #14-1025
Phoenix, Ariz. 85082 USA
Tel./Fax: +1 (602) 604-1524
E-mail: info@nestmann.com
Link: http://www.nestmann.com

Introductions from attorneys are encouraged.

You may download the PGP public key for Mark Nestmann at www.nestmann.com/pgp.htm.

APPENDIX: A GUIDE TO CITATIONS USED IN THIS BOOK

This book cites laws and court cases decided mainly in the U.S. federal court system. Non-attorneys who wish to review these cases may find the following remarks helpful.

A federal statute enacted into law becomes part of the U.S. Code ("U.S.C."). A citation such as 18 U.S.C. 1956 refers has two parts: the volume number or **title** of the code (Title 18 in this example) and the **section** of that title (here, Section 1956).

The U.S. Code is found in many public libraries and law libraries. It is also available online at http://www4.law.cornell.edu.

Many court cases are also cited in this book. The citation lists the name of a case, the date decided, and its location in a "reporter." Federal reporters are also available at libraries, particular law libraries. A law librarian can assist you in retrieving these reporters and looking up the cases cited. They are also found on many Web sites. One of the most comprehensive is http://www.findlaw.com.

A citation such as *United States vs. One 1963 Cadillac,* 250 F. Supp. 183 (W.D. Mo. 1966) has three parts: 1) the case name; 2) the volume number (250) and page number (183) of the reporter in which the case is found ("F. Supp."); and 3) the federal district and year in which the case was decided (western district of Missouri). Where a cited case is also quoted, the citation contains the page number on which the quotation is found after the page reference for the case; e.g., *United States vs. One 1963 Cadillac,* 250 F. Supp. 183, **185** (W. D. Mo. 1966)

The reporter for all published decisions of U.S. district courts is the *Federal Supplement,* abbreviated "F. Supp." Published decisions of the U.S. federal courts of appeal are located in the *Federal Reporter, Second Series* and the *Federal Reporter, Third Series* ("F. 2d" and "F. 3d") respectively.

There are three reporting services for decisions of the U.S. Supreme Court: 1) *United States Reports* ("U.S."); 2) *Supreme Court Reports* ("S. Ct."); and 3) *United States Supreme Court, Lawyer's Edition, Second Series* ("L. Ed. 2d"). Citations in this book for cases decided by the U.S. Supreme Court are from *United States Reports* and *Supreme Court Reports.*

Appeals may be noted in a separate citation connected to the original citation; e.g. *United States vs. Hennsel,* 699 F.2d 18 (1st Cir.), *cert. denied,* 461 U.S. 958 (1983). "Cert. denied," indicates that the decision was appealed to the Supreme Court, but that the Court declined to review it.

Other reporters cited include the *Tax Court Reporter* ("T.C."), the *Bankruptcy Reporter* ("B.R."), *U.S. Treaties in Force* (U.S.T.), the Code of Federal Regulations ("C.F.R."), and various state law and international reporters.

THE NESTMANN GROUP, LTD. 2007-2008 CATALOG

Featuring books and reports by Mark Nestmann
Copyright © 2007, Mark Nestmann. Link: http://www.nestmann.com

The Lifeboat Strategy: Legally Protecting Wealth and Privacy in the 21st Century (3d Ed. 2007)

In 2006 alone, more than nine million Americans had their identity stolen and approximately 2 million were sued. And that's just the beginning of the threats you and your wealth face…. threats of an intensity that would have been unimaginable only a few short years ago:

- Web sites that permit anyone to instantaneously identify any assets you own
- "Data mining" software to analyze your personal and financial affairs to determine your credit-worthiness—but also made available to police (without a warrant) to determine if anything you've done is "suspicious."
- Laws like the USA PATRIOT Act that permit your privacy to be invaded and your property to be confiscated without proof of wrongdoing…

Big Business and Big Brother want to keep you and your wealth in plain sight, to be profitably tracked and conveniently seized. But you CAN fight back… it's perfectly legal to create international "lifeboats" of wealth and privacy that are practically invulnerable to snooping or confiscation. And *The Lifeboat Strategy* shows you exactly what you need to do to counter today's threats to wealth and privacy.

Here's a glimpse of what you'll learn in this book:

- 13 types of public records—available to anyone—that can be used to steal your identity
- Your "right to silence" is narrower than you think!
- Five ways businesses and the government use "data mining" to learn about your interests, sources of income and lifestyle
- The 10 worst electronic eavesdropping threats
- The giant hole in "caller ID blocking"
- Do you fit the definition of a "terrorist?" If you are a member of any of these organizations, you may.
- Tax avoidance vs. tax evasion—what's the difference?
- If you fit any of these 40 "profiles," your assets can be seized, without being convicted of a crime
- Are you a "racketeer?" If you've ever made this simple mistake, you probably are
- How withdrawing lawfully-earned money from your own bank account can land you in jail
- The secret global network that monitors all international telecommunications
- Seven legitimate ways individuals and businesses use offshore centers
- 23 strategies to prevent identity theft
- What to do if police want to search you, your vehicle or your home
- How to avoid looking like a "money launderer"
- 14 ways to preserve postal privacy
- Six tactics for private phone service
- How to obtain insurance privately

- Eight ways to achieve "residential anonymity"
- 22 tactics to audit-proof your tax return
- Nine tips for private banking
- The best private tangible investments
- Five hiding places for your valuables
- An ideal business for privacy seekers
- 19 ways trusts protect privacy and wealth
- Hidden tax traps in offshore mutual funds
- Why Americans should almost never use foreign corporations to hold a securities portfolio
- Three types of international bank accounts—which one is right for you?
- An anonymous safety deposit box
- How to move money privately
- How to invest your IRA or pension internationally
- U.S. laws for reporting wealth held internationally—and strategies to legally avoid them
- Using offshore insurance policies for privacy, asset protection and tax avoidance
- Low cost alternatives to offshore trusts
- How to structure offshore businesses to legally defer profits from U.S. taxes
- The nine best jurisdictions for investing and doing business offshore

The Lifeboat Strategy (3d Ed. 2007, 321 pg., US$95) ISBN 978-1-891266-31-7 (PDF) ISBN 978-1-891266-30-0 (perfect bound).

Austrian Money Secrets (2007)

Austria is one of the world's best-kept financial secrets. Not only does it offer unrivaled access from a euro-zone country to the fast-growing economies of Eastern Europe, but it also has some of the most affordable real estate in Western Europe. Mercer's, a human resources consultancy, rates Austria's historic capital of Vienna as the fourth most desirable city to live in the world. And, speaking of secrets, in Austria, the privacy of banking records is protected by a law with the same legal status as the Austrian Constitution!

Austrian Money Secrets shows you how to use an Austrian bank account as a jumping-off point for access to investment opportunities throughout the world. You'll learn what it's like to live in Austria, as I did for more than two years, and the best ways to qualify for residence and an Austrian passport.

Here's a small sampling of what you'll learn from it:

- Why Austrian bank secrecy laws are superior to those in most other offshore centers
- How to rent anonymous safety deposit box at an Austrian private vault,
- The Austrian bank where the primary language is English
- The Austrian bank with the best English-language online trading platform
- A low-profile method for sending funds abroad—and repatriating them
- A sneaky way the IRS obtains information about offshore bank accounts—and why it doesn't work in
- How to make big profits investing in rent-controlled apartments in Austria
- How to overcome legal restrictions on working in Austria
- How to qualify for "instant" Austrian citizenship and passport
- Why the rich pay very low taxes in Austria

- Why Austria is a tax haven for businesses—and how to make your business qualify

Austrian Money Secrets (2007,146 pg., US$69). Printed edition or e-book (PDF).

War and National Emergencies: The Threats They Pose to Your Wealth (2007)

A little-known network of laws and regulations came into effect after the tragic events of Sept. 11, 2001, that greatly expand the power of the U.S. government to control, direct and even confiscate private wealth.

For instance, in the event of a collapse in the value of the U.S. dollar, the President, at the stroke of a pen, can impose foreign exchange controls restricting the ability to convert U.S. dollars to other currencies, close U.S. banks and/or restrict withdrawals in dollars from bank accounts and impose wage and price controls

This report lays out the history of these powers, under what circumstances they can be used, outlines scenarios for their possible use in the future, and suggests strategies you can take now to deal with them.

War and National Emergencies: The Threats They Pose to Your Wealth (2007, 30 pg., US$39). E-book only (PDF).

The Billionaire's Loophole (2007)

What do Getty Oil heir Tara Getty, Campbell Soup heir John Dorrance III, former Star-Kist Foods Chairman Joseph Bogdanovich, former Wheelabrator-Frye Chairman Michael Dingman, investment manger J. Mark Mobius, Templeton Group founder Sir John Templeton and Carnival Cruise Lines founder Ted Arison and Robert Miller have in common? They've all taken advantage of the "billionaire's loophole:" acquiring foreign citizenship, giving up U.S. citizenship, and as a result saving billions of dollars in future U.S. income, capital gains, gift and estate tax.

You can take advantage of the "billionaire's loophole" as well, and you don't even have to be a billionaire to do it. An entrepreneur with a US$20 million estate could save US$8 million in estate and gift taxes by giving up U.S. citizenship. This report shows you how, step-by-step.

The Billionaire's Loophole (2007, 30 pg., US$39). E-book only (PDF).

The Private Traveler (2007)

Do you have a legal right to travel without undue interference from your government? The answer is an unqualified "yes:" laws in almost every country and a series of international agreements have repeatedly affirmed that right.

But since the events of Sept. 11, 2001, it has become much more difficult to exercise your right to travel without subjecting yourself to intrusive surveillance. Both U.S. citizens and non-U.S. citizens are subjected to secret investigation before they fly. Hundreds of thousands of people have been denied the right to travel because their name appears on a "no fly list."

As this report describes, these initiatives have very little to do with fighting terrorism—they're simply "security theater" that have had near-zero success at identifying terrorists or stopping them at the border.

Fortunately, while governments are imposing more and more restrictions on the right to travel, there still are ways to be a "low profile" traveler. You'll learn how in this report.

The Private Traveler (2007, 35 pg., US$39). E-book only (PDF).

109 Ways to Protect What's Left of Your Privacy and Property Rights (2007)

You're more vulnerable than you might think! This report includes a quiz to determine your vulnerability, and 109 practical and effective ways to protect your Social Security number; home, vehicle, correspondence, telephone, health records, bank, brokerage, and credit card accounts, computer, tax records, travel records and investments.

109 Ways to Protect What's Left of Your Privacy and Property Rights (2007, 32 pg., $39). E-book only (PDF).

E-books are delivered on the http://www.nestmann.com Web site, via e-mail or on CD-ROM in Adobe Acrobat "Portable Document Format." You can download the free "Adobe Acrobat Reader" (necessary to read these e-books) at http://www.adobe.com.

What Others Say About Mark Nestmann

"Nestmann is an authoritative source to learn how to legally protect your assets. His work is must reading for anyone considering asset protection planning." *Brenda Grantland, attorney and co-author, F.E.A.R. Asset Forfeiture Defense Manual.*

"Thank you for the information conveyed in our recent consultation. You have given me a 'road map' to plan for legally protecting my wealth and reducing my taxes offshore." *A consulting client.*

"I found your book to be well-written and informative, and it should be very beneficial to its readers." *Congressman Ron Paul.*

"Mark, it really is a pleasure working with you. I consider you a professional who is very thorough and provides a needed service." *Larry Grossman, Sovereign International Asset Management*

"Your book is an excellent work in its area and I will be recommending it to my clients." *David Lesperance, Canadian Barrister & Solicitor.*

ORDER COUPON

ALL ORDERS COME WITH AN UNCONDITIONAL 30-DAY MONEY-BACK GUARANTEE

QTY.	TITLE	PRICE	TOTAL
___	*The Lifeboat Strategy (2007)* (e-book)	US$95	$___
___	*The Lifeboat Strategy (2007)* (printed edition)	US$95	$___
___	*109 Ways to Protect What's Left of Your Privacy and Property Rights (2006)* (e-book only)	US$25	$___
___	*Austrian Money Secrets* (e-book)	US$69	$___
___	*Austrian Money Secrets* (printed edition)	US$69	$___
___	*War and National Emergencies: The Threats They Pose to Your Wealth (2007)* (e-book only)	US$25	$___
___	*The Billionaire's Loophole Closing at Last? (2007)* (e-book only)	US$25	$___
___	*The Private Traveler (2007) (e-book only)*	US$39	$___
		SUBTOTAL	$___

DELIVERY:

___ *Option 1: E-mail delivery—no shipping charges!* Please deliver my e-book(s) to the following e-mail address: ▓▓▓▓▓▓▓▓▓ @ ▓▓▓▓▓▓ . *(Note: Requires up to 3 megabytes inbox capacity)*

___ *Option 2: Postal delivery.* Please deliver my e-book(s) or printed books via postal mail
US shipping: Add US$5 for e-books, US$10 for printed books　　　　　$___
Canadian shipping: Add US$7.50 for e-books, US$15 for printed books　$___
Rest of world shipping: Add US$10 for e-books, US$25 for printed books　$___

GRAND TOTAL $___

__ **Payment** by cash, check, money order, or Visa/Master Card. Please make checks or money orders payable to **The Nestmann Group, Ltd.**

SHIP TO: _____

ADDRESS _____

CITY _____ STATE/PROVINCE _____ ZIP/POSTAL CODE _____

COUNTRY _____ TEL. _____ E-MAIL _____

Please bill my __ VISA __ Master Card. Card number: _____ Exp. _____

Signature: _____

Credit card billing address (if different from shipping address) _____

ORDER FROM:
The Nestmann Group, Ltd.,
Dept. CA-08LS
2303 N. 44th St. #14-1025
Phoenix, AZ 85008 USA
Tel./Fax: + 1 (602) 604-1524
Web: http://www.nestmann.com

While reliable sources have been sought out in compiling these publications, neither the author nor the publisher can accept liability for the accuracy of the contents nor for the consequences of any reliance placed upon them. Neither Mark Nestmann nor The Nestmann Group, Ltd. are engaged in the practice of law, accounting, financial planning or investment.

NOTES

[1] Council Directive 95/46/EC (Oct. 24, 1995).

[2] Wayne Madsen, *Handbook of Personal Data Protection* (Stockton Press, 1992).

[3] Stephen Pounds, "Company Sued for Giving Private Info to Killer" (*The Palm Beach Post*, August 5, 2000).

[4] Public Law 91-508, Titles I and II, 84 Stat. 1114 (1970)

[5] Robert J. Mintz, *Asset Protection for Physicians and High-Risk Business Owners* (R.J. Mintz, 1999, 2002).

[6] *Jackpot Justice: The True Cost of America's Tort System* (Pacific Research Institute, 2007).

[7] See, e.g., *Greenman vs. Yuba Power Products, Inc.*, 59 Cal. 2d 57; 377 P.2d 897 (1963).

[8] See, e.g., *Walt Disney World Co. vs. Wood*, 489 So. 2d 61 (1986).

[9] Pub. L. 101-336, 104 Stat. 327 (1990)

[10] Pub. L. 90-321, 84 Stat. 1127 (1970).

[11] Pub. L. 91-452, 84 Stat. 941 (1970).

[12] Quoted in Alexander Tabarrok & Eric Helland, "Partisan Judicial Elections and Home Court Advantage" (Independent.org, March 12, 2002).

[13] Renee LePere, "More and More Employers Checking Applicants' Credit" (*Charlotte Sun-Herald* (Florida), Sept. 14, 2003).

[14] Paul Wenske, "Credit Score Could Determine Flight Status" (*Kansas City Star* (Missouri), April 27, 2003).

[15] Quoted in Julie Appleby, "File Safe? Health Records May Not Be Confidential" (*USA Today*, March 23, 2000).

[16] "Your Past, Present and Future Private Medical Records Will Become Open to the Federal Government (HHS), Data-Processing Companies, Insurers, Hospitals, Doctors and Others, without Your Consent, Beginning Oct. 15, 2002" (Press Release from the Institute for Health Freedom, Aug. 26, 2002).

[17] "Face it, You're Toiling in a Fishbowl" (*U.S. News*, Oct. 2, 2000).

[18] "EPIC Urges Accuracy Requirements for Criminal Justice Record Database" (Press Release from the Electronic Privacy Information Center, Feb. 20, 2004).

[19] "FBI Proposes Big Expansion Of Crime-Records Database" (*Privacy Journal*, January 2007).

[20] Dan Eggen, "Justice Dept. Database Stirs Privacy Fears" (*The Washington Post*, Dec. 26, 2006).

[21] *Use and Management of Criminal History Record Information: A Comprehensive Report* (U.S. Department of Justice, 2001).

[22] "U.S. Lifts FBI Criminal Database Checks" (Associated Press, March 25, 2003).

[23] M. L. Elrick, "Police Say Suspended Cop Abused Database" (*The Detroit Free Press*, August 8, 2001).

[24] "Former FBI Employee James J. Hill Pleads Guilty in Connection with the Theft and Sale of FBI Records" (Press Release from U.S. Attorney's Office, Eastern District of New York, Sept. 4, 2001).

[25] "Identity Theft Up 50%" (*Technology News*, March 7, 2007).

[26] "Lesser Known Credit Bureaus Create More Headaches for Identity Theft Victims" (Public Interest Research Group, 1999).

[27] "Identity Thieves" (*ABA Journal*, October 1998).

[28] Joseph Menn, "ID Theft Infects Medical Records" (*Los Angeles Times*, Sept. 25, 2006).

[29] Brad Dorfman, "TJX Card Problem Flags Retail Identify Theft Risk" (*Reuters*, April 1, 2007).

[30] Bob Sullivan, "Online Job Listing an ID Theft Scam" (MSNBC News, Nov. 4, 2002).

[31] "Congressman Cardin Unveils Gamma Ray Scanner at Port of Baltimore" (News Release from Maryland Port Administration, Feb. 10, 2003).

[32] "Airport Delays Scanner that Can See Through Clothing" (Associated Press, Dec. 24, 2006).

[33] Kari L. Dean, "Smartcams Take Aim at Terrorists" (Wired News, June 4, 2003).

[34] *Kyllo vs. United States*, 533 U.S. 27 (2001).

[35] Eric Schmitt, "Liberties Advocates Fear Abuse of Satellite Images" (*The New York Times*, Aug. 17, 2007).

[36] See, e.g., Nicky Jansen, "Compulsory identification in the Netherlands (Radio Netherlands, Dec. 17, 2004).

[37] Pub. L. 109-13, 119 Stat. 231 (2005).

[38] "New Law Furthers *de Facto* National ID Card" (*Privacy Journal*, January 2005).

[39] Audrey Hudson, "Radio Chips Leave Visa Data Unsecured" (*The Washington Times*, Aug. 22, 2006).

[40] Richard Tyler, "Britain is Video Surveillance Capital of the World" (Rinf Alternative News, Dec. 6, 2006).

[41] "'Talking' CCTV Scolds Offenders" (BBC News, April 4, 2007).

[42] "Thousands of Security Webcams Wide Open" (Vnunet News, Jan. 5, 2005).

[43] *United States vs. Moran*, Case No. 1:03-CR-452 (N.D.N.Y. Jan. 5, 2005).

[44] Bob Barr, "OnStar Online to U.S. Government" (*Hawaii Reporter*, Dec. 2, 2003).

[45] Will Wade, "Insurance Rates Driven By GPS" (Wired News, Oct. 3, 2003).

[46] Pete Donahue, "Swiping at Crime: Cases Solved by Tracking MetroCard Use" (*New York Daily News*, Jan. 31, 2000).

[47] "E-Z Pass Now Hard on Adulterers in N.J" (WNBC (New York), Aug. 9, 2007).

[48] Declan McCullagh, "E911—Aid or Intrusion?" (CNET News, Aug. 18, 2003).

[49] "Will GPS Technology Lead to 'Geoslavery'? (*USA Today*, March 7, 2003).

[50] "FBI Apologizes to Lawyer Held in Madrid Bombings," *MS-NBC,* May 25, 2004).

[51] *United States vs. Kincade,* 379 F.3d 813 (9th Cir. 2004), *cert. denied,* 544 U.S. 924 (2005).

[52] See, e.g., Allison Dunfield & Kirk Makin, "Questions Surround Collection of Random DNA Samples" (*The Globe and Mail (Canada)*, May 23, 2003).

[53] "Don't Smile: Get Ready for New Type of Passport" (*Virginian Pilot*, Aug. 7, 2004).

[54] Mark Williams, "Better Face Recognition Software" (*Technology Review*, May 30, 2007).

[55] Deborah Circelli, "Applied Digital Gets FDA Approval on Chip" (*Palm Beach Post* (Florida), Oct. 23, 2002).

[56] Laurie Sullivan, "VeriChip Injects RFID Into Immigration Debate" (*TechSearch*, May 18, 2006).

[57] Valerie Elliot, "Speed Through the Checkout with Just a Wave of Your Arm" (*The Times (U.K.)*, Oct. 10, 2006).

[58] Ryan Naraine, "Triple-Barreled Trojan Attack Builds Botnets" (*E-Week,* June 4, 2005).

[59] Tom Espiner, "Phishing Overtakes Viruses and Trojans" (CNET News. Jan. 30, 2007).

[60] See, e.g., Chris Barylick, "NSA Looking At Social-Networking Spaces" (UPI, June 15, 2006).

[61] Kevin Poulsen, "Reminder: Monday is Wiretap the Internet Day" (*Wired,* May 11, 2007).

[62] Quoted in Doug Thompson, "The Rant" (*Capitol Hill Blue*, Dec. 9, 2005).

[63] For background, see William L. Prosser, "Privacy" (*California Law Review* (1960).

[64] *Wickard vs. Filburn*, 317 U.S. 111 (1942).

[65] *Gonzales vs. Raich*, 545 U.S. 1 (2005)

[66] *Schmerber vs. California*, 384 U.S. 757 (1966).

[67] *United States vs. Dionisio*, 410 U.S. 1 (1973).

[68] *Davis vs. Mississippi*, 394 U.S. 721 (1969).

[69] *United States vs. Mara*, 410 U.S. 19 (1973).

[70] *Cupp vs. Murphy,* 412 U.S. 291 (1973).

[71] *Coddington vs. Evanko,* 112 Fed. Appx. 835 (3d Cir. 2004).

[72] *Semayne's Case,* All ER Rep. 62 (1604).

[73] *United States vs. Dunn,* 480 U.S. 294, 300 (1987).

[74] *Vale vs. Louisiana,* 399 U.S. 30 (1970).

[75] *Kyllo vs. United States,* 533 U.S. 27 (2001).

[76] *United States vs. Dunn,* 480 U.S. 294 (1987) and *Oliver vs. United States*, 466 U.S. 170 (1984).

[77] *United States vs. Hyppolite*, 65 F.3d 1151 (4th Cir. 1995).

[78] *California vs. Greenwood*, 486 U.S. 35 (1988).

[79] *Boyd vs. United States*, 116 U.S. 616 (1886).

[80] *United States vs. Doe*, 465 U.S. 605 (1984)

[81] *United States vs. Ponds*, 454 F.3d 313 (D.C. Cir. 2006)

[82] *California Bankers Association vs. Shultz,* 416 U.S. 21 (1974). *United States vs. Miller*, 425 U.S. 435 (1976).

[83] *Chavez vs. Martinez,* 538 U.S. 760 (2003).

[84] *United States vs. Williams*, 504 U.S. 36 (1992).

[85] Public Law 107-56, 115 Stat. 272 (2001).

[86] *Coffin vs. United States*, 156 U.S. 432 (1895).

[87] *Hamdi v. Rumsfeld*, 542 U.S. 507 (2004).

[88] Pub. L. 109-336, 120 Stat. 2600 (2006).

[89] *Roe vs. Wade*, 410 U.S. 113 (1973).

[90] An example of this line of reasoning is *Griswold vs. Connecticut,* 381 U.S. 479 (1965).

[91] *California Bankers Association vs. Shultz,* 416 U.S. 21 (1974) and *United States vs. Miller*, 425 U.S. 435 (1976).

[92] In *United States vs. Doe*, 465 U.S. 605 (1984), the Supreme Court overruled its prior decision of *Boyd vs. United States*, 116 U.S. 616 (1886).

[93] "Statement of Robert L. Bixby, Executive Director, The Concord Coalition" (Public Hearing, before the President's Commission to Strengthen Social Security, Sept. 6, 2001).

[94] *Miller vs. Reed*, 176 F.3d 1202 (9th Cir. 1999).

[95] "Government Employees Selling Private Info" (Coalition for Constitutional Liberties Weekly Update, Sept. 25, 1998).

[96] Robert Ellis Smith, "Beware Demands For Your Social Security Number" (*Forbes,* Dec. 6, 2006).

[97] Pub. L. 93-579, 88 Stat. 1896 (1974).

[98] Pub. L. 98-369, 98 Stat. 494 (1984), codified at 42 U.S.C. § 1320b-7(a) & (c).

[99] Pub. L. 100-503, 102 Stat. 2507 (1988).

[100] Pub. L. 104-193, 110 Stat. 2105 (1996).

[101] John H. Fund, "Sorry, Mr. President, This Law Applies to You Too" (*The Wall Street Journal,* April 10, 2000).

[102] Spencer S. Hsu, "Cost and Privacy Concerns Cited In New Rules for Driver's Licenses" (*The Washington Post*, March 2, 2007).

[103] Speculative manias are summarized in Charles Kindleberger, *Manias, Panics and Crashes* (3d Ed.) (MacMillan, 1996).

[104] *Hall vs. Geiger-Jones Co.*, 242 U.S. 539 (1917).

[105] Ch. 38, title I, 48 Stat. 74 (1933), codified at 15 U.S.C. 77a et seq.

[106] Ch. 404, 48 Stat. 881 (1934), codified at 15 U.S.C. 78a et seq.

[107] *SEC vs. W. J. Howey Co.*, 328 U.S. 293, 298-99 (1946).

[108] Pub. L. 107-204, 116 Stat. 745 (2002).

[109] Jennifer Haman, "Ron Paul vs. SOX" (Lewrockwell.com, July 26, 2007).

[110] Pub. L. 91-508; 84 Stat. 1128 (1970)

[111] Pub. L. 108-159, 117 Stat. 1952 (2003)

[112] Pub. L. 106-102, 113 Stat. 1338 (1999).

[113] "AutoTrackXP" (Choicepoint.com, Aug. 30, 2007).

[114] "PrivacyActivism Study Finds New Problems for ChoicePoint, Acxiom" (Press release from PrivacyActivism, May 19, 2005).

[115] Kim Zetter, "ID Theft Victims Could Lose Twice" (Wired News, February 22, 2005).

[116] William Safire, "A Snooper's Dream" (*The New York Times*, Nov. 18, 2002).

[117] *Data Mining: Federal Efforts Cover a Wide Range of Uses* (General Accounting Office, May 2004).

[118] Mark Williams, "The Total Information Awareness Project Lives On" (*MIT Technology Review*, April 25, 2006).

[119] Bruce Schneier, "Data Mining for Terrorists" (*Cryptogram*, March 15, 2006).

[120] Pub. L. 89-97, title I, §102(a), 79 Stat. 291 (1965)

[121] "Medicare May be Running Out of Cash" (*USA Today*, March 17, 2003).

[122] Quoted in Mark Nestmann, "Why Doctors are Like Drug Dealers" (*FEAR Chronicles*, November 1992).

[123] Loren Steffy, "Your Medical Data May Not Be as Private as You Think" (*The Houston Chronicle*, Jan. 18, 2007).

[124] Regulation Allows Potential Creditors Access to Medical Records" (*The Denver Business Journal*, April 7, 2006).

[125] "Medical Records Theft Damages Credit Ratings, Threatens Lives" (*AAPS Online*, Oct. 12, 2006).

[126] Codified at 18 U.S.C. 1693-1699 and 39 U.S.C. 601-606.

[127] *United States vs. Van Leeuwen*, 397 U.S. 249 (1970).

[128] James Gordon Meek, "Bush Says Feds Can Open Mail without Warrant" (*New York Daily News*, Jan. 4, 2007).

[129] Robert Bauman, "Where the Business of Snooping Gets Done" (*Sovereign Society Offshore A-Letter*, May 25, 2005).

[130] See, e.g., *Allums vs. State (Ga.)*, 288 S.E. 2d 783 (1982).

[131] Ken Young, "Privacy Group Warns on Print Tracking" (Vnunet News, July 28, 2005).

[132] The procedures for conducting mail covers are discussed in 39 C.F.R. § 233.3.

[133] Mark Benjamin, "The Government is Reading Your Mail" (*Salon*, Jan. 5, 2007).

[134] Richard Miller, *Drug Warriors and Their Prey* (Greenwood Publishing, 1996).

[135] For instance, in *Jones vs. DEA*, 819 F. Supp. 698, 719-21 (M.D. Tenn. 1993), the court concluded that, "the continued reliance of courts and law enforcement officers on [dog sniffs] to separate 'legitimate' currency form 'drug-connected' currency is logically indefensible."

[136] "Domestic CIA and FBI Mail Opening Programs, *Final Report of the Select Committee to Study Governmental Operations with Respect to Intelligence Activities* (U.S. Senate, April 23, 1976).

[137] *Olmstead vs. United States*, 277 U.S. 438 (1928).

[138] Declan McCullagh, "The Privacy Snatchers" (*Time*, Oct. 3, 1997).

[139] *Katz vs. United States* 389 U.S. 347, 350 (1967).

[140] Pub. L. 90-351, 82 Stat. 197 (1968).

[141] 18 U.S.C. § 2518(3).

[142] 18 U.S.C. § 2518(2)(a)(i)

[143] James Ross, "REMOBS" (*Privacy & Security 2001*, September 1999).

[144] *2006 Wiretap Report* (Administrative Office of the U.S. Courts, April 30, 2007)

[145] *FISA Annual Public Report* (2006)

[146] Ryan Singel, "Point, Click ... Eavesdrop: How the FBI Wiretap Net Operates" (Wired News, Aug. 29, 2007).

[147] Declan McCullagh, "FBI Turns to Broad New Wiretap Method" (CNET News, Jan. 30, 2007).

[148] Louis Akin, "Is Someone Eavesdropping on Your Attorney-Client Conversations? (*The Champion*, March 2007).

[149] James Ross e-mail to Mark Nestmann, Feb. 12, 2001.

[150] Janon Fisher, "FBI Fed Gossip Sheets Dirt on Celebrities: Fonda, Astor, Seberg Were Targets of INLET Program" (*ABC News*, Jan. 3, 2000).

[151] James Risen, "Administration Pulls Back on Surveillance Agreement" (*The New York Times*, May 2, 2007).

[152] *United States. vs. Tomero*, Case No. S2 06 Crim. 0008 (LAK) (S.D.N.Y, Nov. 27, 2006).

[153] James Ross, *Privacy & Security 2001* (June 1999).

[154] "Intelligence Activities and the Rights of Americans," *Final Report of the Select Committee to Study Governmental Operations with Respect to Intelligence Activities* (U.S. Senate, April 26, 1976).

[155] Pub. L. 95-511, 92 Stat. 1783 (1978)

[156] "Foreign Intelligence Surveillance Act: Frequently Asked Questions (and Answers)" (Electronic Frontier Foundation, undated).

[157] "Ruling Eases Restrictions On Terror-Suspect Pursuit" (*The Wall Street Journal*, Nov. 19, 2002).

[158] John Solomon, "FBI Provided Inaccurate Data for Surveillance Warrants" (*The Washington Post*, March 27, 2007).

[159] Pub. L. 110-55, 121 Stat. 552 (2007).

[160] James Risen & Eric Lichtblau, "Bush Lets U.S. Spy on Callers Without Courts" (*The New York Times*, Dec. 16, 2005.)

[161] Jason Leopold, "NSA Spying Evolved Pre-9/11" (OpEd News, Jan. 17, 2006).

[162] "U.S. Echelon Spy Network a Fact, European Parliament Told" (Agence France-Presse, Sept. 5, 2001).

[163] *Smith vs. Maryland*, 442 U.S. 735,736 (1979).

[164] *U.S. West Inc. vs. Federal Communications Commission*, 182 F.3d 1224 (10th Cir. 1999).

[165] "Pretexters Could Get 10 Years Under U.S. Law" (CBR Online, Jan. 17, 2007).

[166] Pub L. 99-508, 100 Stat. 1848 (1986)

[167] "Field Guidance on New Authorities that Relate to Computer Crime and Electronic Evidence Enacted in the USA Patriot Act of 2001" (U.S. Department of Justice, Nov. 5, 2001).

[168] Greg Sandoval, "Legal Woes Mount for TorrentSpy" (CNET News, Aug. 29, 2007).

[169] "Secret Monitoring of PC Use is Illegal, Appeals Court Rules" (*The Orlando Sentinel*, Feb. 26, 2005. For a contrasting decision, see Declan McCullagh, "Wife E-Surveilled in Divorce Case" (CNET News, March 1, 2007).

[170] "Q&A: AT&T's Internet Policy" (*USA Today*, June 21, 2006).

[171] Quoted in Austin Bunn, "Playing Telephone: In a Society of Voyeurs, Eavesdropping is an Art" (*The Village Voice*, Feb. 24, 1999).

[172] *United States vs. Mercado-Nava*, Case No. 06-40154-01-SAC (D. Kan., April 12, 2007).

[173] Lucy Sherriff, "Paris Hilton's Sidekick Hacked" (*The Register*, Feb. 21, 2005).

[174] "The Clipper Chip" (Electronic Privacy Information Center, Feb. 1, 2002).

[175] Pub. L. 103-414, 108 Stat. 4279 (1994)

[176] "Carl Cameron Investigates, Part 3" (Fox News, Dec. 14, 2001).

[177] "FBI Probes Espionage at Clinton White House" (*Insight*, May 29, 2000).

[178] Bruce Schneier, *Cryptogram* (March 16, 2006).

[179] Bob Woodward, *Plan of Attack* (Simon & Schuster, 2004).

[180] This agreement is described in James Bamford, *The Puzzle Palace* (Houghton-Mifflin, 1982).

[181] "Spy Network Eavesdropping on Canadians, Says Former Spy" (Canoe News, June 18, 1999).

[182] James Bamford, *The Puzzle Palace* (Houghton-Mifflin, 1982).

[183] *Ibid.*

[184] *An Appraisal of the Technologies of Political Control* (Report to the Director General for Research of the European Parliament, Scientific and Technical Options Assessment Program Office, 1998).

[185] Duncan Campbell, *Interception Capabilities 2000* (Report to the Director General for Research of the European Parliament, Scientific and Technical Options Assessment Program Office, 1999).

[186] Eric Lichtblau & James Risen, "Spy Agency Mined Vast Data Trove, Officials Report" (*The New York Times*, Dec. 24, 2005).

[187] Carl Limbacher, "Clinton Used NSA for Economic Espionage" (NewsMax, Dec. 19, 2005).

[188] Duncan Campbell, "Careful, They Might Hear You" (*The Age (Australia)*, May 23,1999).

[189] Jim Bronskill, "Canada a Key Snooper in Huge Spy Network" (*The Ottawa Citizen*, May 22, 1999).

[190] "EU Parliament OKs 44 Measures to Counter U.S.-Led Spy Group" (Associated Press, Sept. 5, 2001.)

[191] "U.S. Spy Agency Under Fire: Critics Say Memos Suggest Snooping on U.S. Citizens" *USA Today*, June 26, 2000).

[192] Duncan Campbell, "The Spy in Your Server" (*The Guardian*, August 10, 2000).

[193] "EU & FBI Launch Global Telecommunications Surveillance System" (*Statewatch Bulletin*, January-February 1997).

[194] European Parliament and Council Directive 2006/24/EC (March 15, 2006).

[195] Bruno Waterfield, "Electronic Surveillance Enters EU Statute Books" (*EU Politix*, Feb. 21, 2006).

[196] The Council of Europe's Cybercrime treaty is posted at http://conventions.coe.int.

[197] Declan McCullagh & Anne Broache, "Senate Ratifies Controversial Cybercrime Treaty" (CNET News, Aug. 4, 2006).

[198] For background, see http://www.policylaundering.org.

[199] "Gold Clauses: Applicability of Congressional Legislation to Obligations Owed in the United States by Foreign Debtors" (*University of Chicago Law Review*, April 1936).

[200] This background is taken from Steve Forbes, "The Birth of the Tax Beast, Part I" (*The Daily Reckoning*, April 13, 2006).

[201] *Pollock vs. Farmers' Loan & Trust Co.*, 158 U.S. 601 (1895).

[202] See, e.g., *United States vs. Thomas*, 788 F.2d 1250 (7th Cir. 1986); *United States vs. Foster*, 789 F.2d 457 (7th Cir. 1986); *United States vs. Ferguson*, 793 F.2d 828 (7th Cir. 1986).

[203] Marshall Langer, *The Tax Exile Report* (6th Ed.) (Scope Publications, 1997).

[204] "IRS Updates Tax Gap Estimates" (IRS News Release, Feb. 14, 2006).

[205] See, e.g., John A. Andrew III , *The Power to Destroy* (Ivan R. Dee, 2002).

[206] David Barrett, *Final Report of the Independent Counsel in re: Henry G. Cisneros* (D.C. Cir., Jan. 19, 2006).

[207] *Tax Complexity Factbook* (Joint Economic Committee Staff Report, Office of the Chairman, April 2000).

[208] Pub. L. 99-514, 100 Stat. 2085 (1986)

[209] *United States vs. Carlton*, 512 U.S. 26 (1994).

[210] I.R.C. § 7207.

[211] I.R.C. § 7206(1).

[212] 18 U.S.C. § 1001.

[213] *In Matter of Newton,* 718 F.2d 1015 (1983).

[214] Pub. L. 100-647, Subtitle J (1988)

[215] Pub. L. 104-168, 110 Stat. 1452 (1996).

[216] Pub. L. 105-206, title III, 112 Stat. 685 (1998).

[217] The IRS defines a tax shelter as being any structure or investment that doesn't have real economic substance, but is formed for the primary purpose of avoiding tax.

[218] "IRS Made 4.6 Billion Disclosures of Taxpayer Data in 2004, JCT Reports" (*Bureau of National Affairs,* Aug. 22, 2005).

[219] *Semiannual Report to Congress, April 1, 2006 through September 30, 2006* (Office of the Inspector General, U.S. Treasury Department, 2006).

[220] Kevin McCoy, "IRS Workers Could Get Unofficial Access to Data" (*USA Today,* July 26, 2006).

[221] *Tax Shelters and Other Reportable Transactions* (IRS Publication 550, 2006).

[222] Pub. L. 108-357, 118 Stat. 1418 (2004)

[223] "Regulations Governing the Practice of Attorneys, Certified Public Accountants, Enrolled Agents, Enrolled Actuaries, and Appraisers before the Internal Revenue Service" (*U.S. Treasury Department Circular 230,* June 20, 2005).

[224] Stephen L. Feldman, "Alert Regarding Treasury Department Circular 230 Regulations Providing Standards for Written Federal Tax Advice and Sanctions for Noncompliance" (Mondaq News, June 16, 2005).

[225] Vernon Jacobs, "Tax Advisors vs. Taxpayers" (*Offshore Press,* November 2004).

[226] *Atlantic Coast Line vs. Phillips,* 332 U.S. 168, 172-73 (1947).

[227] *Ayrshire Pullman Motor Services & Ritchie vs. CIR,* C.S. 1929, 14 T.C. 754.

[228] Public Law 91-508, Titles I and II, 84 Stat. 1114 (1970)

[229] Penalties for violations of the Bank Secrecy Act are listed in 31 C.F.R. § 103.59 and 31 U.S.C. § 5322.

[230] 31 U.S.C. § 5323.

[231] 31 U.S.C. § 5322(b) provides for enhanced criminal penalties if a violation occurs "while violating another law of the United States or as part of a pattern of any illegal activity involving more than US$100,000 in a 12-month period."

[232] See, e.g., *United States vs. Scanio,* 900 F. 2d 485 (2d Cir. 1990).

[233] 31 U.S.C. § 5324.

[234] See, e.g., "Statement of Interest of the United States." *William T. Wuliger vs. Office of the Comptroller of the Currency,* Case No. 1:05CV0108 (N.D. Ohio, April 5, 2005).

[235] *California Bankers Association vs. Shultz,* 416 U.S. 21 (1974).

[236] *United States vs. Fitzgibbon,* 576 F.2d 279 (10th Cir.), *cert. denied,* 439 U.S. 910 (1978).

[237] *United States vs. Dichne,* 612 F.2d 632 (2d Cir), *cert. denied,* 445 U.S. 928 (1980).

[238] *United States vs. Miller,* 425 U.S. 435 (1976).

[239] *United States vs. Payner,* 447 U.S. 727 (1980).

[240] *United States vs. Noriega,* 746 F. Supp. 1497 (S.D. Fla. 1990).

[241] 12 U.S.C. § 3401-3420.

[242] *Raikos vs. Bloomfield State Bank,* 703 F. Supp. 1364 (S.D. Ind. 1989).

[243] 31 U.S.C. § 5324.

[244] 31 C.F.R. § 103.63 (2006)

[245] Peter J. Kacareb, "An In-Depth Analysis of the New Money Laundering Statutes" (*Akron Tax Journal,* Spring 1991).

[246] *United States vs. Scanio,* 705 F. Supp. 768 (1988).

[247] *United States vs. Aversa,* 84 F.2d 493 (1st Cir. 1993).

[248] *Ratzlaf vs. United States,* 510 U.S. 135 (1994).

[249] Form 104 is available at http://www.fincen.gov/reg_bsaforms.html.

[250] See, e.g., Michael Brick, "U.S. Trust is Fined $10 Million in Bank Secrecy-Law Case" (*The New York Times,* July 14, 2001).

[251] 31 C.F.R. § 103.29.

[252] Forms 8300 and 8362 are available at http://www.fincen.gov/reg_bsaforms.html.

[253] See, e.g., "Car Leasing Owner Sentenced on Money Laundering Charges," in *Automotive Sales Industry: Facts, Figures & Closed Cases* (IRS, March 2007).

[254] See, e.g., *United States vs. Goldberger & Dubin, PC,* 935 F. 2d 501 (2d Cir. 1991) and *United States vs. Leventhal,* 961 F. 2d 936 (11th Cir. 1992).

[255] Form TD F 90-22.1 is available at http://www.fincen.gov/reg_bsaforms.html.

[256] FinCEN Form 105 is available at http://www.fincen.gov/reg_bsaforms.html

[257] "New Suspicious Activity Report Form Required for Money Service Businesses" (IRS News Release, March 7, 2003).

[258] 31 U.S.C. § 5318(g)(3).

[259] "Court Says BSA 'Safe Harbor' Applies Even Where Bad Faith is Alleged" (*Money Laundering Alert,* December 2001).

[260] Adina Postelnicu, "Money Laundering Battle Challenges Legitimate Businesses" (*Marketwatch,* April 14, 2006).

[261] See, e.g., B. E. Hernandez, "RIP to IRP—Money Laundering and Drug Trafficking Controls Score a Knockout Victory

Over Bank Secrecy" (*North Carolina Journal of International Law & Commercial Regulation*, 1993).

[262] *United States vs. Giraldi,* 86 F. 3d 1368 (5th Cir. 1996)

[263] 31 C.F.R. § 103.18 (2006).

[264] Andrew S. Fischer, "I Have Seen Big Brother—and He is Us" (LewRockwell.com, Aug. 6, 2005).

[265] Michael Zeldin, "How to Set Up a Money Laundering Compliance Program" (*Business Crimes Bulletin*, February 1994).

[266] *Money Laundering: A Banker's Guide to Avoiding Problems* (Office of the Comptroller of the Currency, 2002).

[267] "Spotting and Handling Suspicious Transactions" (*ABA Banking Journal*, January 1991).

[268] John Berlau, The Postal Service Has its Eye on You" (*Insight*, July 2, 2001).

[269] Bob Kerr, "Pay Too Much and You Could Raise the Alarm" (*The Providence Journal,* March 28, 2006).

[270] *The SAR Activity Review—by the Numbers*, Issue 7 (Financial Crimes Enforcement Network, November 2006).

[271] Bob Barr, "Americans' Liberties on Endangered List" (*Atlanta Journal Constitution*, August 3, 2005).

[272] Quoted in "Wide Disclosure of SAR Data Endangers Witnesses, Says Merrill Lynch" (*Money Laundering Alert*, February 2000). See also, Robert Lemos, "DEA Data Theft Raises Privacy Concerns" (CNET News, Jan. 24, 2001).

[273] "Reports Catch Few Crooks but Trample Privacy" (*USA Today,* April 3, 2000).

[274] Quoted in Manu Joseph, "Your Money Under More Scrutiny" (Wired News, April 26, 2005).

[275] Jacob J. Finkelstein, "The Goring Ox: Some Historical Perspectives on Deodands, Forfeitures, Wrongful Death and the Western Notion of Sovereignty" (*Temple Law Quarterly*, 1973).

[276] *Ibid.*

[277] For background, see Eric Blumenson & Eva Nilsen, "Policing for Profit: The Drug War's Hidden Economic Agenda" (*University of Chicago Law Review*, Winter 1998).

[278] O. M. Dickerson, *The Navigation Acts and the American Revolution* (University of Pennsylvania Press, 1951).

[279] *The Palmyra*, 25 U.S. (12 Wheat) 1.

[280] *Dobbin's Distillery vs. United States*, 96 U.S. 395 (1878).

[281] *Goldsmith-Grant vs. United States,* 254 U.S. 505 (1921).

[282] *Bennis vs. Michigan*, 517 U.S. 1163 (1996).

[283] Pub. L. 95-633, 92 Stat. 3768 (1978)

[284] Pub. L. 98-473, 98 Stat. 2050 (1984)

[285] 21 U.S.C. § 881(e)(1)(A).

[286] Karen Dillon, "Taking Cash Into Custody Across U.S., Police Dodge State Seizure Laws" (*Kansas City Star,* May 19, 2000).

[287] See, e.g., Jared Shoemaker, "Civil Asset Forfeiture: Why Law Enforcement has Changed its Motto from 'To Serve and Protect' to 'Show Me the Money" (*Justice Policy Journal*, Spring 2007).

[288] *Caplin & Drysdale, Chartered vs. United States*, 491 U.S. 617 (1989).

[289] Pub. L. 99-570, 100 Stat. 3207 (1986)

[290] The civil forfeiture provisions of the money laundering act are provided for at 18 U.S.C. 981.

[291] *United States vs. James Daniel Good Real Property*, 510 U.S. 43 (1993).

[292] *Republic National Bank of Miami vs. United States*, 506 U.S. 80 (1992).

[293] *United States vs. James Daniel Good Real Property*, 510 U.S. 43 (1993).

[294] *Austin vs. United States*, 509 U.S. 602 (1993).

[295] *United States vs. Ursery,* 518 U.S. 267 (1996).

[296] "Tape Reveals Terrifying Campaign in War on Drugs" (*The Knoxville News-Sentinel,* Feb. 6, 2005).

[297] This case is highlighted in Brant Hadaway, "Executive Privateers: A Discussion on Why the Civil Asset Forfeiture Reform Act Will Not Significantly Reform the Practice of Forfeiture" (*University of Miami Law Review*, October 2000).

[298] "Bradenton Police Department Bypassing Courts in Forfeitures" (*The Herald-Tribune* (Bradenton, Fla.), Oct. 22, 2006).

[299] Stefano Esposito, "How Did Two with Criminal Pasts Get Jobs with Devine? (*Chicago Sun-Times,* July 3, 2006).

[300] "NYPD to Begin Seizing Cars of People Arrested for Drunk Driving" (Associated Press, Jan. 21, 1999).

[301] For instance, in *United States vs. $80,760*, 781 F. Supp. 462, 475 & n. 32 (N.D. Tex. 1991), the court held, "[T]here is some indication that residue from narcotics contaminates as much as 96% of the currency currently in circulation."

[302] *United States vs. $124,700*, 458 F. 3d 822 (8th Cir. 2006).

[303] Pub. L. 106-185, 114 Stat. 202 (2000).

[304] Pub. L. 95-223, 91 Stat. 1626 (1978)

[305] Act of Apr. 30, 1790, Ch. 9, 1 Stat. 117.

[306] Pub. L. 91-452, 84 Stat. 941 (1970)

[307] David J. Fried, "Rationalizing Criminal Forfeiture" (*Journal of Criminal Law and Criminology*, Summer, 1988),

[308] Pub. L. 91-513, 84 Stat. 1236 (1970)

[309] Codified at 21 U.S.C. § 848.

[310] David Smith, *Prosecution and Defense of Forfeiture Cases* (Matthew Bender, 1984-).

[311] Pub. L. 99-570, 100 Stat. 3207 (1986)

[312] 18 U.S.C. § 952.

[313] 18 U.S.C. § 1961.

[314] *Alexander vs. United States*, 509 U.S. 544 (1993).

[315] *Caplin & Drysdale, Chartered vs. United States,* 491 U.S. 617.

[316] *In re Billman*, 915 F.2d 916 (4th Cir. 1990).

[317] *United States vs. Gotti*, 155 F.3d 144 (2d Cir. 1998).

[318] *United States vs. Beecroft*, 608 F. 2d 753 (9th Cir. 1979).

[319] Gerard E. Lynch, "RICO: The Crime of Being a Criminal" (*Columbia Law Review*, June 1987).

[320] *RAGS Couture, Inc. vs. Hyatt*, 774 F. 2d 1350 (5th Cir. 1985)

[321] *Sedima, SPRL vs. Imrex Co., Inc.*, 473 U.S. 479 (1985).

[322] *Anza vs. Ideal Steel Supply Corp.*, Case No. 04-433 (U.S. Supreme Court, June 5, 2006).

[323] *H.J., Inc. vs. Northwestern Bell Co.*, 492 U.S. 229 (1989).

[324] Daniel J. Popeo, "Put an End to RICO Abuse" (*The New York Times,* Oct. 23, 2001).

[325] *Religious Technology Center vs. Wollersheim*, 796 F. 2d 1076 (9th Cir. 1986), *cert. denied*, 476 U.S. 1103 (1987).

[326] *Scheidler vs. National Organization for Women, Inc.*, 537 U.S. 393 (2003).

[327] *Evans vs. Dale*, 896 F. 2d 975 (5th Cir. 1990).

[328] *Whitfield vs. United States*, 543 U.S. 209 (2005).

[329] *United States vs. $4,255,625.39*, 551 F. Supp. 314 (1982).

[330] 18 U.S.C. § 1956-57.

[331] *United States vs. Ladum*, 141 F.3d 1328 (9th Cir. 1998).

[332] *United States vs. Tencer,* 107 F.3d 1120 (5th Cir. 1997), *cert. den.* 522 U.S. 960 (1997).

[333] *United States vs. Nattier*, 127 F.3d 655 (8th Cir. 1997), *cert. den.* 118 S. Ct. 1398 (1998).

[334] *United States vs. Gregg*, 179 F.3d 1312 (11th Cir. 1999).

[335] *United States vs. J. David Smith & Steven Dandrea*, Case Nos. 98-6377 & 98-6378 (3d Cir. 1999).

[336] 18 U.S.C. § 1956(c)(7)(D)-(F)

[337] See, e.g., *United States vs. Montague*, 29 F.3d 317 (7th Cir. 1994).

[338] *United States vs. Campbell*, 954 F. 2d 854 (4th Cir. 1992).

[339] Ian Comisky, Lawrence Feld, & Steven Harris, *Tax Fraud and Evasion* (vol. 2) (Warren, Gorham, & Lamont, 1997).

[340] *United States vs. Piervinanzi*, 23 F.3d 670 (2d Cir, 1994), *cert. den.* 513 U.S. 904 (1994).

[341] Ian Comisky & Michael Shepard, "Targeting International Money Laundering: The Uncertain Reach of Current Domestic Law" (*Journal of International Taxation*, May 2000).

[342] *United States vs. Carr*, 25 F.3d 1194 (3d Cir. 1994).

[343] Bruce Zagaris, "U.S. Court Upholds Extraterritorial Enforcement of U.S. Money Laundering Law" (*International Enforcement Law Reporter,* July 2000).

[344] 18 U.S.C. § 981(a)(1)(A).

[345] George Pratt & William Petersen, "Civil Forfeiture in the Second Circuit" (St. *John's Law Review*, 1991).

[346] *United States vs. Daccarett*, 6 F.3d 37 (2nd Cir. 1993).

[347] 18 U.S.C. § 984.

[348] Steven Schwarcz & Alan Rothman, "Civil Forfeiture: A Higher Form of Commercial Law?" (*Fordham Law Review,* 1993).

[349] David Smith, *Prosecution and Defense of Forfeiture Cases* (Matthew Bender, 1984-).

[350] 18 U.S.C. § 984

[351] *United States vs. All Monies ($477,048.62),* 754 F. Supp. 1467 (D. Hawaii 1991).

[352] *United States vs. All the Inventories of the Businesses Known as Khalife Bros. Jewelry*, 806 F. Supp. 648 (E.D. Mich. 1992).

[353] *United States vs. Swank Corp.*, 797 F. Supp. 479 (E.D. Va. 1992).

[354] For background on the Rutgard case, see "Crime and Punishment" (*AAPS* News, October 1996).

[355] *United States vs. Rutgard*, 116 F.3d 1270 (9th Cir. 1997).

[356] *Id.* at 1290.

[357] "Prepared Statement of David B. Smith" (House Judiciary Subcommittee n Crime, Hearing on Money Laundering Act of 1999, Feb. 3, 2000.)

[358] 18 U.S.C. § 1957(f)(1).

[359] David E. Rovella, "Putting Defenders on the Defensive" (*The National Law Journal*, March 28, 2001.)

[360] "Prosecutors End Money Laundering Case Against Attorney" (*The New York Times,* March 19, 2001).

[361] Sharon Harvey Rosenberg, "Banker's Money Laundering Conviction Tossed Out" (*Miami Daily Business Review*, July 20, 2000).

[362] *United States vs. Singleton,* 165 F. 3d 1297 (10th Cir. 1999), cert. denied, 527 U.S. 1024 (1999).

[363] Jennifer Richardson and Bob Brewin, "High Tech Drug Wars" (*Federal Computer Week*, April 23, 1990).

[364] *White House National Drug Control Strategy, 1990* (White House Office of National Drug Control Policy, 1990).

[365] Treasury Department Order No. 105-08 (April 25, 1990).

[366] *Ron Paul Investment Letter*, Aug. 15, 1990.

[367] "Summers Testifies on Drug Trafficking (Says Money Laundering Measures Working)" (*USIA Electronic Journals*, July 1996).

[368] See Ted Senator et al., "The Financial Crimes Enforcement Network AI System (FAIS): Identifying Potential Money Laundering From Reports of Large Cash Transactions" (*Artificial Intelligence*, Winter 1995).

[369] Donald R. Katz, "We Know All About You" (*Esquire*, July 1990.)

[370] 18 U.S.C. § 981(a)(1)(G)

[371] Stefan D. Cassella, "Forfeiture of Terrorist Assets Under the USA PATRIOT Act of 2001" (*U.S. Attorneys Bulletin*, May 2002).

[372] Michael Grebb, "Banks Dig in Along the War's New Front Line in a High Stakes Bid to Stop Money Laundering" (*Bank Technology News,* March 2003).

[373] *Report on Correspondent Banking: A Gateway for Money Laundering* (Minority Staff of the Permanent Subcommittee on Investigations, Feb. 5, 2001).

[374] Dan Eggen & Kathleen Day, "U.S. Probe of Sept. 11 Financing Wraps Up: Terror Money Traced Via ATM, Credit Card Usage" (*The Washington Post*, Jan. 7, 2002).

[375] Brian J. Stammer, "The Gibson Fallout" (*Offshore Finance U.S.A.,* Winter 2003).

[376] "Fishing in the Card Catalogs" (*The New York Times*, June 21, 2005).

[377] *A Review of the Federal Bureau of Investigation's Use of National Security Letters* (U.S. Department of Justice, Office of the Inspector General, March 2007).

[378] Pub. L. 109-177, 120 Stat. 192 (2005).

[379] Robert Block, "Requests for Corporate Data Multiply" (*The Wall Street Journal*, May 20, 2006).

[380] John Solomon, "FBI Finds It Frequently Overstepped in Collecting Data" (*The Washington Post*, June 14, 2007).

[381] Doug Thompson. "White House Keeps Dossiers on More than 10,000 'Political Enemies.'" *Capitol Hill Blue*, Nov. 8, 2005).

[382] *Doe vs. Gonzales,* Case No. 04 Civ. 2614 (S.D.N.Y. Sept. 6, 2007).

[383] See, e.g., "Canadian Universities Find Ways to Keep Private Info From U.S. Patriot Act." *The Canadian Press*, Sept. 19, 2007.

[384] *Youngstown Steel and Tube Company vs. Sawyer*, 343 U.S. 937 (1952).

[385] *U.S. Chamber of Commerce vs. Reich*, 74 F.3d 1322 (D.C. Cir. 1996)

[386] *200 Years of Census Taking: Population and Housing Questions, 1790-1990* (U.S. Bureau of the Census, 1989).

[387] Congress codified these laws in 1954 as Title 13, U.S. Code.

[388] Maria Titze, "Libertarians Urge Filling in Just One Box for Census" (*Deseret News* (Utah), March 7, 2000).

[389] David Burnham, *The Rise of the Computer State* (Random House, 1980).

[390] Steven A. Holmes, "Census Bureau Role Reported in Internment of Japanese-Americans" (*The New York Times*, March 17, 2000).

[391] *Hirabayashi vs. United States*, 320 U.S. 81 (1943).

[392] Eric Lipton, "Panel Says Census Move on Arab-Americans Recalls World War II Internments," *The New York Times*, Nov. 10, 2004.)

[393] Thomas J. DiLorenzo, "The American Gulag" (LewRockwell.com, Sept. 24, 2004).

[394] *Ex parte Merryman*, 17 F. Cas. 144 (1861).

[395] *Ex Parte Milligan*, 71 U.S. (4 Wall.) 2, 120-21 (1866).

[396] *Hepburn vs. Griswold*, 5 U.S. 603 (1870).

[397] Legal Tender Cases (*Knox vs. Lee),* 79 U.S. (12 Wall.) 457 (1871); *Juilliard vs. Greenman*, 110 U.S. 421 (1884).

[398] *Miller vs. United States*, 78 U.S. (11 Wall.) 268 (1871).

[399] Ch. 67, 12 Stat. 696 (1863)

[400] Pub. L. 99-562, 100 Stat. 3153 (1986).

[401] Pub. L. 109-171, 120 Stat. 4 (2005)

[402] Ch. 263, §15, 20 Stat. 152 (1878).

[403] Pub. L. 109-364, 120 Stat. 2355 (2006).

[404] 10 U.S.C. § 331 -335

[405] Ch. 30, 40 Stat. 217 (1917)

[406] For background on the Espionage Act's use in World War I, see "The Experience of the First World War" (*Report of the Commission on Protecting and Reducing Government Secrecy*, U.S. Senate, 1997).

[407] *Schenck vs. United States,* 249 U.S. 47 (1919).

[408] 12 U.S.C. § 95a.

[409] Proclamation 2039 (March 6, 1933).

[410] 73 Stat. 1 (1933).

[411] Executive Order 6102 (April 5, 1933).

[412] Ch. 48, 48 Stat. 112 (1933).

[413] For background, see Charles J. Woelfel, "Gold Clause Cases" (*Encyclopedia of Banking & Finance* (9th Ed.) (1991).

[414] Proclamation 2487 (May 27, 1941).

[415] Ch. 593, 55 Stat. 838 (1941)and Ch. 199, 56 Stat. 176 (1941).

[416] For background, see Michael S. Sweeney, *Secrets of Victory: The Office of Censorship and the American Press and Radio in World War II* (University of North Carolina Press, 2001).

[417] *Bowles vs. Willingham*, 321 U.S. 503 (1944).

[418] *Ex Parte Quirin*, 317 U.S. 1 (1942).

[419] Edward S. Corwin, *Total War and the Constitution* (Knopf, 1947).

[420] Executive Order 8785 (June 14, 1941).

[421] The OFAC "blacklist" is available at http://www.ustreas.gov/ofac.

[422] See, e.g., 21 U.S.C. § 1904(f).

[423] Shirin Sinnar, "How a Treasury Department Terrorist Watchlist Ensnares Everyday Consumers" (Lawyers' Committee for Civil Rights of the San Francisco Bay Area, March 2007).

[424] Executive Order 11490 (Oct. 28, 1969) (revoked by E.O. 12656).

[425] Executive Order 11615 (Aug. 15, 1971) (revoked by E.O. 11788).

[426] Proclamation 4074 (Aug. 15, 1971).

[427] *Emergency Powers Statutes: Provisions of Federal Law Now in Effect Delegating to the Executive Extraordinary Authority in Time of National Emergency* (Report of the Special Committee on the Termination of the National Emergency, U.S. Senate, Nov. 19, 1973).

[428] Pub. L. 94-412, 90 Stat. 1255 (1976)

[429] *Immigration and Naturalization Service vs. Chadha,* 462 U.S. 919 (1983).

[430] *Regan vs. Wald*, 468 U.S. 222 (1984).

[431] 50 U.S.C. § 1701.

[432] *Dames & Moore vs. Regan*, 453 U.S. 654 (1981).

[433] For background, see Jennifer Van Bergen, "How Government Forfeitures are Shutting Down U.S.-Based Muslim Charities" (Findlaw, May 1, 2006).

[434] *Holy Land Foundation vs. Ashcroft*, 333 F.3d 156 (D.C. Cir. 2003), *cert. denied*, 532 U.S. 904 (2004).

[435] Letter from Sean M. Thornton, Chief Counsel (Foreign Assets Control), U.S. Treasury Department, to Chris Powell (August 12, 2005).

[436] Presidential Decision Directives are reviewed in William J. Olson & Alan Woll, *Executive Orders and National Emergencies* (CATO Policy Analysis, Oct. 28, 1999).

[437] Executive Order 12919 (June 3, 1994).

[438] Executive Order 13224 (Sept. 23, 2001)

[439] *Holy Land Foundation vs. Ashcroft*, 333 F.3d 156 (D.C. Cir. 2003), *cert. denied*, 532 U.S. 904 (2004).

[440] *Humanitarian Law Project vs. United States Department of Treasury* (C.D. Calif., Case. No. CV 05-08047 ABC (RMCx), Nov. 21, 2006).

[441] "Bank Data Sifted in Secret by U.S. to Block Terror" (*The New York Times*, June 23, 2006).

[442] Greg Miller & Josh Meyer, "World's Banks Let U.S. Plumb Books" (*The Chicago Tribune*, June 24, 2006).

[443] James Risen, "U.S. Reaches Tentative Deal With Europe on Bank Data" (*The New York Times*, June 29, 2007.)

[444] "CIA Has Access to Swiss Transactions" (*Swissinfo*, June 25, 2006).

[445] "Hawala: An Alternative Banking System and Its Connections To Blood Diamonds, Terrorism, and Child Soldiers" (TED Case Studies No. 119, 2003).

[446] "Detention, Treatment, and Trial of Certain Non-Citizens in the War Against Terrorism" (Military Order of November 13, 2001).

[447] "Bush and Ashcroft Assail Habeas Corpus, Scholar Says" (Cato News, June 20, 2002).

[448] Bruce Zagaris, "U.S. Defense Department Issues Order on Military Commissions" (*International Enforcement Law Reporter*, May 2002).

[449] Dana Priest, "Justice Dept. Memo Says Torture 'May Be Justified'" (*The Washington Post*, June 13, 2004).

[450] "U.S. Report Left Room for Use of Torture" (*Financial Times*, June 8, 2004).

[451] "Justice Issues Rewritten Memo on Torture" (*USA Today*, Dec. 31, 2004).

[452] Andrew Gumbel, "America Admits Suspects Died in Interrogations" (*Independent,* March 7, 2003).

[453] Vikram Dodd, "U.S. Captors' 'Systematic Torture'" (*The Guardian*, Jan. 27, 2005).

[454] *Hamdan vs. Rumsfeld*, Case No. 05-184 (U.S. Supreme Court, June 29, 2006).

[455] Pub. L. 109-336, 120 Stat. 2600 (2006).

[456] "National Security; Prevention of Acts of Violence and Terrorism; Final Rule" (*Federal Register*, pp. 55061-55066, Oct. 31, 2001)..

[457] "Criminal Defense Organization Warns Members, Monitors Intrusions on Attorney-Client Communications" (Press Release from the National Association of Criminal Defense Lawyers, Nov. 9, 2001).

[458] Nina Bernstein, "U.S. Lawyers Keep Silence on Listening In" (*The New York Times*, March 18, 2006).

[459] Marjorie Cohn, "First They Came for Lynne Stewart" (Truthout News, Feb. 15, 2005).

[460] Ron Paul, "Can Freedom be Exchanged for Security?" (*Texas Straight Talk*, Nov. 26, 2001).

[461] Barry Reid, *The Paper Trip* (vols. I, II and III) (Eden Press).

[462] "Al Qaeda Manual Trains Terrorists on Deceiving Financial Institutions" (*Money Laundering Alert*, December 2001).

[463] "Easter Eggs Bypass Security" (*Out-Law News,* April 18, 2006).

[464] 18 U.S.C. § 1001

[465] Solomon L. Wisenberg, "How to Avoid Going to Jail Under 18 U.S.C. Section 1001" (Findlaw, May 11, 2004).

[466] Ted Bridis, "Music-Sharing Subpoenas Targets Parents" (*The Washington Post*, July 24, 2003).

[467] Barbara Goldsmith, *Johnson vs. Johnson* (Knopf, 1987).

[468] Steve Boggan, "Q. What Could a Boarding Pass Tell an Identity Fraudster About You? A. Way Too Much" (*The Guardian,* May 3, 2006).

[469] "The Savings Swipe: What are You Trading for Discounts at the Register?" (*The Morning Call Newspaper*, Jan. 11, 2001).

[470] Deborah Pierce, "Calling All Shoppers On Grocery Store Loyalty Cards" (AlterNet News, July 25, 2002).

[471] Jesse Kalisher, "Art of Noise" (*Brandweek*, June 28, 1999).

[472] *United States vs. Arvizu*, 534 U.S. 266 (2002).

[473] *Hiibel vs. Sixth Judicial Court,* 542 U.S. 177 (2004).

[474] *Horton vs. California,* 496 U.S. 128 (1990).

[475] John Lyon, "Defendant Had no Expectation of Privacy in Vehicle, Court Rules" (*Arkansas News Bureau*, Oct 26, 2006).

[476] *United States vs. Hernandez*, 433 F.3d 1328 (11th Cir. 2005), *cert. denied*, 126 S. Ct. 1635 (2006).

[477] "Police, Drugs, and Corruption" (Drug Policy Alliance, undated).

[478] *Illinois vs. Caballes*, 543 U.S. 405 (2005).

[479] *United States vs. $124,700*, 458 F. 3d 822 (8th Cir. 2006).

[480] Declan McCullagh, "Nifty Surveillance Trend: Cops GPS Track Cars without Warrants" (CNET News, Jan. 20, 2005).

[481] *Horton vs. California,* 496 U.S. 128 (1990).

[482] *Brigham City vs. Stuart*, Case No. 05-502 (U.S. Supreme Court, May 22, 2006).

[483] *United States vs. Coles*, 357 F.3d 780 (9th Cir. 2006).

[484] *Sanchez vs. San Diego County* (Case No. 04-55122, 9th Cir., Sept. 19, 2006).

[485] *Georgia vs. Randolph* (Case No. 04-1067, U.S. Supreme Court, March 22, 2006).

[486] *Hudson vs. Michigan*, 547 U.S. 1096 (2006).

[487] *Gilmore vs. Gonzales* (Case No. 04-15736, 9th Cir., Jan. 26, 2006).

[488] *United States vs. Aukai*, 440 F.3d 1168 (9th Cir. 2006).

[489] *United States vs. Romm*, 455 F.3d 990 (9th Cir. 2006)

[490] Dean Koontz, *CIA Flaps and Seals Manual* (Paladin Press, 1975).

[491] Diane Francis, "Whose Mail is it Anyway?" *Financial Post*, March 14, 2007).

[492] Postal Service Form 1093 is posted at http://www.usps.com/forms/_pdf/ps1093.pdf.

[493] Postal Service Form 1583 is posted at http://www.usps.com/forms/_pdf/ps1583.pdf.

[494] See comments of Justice Cooper in *People vs. Leon*, Case No. B173581 (California Court of Appeal, Aug. 3, 2005).

[495] Francine Brevetti, "Caller ID Tricksters Alarm Privacy Advocates" (*Inside Bay Area*, April 24, 2006).

[496] Bryan Gardiner, "DMCA Exemptions Allow You to Unlock Cell Phones" (*PC Magazine*, Nov. 28, 2006).

[497] Declan McCullagh, "Police Blotter: Judge Orders G-mail Disclosure" (CNET News, March 17, 2006).

[498] Fink is quoted in "Openness on Past Health May Hurt Future Benefits" (*The Chicago Tribune*, Dec. 23, 1990).

[499] "Hiding Tangible Wealth." Dec. 31, 1998. **Link:** http://www.pcisys.net/~y2kgold/hide.htm.

[500] *IRS Fiscal Year 2006 Enforcement and Service Results* (U.S. Treasury Department, Nov. 30, 2006).

[501] Form 526 is available at http://www.irs.gov/pub/irs-pdf/p526.pdf.

[502] Robert E. McKenzie, "Statutes of Limitation" (Mckenzielaw.com, March 3, 2007).

[503] "Giving a Tax Return to an Agent Does Not Constitute Filing" (*Tax Hotline*, January 1999).

[504] Statement of Michael Brostek, "Paid Tax Return Preparers: In a Limited Study, Chain Preparers Made Serious Errors" (Testimony Before the Committee on Finance, U.S. Senate, April 4, 2006).

[505] See, e.g., "Tax Shelter Remediation" (Quatloos Public Archives, undated).

[506] Form 8275 is available at http://www.irs.ustreas.gov/pub/irs-pdf/f8275.pdf.

[507] Form 8822 is available at http://www.irs.gov/pub/irs-pdf/f8822.pdf.

[508] "Use of Pseudonyms by Internal Revenue Service Employees" (*Internal Revenue Manual* § 1.2.4, Sept. 28, 2000).

[509] Albert B. Crenshaw, "Taxpayers' Online Data Protected, IRS Says" (*The Washington Post*, March 27, 2003).

[510] Form 4868 is available at http://www.irs.gov/pub/irs-pdf/f4868.pdf.

[511] You can download Publication 1 at http://www.irs.gov/publications/p1

[512] You can download Publication 556 at http://www.irs.gov/pub/irs-pdf/p556.pdf.

[513] For information on the limits of attorney-client privilege in tax matters, see Martin J. McMahon, Jr. & Ira B. Shepard, "Privilege and the Work Product Doctrine In Tax Cases" (*Tax Lawyer*, Winter 2005).

[514] Form 6209 is available at www.irs.gov/pub/irs-utl/document_6209-2003.pdf.

[515] 31 C.F.R. § 103.34.

[516] "No SSN? No Problem" (*Privacy Journal,* March 2007).

[517] I.R.C. § 6049.

[518] See, e.g., *Report on Money Laundering Typologies, 1998-99* (Financial Action Task Force, 1999).

[519] "Digital Currency Business E-Gold Indicted for Money Laundering and Illegal Money Transmitting" (Press release from U.S. Department of Justice, April 27, 2007).

[520] "Underground Banking" (*Institutional Investor*, January 1999).

[521] See, e.g., Jimmy Burns & Michael Peel, "U.K. Investigates Money Transfer System" (*Financial Times,* July 26, 2006).

[522] Quoted in "Underground Banking and National Security" (*Sapra India Monthly Bulletin*, February 1996).

[523] *Report on Money Laundering Typologies 1999-2000* (Financial Action Task Force, 2000).

[524] This information comes from the Industry Council for Tangible Asset's *Broker Reporting (Form 1099-B) Information Kit.*

[525] Executive Order 6102 (April 5, 1933).

[526] Pub. L. 99-185, Stat. 99-1177 (1985) and Pub. L. 99-61, Stat. 99-115 (1985).

[527] For background, see Franklin Sanders, "What's a Numismatic Coin?" (*The Moneychanger,* July 1996).

[528] Amanda Yarnell, "The Many Facets of Man-Made Diamonds" (*Chemical & Engineering News,* Feb. 2, 2004).

[529] See, e.g., *Hooser v. Superior Court* 84 Cal. App. 4th 997 (2000).

[530] *United States vs. Kovel*, 296 F.2d 918 (2nd Cir. 1961).

[531] *Golden Trade vs. Lee Ansarel Co.*, 143 F.R.D. 514, 518 (S.D.N.Y. 1992).

[532] *North Pacifica, LLC vs. City of Pacifica*, 274 F.Supp.2d 1118, 1127 (N.D. Cal. 2003).

[533] *United States vs. Knoll*, 16 F.3d 1313, 1322 (2d Cir. 1994)

[534] *United States vs. United Shoe Machine Corp.*, 89 F. Supp. 357, 358-59 (D. Mass. 1950).

[535] See, e.g., *United States vs. Rockwell International*, 897 F.2d 1255, 1265 (3d Cir. 1990)

[536] *Hickman vs. Taylor,* 329 U.S. 495 (1947).

[537] *In re Grand Jury Proceedings*, 601 F.2d 162, 171 (5th Cir. 1979).

[538] *Clarke vs. American Commerce National Bank*, 974 F.2d 127, 129 (9th Cir., 1992).

[539] *Magill vs. Superior Court*, 86 Cal.App.4th 61, 111-112 (2001).

[540] *United States vs. BDO Seidman, LLP*, 225 F. Supp. 2d 918, 921 (N.D. Ill. 2002), *aff'd,* 337 F.3d 802 (7th Cir. 2003).

[541] See, e.g., Donald W. Searles & Jay L. Pomerantz, "DOJ Revises Policy on Demanding Waiver of Attorney-Client Privilege" (Mondaq News, Jan. 2, 2007).

[542] Timothy P. Harkness & Darren LaVerne, "Lying to In-House Counsel May Lead to Prosecution" (*The National Law Journal,* July 27, 2006.)

[543] David Axelrod, W. Evan Price II, and Justin Thornton, "What Every Practitioner Needs to Know About Criminal Exposure in the Everyday Practice of Law" (*Criminal Justice,* Fall 1993).

[544] *United States vs. Perlmutter*, 835 F.2d 1430 (2d Cir. 1987).

[545] *United States vs. Connery*, 867 F.2d 929 (6th Cir. 1989).

[546] *Wallace vs. United States*, 281 F.2d 656 (1960) (reversed on procedural grounds).

[547] Axelrod *et al.*

[548] *Ibid.*

[549] Steven Wisotsky, *A Society of Suspects* (Cato Institute, 1992).

[550] *Cheek vs. United States*, 498 U.S. 192 (1991).

[551] *U.S. vs. Hilton Hotels Corp.*, 467 F.2d 1000, 1007 (9th Cir. 1972).

[552] John Hasnas, "Rethinking Vicarious Criminal Liability: Corporate Culpability for White-Collar Crime" (Heritage Foundation WebMemo, Aug. 15, 2006).

[553] This language is suggested by attorney Howard Fisher.

[554] Internal Revenue Ruling 88-76 (Sept. 2, 1988).

[555] See I.R.C. § 703 (a)(2) and (b)(3)).

[556] Internal Revenue Ruling 77-137 (1977)

[557] *Helman vs. Anderson*, 233 Cal. App. 3rd 840 (1991). This decision dealt with limited partnerships but the analysis would likely be similar for a LLC.

[558] "Family Limited Partnerships: New Meaning for Limited" (*Trusts & Estates*, July-August 1993).

[559] *In re Ehmann*, 319 B.R. 200 (Bankr. D. Ariz. 2005).

[560] Ryan Fowler, "LLCs and Charging Order Protection" (*Asset Protection Newsletter*, Jan. 18, 2007).

[561] Internal Revenue Ruling 99-6 (Jan. 14, 1999).

[562] *In re: Albright*, 291 B.R. 538 (Bankr. D. Colo. 2003)

[563] *Strangi vs. Commissioner*, T.C. Memo 2003-14 (May 20, 2003).

[564] See, e.g., Susan Kimsey Smith, "Bulletproofing Family Limited Partnerships and Limited Liability Companies" (*ALI-ABA Estate Planning Course Materials Journal*, December 2004).

[565] Form 2553 may be downloaded at http://www.irs.gov/pub/irs-pdf/f2553.pdf.

[566] I.R.C. § 1361-63.

[567] Form 8832 may be downloaded at http://www.irs.gov/pub/irs-pdf/f8832.pdf

[568] For more information on the limitations of directors and officers liability insurance, see Kate McSweeny, "First in Time, First in Right: When Directors & Officers Liability Coverage Exhausts Before the Litigation Ends" (Mondaq News, July 28, 2006.)

[569] See, e.g., *Suspicious Banking Activities: Possible Money Laundering by U.S. Corporations Formed by Russian Entities* (General Accounting Office, October 2000).

[570] *United States vs. Townley,* Case No. 04-35767 (9th Cir., May 17, 2006).

[571] Gideon Rothschild & Daniel S. Rubin, "Ninth Circuit Treads on an Established Right" (*Trusts & Estates*, November 2006).

[572] Robert Miller, "Offshore Trusts—Trends Toward 2000" (*Trusts & Trustees*, June 1996).

[573] *Restatement of the Law, Third. Trusts*, § 59 (American Law Institute, 2003).

[574] For background, see Mark Merric & Steven J. Oshins, "The Effect of the UTC on the Asset Protection of Spendthrift Trusts" (*Estate Planning*, Aug.-Oct. 2004).

[575] Jay Adkisson, "Domestic Asset Protection Trusts," *The Asset Protection Book* (2004).

[576] "To Trust or Not To Trust?" (*IRS Tax Practitioner Newsletter*, April 17, 2000).

[577] "Revision of Certain Dollar Amounts in the Bankruptcy Code Prescribed Under Section 104(b) of the Code" (*Federal Register*, pp. 7082-7083, Feb. 14, 2007).

[578] Julianne Frank, "Beware of the Involuntary Bankruptcy, Part I" (*Asset Protection Newsletter*, April 3, 2007).

[579] *In re Limperis*, Case No. 06-15791-BKC-JKO (Bankr. S.D. Fla. March 12, 2007).

[580] In *United States vs. Rodgers*, 461 U.S. 677 (1983).

[581] See, e.g., 18 § U.S.C. 1963(a), which stipulates that stipulates that criminal forfeiture shall occur "irrespective of any provision of State law." See also *United States vs. Lot 5, Fox Grove*, 23 F.3d 359 (11th Cir. 1994), in which a Federal Appeals Court affirmed a lower court ruling that federal forfeiture laws aren't preempted by homestead provisions of the Florida constitution.

[582] *United States vs. 15621 SW 209th Ave.,* 894 F.2d 1511 (11th Cir. 1990).

[583] *United States vs. Craft*, 535 U.S. 274 (2002).

[584] *In Re Juan E. Planas*, 199 B.R. 211 (Bankr. S.D. Fla. 1996).

[585] For information on land trusts, see Denis A. Kleinfeld, "Using Florida Land Trusts to Protect Real Estate" (*Offshore Investment*, April 1998).

[586] *In re Estarella,* 2006 Bankr. Lexis 318 (Feb. 23, 2006).

[587] *In re Bosonetto*, 271 B.R. 403 (Bankr. M.D. Fla. 2005).

[588] For more information on IDGTs, see "IRS Powerboosts Intentionally Defective Grantor Trusts" (*Steve Leimberg's Estate Planning Newsletter*, Jan. 17, 2005).

[589] Pub. L. 93-406, 88 Stat. 829 (1974).

[590] *Patterson vs. Shumate*, 504 U.S. 753 (1992).

[591] *United States vs. Sawaf*, 74 F.3d 119 (6th Cir. 1996).

[592] *United States vs. Vondette,* Case No. 02-1528, 02-1529 (2d Cir. December 16, 2003).

[593] Arizona, California, Idaho, Louisiana, Nevada, New Mexico, Texas, Washington, and Wisconsin are community property states. Several other states stipulate that all property acquired and income earned during marriage is considered marital property and subject to "equitable distribution." Equitable doesn't always mean equal, although 50-50 is the norm.

[594] *In re McIntyre*, 222 F.3d 655 (9th Cir. 2000).

[595] See, e.g., Robert Bauman, "Inmates and Demagogues" (*Sovereign Society Offshore A-Letter*, August 4, 2006).

[596] Cited in Walter H. Diamond, "The Changing Image of Offshore Centers" (*The International Offshore & Financial Centers Handbook*, 1994).

[597] Charles Adams, *For Good and Evil: The Impact of Taxes on the Course of Civilization* (Madison Books, 1993).

[598] "The Price of Offshore" (Tax Justice Network, 2005).

[599] For background, see "Regulation S: Raising Offshore Capital in Quasi-Public Offerings" (*C & G Review*, Winter 2005).

[600] Mark Hulbert, "Yes, Foreign Stocks Can Still Reduce a Portfolio's Risk" (*The New York Times,* Feb. 27, 2005).

[601] L. Richard Fischer, *The Law of Financial Privacy* (Warren, Gorham, & Lamont, 1983-)

[602] Dennis Campbell, ed., *International Banking Secrecy* (Sweet & Maxwell, 1992).

[603] Council Directive 95/46/EC (Oct. 24, 1995).

[604] See, e.g., *FTC vs. Affordable Media, LLC et al.* (179 F.3d 1228, 9th Cir. 1999). This case involved an offshore trust but the underlying principle that a person's consent can be coerced to repatriate offshore assets would be the same whether or not there is a structure such as a trust involved.

[605] For background, see "U.S. Inbound: IRS Releases Notice Regarding Qualified Intermediary Program" (*International Tax Review,* May 2006).

[606] *Doe vs. United States*, 487 U.S. 201 (1988).

[607] "FinCEN Report to Congress States that the Reporting of Cross-Border Wire Transfer Data is Technically Feasible for the Government but Requires Further Collaboration" (Press Release from the Financial Crimes Enforcement Network, Jan.17, 2007).

[608] See, e.g., *U. S. Money Laundering Threat Assessment* (U.S. Treasury Department, 2005).

[609] 31 C.F.R. § 103.58.

[610] The requirements are summarized at 31 C.F.R. 103.24.

[611] Form TD F 90-22.1 is posted at http://www.fincen.gov/reg_bsaforms.html.

[612] 31 C.F.R. § 103.57.

[613] 31 U.S.C. § 5322(b).

[614] *United States vs. Mueller*, 74 F.3d 1152 (11th Cir. 1996).

[615] Steven Toscher & Michel R. Stein, "Criminal Enforcement of FBAR Filing Requirements" (*Business Crimes Bulletin*, June 2006).

[616] Vernon Jacobs, *2006 Guide to Reporting Offshore Financial Accounts* (Offshore Press, 2006).

[617] *United States vs. Clines*, 958 F.2d 578 (4th Cir. 1992).

[618] St. Kitts & Nevis Trusts Act, Sec. 21(7), 1996.

[619] See I.R.C. § 2704(b).

[620] *FTC vs. Affordable Media, LLC et al.*, 179 F.3d 1228 (9th Cir. 1999).

[621] For background, see Alexander Bove, "The Protector: Trusty Watchdog or Expensive Exotic Pet?" (*Offshore Investment*, May 2003).

[622] *Grupo Mexicano De Desarrollo, S. A., et al. vs. Alliance Bond Fund, Inc., et al.*, 527 U.S. 308 (1999).

[623] *FTC vs. Affordable Media, LLC et al.*, 179 F.3d 1228 (9th Cir. 1999).

[624] For background, see Gideon Rothschild, "Asset Protection Planning—Current Strategies and Pitfalls" (*Tax Management Estate, Gifts, and Taxes Journal*, September 2005).

[625] *United States vs. Rylander*, 460 U.S. 752 (1983) and *United States vs. Bryan*, 339 U.S. 323 (1950).

[626] Howard Rosen, "Uses and Abuses of Offshore Trusts in Asset Protection Planning" (*Journal of Asset Protection*, September-October 1995).

[627] For background, see Gideon Rothschild, "Did Bankruptcy Reform Law Close the 'Loophole' for the Wealthy?" (*Tax Notes*, April 25, 2005).

[628] *Rahman vs. Chase Bank Trust Company (CI) Ltd.* Jersey Law Review 103 (1991)

[629] I.R.C. §§ 671-679.

[630] For background, see David Kerzner, "Reporting On Transactions With Foreign Trusts and Receipt of Large Foreign Gifts" (*Asset Protection Newsletter*, Nov. 2, 2006).

[631] All these forms are available at http://www.irs.ustreas.gov/formspubs/lists/0,,id=97817,00.html.

[632] For background, see Robert Dunn, Jr., "The Misguided Attractions of Foreign Exchange Controls" (*Challenge*, September-October, 2002).

[633] I.R.C. § 877.

[634] "Notice of Proposed Rulemaking and Notice of Public Hearing: Exchanges of Property for an Annuity" (*Internal Revenue Bulletin*, Nov. 18, 2006).

[635] I.R.C. § 72 and I.R.C. § 817 are the sections of U.S. tax law that apply to variable annuities.

[636] "Diversification Requirements for Variable Annuity, Endowment, and Life Insurance Contracts" (*Internal Revenue Bulletin*, March 1, 2005).

[637] Forms 720 and 8833 are available from http://www.irs.ustreas.gov/formspubs/lists/0,,id=97817,00.html.

[638] Quoted in Vernon Jacobs, *2006 Guide to Reporting Offshore Financial Accounts* (Offshore Press, 2006).

[639] "Diversification Requirements for Variable Annuity, Endowment, and Life Insurance Contracts" (*Internal Revenue Bulletin*, March 1, 2005).

[640] I.R.C. § 817 and I.R.C. § 7702 are the section of the U.S. Tax Code relating to life insurance.

[641] The controlled foreign corporation rules are found at I.R.C. §§ 951-957.

[642] I.R.C. § 952.

[643] For an in-depth and not-too-technical review of the tax rules for CFCs, see Richard Duke & Vernon Jacobs, *A Tax Guide For Owners of Controlled Foreign Corporations and International Business Companies* (Offshore Press, 2007).

[644] I.R.C. § 962.

[645] Christopher Riser, "Asset Protection Planning With Domestic & Foreign Limited Liability Companies" (Offshore Press, 2000).

[646] *A Tax Guide for Owners of Controlled Foreign Corporations and International Business Companies.*

[647] I.R.C. § 951(d)

[648] Benjamin D. Knaupp, "Bearer Shares are a Minefield for U.S. Citizens" (*The Sovereign Individual*, November 1999).

[649] See, e.g., "Anguilla's Immobilization of Bearer Shares Regime—A Practical and Regulatory Sound Approach" (*GCSL Newsletter*, June 2007).

[650] These statistics come from Jay D. Adkisson, *An Introduction to Captives, Closely-Held Insurance Companies, and Risk Retention Groups* (iUniverse, Inc. 2006).

[651] *Carnation Co. vs. Commissioner*, 640 F.2d 1010 (9th Cir. 1981).

[652] I.R.C. § 911(b)(2)(D)(i).

[653] Form 2555 is posted at www.irs.gov/pub/irs-pdf/f2555.pdf.

[654] According to IRS Publication 54, an American employer is: "1) The U.S. Government or any of its instrumentalities. 2) An individual who is a resident of the United States. 3) A partnership of which at least two-thirds of the partners are U.S. residents. 4) A trust of which all the trustees are U.S. residents. 5) A corporation organized under the laws of the United States, any U.S. state, or the District of Columbia, Puerto Rico, the Virgin Islands, Guam, or American Samoa."

[655] For an updated list of the countries in which totalization agreements are in place, along with details of how they operate, see "U.S. International Social Security Agreements" at http://www.ssa.gov/international/agreements_overview.html.

[656] You can download Publication 54 at http://www.irs.gov/pub/irs-pdf/p54.pdf.

[657] W. G. Hill, *PT* (Scope International, 1989).

[658] These procedures are outlined in "U.S. IRS Issues Updated Expatriation Information Statement" (*KPMG Flash International Executive Alert*, March 16, 2005).

[659] See, e.g., Scott Busby, "A Forgotten Human Rights Crisis: Statelessness" (Remarks to a Congressional Human Rights Caucus Members' Briefing, April 19, 2005).

[660] I.R.C. § 877.

[661] For a detailed explanation of the U.S. source income rules as they apply to expatriating U.S. citizens or long-term residents, see Marco A. Blanco & John Kaufmann, "The New Section 877: Everything You Ever Wanted to Know About the Expatriation of Long-Term Permanent Residents Under the New Act but Were Afraid to Ask the Government" (*Tax Notes*, Jan. 3, 2005).

[662] These rules are summarized in Marshall Langer, *The Tax Exile Report* (6th Ed.) (Scope International, 1997).

[663] See "Substantial Presence Test," in *U.S. Tax Guide for Aliens* (IRS Publication 519, 2006).

[664] Immigration and Nationality Act, § 212(A)(10).

[665] "Revision of Tax Rules on Expatriation of Individuals" (Senate Report 110-001, Small Business and Work Opportunity Act of 2007, February 2007).

[666] "Baucus-Grassley Bill Offers Tax Relief to America's Fighting Men and Women" (News Release from U.S. Senate Committee on Finance, June 12, 2007).

[667] For background, see Nick Mathiason, "Welcome to London, the Onshore Tax Haven" (*The Observer*, July 8, 2007).

[668] See http://www.ind.homeoffice.gov.uk/lawandpolicy/immigrationrules for information on how to qualify for U.K. residence.

[669] Robert Lee, "Pressure Mounts on Labour to Scrap U.K. Non-Domicile Tax Status" (Tax News, July 16, 2007).

[670] "Ex-FIBG Insiders Receive Prison Terms in Oregon" (KYC News, Aug. 28, 2007).

[671] David Marchant, "We Expose The Harris Organization's Multi-Million Dollar Ponzi Scheme" (*Offshore Alert*, March 31, 1998).

[672] David Marchant, "The Importance of Due Diligence in Offshore Investing" (*The Sovereign Individual*, July 2000).

[673] Revenue Act of 1937 (Ch. 815, 50 Stat. 813).

[674] Pub. L. 87-834, 76 Stat. 960 (1962).

[675] See, e.g., John R. Griffith, Jr., "The Effect of the Interest Equalization Tax Act and the Interest Equalization Tax Extension Act on Purchases of Long-Term Bonds of Selected Countries Marketed in the United States: 1959 to March 1966" (*Journal of Finance*, June 1969).

[676] *Tax Haven Abuses: The Enablers, The Tools, and Secrecy* (U.S. Senate Permanent Subcommittee On Investigations, Committee on Homeland Security and Governmental Affairs, August 2006).

[677] *Restatement (Third) of Foreign Relations Law of the United States*, § 403(2) (American Law Institute, 1988).

[678] See, e.g., Frank C. Razzano, "Conflicts Between American & Foreign Law: Does the 'Balance of the Interests' Test Always Equal America's Interest?" (*The International Lawyer*, Spring 2003).

[679] *International Estate Planning*, § 9.04 (Matthew Bender & Co., 1994-).

[680] *McDonald vs. Mabee*, 243 U.S. 90 (1917).

[681] *International Shoe Co. vs. Washington*, 326 U.S. 310 (1945).

[682] *McGee vs. International Life Insurance Co.*, 355 U.S. 220 (1957).

[683] *Vault Corp. vs. Quaid Software Ltd.*, 775 F.2d 638 (5th Cir. 1985).

[684] *Calder vs. Jones*, 465 U.S. 783 (1984).

[685] *Doe vs. United States*, 487 U.S. 201 (1988).

[686] *United States vs. Bank of Nova Scotia*, 691 F. 2d 1384 (11th Cir. 1982), *cert. denied,* 462 U.S. 1119 (1983).

[687] *In re Marc Rich & Co.*, 707 F. 2d 663 (2d Cir. 1984).

[688] "Jurisdiction & Liability: The Twin Defenses of Offshore Defendants" (*OAC Update*, March 15, 2007).

[689] See, e.g., "An Overview of the Cuban Assets Control Regulations" (U.S. Treasury Office of Foreign Assets Control, 2006).

[690] See, e.g., "EU Responds to U.S. Extra-Territorial Laws with Blocking Statute" (Europaworld News, Aug. 2, 2001).

[691] *In re Tucker*, 1987-88 Jersey Law Reports 473.

[692] *Restatement (Third) Of Foreign Relations Law* § 483 (1988).

[693] *Pasquantino vs. United States,* 544 U.S. 349 (2005)

[694] Brian Wallach, "All Hands On Deck: Rescuing The Revenue Rule From The Supreme Court's Decision In *Pasquantino*" (*Tax Lawyer*, Winter 2006).

[695] For background, see Cynthia Blum, "Sharing Bank Deposit Information with Other Countries: Should Tax Compliance or Privacy Claims Prevail?" (*Florida Tax Review*, vol. 6, 2005).

[696] "IRS Sets New Audit Priorities" (IRS News Release, Sept. 1, 2002)..

[697] John Doe summonses are authorized in I.R.C. § 7609(f) and discussed in detail in *United States vs. Blackman,* 72 F.3d 1418 (9th Cir. 1995).

[698] Glen Shapiro, "PayPal Ordered To Assist In U.S. Tax Evasion Probe" (Tax News, April 17, 2006).

[699] David Caye Johnson, "Departing Chief Says IRS Is Losing War on Tax Cheats" (*The New York Times*, Nov. 5, 2002).

[700] "Background on the OCCP and OVCI" (Quatloos Public Archives, Nov. 21, 2005).

[701] See, e.g., "Offshore Planner Required to Give Up Client Lists" (*Adkisson & Riser's Developments*, Summer 2006).

[702] "Application Procedures for Qualified Intermediary Status Under Section 1441; Final Qualified Intermediary Withholding Agreement" (IRS Revenue Procedure 2000-12, Jan. 7, 2000).

[703] For details, see "IRS Releases Notice Regarding Qualified Intermediary Program" (*International Tax Review*, May 2006).

[704] Richard Duke, "Foreign Banks Not Investing in U.S. Securities" (*Duke Law Firm Newsletter*, April 2006).

[705] For background, see *Restatement (Third) of Foreign Relations Law of the United States,* § 403.

[706] The OECD Model Convention on Income and Capital is available at http://www.oecd.org.

[707] Marshall Langer, "The Outrageous History of Caribbean Tax Treaty Relationships of the U.S.A. and Other OECD Countries" (*Tax Notes International*, June 10, 2002).

[708] *United States vs. Burbank & Company, Ltd.*, 525 F. 2d 9 (2d Cir. 1975), *cert. denied*, 425 U.S. 934 (1976).

[709] "(U.S.-Switzerland) Treaty on Mutual Assistance in Criminal Matters with Related Notes" (27 UST 2019, TIAS 8302, 1052 UNTS 61, effective Jan. 23, 1977).

[710] See, e.g., "Asset Forfeiture Checks Presented to Various Law Enforcement Agencies" (Press Release from U.S. Attorney's Office, Southern District of Florida, January 2001).

[711] "(U.S.-U.K.) Treaty Concerning the Cayman Islands Relating to Mutual Legal Assistance in Criminal Matters, with Attachments, Protocol and Exchange of Notes" (TIAS 1648, UNTS 179, effective March 19, 1990).

[712] Bradley O. Field, "Comments—Improving International Evidence-Gathering Methods: Piercing Bank Secrecy Laws from Switzerland to the Caribbean and Beyond" (*Loyola (LA) International and Comparative Law Journal*, vol. 15, 1993).

[713] *United States vs. Davis*, 767 F. 2d 1025 (2d Cir. 1985).

[714] *Cardenas vs. Smith*, 733 F. 2d 909 (D.C. Cir. 1984).

[715] *United States vs. Sturman*, 951 F. 2d 1466 (6th Cir. 1991).

[716] *Head Money Cases*, 112 U.S. 580, 598-99 (1884).

[717] *United States vs. Hennsel*, 699 F2d 18, 39 (1st Cir.), *cert. denied*, 461 U.S. 958 (1983).

[718] Jennifer Cantwell, "The Cross-Border Woes Of Conrad Black: The Dilemma of Differing Approaches to Self-Incrimination in Canada and the U.S. (Mondaq News, Sept. 6, 2006).

[719] Bruce Zagaris, "Proposed U.S.-German MLAT Breaks Ground" (*International Enforcement Law Reporter*, March 2005).

[720] See, e.g., *Model Treaty on Mutual Assistance in Criminal Matters* (United Nations General Assembly Resolution 45/117, 1991).

[721] "Flat-Tax Club" (*The Wall Street Journal*, Jan. 6, 2005).

[722] For background, see Daniel J. Mitchell, "A Brief Guide to the Flat Tax" (*Heritage Foundation Backgrounder No. 1866*, July 7, 2005).

[723] *Harmful Tax Competition: An Emerging Global Issue* (OECD, 1998).

[724] Marshall J. Langer, "Harmful Tax Competition—The Real Tax Havens" (*Tax Notes International*, Dec. 18, 2000).

[725] The countries identified as "tax havens" by the OECD in 2000 were Andorra, Anguilla, Antigua and Barbuda, Aruba, the Bahamas, Bahrain, Barbados, Belize, British Virgin Islands, Cook Islands, Dominica, Gibraltar, Grenada, the Channel Islands (Guernsey/Sark/Alderney/Jersey), Isle of Man, Liberia, Liechtenstein, Maldives, the Marshall Islands, Monaco, Montserrat, Nauru, Netherlands Antilles, Niue, Panama, Samoa, the Seychelles, St Lucia, St. Christopher & Nevis, St. Vincent & the Grenadines, Tonga, Turks & Caicos Islands, U.S. Virgin Islands and Vanuatu. For the current list of jurisdictions the OECD deems to be engaged in harmful tax competition, see http://www.oecd.org.

[726] These provisions are contained in the Cayman Islands Monetary Authority (Amendment) (International Cooperation) Law (2000).

[727] "O'Neill Limits Information Exchange In OECD Letter" (Tax News, June 18, 2001).

[728] "U.S. & OECD Carve-up Offshore Financial Privacy" (*The Washington Post*, June 27, 2001).

[729] "List of Uncooperative Tax Havens" (OECD Centre for Tax Policy and Administration, August 7, 2007).

[730] The current membership of the EU is listed at http://www.europa.eu.

[731] Council Directive 2003/48/EC (June 3, 2003).

[732] Charlotte Denny & Andrew Osborn. "EU Deal on Tax Dodging Leaves Loopholes" (*The Guardian*, Jan. 22, 2003).

[733] Robert Budden & James Mawson, "Tax Haven Clampdown Spurs Cash Outflow" (*Financial Times*, July 1, 2005).

[734] Ulrika Lomas, "Switzerland Reveals EU Savings Tax Directive Revenues" (Tax News, April 25, 2007).

[735] *Report of the High-Level International Intergovernmental Consideration of Financing for Development* (United Nations General Assembly, 2001).

[736] "What If There Were an International IRS?" (*National Review*, March 10, 2006).

[737] "Joint International Tax Shelter Information Center Expands and Opens a Second Office in the United Kingdom" (IRS News Release, May 23, 2007).

[738] The G-7 (now the G-8) consists of the United States, the United Kingdom, France, Italy, Japan, Germany, and Canada. Members of the FATF are: Argentina, Australia, Austria, Belgium, Brazil, Canada, Denmark, European Commission, Finland, France, Germany, Greece, Gulf Co-operation Council, Hong Kong, China, Iceland, Ireland, Italy, Japan, Luxembourg, Mexico, Kingdom of the Netherlands, New Zealand, Norway, Portugal, Singapore, Spain, Sweden, Switzerland, Turkey, United Kingdom and the United States.

[739] *40 Recommendations of the Financial Action Task Force to Fight Money Laundering* (Financial Action Task Force, 1990, 1996).

[740] These initiatives are summarized in the *1998-1999 Report on Money Laundering Typologies* (Financial Action Task Force, 1999)

[741] *Special Recommendations on Terrorist Financing* (Financial Action Task Force, 2004).

[742] *Review to Identify Non-Cooperative Countries or Territories: Increasing the Worldwide Effectiveness of Anti-Money Laundering Measures* (Financial Action Task Force, 2000).

[743] The 15 countries originally listed as "non-cooperative" were the Bahamas, Cayman Islands, Cook Islands, Dominica, Israel, Lebanon, Liechtenstein, Marshall Islands, Nauru, Niue, Panama, Philippines, Russia, St. Kitts & Nevis and St. Vincent & the Grenadines. All have now been removed from the blacklist.

[744] FinCEN advisories are posted at http://www.fincen.gov.

[745] "What is Money Laundering?" (Financial Action Task Force, undated).

[746] *Report on Non-Cooperative Countries and Territories* (Financial Action Task Force, Feb. 14, 2000) (Annex).

[747] Amanda Banks, "Economic Survey Paints Gloomy Picture For Bahamas" (Tax News, March 17, 2003).

[748] Nand C. Bardouille, "The OECD Harmful Tax Initiative: Impact of the Proposals on Small and Developing CARICOM States" (Caribbean Trade Reference Center, undated).

[749] "FATF Told: 'Physician, Heal Thyself'" (Tax-News.com, Oct. 31, 2002).

[750] See http://www.fincen.gov/int_egmont.html for a current list of members of the Egmont Group.

[751] "On Her Majesty's Not So Secret Service" (*Offshore Alert*, Jan. 31, 2003).

[752] Council Directive 91/308/EEC (June 10, 1991).

[753] Council Directive 2005/60/EC (Oct. 26, 2005).

[754] "EU Money Laundering Directive Could Jeopardise City Growth" (Press Release from the Society of Trust and Estate Practitioners, Jan. 17, 2007).

[755] The vast majority of common law jurisdictions are members of the Commonwealth Secretariat, which has 53 members. The current list is posted at http://www.thecommonwealth.org/Internal/142227/members.

[756] "Cayman Islands Yield to European Union" (*Caribbean Net News,* Feb. 17, 2004).

[757] See, e.g., "Bahamas: Privy Council Abolishes Mandatory Death Sentence" (Press Release from Amnesty International, March 6, 2006).

[758] *Tournier vs. National Provincial and Union Bank of England* [1924] 1 K.B. 461.

[759] Dennis Campbell, ed., *International Banking Secrecy* (Sweet & Maxwell, 1992).

[760] *Bertoli vs. Malone* (1990-91 *Cayman Islands Law Report* 58).

[761] *Mareva Compania Naviera SA vs. International Bulkcarriers SA* [1975] 2 Lloyd's Rep. 509.

[762] Jeremy Walton, "The Enforcement of Asset-Freezing Orders Abroad" (Mondaq News, August 11, 2006.)

[763] *Grupo Mexicano de Desarrollo, SA, et al. vs. Alliance Bond Fund Inc., et al.* 527 U.S. 308 (1999).

[764] *Re Butterworth,* 19 CH D 588 (1882).

[765] Fax from Anthony B. Travers to Mark Nestmann, June 24, 1994.

[766] "(U.S.-Belize) Treaty on Mutual Legal Assistance in Criminal Matters" (July 2, 2003).

[767] See, e.g., "80 Belizeans Could Lose Jobs, Despite Newest Court Ruling" (Belize News, March 5, 2004).

[768] "Commitment of Belize" (Letter to Donald Johnston, OECD Secretary-General, from Ralph H. Fonseca, Minister responsible for international financial services, March 8, 2002).

[769] "Belize Vanishes From Telecommunications" (*National Business Review* (New Zealand), April 21 2005.)

[770] "Belize International Bonds Tumble on Default Concern" (*Bloomberg,* Aug. 9, 2006).

[771] *Belize: Assessment Letter for the International Financial Community* (International Monetary Fund, Dec. 20, 2006).

[772] "Bermuda" (*CIA World Factbook,* 2007).

[773] Roger Crombie, "Still in the Lead: Bermuda" (*Risk & Insurance*, Oct. 1, 2005).

[774] Letter to Donald J. Johnston, OECD Secretary-General, from C. Eugene Cox, Deputy Premier and Minister of Finance (May 15, 2000).

[775] "(U.S.-U.K) Agreement (on Behalf of the Government of Bermuda) for the Exchange of Information with Respect to Taxes" (TIAS 11986, Dec. 2, 1988).

[776] Matthew Taylor, Bermuda Avoids EU Tax Legislation, for Now" (*The Royal Gazette,* July 23, 2004).

[777] Michael Peel, "Corruption Claims Taint Island Tax Haven" (*Financial Times,* Aug. 8, 2007).

[778] "Cayman Islands: Advance Commitment Letter" (Letter to Donald Johnston, OECD Secretary-General, from P.J. Smith, Governor, March 8, 2002).

[779] "(U.S.-U.K.) Treaty Concerning the Cayman Islands Relating to Mutual Legal Assistance in Criminal Matters, with Attachments, Protocol and Exchange of Notes" (TIAS 1648, UNTS 179, effective March 19, 1990).

[780] "Agreement between the Government of the United Kingdom of Great Britain and Northern Ireland, Including the Government of the Cayman Islands, and the Government of the United States of America for the Exchange of Information Relating to Taxes" (Cm 6628, effective March 10, 2006).

[781] *515 South Orange Grove Owners Assoc. vs. Orange Grove Partners*, Case No. 208/94 (Cook Islands).

[782] This case is discussed in "The Value of Marital Assets Placed in an Offshore Trust is Subject to Equitable Distribution in Divorce" (*Asset Protection Journal*, Winter 1999).

[783] *Riechers vs. Riechers*, 679 N.Y.S. 2d 233 (1998).

[784] "Commitment of the Cook Islands" (Letter to Donald Johnston, OECD Secretary-General, from Dr. Robert Woonton, Prime Minister, March 22, 2002).

[785] "Cook Islands," *International Narcotics Control Strategy Report* (U.S. Department of State, 2007).

[786] *Cook Islands" (CIA World Factbook,* 2007).

[787] Statement by Dr. Denzil L. Douglas, Prime Minister and Minister of Finance, Planning, Development and National Security, on the OECD Harmful Tax Competition Initiative (March 5, 2002).

[788] "(U.S.-St. Kitts & Nevis) Treaty on Mutual Legal Assistance in Criminal Matters, with Related Exchange of Notes" (effective Feb. 23, 2000).

[789] *St. Kitts and Nevis: 2006 Article IV Consultation—Staff Report; Staff Statement; and Public Information Notice on the Executive Board* (IMF Country Report No. 07/141, April 2007).

[790] Philip R. Weems, "Guidelines for Enforcing Money Judgments Abroad" (*International Business Lawyer*, December 1993).

[791] *European Savings Tax Directive* (Lowtax Intelligence Reports, 2005).

[792] "(U.S.-Austria) Convention for the Avoidance of Double Taxation and the Prevention of Fiscal Evasion with Respect to Taxes on Income, with Memorandum of Understanding" (TIAS 2009, UNTS 309, effective Feb. 1, 1998).

[793] "(U.S.-Austria) Treaty on Mutual Legal Assistance in Criminal Matters, with Attachments" (TIAS 2029, UNTS 153, effective Aug. 1, 1998).

[794] For background, see J. H. Merryman & D. S. Clark, *Comparative Law: Western European and Latin American Legal Systems, Cases and Materials* (Bobbs-Merrill Co., 1978).

[795] *Liechtenstein Company Law* (Liechtenstein Verlag), translated by Bryan Jeeves, is an English translation of selected portions of the PGR.

[796] "The Principality of Liechtenstein in the European Economic Area (EEA)—Taking Stock and Looking Forward" (*PA News*, November 1999).

[797] "Liechtenstein, `Uncooperative' Tax Haven, to Keep Bank Secrecy" (*Bloomberg*, March 20, 2006).

[798] Roger Frick, "Liechtenstein and the European Union (EU) Savings Tax Directive" (Mondaq News, Sept. 6, 2006).

[799] Andreas Batliner, "Mutual Assistance by Liechtenstein in Criminal Matters" (*Memo to Clients*, October 1997).

[800] Carla Johnson, "Liechtenstein No Longer On FATF's Radar" (Tax News, July 3, 2002).

[801] "(U.S.-Liechtenstein) on Mutual Legal Assistance in Criminal Matters, with Exchange of Notes (effective Aug. 1, 2003).

[802] 26 C.F.R. § 301.7701-2(b)(8).

[803] Letter to Donald Johnston, OECD Secretary-General, from Norberto Delgado Duran, Ministry of Economy and Finances (Panama) (April 15, 2002).

[804] "International Mutual Legal Assistance in Criminal Matters" ((Swiss) Federal Department of Justice and Police, August 23, 2007).

Printed in the United States
104040LV00008B/25-74/A

9 781891 266300